From Babylon to the Silicon Valley—The Origins and Evolution of Intellectual Property

From Babylon to the Silicon Valley—The Origins and Evolution of Intellectual Property

A Sourcebook

Nuno Pires de Carvalho

Wolters Kluwer

Published by:
Kluwer Law International B.V.
PO Box 316
2400 AH Alphen aan den Rijn
The Netherlands
E-mail: international-sales@wolterskluwer.com
Website: lrus.wolterskluwer.com

Sold and distributed in North, Central and South America by:
Wolters Kluwer Legal & Regulatory U.S.
7201 McKinney Circle
Frederick, MD 21704
United States of America
Email: customer.service@wolterskluwer.com

Sold and distributed in all other countries by:
Air Business Subscriptions
Rockwood House
Haywards Heath
West Sussex
RH16 3DH
United Kingdom
Email: international-customerservice@wolterskluwer.com

ISBN 978-94-035-1754-4

e-Book: ISBN 978-94-035-1805-3
web-PDF: ISBN 978-94-035-1853-4

For Ana
for ever

> But intellectual property is not only about those wonderful inventions that one day will take the human being to the stars, or the complex, sophisticated molecules that save lives, or those quasi magical devices that permit us to live with comfort and communicate instantaneously with the other side of the planet. Intellectual property is not only about that, but it is also about the differentiating assets of the small traders, the breeders, the honest merchants who carry out their lives by asserting their identities and luring customers in small markets of poor, remote villages.
>
> This adds to the complexity of intellectual property, which, like a kaleidoscope, captures the essence of the life of persons at work, carrying their professions in the four corners of the world.

Francis Gurry, *in* WIPO, INTRODUCTION TO INTELLECTUAL PROPERTY—THEORY AND PRACTICE, at xxix (Preamble) (2nd ed., Wolters Kluwer, 2017).

> Intellectual property: property, which, from its immateriality, can be stolen through a window without cutting out a pane of glass; which can be carried off by the eye without being traced or found upon the person; and which, at present, is guarded neither by high moral feeling nor the dread of moral reproach.
>
> J. Emerson Tennent, A Treatise on the Copyright for Designs for Printed Fabrics, with Considerations on the Necessity of its Extension, at 94 (Smith, Elder and Co., 1841).

Table of Contents

Introduction

Intellectual property is a branch of law that gathers many different subjects, from copyrights and related rights (such as artists' performances) to patents, trademarks and the repression of unfair competition. All intangible features, elements or devices used by merchants and producers to differentiate their articles and businesses from those of competitors are the subject matter of the branch of law that is known as intellectual property.

Intellectual property exists in an environment of commercial rivalry only. Intellectual property is about differentiation, and so it has been since Ancient Times when the first merchants and artisans began carrying out their trades privately. Intellectual property, therefore, arises spontaneously whenever and wherever entrepreneurs carry out their professions in an environment of competition with other businesses.

The first differentiating assets appeared naturally in those early economies that permitted merchants and artisans to carry out their enterprises privately and competitively—in the south of Anatolia, around 4,000 BC, and a few centuries later, in Mesopotamia. The first elements of intellectual property that emerged from such a commercial environment were the firms of merchants and artisans. By then, not only entrepreneurs had set several differentiating assets that enabled them to carry on their businesses with legal security and predictability, but also societies had already established certain legal mechanisms acknowledging those firms, in a pictorial form (seals), as legitimate businesses' legal components. In this token, public records of the transfer of a seal from a father to his son, and of the replacement of a seal lost by a merchant, have been found in Sumer. Vestiges implying the formal, albeit indirect, acknowledgement of a mechanism of appropriation of differentiating technical knowledge have also reached us in the form of precepts in at least two Sumerian codifications of jurisprudence.

From Babylon, the use of the intellectual property has expanded to the regions with which it maintained trade links: the Indus Valley, and the Near East. By contrast, only relatively rare eruptions of differentiating assets can be found in Egypt or China. The reason is that these two civilizations thrived on essentially centralized economies, merchants and artisans mainly operating for the rulers or on their behalf. There were some cases of small artisans using their marks, but those were few (as compared to the seals found in Mesopotamia, and the Indus Valley), and they were confined to specific industries, like pottery. Most seals in Egypt and China would identify the rulers, not the merchants or the artisans. They were not intellectual property.

From the Near East, intellectual property, as a spontaneous tool of commercial rivalry, spread around the Mediterranean basin: Phoenicians, Minoans, Greeks, and Romans, used to incorporate differentiating assets to their daily businesses. Business identifiers—trademarks, geographical indications, slogans, trade dress, firms—gained importance and became abundant, almost trivial, tools of differentiation. But, by contrast, technical elements of differentiation—such as new products and new shapes of known products—were not privately appropriated. And yet in Greece and, in particular, in Rome, technological advances played a significant role, not only in the form of new machinery but also of consumer goods. However, neither of those societies had artisans and inventors in special consideration. Inventors would be remunerated with salaries and, eventually and exceptionally, with prizes. The idea of recognizing the private appropriation of knowledge was still unknown, with the single exception of Sybaris, *circa* sixth century BC—but then with a religious motivation. By contrast, writers had prestige (some of them were politicians of a high social ranking), but due to technical limitations and spread illiteracy, their works would reach a limited number of readers. Therefore, they needed to rely on prizes and other forms of public and private patronage. The same can be said of artists, such as painters and sculptors. Roman law had rules on their right to inscribe their names on works based on priority, but ultimately the works would belong to their patrons.

After the demise of the Roman Empire, and the consequent decrease of trade in Europe, intellectual property ceased to be necessary. Populations gathered around convents and monasteries, and agricultural and handicraft productions were essentially self-sufficient. Roads built by the Romans for their legions crumbled into ruins and maritime routes were blocked by the Vikings, in the North, and the Muslims, in the South. Trade beyond local exchange has been reduced to a very minimum and impulse for introducing technical improvements disappeared.

However, it was in monasteries that hand labor gained prestige because it would be integrated into the rules of various religious orders as part of their collective discipline. The work (creative or not) of artisans and artists thus gained social consideration.

Through the Middle Ages, specialized labor was organized as corporations or guilds, with their own sets of rules. Intangible differentiating assets were used by those guilds as elements of rivalry with manufacturers and merchants from other cities and countries, but competition within each city was scarce, as it would affect the privileges of each guild. Rulers, eager to promote the growth of their cities' tax base, started granting industrial privileges to encourage the immigration of skilled foreign artisans. In doing so, those rulers were in conflict with the rationale of corporatism. This explains why those foreign artisans would be granted *privileges* (for they would be out of reach of local guilds' rules) through *patent letters* (the publicity of those letters would make the privileges enforceable). At the same time, the birth of the Commercial Revolution, fostered by the southern European cities that engaged in trade with

Muslims, led to the creation of new legal tools in support of trade—trademarks and their registries being one of those.

The Renaissance saw the rise of global trade and the birth of the Scientific Revolution. Global trade created the premises for the intensification of the use of business identifiers—and, with it, the first movements towards international recognition of those identifiers. And the Scientific Revolution set the foundations of organized science and the constant flow of innovative products. The granting of industrial privileges became intense throughout Europe, with a profusion of genuine inventors and introducers of new techniques claiming the corresponding benefits. Some European countries hesitantly moved towards setting some norms on those grants, namely Venice, at the end of the fifteenth century, and England, in the first half of the seventeenth century. A parallel regime of privileges was also put in place to accompany the emerging and wide dissemination of the printing industry.

The Industrial Revolution has transformed the laws of industrial privileges into modern patent law. The change has resulted from the adoption of the *laissez-faire, laissez-passer* ideology, which English and United States courts transposed into law by setting several basic standards ensuring the role of patent rights in promoting technological differentiation and free competition. From the guild regime of the Middle Ages, the economy moved to one of individual (relative) freedom. Those medieval special privileges were no longer needed. Patents, especially after the French Revolution, became grants of rights to exclude, rather than of rights to use.

The increasing need for the dissemination of scientific, religious, and philosophical literature and the manifest inadequacy of printing privileges for the protection of authors' rights and interests have given rise to a new legal framework for printed works—copyright law started crawling then.

The success of the Industrial Revolution has led to gradual improvement and complication (or sophistication, if you will) of patent laws. It also has led to the globalization of trade, as an ultimate consequence of the industrial surpluses generated by improved processes and advanced technologies. The need for multilateral, harmonized international protection of intellectual property was thus born.

The paragraphs above summarize 6,000 years of the historical evolution of intellectual property. It was born as a spontaneous need for merchants and artisans to differentiate themselves and their articles as well. 6,000 years later, the role and nature of intellectual property have not changed. The way governments use intellectual property laws as tools of public policy (and frequently as tokens of internationally commercial bargaining) may have changed. But not its core. As far as that core is concerned, today intellectual property is the same as it was 6,000 years ago: an instrument for the assertion of the identities of merchants and manufacturers in their struggle to lure customers. In other words, intellectual property "like a kaleidoscope, captures the essence of life of persons at work, carrying their professions in the four corners of the world" (*see* the Epigraph).

Intellectual property continues evolving by small, imperceptible steps that result from the daily practices of merchants and manufacturers carrying their businesses. Be it in Silicon Valley or in small markets of poor, remote villages; entrepreneurs endeavor to affirm their identities and lure customers to acquire the articles and services they make and sell. For that purpose, they use old differentiating elements, or they test new ones, in a spontaneous manner.

The sources in the chapters that follow will show how intellectual property tools have been and continue being created by entrepreneurs in a setting of commercial rivalry. Social forces have dominated and continue dominating the creation and development of those tools, accepting ones and repudiating others. But in all cases, the common denominator in all the subject matters of intellectual property is the need for commercial rivals to differentiate their products and lure customers with honesty and fairness. This is true whether we are looking at copyrighted works, patented inventions, registered marks and trade names, secrets, reputation, origin, whatever.

Having said this, let me now make a few editorial notes:

(1) This book is about how intellectual property emerged and evolved in the last 6,000 years. It is a fascinating story that comes to us through the voices of the past and the present. Those are the voices of writers, of inventors, of merchants, of artisans, of kings, of parliaments, of lawyers, of judges, and they tell us a story of human beings making a living from their honest work.

In selecting those voices, my concern was of detecting those important snapshots that illustrate the creation or changes in the evolution of intellectual property. The selection, of course, reveals my own perceptions, which may not always correspond to mainstream views. Moreover, in order to avoid an excessive long book, I have tried to select texts of more relevance. Here, again, my own perceptions may have been determinant in distinguishing what is more relevant from what is not. Some texts may seem repetitive, but I have included them anyway because they reveal subtle differences, small steps, almost imperceptible, in the social construction of intellectual property.

On the other hand, the exponential growth of global trade that started in the middle of the nineteenth century has generated a likewise exponential growth of the debates, texts and cases concerning intellectual property. Therefore, in preparing this book, it has been difficult to find significant sources from Antiquity and the Middle Ages, but, because of their scarcity, it has been easy to select them. By contrast, given their abundance, it has been very easy to find sources on intellectual property from the Modern Age forward, but it has been difficult to select them.

Readers may find it surprising that a large proportion of the texts come from Rome, as far as Antiquity is concerned; from France and England, as far as the Middle Ages and modern times are concerned; and from the United States, concerning today. The references to Egypt are rare, and no text concerns China, even if those were centers of the greatest civilizations of Ancient Times. The reason was given above: intellectual property is specific to free markets, where merchants and manufacturers exercise commercial rivalry. Such rivalry was nonexistent or very scarce in both Egypt and China, where the economy was heavily centralized, with the manufacture and commercial distribution remaining in the hands of authorities and temples. The same can be said of the Islamic world, which after the seventh century AD, and for almost five centuries, dominated a vast proportion of the Mediterranean basin. In spite of its enormous scientific and cultural influence on Europe, the economy of the Islamic civilization was essentially based on centralized government. This does not mean that some artisans would not resort to business identifiers to designate and distinguish the articles they produced, but those would be, in general, limited to a few industrial sectors, and they would be enforced through the courtesy of the trade, rather than by courts.

As to modern times, we should not forget that through several centuries from the Middle Ages until the Industrial Revolution, France was by far the greatest economic power of Europe, with England acting as its rival and main competitor. So, it should not be a surprise that most tools of intellectual property that have reached us were created and tested in those two European centers of development. In parallel, in other emerging economic powers that, albeit more or less fleetingly, reached great success and influence, such as the Italian Republics and the Portuguese and Spanish maritime empires, intellectual property tools were also used, if not created anew, in profusion. Accordingly, voices from those countries will be heard in this book. But it was for the sake of keeping the number of sources within a reasonable limit that this book did not include texts from other great economic powers, such as Germany, the Netherlands, and Russia, where intellectual property was also used with intensity. Moreover, the respective sources are not as easily accessible as those that have been selected.

An overall concern has presided over the selection of sources: with a very few exceptions, related to early times, the sources refer to intellectual property, i.e., to differentiating intangible tools. Otherwise, this book deals basically with differentiation and commercial rivalry. This explains why some expressions of intellectual creations that are similar to intellectual property have been left out, such as traditional knowledge and traditional cultural expressions—after all, unless in very narrow contexts, traditional communities do not compete with each other to sell the practical products of their traditions. Likewise, the regime that protects names that identify political parties, for example, has many similarities with trademark law, but those names are not trademarks, for the simple reason that political parties are rivals, but not in a commercial context.

(2) The selected sources follow a criterion of separation of intellectual property specialties, but only to a limited extent. The reason is that very often, the borders between areas of intellectual property are very blurred, and thus it becomes very difficult to distinguish them. As we will see, in the Chapter on trade secrets, there are texts that speak to patent law as much as they concern trade secrets. Also, in the Chapter dedicated to copyright, several sources speak to trademark law. The reason is that distinctive signs, such as trademarks, trade names, and shop signs, were for some time used as a supplementary way of preventing the unauthorized reproduction of works. From a legal perspective, the borders between artistic creations and industrial designs are extremely thin—in some countries, they do not exist. For many years, authorities and courts would not make a distinction between trademarks, shop signs and certification marks—that is why they have all been reunited in a single chapter under the general notion of business identifiers.

Anyway, I am aware that the organization of the sources in this book under five chapters is largely artificial. The choices made have tried to find and follow consistency between the different areas of intellectual property that show more affinity, but arbitrariness in that choice can never be eliminated.

Moreover, this book has left many areas of intellectual property out, such as plant variety protection, layout designs of integrated circuits, and repression of unfair competition—the broadest and perhaps oldest of them all—to mention three. Once again, this was the fruit of an arbitrary choice. But as regards the field of repression of unfair competition, here and there it is reflected under the five chapters.

(3) Most texts are preceded by notes that explain their respective contexts. However, I have tried to keep those notes as much succinct as possible, so as to give preeminence to the sources. Hopefully, the sources selected will be able to speak for themselves.

(4) Finally, many of the sources in this book have been translated. When the translations are not mine, translators' names are provided in the Credits section. But because a majority of those are indeed mine (with, in some cases, the assistance of Google Translation—a superb tool), a word of caution is appropriate: given that translation is (re)creation, eventual inaccuracies in those translations are entirely my fault. I only hope they are not too many.

I cannot close the presentation of this book, which has taken almost five years of my life, without saying a special word of thanks to my wife, Ana. I thank her for her enormous patience while I walked through a lot of museums, ancient ruins, medieval cathedrals, castles, markets, and libraries, mostly digital (Gallica, Archive.org, la Biblioteca Digital de España, etc.), in search for clues of times past. She has given this book—as well as my life—the only meaning that counts, and that is love.

Arraial d'Ajuda (Bahia, Brazil), November 28, 2019

CHAPTER 1

Patents

§1.01 AMENEMHET, AN EGYPTIAN INVENTOR

Sixteenth Century BC

In his autobiography, inscribed on the wall of his tomb, Amenemhet claims the invention of a water clock, which pharaoh Amenhotep I (18th Dynasty, sixteenth century BC) received with great favor. As it was the practice then, the inventor was generously rewarded by the king. The idea of privately appropriating his invention would be very strange at that time, since in Ancient Egypt there was not a private market for those devices, and the inventor, therefore, did not have to fear the commercial rivalry of other clock makers.

(6) [...] The first time I was praised was under the Majesty of the King of Upper- and Lower Egypt [Djeserkare, or Amenhotep I]

(7) [...] I studied by reading in all writings of the god's words.

(8) [...] I found that the night of the season of Akhet was of 14 hours, while the night in Summer consists of 12 hours.

(9) [...] I verified an increase month by month, followed by a decrease month by month.

(10) [...] I followed the movements of Re [the sun] and Aah [the moon], in their conjunction.

(11) [...] The ankh [a cross, symbol of life] is in her hands as it is the usage.

(12) [...] Re, when he moves close to Nekhbet. She goes to Re on

(13) [...] so as to tend the symbol of life and power which is in her hand to the nose of His Majesty, who has descended on two strings

(14) Re is rejoicing when he sees these goddesses going up and down in front of him. I made a Merkhet [a timekeeping device] calibrated upon the year. It seemed beautiful to the king of Upper and Lower Egypt, vindicated.

(15) It was calibrated in view of each of its seasons. Never before had something like that been made since the primeval time of the land. I made this august measuring device in the favor of the king of Upper and Lower Egypt, vindicated, parted into half

(16) and third. It was counted (i.e. correct) when entering Summer, during Harvest, in the phases of the moon, who arrives at his hour, each hour according to its day. The water comes out via one pipe.

§1.02 IN SYBARIS, AN EARLY EPISODE OF PRIVATE APPROPRIATION OF KNOWLEDGE

Sixth Century BC

Athenaeus of Naucratis (end of the second, beginning of the third century AD), in his BANQUET OF THE LEARNED, quoting from Phylarcus, a Greek historian of the third century BC, puts in the mouth of a banquet participant a description of the luxurious habits of the Sybarites and implies the great prestige that cooks who catered to public banquets had in that city. Sybaris was a Greek colony, located in the Gulf of Taranto, south of Italy. It was founded in 720 BC and destroyed by a neighboring city, Kroton, around three centuries later. Sybaris was a very wealthy colony, due to its productive agriculture and strategic geographic location. A great part of its revenue came from tolls the city would charge on merchant ships that navigated through the safer waters across. The statute of Sybaris mentioned by Athenaeus had a very specific purpose of promoting the creation of new and especially tasty dishes in the context of public banquets, which had a religious nature.

[The Sybarites] also celebrate in public numbers of feasts; and they honour those who display great magnificence on such occasions with golden crowns, and they proclaim their names at the public sacrifices and games; announcing not only their general goodwill towards the city, but also the great magnificence which they had displayed in the feasts. And on these occasions they even crown those cooks who have served up the most exquisite dishes. . . .

And if the confectioner or cook invented any peculiar and excellent dish, no other artist was allowed to make this for a year; but he alone who invented it was entitled to all the profit to be derived from the manufacture of it for that time; in order that others might be induced to labour at excelling in such pursuits. . . .

§1.03 DIONYSIUS OF SYRACUSE HIRED INVENTORS AND ENCOURAGED THEM WITH SALARIES AND AWARDS

Fifth Century BC–Fourth Century BC

. . . At once, therefore, he [Dionysius, the tyrant of Syracuse] gathered skilled workmen, commandeering them from the cities under his control, and attracting them by high wages from Italy and Greece as well as Carthaginian territory. For his purpose was to make weapons in great numbers and every kind of projectiles, and also quadriremes and quinquiremes, no ship of the latter size having yet been built at that time. After collecting many skilled workmen, he divided them into groups in accordance with their skills, and appointed over them the most conspicuous citizens, ...

In fact, the catapult was invented at this time in Syracuse, since the ablest skilled workmen had been gathered from everywhere into one place. The high wages as well as the numerous prizes offered the workmen who were judged to be the best stimulated their zeal. And over and above these factors, Dionysius circulated daily among the workers, conversed with them in kindly fashion, and rewarded the most zealous with gifts and invited them to his table. Consequently the workmen brought unsurpassable devotion to the devising of many missiles and engines of war that were strange and capable of rendering great service. . . .

§1.04 ARCHIMEDES, ASHAMED OF HIS INVENTIONS

Third Century BC

The absence of legal provisions in Greece and in Rome on rewards and incentives to artisans and inventors was a natural consequence of the low esteem that professions related to arts and crafts generally received from society. Archimedes, one of the greatest inventors of all times, despised his own inventive activities, according to the testimony of the Roman historian Plutarch (first-second centuries AD). His inventions were due to a purely philosophical spirit of entertainment and acquisition of knowledge.

These machines he had designed and contrived, not as matters of any importance, but as mere amusements in geometry; in compliance with King Hiero's desire and request, some little time before, that he should reduce to practice some part of his admirable speculations in science and, by accommodating the theoretic truth to sensation and ordinary use, bring it more within the appreciation of people in general. . . .

Yet Archimedes possessed so high a spirit, so profound a soul, and such treasures of scientific knowledge, that though these inventions had now obtained him the renown of more than human sagacity, he yet would not deign to leave behind him any commentary or writing on such subjects; but, repudiating as sordid and ignoble the whole trade of engineering, and every sort of art that lends itself to mere use and profit, he placed his whole affection and ambition in those purer speculations where there can be no reference to the vulgar needs of life.

§1.05 IN THEBES, INVENTORS WERE REWARDED

First Century BC

Diodorus of Sicily (First century BC) reports that in the city of Thebes, which god Osiris would have founded, artisans were well rewarded for their inventions, when useful. The historian mentions rivalry among the inventors. This suggests that somehow their inventions would be examined so as to compete for the existing rewards.

Special esteem at the court of Osiris and Isis was also accorded to those who should invent any of the arts or devise any useful process; consequently, since copper and gold mines had been discovered in the Thebaid, they fashioned implements with which they killed the wild beasts and worked the soil, and thus in eager rivalry brought the country under cultivation, and they made images of the gods and magnificent golden chapels for their worship.

§1.06 VITRUVIUS IN SUPPORT OF AUTHORS AND INVENTORS

First Century BC-First Century AD

Vitruvius (first century BC-first century AD), in his work The Ten Books of Architecture, recommends Cesar that authors and inventors be rewarded.

Since, therefore, these great benefits to individuals and to communities are due to the wisdom of authors, I think that not only should palms and crowns be bestowed upon them, but that they should even be granted triumphs, and judged worthy of being consecrated in the dwellings of the gods.

Of their many discoveries which have been useful for the development of human life, I will cite a few examples. On reviewing these, people will admit that honors ought of necessity to be bestowed upon them. . . .

For Diagnetus was a Rhodian architect, to whom, as an honour, was granted out of the public treasury a fixed annual payment commensurable with the dignity of his art. At this time an architect from Aradus, Callias by name, coming to Rhodes, gave a public lecture, and showed a model of a wall, over which he set a machine on a revolving crane with which he seized an helepolis as it approached the fortifications, and brought it inside the wall. The Rhodians, when they had seen this model, filled with admiration, took from Diagnetus the yearly grant and transferred this honour to Callias.

§1.07 PLINY THE ELDER, ON PRIZES FOR INVENTIONS

First Century AD

Pliny the Elder reported on a proposal by Apicius to establish a prize for those who invented a sauce made of the liver of rougets, a fish from the Mediterranean. Marcus Gavius Apicius, a Roman millionaire, was a gourmet and lover of refined luxury. He lived in the first century AD during the reign of Tiberius.

In another passage, Pliny told about a great inventor, Sergius Orata, who became rich from selling his invention, the suspended bath. Orata also has proposed the organization of a competition for the invention of a sauce.

XXX. Mr. Apicius, admirable for the inventions of luxury items, thought that an excellent preparation was of letting [the rougets] die in the brine, called *garum of the allies* [...] (because this thing even got a nickname); and he proposed a prize for one who would invent a brine with the liver of the rouget. It is easier to remember the proposition than to say who won the prize.

LXXIX. The oyster beds were first made by Sergius Orata at Baïes, in the time of the orator L. Crassus, before the war of the Marses; and he establishes them not for a gastronomic purpose, but to earn money. Such inventions, for which his mind was ingenious, brought him large revenues; it was he who, having first imagined the suspended baths, sold country houses after having furnished them with this apparatus.

§1.08 ONE RULE IN THE CODE OF JUSTINIAN IN FAVOR OF ARTISANS

Fourth Century AD

The social attitude against those who embraced technical professions started to change towards the end of the Roman empire.

Code of Justinian, Book X, Title 64. Concerning the excuses of artisans.

The Emperor Constantine to Maximus.

We order that artisans engaged in the trades hereinafter specified, and who reside in different cities, shall be exempt from all civil duties, above all, if their leisure is employed in perfecting themselves in occupations by which they may become more skillful, and their sons be instructed. . . .

Given on the fourth of the *Nones* of August, during the Consulate of Felicianus and Titian, 337.

§1.09 THE FIRST INDUSTRIAL PRIVILEGE GRANTED TO A FOREIGN ARTISAN

March 2, 1236

In 1236, Henry III, of England, confirmed an industrial privilege that the city of Bordeaux had granted to Bonafusus de Sancta Columba. Like all privileges of this kind that were granted between the thirteenth and the eighteenth centuries, this was basically an administrative license for Bonafusus to carry his manufacture and trade. By contrast with modern patents, which provide primarily a right to exclude—and never a right to use, because this right results from the laws on economic freedom—industrial privileges were essentially the grant of a right to use. This explains the specific language of the privilege, which provided for "a licence by Galcelinus' Columb', the mayor, and the jurats of the commune of Bordeaux, for the said Bonafusus."

Apparently Bonafusus and his family have made good use of his privilege, his name having climbed from the status of an artisan to the ranking of city counselor and magistrate. Indeed, the name of Bonafusus de Sancta Columba (probably referring to a son or grandson) appears as a "jurat" (counsellor) of the city of Bordeaux in a document reflecting the oath of loyalty to the French king Philippe the Beau, on May 22, 1293.

Inspeximus and confirmation to Bonafusus de Sancta Columba, citizen of Bordeaux, of letters patent to him, sealed with the common seal of Bordeaux, dated 1234, 2 Kal.

April by P. Calhu, the mayor, and the jurats of the commune of Bordeaux, being a ridimus of a licence by Galcelinus' Columb', the mayor, and the jurats of the commune of Bordeaux, for the said Bonafusus, granted in the presence of the said mayor and jurats, and of the consuls of that city; to make cloths of Bordeaux, for fifteen years, to wit, for him and such of his fellows as he shall see fit to join with him on the following conditions:—it shall be lawful for him and his fellows to be (*evenire*) weavers, engage fullers, dyers and other workers of woollen cloths, and make cloths of divers colours after the manner of the Flemings, the French or the English, and for him only and his fellows. Any women, however, may spin and prepare wool in any other way without requiring licence from them. Grant also that wool or dye or any apparatus necessary for making colours of cloth or cloths, borne to Bordeaux within the said term, shall be bought by him and his fellows only, so that no one may buy the same unless he be of them or obtain their licence. Grant especially to him and his fellows, that they may use any plates, stone courtyards (*atriis litiis*), enclosure within the walls and other common pastures (*paduentiis*) of the city of Bordeaux freely and quietly, for making, drying, stretching or in other ways preparing cloth, on condition, however, that houses, roofs or other lasting impediments be not made in the above mentioned places, nor water kept back from its course or diverted, except by the will of the mayor and jurats and only with respect to the pastures and waters of the town of Bordeaux or within the banlieu. At the expiration of the term of fifteen years, anyone is to be at liberty to make any and as many clothes as they please, and the said Bonafusus and his fellows are to have no advantage in any of the above particulars.

§1.10 ENGLAND INAUGURATES A SYSTEM OF INCENTIVES TO LURE FOREIGN ARTISANS

July 23, 1331

The Commercial Revolution, in the eleventh and twelfth centuries, benefited some regions of Europe more than others—Italy and Flanders being the first winners. The economic imbalances that resulted from the different speeds of countries' economic growth persuaded a number of national leaders to introduce measures so as to lure foreign skilled artisans to their realms in order to open new fronts of industrial production, thus expanding national tax bases. In the fourteenth century England took the first measures to establish manufactures of wool cloth, which would allow the country to exploit the raw materials it had in abundance and that it exported to Continental Europe. The text that follows is the first industrial privilege with a broad application (it was granted to John Kempe, but it promises equal favors to other artisans) that encourages the immigration of skilled foreign artisans.

The king to all bailiffs, etc., to whom these letters may come, greeting. Know that, whereas John Kempe, of Flanders, weaver of woollen cloths, has come to dwell within our realm of England for the sake of exercising his craft therein and of instructing and informing those who wish to learn the same, and has brought with him certain men and servants and apprentices of that craft:

We take this John, his men, servants, and apprentices aforesaid, together with all their goods and chattels, into our protection, and we promise to other men of that craft, as well as to dyers and fullers, wishing to come from across the sea to dwell within our kingdom for the same cause, that similar letters shall be granted.

Witness the king, at Lincoln, the 28th day of July.

§1.11 THE CLOTH ACT—A STATUTE THAT PROVIDED FOR INCENTIVES TO FOREIGN ARTISANS

1337

In 1331 England had already granted an industrial privilege to a foreign artisan with the general purpose of importing a new industry to the country—that of wool cloth manufacturing. That privilege (*see* Text 1.10) came with a general promise to all artisans in the same circumstances. Six years later Edward III moved that promise further and included it in a statute, The Cloth Act (11 Edw. 3, c. 2), thus overcoming the resistance that London-based cloth makers had offered against the 1331 privilege.

Item, It is accorded, That all the Cloth-works of strange Lands, of whatsoever country they be, which will come into England, Ireland, Wales and Scotland, within the King's Power, shall come safely and surely, and shall be in the King's protection and safe Conduct, to dwell in the same Lands, choosing where they will; and to the Intent the said Cloth-workers shall have the greater Will to come and dwell here, our Sovereign Lord the King will grant them Franchises, as many and such as may suffice them.

§1.12 THE PRACTICE OF GRANTING INDUSTRIAL PRIVILEGES EXPANDS TO ITALY

1355

In 1355 the Prince of Ferrara granted Jacopo di Dondi (known for his invention of an intricate mechanical clock) a privilege for the extraction of salt from the hot mineral springs that are found near Padua. The text that follows is an excerpt from a notice on that privilege written by Francesco Scipione.

Our Jacopo, in that occasion, reveals his invention on producing salt to the Prince [of Ferrara], who in his good disposition decides to grant him the permission to make it, through an honorific Decree that accorded him the exclusive right [of making it] and transport it to wherever he saw fit, with exemption of any duties and taxes.

In the following year, in order to contest his enemies and describe how to make that Salt, he wrote a brief treatise on this topic. Here is the title: *Consideratio Jacobi de Dondis de causa salsedinis aquarum, & de modo conficiendi sal ex eis* [Treatise by Jacobi de Dondis on the cause of the saltiness of the water, and mode of making salt from it]. . . . In order, says Jacopo [in the Preamble of his treatise] to repress the calumnies of my enemies & envious detractors of the work that is more the product of divine grace than of human ingenuity, I am obliged to write a treatise on a method that I recently invented of extracting salt from the hot springs near Padua, [divided into four chapters]. . . .

§1.13 PRIVILEGE GRANTED TO FILIPPO BRUNELLESCHI BY THE CITY OF FLORENCE

June 19, 1421

In 1421, architect and inventor Filippo Brunelleschi requested, and obtained, an industrial privilege from the city of Florence, for the design of a particular type of boat to transport marble on the Arn river. The privilege makes an interesting reference to the disclosure of the invention as a quid pro quo *to the exclusivity.*

Although he was a prolific and successful inventor while orienting the construction of the Dome of Florence's cathedral, this was the only time Brunelleschi asked for an industrial privilege. Most of his other inventions would be rewarded through prizes for competitions that the Guild of Wool Merchants of Florence would call for when a particularly technical difficulty would appear in the construction. Brunelleschi would also not be a strange to protecting pieces of his knowledge through secrecy—for example, the method he used to build the Dome in a manner that avoided that if fell inwards, by using a web of fixed and mobile chains, was found a few years ago, by an Italian architect, Massimo Ricci.

His idea for requesting a privilege for the boat came probably from his supposition that he would be able to obtain more revenues directly from the market, by selling marble transportation services, not only for the Dome he was building, but for other construction sites as well.

The design of the boat is not known. It seems that it was an unfortunate commercial adventure, because the boat (known as the Badalone, the monster) sunk in its first travel.

The Magnificent and Powerful Lords, Lords Magistrate, and Standard Bearer of Justice:

Considering that the admirable Filippo Brunelleschi, a man of the most perspicacious intellect, industry, and invention, citizen of Florence, has invented some machine or kind of ship, by means of which he thinks he can easily, at any time, bring in any merchandise and load on the river Arno and on any other river or water, for less money than usual, and with several other benefits to merchants and others, and that he refuses to make such machine available to the public, in order that the fruit of his genius and skill may not be reaped by another without his will and consent; and that, if he enjoyed some prerogative concerning this, he would open up what he is hiding and would disclose it to all;

And desiring that this matter, so withheld and hidden without fruit, shall be brought to light to be of profit to both said Filippo and our whole country and others, and that some privilege be created for said Filippo as hereinafter described, so that he may be animated more fervently to even higher pursuits and stimulated to more subtle investigations, they deliberated on 19 June 1421;

That no person alive, wherever born and of whatever status, dignity, quality, and grade, shall dare or presume, within three years next following from the day when the present provision has been approved in the Council of Florence, to commit any of the following acts on the river Arno, any other river, stagnant water, swamp, or water running or existing in the territory of Florence: to have, hold, or use in any manner, be it newly invented or made new in form, a machine or ship or other instrument designed to import or ship or transport on water any merchandise or any things or goods, except such ship or machine or instrument as they may have used until now for similar operations, or to ship or transport, or to have shipped or transported, any merchandise or goods on ships, machines, or instruments for water transport other than such as were familiar and usual until now, and further that any such new or newly shaped machine, etc. shall be burned;

Provided however that the foregoing shall not be held to cover, and shall not apply to, any newly invented of newly shaped machine, etc. designed to ship, transport or travel on water, which may be made by Filippo Brunelleschi or with his will and consent; also, than any merchandise, things, or goods which may be shipped with such newly invented ships, within three years next following, shall be free from imposition, requirement, or levy of any new tax not previously imposed.

§1.14 INDUSTRIAL PRIVILEGE GRANTED TO JOHN UTYNAM

April 3, 1444

In the fifteenth century, the practice of granting industrial privileges was already spread through Europe, with countries competing for luring skilled foreign artisans. Henry VI, who founded the Eton College, in 1440, hired John Utynam, a coloured glass maker from Flanders, to work in its construction. In 1444 he granted Utynam an industrial privilege, with license and exclusivity to use a new process of painting glass.

Two elements in this privilege are of particular interest: the mention of novelty ("because the said art has never been used in England") and the artisan's promise he would teach his art to local artisans—an early expression of patents as tools of technology transfer.

Licence for life for John Utynam, born in Flanders, who has returned of late to England at the king's command, to stay in the realm with his wife and children, sons and daughters, and servants, as any liege of the king, and protection for the same; grant also to him for life that he may engage in all acts, works and sciences lawful and liberal without impediment, and since he has come to make glass of all colours for the windows of Eton college and the college of St. Mary and St. Nicholas, Cambridge, appointment of him to take artificers, workmen and labourers and to set them to work at the king's wages, and wood, clay (*lutum*), stones, ashes, metals and carriage therefor, and to commit to prison all rebellious herein to stay until they find security to serve faithfully; and grant that all glass made at his own costs and not for the use of the colleges may be exposed by him for sale without payment of customs or subsidies thereon; and because the said art has never been used in England and John intends to instruct divers lieges of the king in many other arts never used in the realm beside the said art of making glass, the king retains him, therefore, for life at his wages and fees and grants that no liege of the king learned in such arts shall use them for a term of twenty years against the will and assent of John, under a penalty of 200l, whereof two parts shall be rendered to the king and one part to John, any liege who cannot levy that sum to suffer imprisonment without delivery save by the king's special command.

§1.15 THE PARTE OF 1474, OF VENICE, ON INDUSTRIAL PRIVILEGES FOR INVENTIONS

March 19, 1474

In the fifteenth century, Venice was at the peak of its commercial success. As a commercial power, it controlled trade in the Eastern Mediterranean and the flow of Asian spices into Europe. Wealth thus obtained was used in support of a growing industrial and technological base, of which the glass industry in Murano and naval construction, in the Arsenal, are examples.

Venice was perhaps the first State where economic liberalism was adopted as the official ideology, for Venetian merchants and manufacturers could carry out their businesses in great part without the constraints of corporatism. This explains the Parte of 1474, which could be seen as the first serious ancestor of modern patent law—a very remote one, however. Unlike the Cloth Act, of 1337 (*see* Text 1.11), the Parte aims at specific inventions rather than to general knowledge of a given industry.

We have among us men of great genius, apt to invent and discover ingenious devices; and in view of the grandeur and virtue of our City, more such men come to us every day from diverse parts. Now, if provision were made for the works and devices discovered by such persons, so that others who may see them could not build them and take the inventor's honor away, more men would then apply their genius, would discover, and would build devices of great utility and benefit to our commonwealth. Therefore:

Be it enacted that, by the authority of this Council, every person who shall build any new and ingenious device in this City, not previously made in our Commonwealth, shall give notice of it to the office of our General Welfare Board when it has been reduced to perfection so that it can be used and operated. It being forbidden to every other person in any of our territories and towns to make any further device conforming with and similar to said one, without the consent and license of the author, for the term of 10 years. And if anybody builds it in violation hereof, the aforesaid author and inventor shall be entitled to have him summoned before any magistrate of this City, by which magistrate the said infringer shall be constrained to pay him hundred ducats; and the device shall be destroyed at once. It being, however, within the power and discretion of the Government, in its activities, to take and use any such device and instrument, with this condition however that no one but the author shall operate it.

§1.16 PRIVILEGE GRANTED BY ISABEL OF SPAIN, IN 1478, TO HER PHYSICIAN, PEDRO AZLOR

February 24, 1478

With the practice of industrial privileges consolidated and spread throughout Europe, in the fifteenth century, each country would add its own idiosyncrasies and specificities to the mechanism. For example, this privilege granted by Queen Isabel of Spain to her physician acknowledges that the invention to be protected did not exist yet, it was just a promise. Eventually, the technique to be used by the grantee did not concern a genuine invention in strict terms, but rather a known technique with some improvements.

That the privilege was granted to someone that belonged to the inner circle of Queen's relations might be an expression (found in many other privileges) of explicit favoritism.

Lady Isabel, by the grace of God, Queen of Castilla, of León, of Toledo, of Sicily, of Portugal, of Galicia, of Sevilla, of Córdova, of Murcia, of Jahen, of the Algarves, of Algeziras, of Gibraltar, princess of Aragón and Lady of Viscaya and of Molina.

To the infants, dukes, marquises, counts, elected, masters of the orders, priors, commanders and sub-commanders, mayors of the castles and strong and flat houses and rich men and to the councils and councilors, assistants, mayors, magistrates, civil servants, twenty fours [a special post in certain municipalities], squires and officers and good men of the very loyal city of Seville, as well as of the other cities, villages and places of my Realms and Ladyships and to any other of my vassals and subjects and to each and any of you to whom this letter of mine or its transcription signed by a public notary will be shown.

Health and grace: Know that Dr. Pedro Azlor, my physician, has informed me that he wanted to invent and make in my Realms and Ladyships new buildings of mills and grinds for grinding bread, which he says will result in great benefit and utility of the public affairs of my Realms and Ladyships, and that he fears and dreads that, after having invented and shown the said grindings, some people seeing his industry and care that he in them has, soon will want to make the same things in the manner that he had done them, being the first that to these Realms of mine brought and created them. And having spent many costs of maravedís in this and in its working and inventing, trusting to take advantage of his knowledge, and that if another person were to take his invention, he would lose all his work and could not extract from it the costs that he would put in it. Who, if it so happened, says he would receive great injury and damage, because he has worked and spent his time in building and will incur in expenses in it, for which cause he begged me and asked for mercy on him, provided him with the order that within a certain period no one would dare to make or build grinds according to the new manner he had built it about the said grinds for grinding bread, of water as of men, or the force of beasts or of the wind, in the new manner that he had invented it, and begged me that I granted him in respect of it. And I have agreed, thus I command you that since the day that said Pedro Azlor builds or shows the shape of the said grinds of his new manner, during the next first twenty years, do not consent nor permit that any people dare to make or make grinds or mills in such a manner that the said Pedro Azlor makes. And allow and consent that he makes and builds in any proper place of my Realms and Ladyships any mills and grinds that he wants to make, provided that it does not cause harm or damage to any other. And during this period, that [in respect of the above mentioned invention] or part of it do not impose nor consent to impose obstacles or any difficulty. And if other people want to make it, that you, judges, do not only refuse your consent or approval, but also destroy it. And the twenty thousand maravedís for the said doctor, it will be levied in such a manner that no cost remains from it during the said term of twenty years as from the day the said doctor Pedro Azlor starts discovering the art of the buildings of the said grinds or erecting them in a way that he can use the said devices for twenty years, as it is said. And do not prevaricate, under penalty of my grace and of thirty thousand maravedís for the city hall.

Given in the very noble and loyal city of Sevilla on the twenty-fourth day of February, year of the birth of our Lord Savior Jesus Christ of one thousand four hundred and seventy eight years. I, the Queen, had made it written by order . . . (Signed).

§1.17 PRIVILEGE GRANTED BY JOHN II, OF PORTUGAL, TO HIS WIFE'S CHAPLAIN AND OTHERS

August 22, 1490

This privilege for a machine to extract water from wells and ponds included one exception to the rights granted, namely that the grantees could not refuse to license the use of the machine "to anyone who wanted to draw water with that device for the service of their house, for which license they would receive two gold florins, or their fair value." This was a sort of a compulsory license.

Martim Gil, chaplain to queen D. Joana, of Castilla, sister of João II, of Portugal, and canon in Santa Maria de Málaga; Master Anes, servant and gunner of the King of Castilla; Master Pedro, neighbor of Málaga; Afonso Fajardo; and Pedro Catalão, barber of João II, had represented to the king that they knew how to make such devices and contraptions with which water could be drawn from wells and ponds, and everywhere else where it could be found, without beasts or living things to move them. John, recognizing the usefulness of the invention, orders the issuance of a letter to the discoverers, dated August 22, 1490, by which he confers them the following privileges:

> In the case of making such devices and contraptions in the manner they claimed, and they being the first introducers and manufacturers of those devices in Portugal, no other person, within the period of 40 years from this letter's date, could make such devices without a license by the inventors; on the understanding, however, that they could not deny it to anyone who wanted to draw water with that device for the service of their house, for which license they would receive two gold florins, or their fair value; and if the owners of other houses were to take advantage of that water, each of them should also pay two florins. Anyone who wanted to draw water with the device to water gardens, meadows, or any other fields, could also obtain a license paying a third of the expense he would have to incur in one year to draw water with animals or otherwise; this expenditure would be determined under oath by two knowledgeable persons.
>
> If the water extracted with the device could be used to build mills, tramples or any similar works, the inventors would have no obligation to license [their invention]; its licensing would be entirely subject to agreement between the interested parties. [...]

With the consent of the petitioners it was also established that out of all the net profit that the society generated, one-third would revert to the king's chamber, and the rest to them. The rights of the partners constituted their property, which would be transmitted, like any other, to their heirs and successors.

The privilege concludes by imposing upon those who made the devices without a license a fine of 20,000 reais, equally divided between the treasury and the inventors, as well as the loss of the work along with the house or place where it had been made.

§1.18 AN INDUSTRIAL PRIVILEGE GRANTED BY THE MUNICIPALITY OF AMIENS, FRANCE

April 18, 1539

> This privilege granted by the city of Amiens to an inventor also included a compulsory license, ensuring that the grantee was entitled to a reasonable remuneration. The privilege did not entail exclusivity, but a reward from the city.

At the meeting of the aldermen of Thursday, April 18, 1539, Hector de Palet or Palot, after having undertaken to produce saltpeter for the city, offers to make furnaces for the brewers and the dyers. It is agreed to give ten écus as a reward if this kind of furnace is found to be useful. If the dyers and the brewers want to order the making of similar ones, Hector will be obliged to have those made for them, being reasonably satisfied for the labor.

§1.19 ANOTHER INDUSTRIAL PRIVILEGE GRANTED BY THE CITY OF AMIENS

March 27, 1543

> Thursday, March 27, 1543.—Pierre Gestin and Robert de la Roche, residing in Amiens, having invented and found the manner of calendering satin without the

help and expenses of horses, but with the assistance of one or two men only, request the exclusive privilege of making those machines during four years. The privilege is granted to them for three, and it is permitted that they use four counterweighs that belong to the city so as to load their calender.

§1.20 ONE OF THE MANY PRIVILEGES THAT HENRY IV, OF FRANCE, GRANTED TO INVENTORS

March 1, 1585

This text concerns the patent letters signed by Henry IV, of France, granting exclusivity to three self-proclaimed inventors in the right to use a number of undescribed (and undisclosed) inventions—including the perpetual motion. The letter does not describe the inventions, only their proclaimed advantages, even if the inventors offered to provide a demonstration of how they worked, at their own expenses.

This letter presents two elements of interest. The first element is that it does not follow what today is called the "rule of unity," under which patents are granted to one single inventive concept.

The second element is that the rights granted by this privilege cover not only direct and indirect infringement, but also contributory infringement—in this, thus, it is a very modern document.

Henry, by the grace of God, King of France and Poland, to our beloved and seer counselors holding our great council, courts of parliament, bailiffs, seneschals and provosts, or their lieutenants, and to all our other law enforcers and officers to whom it will concern, greetings and affection.

Our dear and beloved Nicolas Wasseur Hun, bourgeois of Basel in Switzerland, Jehan Desponde and Paul Latreille, have made it shown to us that after having long sought the means to be able to raise the waters from a low and deep place to the top, they have arrived by the grace of God to the knowledge of the true secret, so much so that they have the means to raise the water of the wells as high and in such quantity as they wish, and to make of each well a fountain running continuously, and this without the help from any man or animal, thus by itself. Moreover, they have other ways of making of each well a mill of wheat, of cloth, of tanning, of beating the gunpowder, of making paper, of sawing the wood, of operating the bellows of all forges, the whips to refine iron and forge it after its fusion, as well as all other gold and silver mines, and all other metals that need the violence of water. Furthermore they can make fountains for our good city and municipality of Paris in all the places that will be necessary, which will continuously gush as much water as one wants, and this by means of a channel that they will open from the river, which water will be clearer, cleaner and healthier to drink than that of the said river, a very useful and necessary thing in our said city of Paris, as well as in several of our fortresses, which have great lack of the above mentioned fountains and mills, which is often the cause for their being forced to surrender when besieged. And because many people promising the same things could be presented to us without however having been able to achieve their undertaking, the said petitioners offer to demonstrate it at their own costs and expenses, which is the real way to remove the error and distrust from them and their invention. And furthermore they have the means of plowing more land in one day with two horses or other animals which are not accustomed to do it than with two pairs of oxen; and also to pull and lead any wagons whatsoever more easily with six horses, or even with less, than is commonly done with thirty; and they will make that a single man can raise more weight than fifty men together would be able to do, so much so that the force of a man will be sufficient by their craft to raise a double cannon. And they will also make boats to sail a river, wide or narrow, against the current with two-thirds less men and horses than are currently usually employed, which will bring great savings and cause that all goods, both those transported by water and those transported by land, will be at a better price. They can likewise save half the wood that is consumed by dying, steaming and washing, brewing beer, cooking, and other things on which there has been the custom of burning a lot of wood. Moreover, they have found perpetual motion, which can serve an infinity of good things and very important conveniences of us and our subjects. And although part of them are our subjects and the other part Germans, and having requested for this purpose in several places of Germany, such as Auxbourg, Strasbourg and other places, nevertheless those of them which are our subjects have always retained their German companions so fond of our service that they did not want to communicate their said invention to any prince, republic or city of Europe, that firstly they were offered to us to embellish, if we please, our city and municipality of Paris, as the first of our said kingdom, which we honor by our ordinary residence, by means of the mentioned fountains, to be kept much healthier and clearer than it is at present, in consequence of which the residents would be provided with good waters, of which they have great lack, more than the other cities and places of our State; for what reasons and the great good that the said invention can bring to all this kingdom, the said petitioners having not been invited to present themselves to us other than by the natural duty that they have at our service, ornament of their country and affection that they all together bring to its good, they have very humbly begged and requested to permit them and those to whom they will give charge and power to do this, and to prohibit all others to use the said invention in our country, lands and lordships of our obedience, during the time of thirty years, directly or indirectly, in any way whatsoever, without their leave or permission, under penalty of confiscation of bodies and property assignable to them, both against the workers who will, without their permission, make and imitate their machines, and those who will use and put them into practice, and for these purposes grant them our letters to this necessary;

We, for these reasons, wishing to help the said exponents in the execution of such a laudable and holy will, have, by liberally inclining to their request, and not for remunerating them in any manner whatsoever, allowed and accorded and granted, by our graces, special, full power and royal authority, allow them, accord, grant, want and please us, by these present, that up to thirty years, starting from the day and date of these, that they can, and only those that will receive from them charge, authorization and capacity to do and fulfill the content of the above by all the places and sites of this our said kingdom, country, lands and lordships of our obedience, that will be required, without, during the said period, any other, of whatever state, quality, and condition that they may be, may in any way whatsoever imitate or counterfeit their said invention, nor to use it, directly or indirectly, without their permission, which we prohibit them very expressly, under the penalty, both to the workers who will have made the machines and works serving the things above, and those who have had them made and put or will want to put at work and service in any way whatsoever, of confiscation of bodies and property assignable to said petitioners by these said present, the content of which we want and order you that you make them, obey and let enjoy and use plainly and peacefully, as it is said, ceasing and putting an end to all disturbances and hindrances to the contrary, without the said petitioners being required, in order to do so, to obtain verification and confirmation of these present [letters] other than in our great council, and which verification that will follow we further wish to be of such virtue and execution as if it was done in all our other courts.

Given in Paris, the first day of March, the year of grace one thousand and five hundred eighty-five.

And of our kingdom, the eleventh. Signed by the King at his council.

§1.21 HENRY IV, OF FRANCE, SETTLES A DISPUTE OVER INVENTORSHIP

March 6, 1610

This text is the judgment by the State Council of Henry IV, settling a dispute on the true inventorship of an invention initially claimed by Claude du Caire. Of particular interest, besides the specifics of the various allegations made and the manner of sorting out who was right, was the implication that the entitlement to the industrial privilege belonged to the true inventor, regardless of the fact that the challenger had alleged being able to produce better results.

In 1610, Claude du Caire obtained a patent for the same invention from the Senate of Venice.

Judgment of the State Council and Letters Patent of the King, of March 6, 1610, containing the privilege granted to Claude du Caire, his heirs, and successors, to disclose, and teach the use of furnaces by him newly invented, for the saving of half the wood usually consumed by other furnaces, with the advice of the Provost of the Merchants and Echevins of Paris, and Judgment of the Court of Parliament, containing the verification of said letters.

Extract from the Records of the State Council:

Seen by the King in his Council, the certificate [*brevet*] of his Majesty of September 22, 1608, by which he has allowed Claude du Caire, one of the entrepreneurs of the mining companies of France, and his associates, to show the way and the construction of stoves and furnaces of their invention to all those who wish to use them in this Kingdom, by means of which half of the wood that is consumed in stoves and furnaces will be saved, against reward that will be mutually agreed, with defenses to all persons who wish to use the said invention during the term of fifteen years, from the day and date of the publication of the letters that will be issued, without the consent and permission of said du Caire, or his associates, on penalty of a fine of fifteen hundred pounds, for the first time, one-third being applicable to his Majesty, one-third to the inventors, and one-third to the whistle-blowers, and of all expenses, damages, and interest.

Motion by Denis Thouin, requesting that the privilege of the reformation and new construction of the said stoves and furnaces for the saving of wood, granted by his Majesty to the said du Caire, be adjudicated to the one of the two who will have made the best proof of his invention in the presence of experts, and which in any case will make the condition of his Majesty better and more advantageous. The judgment given to the said Council on the twenty-ninth of October 1609 ordered that the said Motion would be served on the said du Caire, and the day assigned to the parties to give proof of the experience of their invention, in the presence of Sieur de Suilly, peer and Grand Voyeur de France, whom his Majesty would have appointed to attend and report to the said Council, in order that afterwards the preference over the said privilege be granted to that whose proof of the invention would be better and more certain, and whose condition to his Majesty and the public would be more advantageous. . . . Three instructions by the said Sieur Duc de Suilly, . . . to summon before him the said Thouin and du Caire, to certify in writing, each signed by his hand, the invention which they claim to put in use for the saving of the wood of the said stoves and furnaces, . . . Report of their appearance before the said sieur Duc de Suilly, containing their statements and demonstrations. Statement certified in writing, by the said du Caire, on the saving of about half of the wood which is usually consumed by the bakers and pastry-cooks by means of the ovens of his new invention, which are manufactured on one another, and for all dyes, beer brewers, soap manufactures, laundries, ovens and stoves, and for salt-works, for which he requires no other reward than those who will deem the said inventions to be useful and profitable to them, and wish to use it, would willingly accord him. Motion presented by sieurs de la Fin, Beringhen, Demouillepied, and by Gilles de l'Île. At the expectation that they are the first authors and operators of the said invention, it be the pleasure of the King to order that, to the exclusion of the said du Caire, and his said associates, the privilege of building the said furnaces, will be issued in their favor under the name of the said de l'Île, to be enjoyed by them during the term of thirty years, or such other time as it will please his Majesty. . . .

The King in his Council has ordered and orders that the said du Caire during the term of fifteen years will enjoy the said privilege of constructing new stoves and furnaces, and other inventions contained and specified by the said certificate, under the conditions proposed by him, and that for this purpose all letters and provisions will be issued in his favor. And as regards the other proposed inventions not comprised in the said certificate, his Majesty orders that new proof will be made of them, in the presence of sieur du Sully, designated for this effect, so that, in accordance with his report, to be adjudicated to those whose proof will be found to be the best and more certain. . . . Done in the King's State Council held in Paris, on the sixteenth day of March, one thousand six hundred and ten. . . .

§1.22 A FRENCH COURT AFFIRMS THE PRINCIPLE OF ALTERNATIVENESS AS THE JUSTIFICATION OF THE PATENT SYSTEM

May 3, 1610

The text that follows was produced by an administrative body of the Municipality of Paris, in connection with the confirmation of the patent letters signed by Henry IV as regards the dispute over Claude du Caire's privilege (*see* the previous Text). This is a text of enormous significance because for the first time the principle of alternativeness is affirmed as a justification of the patent system: patent rights are not monopolist because third parties may always prefer to use those techniques that were available before the grant (or that can be created afterwards). Consequently no patent can cover a solution that is the only one possible for a given technical problem.

This important concept, which avoids the creation of monopolies by the patent system (unless government regulation provides otherwise) would be later enunciated by other courts, in other places, but with the same meaning (*see* Texts 1.42 and 1.47).

Extracted from the Records of the Hotel of the City of Paris:

The Provosts of the Merchants and the Aldermen of the said city, who saw the letters patent of the King, given in Paris on March 6 last, signed Henry, and on the fold by the King, and sealed on double tail of yellow wax, obtained by Claude du Caire, lord of Poippes, general contractor of the Mines of France, by which and for the causes contained, his Majesty gave and granted to the said du Caire, his heirs, employees, and successors in title, privilege, power, faculty, capacity, and freedom to bring and have brought to light, and evidence, to show and teach, when it suits him, to practice and to have practiced through all Kingdoms, countries, lands, and lordships of his obedience, the inventions and secrets of certain construction of stoves, which can bring savings of about half of the wood that is customarily consumed by the bakers, pastry cooks, dyers, beer brewers, laundry operators, soap makers, furnaces, ovens and others of all sorts of people's conditions, with the help of stoves and furnaces, to all those who will want to use and be served by them, for a reasonable reward, that they will be obliged to lease from the said du Caire and his employees, which they will contract by mutual agreement, and this for the time and space of fifteen years, from the day and date of verification of said letters, making express inhibitions and prohibitions to all persons of any quality and condition whatsoever to use or to be served by said inventions, to have any stoves and furnaces built or erected, except by the permission of the said du Caire, his employees, and successors in title, for the said period of fifteen years, under the penalty of a fine of one thousand pounds, in accordance with what is extensively mentioned by the said letters sent to them by our lords of the Court of Parliament, for giving advice on them.

They say that it seems that the confirmation of the said letters cannot injure the public, since these are in liberty and willingness to use, or not, the said invention, in addition to the evident convenience arising from the said letters, that the artisans will receive by means of the reduction and management of the use of the wood, and therefore they report to our said Lords of the Court of Parliament to command it, as they will find it to be good. Done at the office of the city, the third day of May, one thousand six hundred and ten.

§1.23 ANOTHER FRENCH INDUSTRIAL PRIVILEGE

June 30, 1611

These patent letters (signed in Paris, June 30, 1611, and registered in Parliament on March 2, 1612) inform that the invention in question has been disclosed to and its utility examined by a committee designated by the king. In following the then applicable regime of privileges, the letter starts by according an authorization for building the mills. Such an authorization was limited, however, because it should not affect those lands whose owners enjoyed the "droit de moulin" (or right to have a mill—according to which they would charge a fee from those farmers and villagers who wished to have grains ground).

This privilege presents two interesting aspects. First, it provides for a sanction in the case the invention reduces the value of any of the crown's mills.

This is a strange notion of utility, but today the solution would not be much different. Today, if the operation of a given invention reduces the value of public property, the correspondent patent will be subject to a compulsory license or its commercial exploitation will be prohibited.

Second, the letter grants the inventors the exclusive right in building the new windmills (on public lands only), but not the exclusive right to use the mills, i.e., to grind grains. This corresponds to the old "droit de moulin," but, with hindsight, one could see here a sort of exhaustion of patent rights.

Also worth of notice is the statement that the inventors, having received offers from foreign authorities to disclose and practice their inventions in their dominions, have preferred to keep the secret and apply for the patent in France. The patent letter of 1585, addressed to Hun, Desponde and Latreille (*see* Text 1.20), made the same affirmation. At that time, there was no requirement of novelty, and industrial privileges have indeed been obtained for the same invention in various countries regardless of their having been disclosed or kept secret. As in the previous case, the intention of the applicants was to please the King, and obtain a more sympathetic disposition from him.

Louis, etc. Our dear and beloved Jehan de Bras de Fer, esquire, lord of Châteaufort, made it said and demonstrated to us that in the last fifteen to twenty years he would have, with Adam Faucheron, carpenter, and others, employed all his time and wealth in search of several secrets and inventions still not found or discovered, no less necessary to the public than rare, which he would have been summoned to show by several foreign princes and lords who would have had his advice with offers of great favors and rewards, which he always have refused so as to give them to our kingdom, his homeland.

Among which inventions he found that of a hand-mill which will grind by means of a man, a horse or a donkey, which is of such, so rare and convenient ingenuity that he can at any time and season to continually turn and serve both to grind the wheat, to make paper, to tread cloth and other things, as well as to beat oak bark, powders, pound hemp and other things where there is the necessity of whips, mallets, gavels, and hammers, and to spin millstones for all sorts of things, whether for cutting diamonds, or for grinding all kinds of grains, for making oils, as well as for raising water; likewise for making mills suitable for milling on the boats and vessels that go over the sea and the rivers, the maintenance and the expenses being much less than those that are now in use, and with the effect of being able to avoid to be delayed in any way in the lowlands by lack of wind, or in the valleys by drought, ice and water shortages, having nothing to do with water or wind, to the great good and relief of the people, who are often forced to go far away in search of mills, which they may have from now on by means of the said invention, near their dwellings, continually working with ease and little expense.

Furthermore that if one wants, by means of the said invention, to prevent that several small rivers be blocked by road locks or otherwise, by disposing the water to the favor and use of the said mills sitting on those, [the inventions] can be used to carry boats and cars and by this means to be more useful to the public than they are in the use of the mills that they make grind, the ingenuity and invention of the said Bras de Fer satisfying and supplying instead of water and wind.

On the basis of which, in order not to omit anything that depends on our authority, for the good, the advantage and the convenience of our subjects, we have had the said proposal put into consideration and deliberation, and ordered senior members of our council to see and examine the effect of said invention; which they would report to us they had seen it grinding and reducing the wheat into good, fair and of market value flour, by the ingenuity of the said Bras de Fer, and advise to authorize and highlight it.

For these reasons, and also wishing to gratify the said Bras de Fer:

(1) We have, by the advice of the queen regent, our very honored lady and mother, and of the senior members of our council, allowed and granted, allow and grant that he and his associates, or those to whom he will give permission, may have the mills of his invention built and erected, and to use it for all the things that are here declared, in all the cities, towns, villages and places of our kingdom, lands and countries of our obedience, accepting or leasing the places he wants to build or erect the mills of his invention.

(2) However, he will not be allowed to build the said mills on the lands of the lords and gentlemen having the *droit de moulin*, nor on private vessels, without their agreement and consent; which mills of his invention shall belong to him, to his associates and to those to whom he will give permission to make build the said invention, their heirs, representatives or successors in title, as their own true and natural thing, and dispose of it as they see fit, provided that they have satisfied the owners of the places and sites in which the said mills will be built, on the condition that, in the event that any of the mills brings less value to any of ours, the said Bras de Fer, its associates and those who will have his permission will pay, for each year, the whole lease and rent to which they would have been obliged by our officers, taking by themselves the mills, which they will use, as they will see fit to be.

(3) Prohibiting all persons, of whatever quality and condition they may be, to order the building of the mills of his invention, even on boats, to make or to counterfeit or to imitate them, either wholly or in part, and to use in any way, for any purpose whatsoever, the said invention and ingenuity, even in the watermills or windmills presently built, without his express leave or permission, under the penalty of a fine of ten thousand pounds and confiscation of the mills and invention made or counterfeited, half of which assignable to us and the other half to the said Bras de Fer and his associates, the said Bras de Fer not needing another permission or grant for the construction of the said mills, either from us or from the cities, towns, villages or other places belonging to us, other than these letters, and this during the period of twenty years.

(4) And so that the said Bras de Fer be not disturbed or prevented by anyone, claiming to have had and obtained from the late kings our predecessors, that God absolve, such power and permission to build some mills, the invention of which they would have not been able to see, not even any evidence or experience of those in the presence of any commissioner deputy of our council, as a fake or imagined thing, we have revoked the power and all the letters granted for that purpose, and revoke them as null and void, making very express prohibitions to all people to use or be served by them, under the same penalties as above.

We want this and command you, etc.

§1.24 IN THE EARLY SEVENTEENTH CENTURY FRANCE HAD ALREADY DEVELOPED A SORT OF A TEMPLATE FOR INDUSTRIAL PRIVILEGES

October 10, 1612

The similarity of the language used in the following privilege with the previous one implies that in the early seventeenth century France had already developed a sort of a legal formula for those titles, even if the country had still to wait six decades to have its own first patent statute.

Three elements in this patent letter are of significance. First, it is still very much a privilege in the strict sense of the word, given that the king invokes the inventor's good services in other fields ("inventions of mathematics that he found both for war and for other occasions"), thus meaning that the patent has not been granted just because of the invention made.

Second, the exclusivity is granted for the whole invention or for any "particularity" of it. With hindsight, one could see here a sort of a precedent of today's practice of writing patent applications, dividing the whole inventive concept into independent claims. Patent infringement does not require that the whole invention be used—the unauthorized use of one particularity may suffice.

Third, the granted exclusivity does not affect those who may have acquired patents for inventions "for the same effects" from previous kings. Is this a disclaimer of responsibility—which is common today—in the case this patent overlaps previous titles for the same invention? Or does that language imply that the patent is granted with reference to the specific characteristics of the claimed invention, but does not harm the rights of those who may have invented different technical solutions, albeit with the same or similar results? If the second option was true, then this letter presents already some aspects of modernity.

Paris, 10 October 1612. Registered in the Parliament, 3 January 1619.

Louis, etc. Our dear and well-beloved J. Regnault Dezanville has humbly demonstrated to us that, wishing to serve the public, industriously found an invention which has not yet been practiced to avoid that rooms get smoky.

Very humbly begging and requesting us that we grant him a privilege to serve the public with his invention, and to prohibit all people, for twenty years, to make or counterfeit it, or any particularity contained in it, and to use or being served by it without his permission, or of those who will have received the authorization from him, under the penalty of a fine of one hundred écus, half assignable to us, and the other half to the whistleblower.

Whereas Dezanville has worked for the public in this respect, and also considering the good and pleasant services he has given us in the mathematical inventions he has found both for the war and for other occasions,

(1) To that Dezanville, his heirs and successors in title, we have permitted, granted and accorded, and by the present [letters], signed by our hand, we give, grant and accord the permission to put into use the said invention through all the places and sites of this kingdom, country, lands, and lordships of our obedience, and derive from it the profit that is due to him for twenty years: allowing him to associate by license or assignment of this privilege, with such persons as it pleases him, so as to enjoy it through them and to avail themselves of it, jointly or separately, and in all places which they have agreed

upon, during those twenty years, starting in each of your areas and jurisdictions on the day that these presents have been therein published and verified.

(2) And for this, we have made and make very express prohibitions to all our subjects and others, of whatever state, quality and condition that they may be, to make or to order the making of the said invention in any place of our kingdom, country, lands and lordships of our obedience, or of any particularity contained in it, or to use it, under the penalty of a fine of one hundred écus, half payable to us and the other half to the whistleblower, unless as per the permission of the said Dezanville or of those who will have received the power from him, without however prejudicing those who, before these present [letters], would have obtained privileges from our predecessors or from ourselves for the same effects.

We thus command you, etc.

§1.25 THE STATUTE OF MONOPOLIES: STILL A LAW ON PRIVILEGES, BUT THE FOUNDATION OF MODERN PATENT LAW

1623

The language of this Statute has still the taste of old medieval privileges, but its laconic style had the advantage of leaving room for courts to resort to common law for filling its gaps and loopholes. It was thus that, gradually, along the two next centuries, English courts built the foundations of modern patent law, on which the Industrial Revolution would evolve.

The Statute sets a term of protection of industrial privileges of fourteen years, which, as a multiple of seven, has Biblical origins.

The Statute of Monopolies, England, 1623. 21 James I, c. 1, 3, 1623.

Forasmuch as your most excellent Majesty in your royal judgment and of your blessed disposition to the well and quiet of your subjects, did, in the year of our Lord God one thousand six hundred and ten, publish in print to the whole real and to all posterity, that all grants of monopolies and of the benefit of any penal laws, or of power to dispense with the law, or to compound for the forfeiture, are contrary to your Majesty's laws, which your Majesty's declaration is truly consonant and agreeable to the ancient and fundamental laws of this your realm: And whereas your Majesty was further graciously pleased expressly to command that no subject should presume to move your Majesty for matters of that nature; yet nevertheless upon misinformations and untrue pretenses of public good, many such grants have been unduly obtained and unlawfully put in execution, to the great grievance and inconvenience of your Majesty's royal and blessed intention so published as aforesaid: for avoiding whereof and preventing of the like in time to come, may it please your most excellent Majesty at the humble suit of the lords spiritual and temporal and the commons in this present Parliament assembled, that it may be declared and enacted, and be it declared and enacted by the authority of this present Parliament, that all monopolies and all commissions, grants, licences, charters, and letters patent heretofore made or granted, or heretofore to be made and granted to any person or persons, bodies, politic or corporate whatsoever for the sole buying, selling, making, working, or using of anything within this realm or the dominion of Wales, or of any other monopolies, or of power, liberty, or faculty to dispense with any others, or to give licence or toleration to do use, or exercise anything against the tenor or purport of any law or statute, or to give or make any warrant for any such dispensation, licence, or toleration to be had or made, or to agree or compound with any others for any penalties or forfeitures limited by any statute, or of any grant or promise of the benefit, profit, or commodity of any forfeiture, penalty, or sum of money that is or shall be due by any statute before judgment thereupon had, and all proclamations, inhibitions, restraints, warrants of assistance, and all other matters and things whatsoever any way tending to the instituting, erecting, strengthening, furthering, or countenancing of the same or any of them, are altogether contrary to the laws of this realm, and so are and shall be utterly void and of none effect, and in no wise to be put in use or execution. . . .

VI. Provided also and be it declared and enacted, that any declaration before mentioned shall not extend to any letters patent and grants of privilege for the term of fourteen years or under, hereafter to be made of the sole working or making of any manner of new manufactures within this realm, to the true and first inventor and inventors of such manufactures, which others at the time of making such letters patent and grants shall not use, so as also they not be contrary to the laws nor mischievous to the state, by raising prices of commodities at home, or hurt of trade, or generally inconvenient; the said fourteen years to be accomplished from the date of the first letters patent or grant of such privilege hereafter to be made, but that the same shall be free of such force as they should be if this Act had never been made, and of none other. . . .

§1.26 IN FRANCE, COLBERT ESTABLISHES A RULE: PATENTS ARE ONLY TO BE GRANTED FOR INVENTIONS THAT ARE GENUINELY NEW

February 17, 1679

In this letter, Jean-Baptiste Colbert, minister of Finance of Louis XIV, states his (and the King's) policy concerning industrial privileges: they would not be granted unless the matter to be protected were new technology. Possibly it was this idea that led Colbert to support and sponsor the Academy of Sciences and its role of examining patent applications as to their novelty and utility (*see* Text 1.27).

To Mr. Dalliez, Director of the Compagnie du Levant.

Saint-Germain, February 17, 1679

I will examine the proposals you make to me concerning the manufacture of pancakes; but as it has been some time since I have had its current situation examined, I am almost persuaded that it will be maintained by allowing to the public the freedom to work in it, and by revoking the privilege of Mr. Dupuy. You must be assured that whenever I find either a greater advantage, or an equal advantage, I do not hesitate to take away all privileges, especially since you see that that of Mr. Dupuy has not been successful.

I will let you know my feelings on the proposal you have submitted to me for a manufacture of earthenware. But you must reckon that there will always be great difficulty in obtaining exclusive privileges for all the manufactures that are established in the kingdom, and that they will be obtained only for those whose knowledge is entirely unknown.

§1.27 JEAN-BAPTISTE COLBERT INAUGURATES THE FIRST PATENT OFFICE

January 26, 1699

In 1666, the Academy of Sciences (which until then was part of the Academy of Letters), became an independent organization and moved to a special room in the King's library, then sieged in a house owned by Colbert. In 1699 Colbert moved the Academy to a gallery at the Louvre Palace and, on January 29 of that year, the king approved its by-laws, which included the task of examining patent applications as to novelty and utility. The text that follows is an excerpt from those by-laws.

But, even in the absence of a written rule, the Academy had had the attribution of examining the merit of applications for privileges since its foundation, in 1666 (not coincidentally, one year after Colbert became minister of Finance of Louis XIV).

Between 1666 and 1699, the Academy had already examined and approved 47 applications.

As the King wishes to continue to give marks of his affection to the Royal Academy of Sciences, His Majesty has resolved the present regulations, which He wishes to be exactly observed. . . .

XXXI.—The Academy shall examine, if the King so orders, all the machines for which privileges will be solicited from His Majesty. It will certify whether they are new and useful, and the inventors of those that will be approved shall be required to leave a model for it.

§1.28 A PORTUGUESE DECREE INCENTIVIZING THE IMMIGRATION OF INVENTORS

April 18, 1761

José I, of Portugal, had the Marquis of Pombal as his Prime Minister, a man who performed as regards the Portuguese economy a role not dissimilar to that of Colbert in France: he was a reformist, and a strong promoter of the national industry. The text that follows is not about the appropriation of knowledge, in spite of its reference to inventions. But it reflects a policy of establishing favors to inventors.

By Decree of 9 February of this year, which was sent to the Chamber's Senate, I was served to permit that all, and any persons working in this Court, or in any place of this Kingdom, who had obtained permission from the Board of Trade of these Realms and their Domains, to work on cast works of Tin, Brass, and other metals, be issued the necessary permits in their favor by the same Senate; in such a manner that the Officers of its jurisdiction could not cause to them the slightest hindrance. And bearing in mind that the advancement of the Mechanical Arts in this Kingdom may be accomplished by facilitating the foreign Artificers with the permits that they ask: I think it best as well to extend the same permission to all, and any outstanding artificers, whether national or foreign, so that, when submitting licenses from the aforementioned Board to work on works of new invention, or of known utility to the Kingdom, the Senate orders the issuance of the necessary licenses to them. The same Chamber's Senate, having understood it in the same way, and have it executed.

Nossa Senhora da Ajuda, April 18, 1761. With the Initials of His Majesty.

§1.29 FRANCE REVISES AND CONSOLIDATES ALL INDUSTRIAL PRIVILEGES GRANTED UNTIL 1762

1762, December 24

The inadequacy of the old industrial privilege regime to support the movement of a country into the Industrial Revolution has become evident to the French by the end of the seventeenth century. The text that follows enumerates some of the major shortcomings of such a regime. By revoking those privileges, the king ordered that new privileges would obey a system of disclosure and follow a fixed term. Their maintenance would also require the commercial exploitation of the invention. France was thereby getting closer to a modern system of patents.

Louis, etc. Commercial privileges, which are intended to reward the industry of inventors or to excite that which languished in competition without emulation, do not always have the success that can be expected, either because these privileges, granted for unlimited time, seem to be a hereditary asset rather than a personal reward to the inventor, either because the privilege can be subsequently assigned to people who do not have the required capacity, or finally because the children, heirs and successors of the privileged person, called by law to the privilege's enjoyment, neglect to acquire the necessary talents.

The lack of exercise of these privileges may also have all the more inconveniences as they hinder freedom without providing the public with the resources it waits for; finally, the lack of publicity of the title of the privilege often gives the privileged person the opportunity to extend it and unduly hinder the industry and the work of our subjects. For these causes, etc., we want and please the following:

1. All commercial privileges, which have been or will be granted to individuals, either in their own name or in their and their company's name, for fixed and limited periods, shall be carried out according to their form and content, until the end of the term set by the titles of their concession.
2. All the said privileges, which have been or would be subsequently granted indefinitely and without term, are and will remain fixed and reduced to the term of fifteen years of enjoyment from the title of grant, except when the privileged persons obtain the extension of said privileges, if that occurs; however, we do not intend to innovate with respect to the grants by us made as regards every real estate, either in *franc-aleu*, or in *fief*, or at the expense of annual fees.
3. Privileges unlimited in their titles of grant and fixed by the preceding article to the term of fifteen years, which will expire, or [which are] in the fourteenth year of their exercise, on the day of the present Ordinance, shall be extended until the end of three years, counting from the day of the said publication, except if the privileged person obtains a further extension, if that occurs.
4. The privileged person may during his life assign the exercise of his privilege to his children or grandchildren, but he may not assign it to others, without being especially authorized by us to do so.
5. In the event of the death of the privileged person during his privilege's term, his direct or collateral heirs, universal legatees, individuals, or other successors, cannot succeed to the said privileges without having obtained from us a confirmation, after justifying their capacity, and this notwithstanding any clauses, no matter what they may be, which could be found either in the title

of grant, or in subsequent titles and acts, which we have expressly derogated by this Ordinance.

6. All privileges in respect of which the privileged persons have in vain attempted to be successful, or whose use and exercise during one year they have neglected, as well as the decisions and patent letters, grants or other titles constitutive of the said privileges, will be and will remain null and revoked, unless the exercise of the said privileges has been suspended for some legitimate causes or impediments that the privileged person shall be bound to justify.
7. And so that the said privileges are known to all those who may be interested, we wish that after the registration of the said privileges in our courts, at the diligence of our attorneys-general, a verified copy of these be sent to the offices of the bailiffs, in whose jurisdiction they must be executed. Thus we accord, etc.

§1.30 ENGLAND'S CHIEF JUSTICE, LORD MANSFIELD, ASSERTS THE ENABLING DISCLOSURE REQUIREMENT AS PART OF THE DEAL BETWEEN SOCIETY AND THE PATENTEE

1778

In the process of adapting patent law to the economic and technical scenario of the Industrial Revolution, English courts introduced the requirement of the detailed description of inventions, and the precise identification of the technical characteristics that inventors believe to constitute their invention, i.e., the claims. In this way, the patent served to teach the invention, so that, once the patent expired, society could use it.

Liardet v. Johnson

Before Lord Mansfield, C. J. 1778

This was an action brought for an infringement of the plaintiff's patent, granted 1773, for a composition or stucco for the covering the walls of houses. This patent was set aside in consequence of insufficiency of the specification.

Lord Mansfield, in delivering judgment, said, the general questions on patents are, 1st, whether the invention was known and in use before the patent; and, 2nd, whether the specification is sufficient to enable others to make it up. The meaning of the specification is, that others may be taught to do the thing for which the patent is granted; and if the specification is false the patent is void, for after the term the public ought to have the benefit of the discovery. Hence the law requires as the price the patentee should pay to the public for his monopoly, that he should, to the very best of his knowledge, give the fullest and most sufficient description of all the particulars on which the effect depends.

§1.31 AN EARLY ATTACK AGAINST THE PATENT SYSTEM, AND PHARMACEUTICAL PATENTS IN PARTICULAR

1780

Although European countries and the United States gradually embraced the patent system as a mechanism to bring technical and economic progress, not all citizens would be happy with it. As a matter of course, there might have strong reasons to be suspicious of such a system: patents were still basically privileges, and many of them—especially those granted for medicines—would be kept under secrecy.

In England the regular patenting of medicines started after the passing of the Statute of Monopolies. However, the term "patent medicine" could also mean a medicine that received a patent letter authorizing its commercialization and advertisement. In both cases, the pharmacists were required to disclose the composition of the products. But this did not avoid the proliferation of quack medicines.

The text that follows is an interesting and funny expression of that suspicion.

The Patent, a Poem (excerpt), by W. Woty, 1780

Happy the Man, who duly pays his debts,
He still more happy, who a Patent gets.
This prose enlivens, and adorns the rhime,
Lifts the low thought, and stamps it with sublime;
Catches the eye, allures that erring sense,
Ere steady Judgment can her reign commence,
Like Copper-plates, at which Men-children look,
And praise the Prints, before they read the book.
Hail to the Patent! which enables Man
To vend a Folio—or a Warming-pan.
This makes the Windlass work with double force
And smoke-jacks whirl more rapid in their course;
Confers a sanction on the Doctor's pill,
Oft' known to cure, but oft'ner known to kill.
What man would scruple to resign his breath,
Provided he could die a Patent death! . . .
The time may come, when nothing will succeed,
But what a previous Patent hath decreed;
And we must open, on some future day,
The door of Nature with a patent Key. . . .

§1.32 AN ENGLISH COURT IMPOSES THE REQUIREMENT OF THE BEST MODE DESCRIPTION

February 5, 1787

This is an important opinion clarifying to what extent the description of the invention is required. After *Liardet v. Johnson* (*see* Text 1.30), English courts would often be called to scrutinize the quality of patent specifications. In this case, the King's Bench went further, and invalidated a patent on the failure to describe the best mode.

Turner v. Winter

King's Bench, February 5, 1787

The action was a case for infringement of a patent dated February 26, 1780, for a method of producing yellow color for painting in oil or water, making white lead, and separating the mineral alkali from common salt, all to be performed in a single process. . . .

Ashurst, J. I think that, as every patent is calculated to give a monopoly to the patentee, it is so far against the principles of law, and would be a reason against it, were it not for the advantages which the public derive from the communication of the invention after the expiration of the time for which the patent is granted. It is, therefore, incumbent on the patentee to give a specification of the invention in the clearest and most unequivocal terms of which the subject is capable. And if it appear that there is any unnecessary ambiguity affectedly introduced into the specification, or anything which tends to mislead the public, in that case the patent is void. Here it does appear to me that there is at least such a doubt on the evidence that I cannot say this matter has been so fully and fairly examined as to preclude any farther investigation of the subject. . . .

But in truth, the patent is for making white lead and two other things by one process. Therefore, if the process, as directed by the specification, does not produce that which the patent professes to do, the patent itself is void. It is certainly of consequence that the terms of a specification should express the invention in the clearest and most explicit manner, so that a man of science may be able to produce the thing intended without the necessity of trying experiments.

Buller, J. Many cases upon patents have arisen within our memory, most of which have been decided against the patentees, upon the ground of their not having made a full and fair discovery of their inventions. Whenever it appears that the patentee has made a fair disclosure, I have always had a strong bias in his favor, because, in that case, he is entitled to the protection which the law gives him. How far that law which authorizes the king to grant patents is politic, is not for us to determine. When attempts are made to evade a fair patent I am strongly inclined in favor of the patentee; but where the discovery is not fully made, the court ought to look with a very watchful eye to prevent any imposition on the public. Then the question is, whether the present plaintiff has made a fair discovery. . . . So if he [the plaintiff] make the article for which the patent is granted with cheaper materials than those which he has enumerated, although the latter will answer the purpose equally well, the patent is void, because he does not put the public in possession of his invention, or enable them to derive the same benefit which he himself does.

Now, on either of these grounds the patent is void. . . .

§1.33 JAMES MADISON'S VIEWS ON THE PATENT CLAUSE OF THE UNITED STATES CONSTITUTION

October 1787–May 1788

The project for a Federal Constitution of the United States was subject to attacks by powerful antagonists who were not pleased with the loss of autonomy of States. In response to those attacks, and wishing to influence voters towards the ratification of the Constitution, three eminent politicians, James Jay, Alexander Hamilton, and James Madison, produced a series of essays defending the Constitution. Those essays, designated as The Federalist, were published in newspapers of New York City under the pseudonym Publius between 1787 and 1788. In The Federalist Paper No. 43, in defending the Union's authority to grant patents and copyrights, as opposed to individual States, James Madison produced a strong and eloquent, albeit short, defense of the two systems.

The fourth class [of powers lodged in the general government by the Constitution] comprises the following miscellaneous powers:

1. A power "to promote the progress of science and useful arts by securing, for a limited time, to authors and inventors the exclusive right to their respective writings and discoveries".

The utility of this power will scarcely be questioned. The copyright of authors has been solemnly adjudged in Great Britain to be a right of common law. The right to useful inventions seems with equal reason to belong to the inventors. The public good fully coincides in both cases with the claims of individuals. The States cannot separately make effectual provision for either of the cases, and most of them have anticipated the decision of this point by laws passed at the instance of Congress.

§1.34 THE CONGRESS OF THE UNITED STATES PASSES THE FIRST MODERN PATENT STATUTE

April 10, 1760

In 1790, on the authority of the Patent Clause of the Constitution, the Congress of the United States enacted the first modern patent statute. It was not the first statute in the New World, because some States, such as Virginia, had their own patent statutes. Congress itself had already granted individual privileges, on a case-by-case basis. Three years later this Act was replaced by the 1793 Act, simplifying the prosecution of patent applications.

Patent Act of 1790, Ch. 7, 1 Stat. 109-112 (April 10, 1790)

An Act to promote the progress of useful Arts

Section 1.

Be it enacted by the Senate and House of Representatives of the United States of America in Congress assembled, That upon the petition of any person or persons to the Secretary of State, the Secretary for the Department of War, and the Attorney

General of the United States, setting forth, that he, she, or they, hath or have invented or discovered any useful art, manufacture, engine, machine, or device, or any improvement therein not before known or used, and praying that a patent may be granted therefor, it shall and may be lawful to and for the Secretary of State, the Secretary for the Department of War, and the Attorney General, or any two of them, if they shall deem the invention or discovery sufficiently useful and important, to cause letters patent to be made out in the name of the United States, to bear teste by the President of the United States, reciting the allegations and suggestions of the said petition, and describing the said invention or discovery, clearly, truly and fully, and thereupon granting to such petitioner or petitioners, his, her or their heirs, administrators or assigns for any term not exceeding fourteen years, the sole and exclusive right and liberty of making, constructing, using and vending to others to be used, the said invention or discovery; which letters patent shall be delivered to the Attorney General of the United States to be examined, who shall, within fifteen days next after the delivery to him, if he shall find the same conformable to this act, certify it to be so at the foot thereof, and present the letters patent so certified to the President, who shall cause the seal of the United States to be thereto affixed, and the same shall be good and available to the grantee or grantees by force of this act, to all and every intent and purpose herein contained, and shall be recorded in a book to be kept for that purpose in the office of the Secretary of State, and delivered to the patentee or his agent, and the delivery thereof shall be entered on the record and endorsed on the patent by the said Secretary at the time of granting the same.

Sec. 2.

And be it further enacted, That the grantee or grantees of each patent shall, at the time of granting the same, deliver to the Secretary of State a specification in writing, containing a description, accompanied with drafts or models, and explanations and models (if the nature of the invention or discovery will admit of a model) of the thing or things, by him or them invented or discovered, and described as aforesaid, in the said patents; which specification shall be so particular, and said models so exact, as not only to distinguish the invention or discovery from other things before known and used, but also to enable a workman or other person skilled in the art or manufacture, whereof it is a branch, or wherewith it may be nearest connected, to make, construct, or use the same, to the end that the public may have the full benefit thereof, after the expiration of the patent term; which specification shall be filed in the office of the said Secretary, and certified copies thereof, shall be competent evidence in all courts and before all jurisdictions, where any matter or thing, touching or concerning such patent, right, or privilege, shall come in question.

Sec. 3.

And be it further enacted, That upon the application of any person to the Secretary of State, for a copy of any such specification, and for permission to have similar model or models made, it shall be the duty of the Secretary to give such copy, and to permit the person so applying for a similar model or models, to take, or make, or cause the same to be taken or made, at the expense of such applicant.

Sec. 4.

And be it further enacted, That if any person or persons shall devise, make, construct, use, employ, or vend within these United States, any art, manufacture, engine, machine or device, or any invention or improvement upon, or in any art, manufacture, engine, machine or device, the sole and exclusive right of which shall be so as aforesaid granted by patent to any person or persons, by virtue and in pursuance of this act, without the consent of the patentee or patentees, their executors, administrators or assigns, first had and obtained in writing, every person so offending, shall forfeit and pay to the said patentee or patentees, his, her or their executors, administrators or assigns such damages as shall be assessed by a jury, and moreover shall forfeit to the person aggrieved, the thing or things so devised, made, constructed, used, employed or vended, contrary to the true intent of this act, which may be recovered in an action on the case founded on this act.

Sec. 5.

And be it further enacted, That upon oath or affirmation made before the judge of the district court, where the defendant resides, that any patent which shall be issued in pursuance of this act, was obtained surreptitiously by, or upon false suggestion, and motion made to the said court, within one year after issuing the said patent, but not afterwards, it shall and may be lawful to and for the judge of the said district court, if the matter alleged shall appear to him to be sufficient, to grant a rule that the patentee or patentees, his, her, or their executors, administrators or assigns, show cause why process should not issue against him, her, or them, to repeal such patents; and if sufficient cause shall not be shown to the contrary, the rule shall be made absolute, and thereupon the said judge shall order process to be issued as aforesaid, against such patentee or patentees, his, her, or their executors, administrators, or assigns. And in case no sufficient cause shall be shown to the contrary, or if it shall appear that the patentee was not the first and true inventor or discoverer, judgment shall be rendered by such court for the repeal of such patent or patents; and if the party at whose complaint the process issued, shall have judgment given against him, he shall pay all such costs as the defendant shall be put to in defending the suit, to be taxed by the court, and recovered in such manner as costs expended by defendants, shall be recovered in due course of law.

Sec. 6.

And be it further enacted, That in all actions to be brought by such patentee or patentees, his, her, or their executors, administrators or assigns, for any penalty incurred by virtue of this act, the said patents or specifications shall be prima facie evidence, that the said patentee or patentees was or were the first and true inventor or inventors, discoverer or discoverers of the thing so specified, and that the same is truly specified; but that nevertheless the defendant or defendants may plead the general issue, and give this act, and any special matter whereof notice in writing shall have been given to the plaintiff, or his attorney, thirty days before the trial, in evidence, tending to prove that the specification filed by the plaintiff does not contain the whole of the truth concerning his invention or discovery; or that it contains more than is necessary to produce the effect described; and if the concealment of part, or the addition of more than is necessary, shall appear to have been intended to mislead, or shall actually mislead the public, so as the effect described cannot be produced by the means specified, then, and in such cases, the verdict and judgment shall be for the defendant.

Sec. 7.

And be it further enacted, That such patentee as aforesaid, shall, before he receives his patent, pay the following fees to the several officers employed in making out and perfecting the same, to wit: For receiving and filing the petition, fifty cents; for filing specifications, per copy-sheet containing one hundred words, ten cents; for making out patent, two dollars; for affixing great seal, one dollar; for indorsing the day of delivering the same to the patentee, including all intermediate services, twenty cents.

§1.35 REPORT ON THE PROPERTY OF DISCOVERIES AND INVENTIONS IN ALL SORTS OF INDUSTRY, SUBMITTED TO THE NATIONAL ASSEMBLY OF FRANCE BY M. DE BOUFFLERS

December 30, 1790

On the other side of the Atlantic Ocean, France, liberated by the Revolution from the constraints of the corporatist regime, prepared itself to embrace a modern patent system. It did so by unequivocally attributing the nature of property to the rights of inventors in their inventions. The text that follows are excerpts from the Report prepared for the French Parliament by the politician and poet, Stanislas de Boufflers (1738-1815), whose views were the basis for the law to be enacted (*see* Text 1.36).

If there is for a man a real property, that is his thought; that, at least, seems beyond reach; it is personal, it is independent, it is prior to all transactions, and the tree that grows in a field does not belong to that field's owner as much undeniably as the idea that comes to the spirit of a man belongs to its author. Invention, which is the source of arts, is also that of property: it is the original property; all others are not more than conventions. . . .

Whereas an inventor does not reveal his secret that he owns, and nothing prevents him from either keeping it concealed, or of fixing the conditions under which he consents to reveal it, he is free, when he contracts with society, as much as society is when it contracts with him; . . . .

If I am not wrong, it is to this that the first contract between the inventor and society can be reduced. The inventor wants to be allowed to enjoy peacefully something that comes from inside him, that belongs to him; and the proof he has is that only he knows it; he asks therefore that any other person be prohibited in advance to appropriate it after he revealed it, and it is only under this original condition that he will reveal what he calls his discovery.

§1.36 THE FRENCH NATIONAL ASSEMBLY PASSES ANOTHER MODERN PATENT STATUTE

January 7, 1791

The second modern patent statute, the French Act of January 7, 1791, was designed to support France's dispute with England on commercial and technological supremacy. It is this dispute—and the use of the patent system as one of its instruments—that explains the coexistence in the 1791 Act of modern aspects of patent law (such as the acknowledgment of proprietary rights, disclosure, access to information, enforcement, and aspects dealing with patentees' abuses), with elements that otherwise could appear unfit and displaced. One of those elements is the possibility given to the patentee to keep his/her invention secret. The other is the forfeiture of the French patent if the inventor takes a patent for the same invention in another country. Both features aim at avoiding that technology with eventual strategic importance be transferred or communicated to English rivals.

Law Relating to Useful Discoveries, and the Means of Ensuring their Ownership to Those Who Will Be Recognized as their Authors

Louis, by the grace of God, etc.:

Considering that any new idea, whose expression or development may become useful to society, belongs originally to the person who conceived it, and not acknowledging an industrial discovery as the property of its author would mean to attack human rights in their essence; considering, at the same time, how the absence of a positive and authentic declaration of this truth may have contributed so far to discourage the French industry, causing the emigration of several distinguished artists, and causing the transfer abroad of a great number of new inventions, from which this kingdom should have extracted the first advantages; considering finally, that all the principles of justice, public order and national interest, imperiously command that the opinion of French citizens on this kind of property be established from now on by a law that acknowledges and protects it, we order what follows:

I. Any discovery or new invention, in all kinds of industry, is the property of its author; consequently, the law guarantees him full and complete enjoyment, according to the mode and for the time that will be hereinafter determined. . . .

III. Whoever is the first to bring to France a foreign discovery will enjoy the same advantages as if he were the inventor.

IV. Whoever wishes to preserve or assure an industrial property of the kind of those stated in the preceding articles will be required,

1° To address to the secretariat of the directorate of his department, and to declare in writing whether the object he presents is of invention, of improvement, or merely of importation;

2° To file under seal an exact description of the principles, means and processes that constitute the discovery, as well as the plans, sections, drawings and models that could relate thereto, so as the mentioned file be opened at the moment when the inventor receives his title of ownership.

V. As for objects of general utility, but of a very simple execution and a too easy imitation so as to justify the establishment of any commercial speculation, and in any case, when the inventor prefers to deal directly with the government, he will be free to address either the administrative assemblies or the legislative body, if necessary, to confide his discovery, demonstrating its advantages and to solicit a reward.

VI. When an inventor prefers to the personal advantages assured by the law the honor of making the enjoyment of the fruits of his discovery or invention forthwith, and when he proves by public knowledge, and by legal proofs, that this discovery or invention is of real utility, an award may be granted to him from the funds intended for the encouragement of the industry.

VII. In order to ensure to any inventor the property and temporary enjoyment of his invention, he shall be granted a certificate or a patent, in the form indicated in the regulations to be set for the implementation of this Act.

VIII. The patents will be given for five, ten or fifteen years, at the choice of the inventor; but this last term can never be extended without a special decree of the legislative body.

X. The exercise of patents granted for a discovery imported from a foreign country cannot extend beyond the term fixed in that country for the exercise of the first inventor.

XI. It will be open to any citizen to go to the secretariat of his department to consult the catalog of new inventions; it shall likewise be free for any domiciled citizen to consult, at the general archive established for that purpose, the specifications of the various patents currently in force; however, the descriptions shall not be communicated in cases where the inventor, having understood that political or commercial reasons require the secrecy of his discovery, would have presented himself to the legislative body to explain his motives, and would have obtained a particular decree on this subject.

In cases where it will be declared that a description shall remain secret, commissioners will be appointed to ensure the accuracy of the description as regards means and processes, without the author ceasing afterwards to be responsible for that accuracy.

XII. The proprietor of a patent shall privately enjoy the exercise and the fruits of the discovery, the invention or the improvement for which the said patent has been obtained; as a result, he may, by providing good and sufficient security, request the seizure of counterfeit goods and bring the infringers before the courts; when the counterfeiters are convicted, they will be sentenced, in addition to the seizure, to pay the inventor of the damages proportionate to the importance of the counterfeit, and in addition to pay to the charity of the poor of the district a fine fixed at a quarter of the amount of the said damages, but such fine may not exceed the sum of 3,000 pounds, and the double in the event of recurrence.

XIII. In case the claim for counterfeiting, according to which the seizure has taken place, is found to be devoid of evidence, the inventor shall be condemned to pay to the other party damages and interests proportionate to the disturbance and the prejudice that it may have experienced, and in addition to pay a quarter of the amount of the said damages and interests to the charity of the poor of the district, but such fine may not exceed the sum of 3,000 pounds, and the double in the event of recurrence.

XIV. Every patent owner shall have the right to open business establishments throughout the kingdom, and even to authorize other private persons to apply and use those means and methods; and in any case, he may dispose of his patent as personal property.

XV. At the expiration of each patent, considering that the discovery or invention must belong to society, the description will be made public, and its use will be allowed throughout the kingdom, so that any citizen can freely exercise and enjoy it, unless a law has extended the patent term, or determined its secrecy in the cases mentioned in Article XI.

XVI. The description of the discovery set out in a patent shall also be made public, and the use of the means and processes relating to this discovery shall also be declared free throughout the kingdom when the owner of the patent is deprived of it, which will not take place except in the following cases:

1° Any inventor, held responsible for having, in submitting his description, concealed the real means of its execution, will be deprived of his patent.

2° Every inventor, held responsible for having used in his manufacture secret means that were not detailed in his description, or regarding which he has not declared to be added to those stated in his description, will be deprived of his patent.

3° Any inventor, or who claims to be such, who will be held responsible for having obtained a patent for discoveries already stated and described in printed and published works, will be deprived of his patent.

4° Any inventor who, in the period of two years, from the date of the patent, has not put his discovery in operation, and who has not justified the reasons for his inaction, will be deprived of his patent.
5° Any inventor who, having obtained a patent in France, is found to have taken one for the same object in a foreign country, will be deprived of his patent.
6° Finally, any acquirer of the right to exploit a discovery covered by a patent shall be subject to the same obligations as the inventor, and, if he contravenes them, the patent shall be revoked, the discovery published, and the use thereof shall become free in all the kingdom. . . .

§1.37 A FRENCH PATENT FOR A SAVINGS PLAN

August 22, 1791

The text that follows is an excerpt from the patent letter for a savings plan, known as La Caisse Lafarge, which several years later proved to be a Ponzi scheme, and went wrong, leaving thousands of investors penniless. This patent would be invalidated one year later by a law of 1792 (see Text 1.38).

The fact that the inventor has applied for the patent for a short term (of five years only, when he could have requested a fifteen-year term) suggests that he was seeking for a stamp of approval of the savings plan, rather than for the exclusivity of his invention. Indeed, the idea that patents represented administrative approvals and licenses to use, which emerged in the Middle Ages in association with industrial privileges, remained in the minds of many. It was that same idea that was the basis of the reluctance of the French Parliament to grant patents for pharmaceutical inventions—those patents would be in conflict with the requirement that medicines be subject to a technical examination prior to their commercialization. And indeed, in 1844, their patentability would be excluded. (*see* Text 1.45).

Patent for the establishment of the Savings and Charity Fund of Mr. Joachim Lafarge.

Louis, by the grace of God and by the Constitutional Law of the State, King of the French: To all present and to come, greetings:

Messrs. Joachim Lafarge and Louis-Charles Mitouflet, citizens of Paris, having stated to us that they wish to enjoy the property rights accorded by the Law of January 7, 1791, to the authors of discoveries and inventions in any kind of industry, and consequently to obtain a patent of invention which will last five years, to establish in Paris and in all the kingdom, the offices of a Fund of savings and charity, of which Mr. Lafarge has been declared the inventor and Mr. Mitouflet his associate, as it results from the records filed with the secretariat of the Department of Paris, on the eighteenth day of August 1791:

Having regard to the request of the said Messrs. Lafarge and Mitouflet, together with an Explanatory Memorandum, the printed Brochure of the said Fund, the statutes also printed, and a handwritten booklet containing additions to the said statutes, whose contents follow.

Memorandum:

Joachim Lafarge, officer of the King, is the author of a plan of investments, known today under the name of Fund of Savings and Charity [*Caisse d'épargne et bienfaisance*].

In his works he was guided by three purposes:

> The first, to lead the indigent class, by the hope of a very advantageous enjoyment, to making savings, the fruits of which they will reap at the age of repose and need;
>
> The second, to make the wealthy class contribute for the prosperity of this establishment, to improve the fate of the poor;
>
> The third, to extinguish a portion of the debt of the State, at no cost to the nation.
>
> After having seen the plans approved by the municipality of Paris, and the committees of finance and poverty of the National Assembly, he has formed his establishment both in Paris and in the provinces, and distributed the Brochure that contains its development, as well as the by-laws that are the general law of the Fund and of those who are interested in placing funds in it.
>
> But the publicity that he has given to his work would make him fear that his property could be put in danger, under the pretext that he has not obtained a patent, and therefore he applies for the patent, to enjoy it for five years with the exclusive privilege that the law attaches to it.
>
> He attaches to this memorandum a printed copy of the Brochure, a likewise printed copy of the by-laws and a certified copy of an addition to those by-laws, at a general meeting of the interested parties.
>
> In Paris, this 17th of August, 1791.
>
> [The texts of the Brochure and the By-laws follow]. . . .

§1.38 THE FRENCH STATUTE THAT CANCELLED PATENTS FOR SAVINGS PLANS

September 20, 1792

Fourteen patents for saving and other investment plans were granted in France after the entry of the 1791 Act in force. The justification for those grants was a very liberal interpretation of the term "in any kinds of industry." Just one year later, and upon the complaints of opponents of the patent system, including parliamentarians, the National Assembly revoked all patents granted for those type of inventions (and prohibited the granting of new titles), on the ground that the word "industry" in the 1791 law referred to arts and crafts, not to abstract ideas.

The Caisse Lafarge survived the revocation of its patent for some decades, until it was liquidated. In other words, the patent was irrelevant for the success (or failure) of the plan. As said, the intention of Joachim Lafarge in applying for a patent was not that of securing exclusivity in his financial scheme, but in using the patent as a sort of public recommendation of the organization.

Law concerning the patents for inventions granted to financial institutions.

September 20, 1792

The National Assembly, considering that the patents of invention that are authorized by the law of January 7, 1791, cannot be granted other than to the authors of all discoveries or new inventions, in all the kinds of industry, only as regards arts and crafts; that the patents of invention which could be granted to financial institutions would become dangerous, and that it is important to take measures to stop the effect of those that have already been issued or that could be so thereafter; decrees that the executive branch will no longer be authorized to grant patents of invention to finance institutions, and eliminates the effect of those that might have been granted.

§1.39 A BRITISH COURT INTRODUCES THE REQUIREMENT OF INDUSTRIAL APPLICABILITY (UTILITY)

January 25, 1799

The Statute of Monopolies was still in force when British courts set the susceptibility of industrial application as a condition of patentability. The pretext was a debate over the nature of one of the improvements introduced by James Watt to his steam engine—an improvement basically consisting of a process of using that machine. The discussion that arose was whether a process, i.e., a particular arrangement of procedures, could be deemed a manufacture, or something that involved the employment of human hands.

The condition of utility (or susceptibility of industrial application, or materiality) of inventions was extensively discussed by the four judges of the Court of Common Pleas in Boulton and *Watt v. Bull*, May 16, 1795. But, because the Court was equally divided as to the validity of the patent, no judgment was given. The matter was decided subsequently by the Court of King's Bench in the judgment that follows.

Hornblower and Maberley v. Boulton and Watt, in error

In the Court of King's Bench, January 25, 1799

This was an action on the case, brought in the Court of Common Pleas, by the defendants in error, against the plaintiffs in error, for infringing a patent. . . .

Lord Kenyon, Chief Justice.—. . . I confess I am not one of those who greatly favour patents; for though in many instances, and particularly in this, the public are benefited by them, yet, on striking the balance upon this subject, I think that great oppression is practised on inferior mechanics by those who are more opulent. The principal objection made to this patent by the plaintiffs in error is, that it is a patent for a philosophical principle only, neither organized or capable of being organized; and if the objection were well founded in fact, it would be decisive: but I do not think it is so. No technical words are necessary to explain the subject of a patent; as Lord Hardwicke said, upon another occasion, "there is no magic in words." The questions here are, whether, by looking at the patent, explained as it is by the specification, it does not appear to be a patent for a manufacture, and whether the specification is not sufficient to enable a mechanic to make the thing described? . . . By comparing the patent and the manufacture together, it evidently appears that the patentee claims a monopoly for an engine or machine, composed of material parts, which are to produce the effect described, and that the mode of producing this is so described as to enable mechanics to produce it. . . . But having now heard everything that can be said on the subject, I have no doubt in saying that this is a patent for a manufacture, which I understand to be something made by the hands of man. . . .

Mr. Justice Grose— . . . The subject is new to me, not affecting to be a mechanic, and I have had great difficulties in making up my mind upon it. I am inclined, however, to think that a patent cannot be granted for a mere principle; but I think that although, in words, the privilege granted is to exercise a method of making or doing anything, yet if that thing is to be made or done by a manufacture, and the mode of making that manufacture is described, it then becomes in effect (by whatever name it may be called) not a patent for a mere principle, but for a manufacture, for the thing so made, and not merely for the principle upon which it is made. . . . Mr. Justice Laurence— . . . Some of the difficulties in the case have arisen from considering the word engine in its popular sense, and that the Legislature so understood it, is evident from the words "engine" and "method" being used as convertible terms. Now there is no doubt but that for such a contrivance a patent may be granted, as well as for a more complicated machine; it equally falls within the description of a "manufacture" . . . .

Judgment affirmed.

§1.40 BRAZIL ENACTS ITS FIRST PATENT STATUTE

April 28, 1809

The trend of setting the patent system as a mechanism for promoting the development of the industry arrived in Brazil as early as 1809—prior to many countries that were already engaged in the Industrial Revolution, and even before Brazil acquired its independence (which would happen in 1822). The reason was that the war between France and England led the king of Portugal (then Prince regent), John VI, with an escort of the British navy, to move to Rio de Janeiro and fix temporary residence therein. The Continental Blockade imposed by Napoleon and the tense relations between England and the United States persuaded the leaders of Great Britain of Brazil's commercial interest. In the context of these political concerns, a secret treaty between Portugal and Great Britain was signed in 1807, establishing that a treaty of free commerce would be negotiated (it would be signed in 1810). In 1809, the Prince regent introduced a statute promoting the industrialization of Brazil, including a clause on patents for inventions—similar (not by coincidence, given that its inspiration was clearly English) to the patent clause of the Statute of Monopolies of 1623, but with some French influence (such as the combination of patents and financial rewards).

Decree (*Alvará*) of April 28, 1809

Exempts from duties the raw materials used by factories and grants other favors to manufacturers as well by national navigation.

I, the Prince Regent, make it known to those who see the present Decree, that the promotion of the public happiness of my faithful Vassals being the first and foremost object of my paternal care; and having established with this purpose liberal principles for the prosperity of this State of Brazil, and which are essentially necessary to foster agriculture, encourage trade, advance navigation, and increase the population, becoming more extensive and analogous to the greatness of the same State: . . . having heard the advice of Ministers of my Council, and of other zealous persons of my service; extending and renewing the many measures already established in this regard, and in order that they may have prompt and exact observance for the general and individual prosperity of my faithful Vassals, which I very much wish to advance and promote, as the greatness and consideration of my Royal Crown and the Nation depend upon it; I am served to determine the following: . . .

VI—Being very convenient that the inventors and introducers of some new machine, and invention in the arts, enjoy the exclusive privilege in addition to the right that they may have to the pecuniary favor, which I am served to establish for the benefit of the industry and the arts; I command that all persons who are in that case to present the plan of their new invention to the Royal Board of Commerce; and that, recognizing the truth and ground of it, [the Board] grants them the exclusive privilege for fourteen years, being obliged to publish it later, so that at the end of that period the whole nation will enjoy the fruit of this invention. I further order that an exact revision be made of those which are currently granted, making public in the order set forth above, and revoking all those who, by reason of false claim, or without good reason, have obtained similar grants.

§1.41 THE COURT OF CHANCERY HOLDS THAT THE INVENTION DISCLOSURE REQUIREMENT IS EMBEDDED IN THE RATIONALE OF THE PATENT SYSTEM

July 25, 1816

As seen above (*see* Text 1.36), the French patent act of 1791 admitted that some inventions could be patented without the need for their disclosure. This rule was in part explained by the intent of the French to use the patent system to their advantage in the dispute they had with England for industrial and technological supremacy. By contrast, English common law was much stricter in requiring that inventions' specifications be disclosed. The text that follows is a report of a judgment holding that disclosure of British patented inventions was too important for being dispensed with, even if it gave some advantage to the French industry. Actually, this was not the first opinion holding the requirement of disclosure. In a judgment of January 22, 1802, in *Ex Parte Koops,* the same Court of Chancery, invoking the rationale of the patent system, had already expressed reluctance in approving petitions for the late submission of the specifications, or for keeping them secret.

In Re Lacy's Patent

In the Court of Chancery—July 25, 1816

Mr. Bell stated, that this was an application to the Court, praying that his Lordship would not put the great seal to a patent which Mr. Lay, of Nottingham, had sought to obtain for making lace by a machine, to be worked by a steam-engine. The ground objection to the patent was, that Mr. Lacy wanted to keep his specification secret for the space of fifteen months, which was contrary to the policy of the law, and great injustice to the king's subjects in general. . . .

The Lord Chancellor Eldon said, that he could not put the great seal to a patent which gave the party fifteen months to make out his specification. In the present reign thousands of patents had been granted, and this indulgence was extended only in two or three of them. Where the letters patent were for an invention to be used in England, Scotland, and Ireland, the usual period for the specification was six months; but where they were confined to England only, two months was the given time. Mr. Lee's case was a very peculiar one; it was for securing to the State, in a time of war, the benefit of a most important discovery. If Mr. Lacy could make out that the State was to be benefitted by his invention in any peculiar way, as in the case of preparing hemp and flax, it might be doubtful whether he might not have a secret specification. His Lordship was of opinion, however, that the Legislature would pause a long time before they passed such an Act in future; and he thought he might venture to say, that if Mr. Lacy were to apply for such an Act he would not procure it. The gentleman had said, that if this specification was not kept secret the French might copy it; but his Lordship could not establish a new principle merely to prevent the French from smuggling; neither could he put the great seal to a patent without seeing the specification, for it might turn out not to be worth a farthing, and then public genius would be discouraged merely for the benefit of the patentee. Many cases of this nature had occurred. The patent could not pass without the responsibility of the great seal; and if his Lordship could bring himself to pass it, he might be called upon to give an account in Parliament why he had extended this particular privilege to this individual. It was certainly contrary to the general policy of the law, and he could not in justice to the King's subjects affix the great seal to it merely because it was a manufacture which other countries had in common with this.

§1.42 A BRAZILIAN COURT AFFIRMS THE PRINCIPLE OF ALTERNATIVENESS

1820

As seen, the patent statute of Brazil, of 1809 (Text 1.40), attributed to the Royal Board of Commerce, Agriculture, Manufactures and Navigation, the task of examining patent applications. In carrying their task, looking at an application on a machine for cotton bagging and baling, filed by José Joaquim Machado, the Board, in a *dictum* (supporting a French-like system without prior examination), affirmed the same doctrine of alternativeness that the French State Council had pronounced two hundred years earlier (Text 1.22).

. . . The Court of the Royal Board of Commerce decides to accept the information of the Deputy Inspector of Factories and his opinion that it is in the spirit of Your Majesty's generous system to encourage and favor the progress of the general industry, even in any improvement of saving time and labour, of which this Kingdom is so much in need. . . . Besides, in accordance with the more liberal and practical system under which the governments of the nations known for their superior industry, considering that any, albeit slight, new advances in the machines and processes of useful work are not indifferent to the national interest, grant with absolute frankness and immediately the exclusive temporary privilege to any inventor, or first introducer of improvements added to previous ones, without any comparison and inquiry, which experience has shown to be harmful or useless in the present progressive pace of invention in all arts and activities, which should not be obstructed, as long as neither is the use of ordinary machinery and methods prohibited, nor is the right of anyone to show that the intended invention is entirely false and already of common use of society, which is already foreseen in paragraph 6 of the mentioned Decree of April 28, 1809, given that by this mechanism the society may immediately obtain possession of the improvement, the inventor immediately enjoys with just title the reward for his invention, investment and inventive risk, and those who use or wish to use the [patented] methods have no sound reason to complain, because it is free to all parties to prefer the old over the new technique.

§1.43 THE UNITED STATES CREATES THE PATENT OFFICE

1836

In 1836 the United States Congress passed a statute creating the patent office and determining its functions of examining patent applications and recording patents granted. The 1836 Act eliminated the discriminatory treatment that the 1832 Act reserved to foreign inventors (only those foreigners who resided in the United States and submitted under oath that within one year they would apply for citizenship would qualify to obtain patents), but it kept it as regards the possibility of applying for provisional protection "till he shall have matured his invention."

An Act to promote the progress of useful arts, and to repeal all acts and parts of acts heretofore made for that purpose.

Section 1. Be it enacted by the Senate and House of Representatives of the United States of America in Congress assembled, That there shall be established and attached to the Department of State, an office to be denominated the Patent Office; the chief officer of which shall be called the Commissioner of Patents, to be appointed by the President, by and with the advice and consent of the Senate, whose duty it shall be, under the direction of the Secretary of State, to superintend, execute, and perform, all such acts and things touching and respecting the granting and issuing of patents for new and useful discoveries, inventions, and improvements, as are herein provided for, or shall hereafter be, by law, directed to be done and performed, and shall have the charge and custody of all the books, records, papers, models, machines, and all other things belonging to said office. . . .

Section 5. And be it further enacted, That all patents issued from said office shall be issued in the name of the United States and under the seal of said office, and be signed by the Secretary of State, and countersigned by the Commissioner of the said office, and shall be recorded, State, and by together with the descriptions, specifications, and drawings, in the said office, in books to be kept for that purpose. Every such patent shall contain a short description or title of the invention or discovery, correctly indicating its nature and design, and in its terms grant to the applicant or applicants, his or their heirs, administrators, executors, or assigns, for a term not exceeding fourteen years, the full and exclusive right and liberty of making, using, and vending to others to be used, the said invention or discovery, referring to the specifications for the particulars thereof, a copy of which shall be annexed to the patent, specifying what the patentee claims as his invention or discovery.

Section 6. And be it further enacted, That any person or persons having discovered or invented any new and useful art, machine, manufacture, or composition of matter, or any new and useful improvement on any art, machine, manufacture, or composition of matter, not known or used by others before his or their discovery or invention thereof, and not, at the time of his application for a patent, in public use or on sale, with his consent or allowance, as the inventor or discoverer; and shall desire to obtain an exclusive property therein, may make application in writing to the Commissioner of Patents, expressing such desire, and the Commissioner, on due proceedings had, may grant a patent therefor. But before any inventor shall receive a patent for any such new invention or discovery, he shall deliver a written description of his invention or discovery, and of the manner and process of making, constructing, using, and compounding the same, in such full, clear, and exact terms, avoiding unnecessary prolixity, as to enable any person skilled in the art or science to which it appertains, or with which it is most nearly connected, to make, construct, compound, and use the same; and in case of any machine, he shall fully explain the principle and the several modes in which he has contemplated the application of that principle or character by which it may be distinguished from other inventions; and shall particularly specify and point out the part, improvement, or combination, which he claims as his own invention or discovery. He shall, furthermore, accompany the whole with a drawing, or drawings, and written references, where the nature of the case admits of drawings, or with specimens of ingredients, and of the composition of matter, sufficient in quantity for the purpose of experiment, where the invention or discovery is of a composition of matter; which descriptions and drawings, signed by the inventor and attested by two witnesses, shall be filed in the Patent Office; and he shall moreover furnish a model of his invention, in all cases which admit of a representation by model, of a convenient size to exhibit advantageously its several parts. The applicant shall also make oath or affirmation that he does verily believe that he is the original and first inventor or discoverer of the art, machine, composition, or improvement, for which he solicits a patent, and that he does not know or believe that the same was ever before known or used; and also of what country he is a citizen; which oath or affirmation may be made before any person authorized by law to administer oaths.

Section 7. And be it further enacted, That, on the filing of any such application, description, and specification, and the payment of the duty hereinafter provided, the Commissioner shall make or cause to be made, an examination of the alleged new invention or discovery; . . .

Section 12. And be it further enacted, That any citizen of the United States, or alien who shall have been resident in the United States one year next preceding, and shall have made oath of his intention to become a citizen thereof, who shall have invented any new art, machine, or improvement thereof, and shall desire further time to mature the same, may, on paying to the credit of the Treasury, in manner as provided in the ninth section of this act, the sum of twenty dollars, file in the Patent Office a caveat, setting forth the design and purpose thereof, and its principal and distinguishing characteristics, and praying protection of his right till he shall have matured his invention; . . .

§1.44 THE INTEGRATION OF INVENTORS INTO FACTORIES' LABOR FORCE GIVES RISE TO CONFLICTS ON THE OWNERSHIP OF PATENTS AND THE REMUNERATION OF INVENTION

January 1843

Patents are tools of private entrepreneurship. As such, they have been specifically design to support capitalism. But, until the second half of the nineteenth century, a feature was still missing in patent law. Indeed, the majority of the great inventions of the 17th and 18th centuries, when the Industrial Revolution was already in full swing in some countries, was made by industrialists, who put their energies and minds into new products and new processes—in many cases in association with wealthy investors. The system worked well in the beginning, but it became manifestly insufficient for the new economy of the nineteenth century, with its widespread innovation spirit and, importantly, the increasing demand of consumers for a constant flow of improvements. It was then that capitalists brought inventors into their factories' work forces, where they joined hands with brown and white collar works. As a logical consequence, at some point employers and employees started fighting over the ownership and the gains from inventions made as part of employment contract obligations. The opinion of the United States Supreme Court that follows was one of the first court decisions on that topic. It affirmed one of the doctrines that buttress today's regime of employees' inventions—that of a license accorded by the employee to the employer. Later other explanations would be found in the United States and other countries as well.

McClurg v. Kingsland

42 U.S. 202 (1843)

. . . Mr. Justice Baldwin delivered the opinion of the court.

This case comes here on a writ of error to the Circuit Court for the Western District of Pennsylvania, in an action brought by the plaintiffs, assignees of James Harley, against the defendants, for the infringement of a patent granted to Harley for an improvement in the mode of casting chilled rollers and other metallic cylinders and cones, in which judgment was rendered for the defendants.

. . . The novelty of the invention was much contested at the trial, but as the case turned on other points, that became an immaterial question; and the case comes before us, on exceptions to the charge of the court, which assumed that Harley was the original and true inventor of the improvement, and put the case to the jury on the following facts, which were in full proof, in nowise contradicted, and admitted to be true:

That Harley was employed by the defendants at their foundry in Pittsburg, receiving wages from them by the week; while so employed, he claimed to have invented the improvements patented and after several unsuccessful experiments made a successful one in October, 1834. The experiments were made in the defendants' foundry, and wholly at their expense, while Harley was receiving his wages, which were increased on account of the useful result. Harley continued in their employment, on wages, until January or February, 1835, during all which time he had made rollers for them. He often spoke about procuring a patent, and prepared more than one set of papers for the purpose. Made his application the 17th February, 1835, for a patent. It was granted on the 3rd of March, and assigned to the plaintiffs on the 16th of March, pursuant to an agreement made in January.

> While Harley continued in the defendants' employment, he proposed that they should take out a patent and purchase his right, which they declined. He made no demand on them for any compensation for using his improvement, nor gave them any notice not to use it, till, on some misunderstanding on another subject, he gave them such notice about the time of his leaving their foundry, and after making the agreement with the plaintiffs, who owned a foundry in Pittsburg, for an assignment to them of his right. The defendants continued to make rollers in Harley's plan. The present action was brought in October, 1835, without any previous notice by them. . . .
>
> . . . The case before us is one of this description: the defendants use the invention of Harley for four months before his application of the patent; this use was public; and not only with his express consent and allowance, but he himself made the rollers, on the plan he invented, during those months, from the time when he had ascertained the utility of his invention.
>
> It would, therefore, be no strained, if not the fair construction of this act, if, under such and the other circumstances in evidence in the cause, the court charged the jury that, if they believed the witnesses, the patent subsequently was void. The Circuit Court, however, did not go so far. They held that the defendants might continue to use the invention, without saying that the public might use it without liability to the plaintiffs, in which we think there was no error in their direction to the jury; that they might presume a license or grant from Harley, or on the legal effect of the uncontroverted evidence as to the right of recovery, by the plaintiffs, or on the construction of the acts of 1793, 1800, 1832, and 1836.

The remaining exception is to the charge of the court below, on the effect of the 7th section of the act of 1839, which is in these words:

> That every person or corporation who has or shall have purchased or constructed any newly invented machine, manufacture, or composition of matter, prior to the application by the inventor or discoverer of a patent, shall be held to possess the right to use and vend to others to be used, the specific machine, manufacture, or composition of matter so made or purchased, without liability therefore to the inventor or any other person interested in such invention, and no patent shall be held invalid by reason of such purchase, sale, or use prior to the application for a patent as aforesaid, except on proof of abandonment of such invention to the public, or that such purchase, sale, or prior use has been for more than two years prior to such application for a patent.
>
> The object of this provision is evidently twofold—first, to protect the person who has used the thing patented, by having purchased, constructed, or made the machine &c., to which the invention is applied, from any liability to the patentee or his assignee; second, to protect the rights, granted to the patentee, against any infringement by any other persons. This relieved him from the effects of former laws and their constructions by this Court, unless in case of an abandonment of the invention or a continued prior use for more than two years before the application for a patent, while it puts the person who has had such prior use on the same footing as if he had a special license from the inventor to use his invention, which, if given before the application for a patent, would justify the continued use after it issued without liability. . . .

§1.45 FRANCE UPDATES ITS PATENT LAW, REDUCING THE SCOPE OF PATENTABILITY AND ELIMINATING SECRECY

July 5, 1844

In 1844, in response to the criticisms against the dated patent law of 1791 (see Text 1.37), France introduced a new statute. One of its major substantive changes was the exclusion of pharmaceutical inventions from patentability (in addition to the exclusion of financial and credit plans, which had already been set in 1792—*see* Text 1.38).

The law provided that the exclusion from patentability did not supersede any administrative requirements concerning authorizations for the commercialization of pharmaceuticals, including secret medicines, the commercialization of which was, under a Decree of 1810, dependent on a technical examination as to their safety and efficacy. The Decree also determined that the formulae of those medicines that were approved by a special commission because of their useful effects would be acquired by the government and publicly disclosed. The remuneration to be paid to the inventors should take into account the merits of the inventions and the financial gains that the inventors might expect.

The statute maintained the practice of granting patents without prior examination as to the merits of the claimed inventions.

The statute eliminated the automatic invalidation of the patent in the case the inventor obtained another patent for the same invention in another country. This might seem an opening towards international trade, but it was not: in 1844, that rule was replaced with the automatic lapse of patents in the case the inventor imported the patented objects or similar if made abroad. In doing so, France may have eliminated an obstacle to the circulation of technology but put a barrier to trade in its place.

Law of July 5, 1844 on patents for inventions

Title I

General provisions

Article 1. Every new discovery or invention in every kind of industry confers to its author, under the conditions and for the term herein determined, the exclusive right of exploiting for his own benefit such discovery or invention.

This right is established by titles issued by the Government under the name of *patents for invention*.

Art. 2.—[The following] Will be considered as inventions or new discoveries:

Inventions of new industrial products;
The invention of new means or the new application of known means for the obtaining of a result or of an industrial product.

Art. 3.—[The following] Are not patentable:

1° Pharmaceutical compositions or medicines of any kind, said objects remaining subject to special laws and regulations on that matter, and in particular to the decree of August 18, 1810, concerning secret medicines.
2° Plans and combinations of credit or finance.

Art. 4.—The duration of patents will be of five, ten or fifteen years. . . .

Art. 11.—The patents whose application has been regularly filed will be issued, without prior examination, at the risk and peril of the applicants, and without guarantee of the reality, the novelty or the merit of the invention, nor of the faithfulness or the exactitude of the description.

An order of the Minister stating the regularity of the application will be issued to the applicant and will constitute the patent of invention. . . .

Title IV

On invalidation and forfeiture and related actions

Section 1

On invalidation and forfeiture. . . .

Art. 33. [The following] will have their rights forfeited:

1° The patentee who has not paid his annuity before the beginning of each year of the term of his patent.

2° The patentee who has not started the exploitation of his discovery in France, within two years from the date of signature of the patent, or who ceases to exploit it for two consecutive years, unless, in either case, he justifies his inaction.

3° The patentee who has introduced in France objects made in a foreign country and similar to those guaranteed by his patent.

Nevertheless, the Minister of Agriculture, Trade and Public Works may authorize the introduction of:

1. Models of machines;
2. Articles made abroad, intended for public exhibitions or essays made with the approval of the Government. . . .

§1.46 THE UNITED STATES SUPREME COURT SETS NONOBVIOUSNESS AS A REQUIREMENT OF PATENTABILITY

1850

As patent law was being modernized and adapted to the new economic environment that resulted from the Industrial Revolution, a refined, more rigorous, concept of novelty emerged—protection being denied to trivial differences between the state of the art and the new invention. This means that courts would require that inventions, in order to qualify for patent protection, should not only present significant novelty, but should also produce unexpected results when compared to the state of art. In other words, inventions should result from the exercise of significantly creative ingenuity. Novelty, therefore, ceased to be enough--as well as trivial inventiveness, for that matter. Instead, significant inventiveness, or nonobviousness, has become a requirement. The justification of this apparent strictness was the need to free the operation of businesses of the clog that a multitude of exclusive rights covering trivial matter could generate (and were generating indeed, when a sort of a frenzy of frivolous patenting got hold of the United States in the second half of the nineteenth century and which led to the patent wars in the agro and railroad industries) (*see* also Texts 1.48 and 1.50).

With this opinion, the Supreme Court of the United States has raised the standard of required inventiveness, rejecting the patentability of trifling devices.

Hotchkiss v. Greenwood

52 U.S. 248 (1850)

Mr. Justice Nelson delivered the opinion of the Court

. . . Now it may very well be, that, by connecting the clay or porcelain knob with the metallic shank in this well-known mode, an article is produced better and cheaper than in the case of the metallic or wood knob; but this does not result from any new mechanical device or contrivance, but from the fact, that the material of which the knob is composed happens to be better adapted to the purpose for which it is made. The improvement consists in the superiority of the material, and which is not new, over that previously employed in making the knob.

But this of itself can never be the subject of a patent. No one will pretend that a machine, made, in whole or in part, of materials better adapted to the purpose for which it is used than the materials of which the old one is constructed, and for that reason better and cheaper, can be distinguished from the old one, or, in the sense of the patent law, can entitle the manufacturer to a patent.

The difference is formal, and destitute of ingenuity or invention. It may afford evidence of judgment and skill in the selection and adaptation of the materials in the manufacture of the instrument for the purposes intended, but nothing more. . . .

§1.47 THE SUPREME COURT OF THE UNITED STATES ALSO SET ALTERNATIVENESS AS A PRINCIPLE OF PATENT LAW

1852

After the State Council of France, in 1610 (*see* Text 1.22), and the Board of Commerce of Brazil, in 1820 (*see* Text 1.42), the United States Supreme Court, in 1852, also reached the conclusion that patent law is one of the foundations of a free and competitive economy, provided patents are not granted for solutions that do not admit technical alternatives. This notion has put aside once and for all the idea that patents generate monopolies.

Only the State has the authority to disturb alternativeness, when it regulates the manner in which the market works. In some cases, governments require that a certain technical solution (eventually covered by a patent) become a technical standard of obligatory observation by the industry. In other cases, governments delay the entry of new inventions into the market, by imposing conditions on their quality, effectiveness and safety, which naturally accords to the inventors a significant head start.

In doing so, although they may be pursuing relevant public policies, governments destroy the procompetitive effects of the patent system.

Le Roy v. Tatham

United States Supreme Court, 1852

55 U.S. 156 (1852)

. . . It is admitted that a principle is not patentable. A principle, in the abstract, is a fundamental truth; an original cause; a motive; these cannot be patented, as no one can claim in either of them an exclusive right. Nor can an exclusive right exist to a new power, should one be discovered in addition to those already known. Through the agency of machinery a new steam power may be said to have been generated. But no one can appropriate this power exclusively to himself, under the patent laws. The same may be said of electricity, and any of other power in nature, which is alike open to all, and may be applied to useful purposes by the use of machinery.

. . . In all such cases, the processes used to extract, modify and concentrate natural agencies, constitute the invention. The elements of the power exist; the invention is not discovering them, but in applying them to useful objects. Whether the machinery used be novel, or consist of a new combination of parts known, the right of the inventor is secured against all who use the same mechanical power, or one that shall be substantially the same.

. . . A patent is not good for an effect, or the result of a certain process, as that would prohibit all other persons from making the same thing by any means whatsoever. This, by creating monopolies, would discourage arts and manufactures, against the avowed policy of the patent laws. . . .

§1.48 THE UNITED STATES SUPREME COURT ESTABLISHES THAT THE PATENT SYSTEM WAS NOT DESIGNED TO PROTECT TRIFLING DEVICES

1883

After deciding that patents should observe alternativeness and nonobviousness, the Supreme Court of the United States moved a step further and imposed an element of quantification of the amount of inventiveness required. By contrast with copyright, which requires a modicum of creativity, patents demand that inventiveness be exercised in a manner that leads to the finding of technical solutions of a certain technical and economic significance.

Atlantic Works v. Brady

Supreme Court of the United States, 1883

107 U.S. 192 (1883)

Mr. Justice Bradley delivered the opinion of the court.

. . . The most important question, and first to be considered, is the validity of the patent.

It is obvious from reading the specification that the alleged invention consists mainly in attaching a screw (which the patentee calls a mud-fan) to the forward end of a propeller dredge-boat, provided with tanks for settling her in the water. It is operated by sinking the boat until the screw comes in contact with the mud or sand, which, by the revolution of the screw, is thrown up and mingled with the current. The use of a series of tanks for the purpose of keeping the vessel level whilst she settles is an old contrivance long used in dry-docks, and is shown, by the evidence, to have been used in many light-draft monitors during the late war. . . .

It may well be asked, at this point, Where was there any invention in the device described in the patent? Was it invention to place a screw for dredging at the stem of the boat? Nothing more than this was in reality suggested by the patentee. . . .

The process of development in manufactures creates a constant demand for new appliances, which the skill of ordinary head-workmen and engineers is generally adequate to devise, and which, indeed, are the natural and proper outgrowth of such development. Each step forward prepares the way for the next, and each is usually taken by spontaneous trials and attempts in a hundred different places. To grant to a single party a monopoly of every slight advance made, except where the exercise of invention, somewhat above ordinary mechanical or engineering skill, is distinctly shown, is unjust in principle and injurious in its consequences.

The design of the patent laws is to reward those who make some substantial discovery or invention, which adds to our knowledge and makes a step in advance in the useful arts. Such inventors are worthy of all favor. It was never the object of those laws to grant a monopoly for every trifling device, every shadow of a shade of an idea, which would naturally and spontaneously occur to any skilled mechanic or operator in the ordinary progress of manufactures. Such an indiscriminate creation of exclusive privileges thuds rather to obstruct than to stimulate invention. It creates a class of speculative schemers who make it their business to watch the advancing wave of improvement, and gather its foam in the form of patented monopolies, which enable them to lay a heavy tax upon the industry of the country, without contributing anything to the real advancement of the arts. It embarrasses the honest pursuit of business with fears and apprehensions of concealed liens and unknown liabilities to lawsuits and vexatious accountings for profits made in good faith. . . .

Our conclusion is, that the patent sued on cannot be sustained, and that the decree of the Circuit Court must be reversed, and the cause remanded with instructions to dismiss the bill of complaint.

Decree reversed accordingly.

§1.49 THE BIRTH OF MULTILATERAL PROTECTION FOR PATENTS—THE PARIS CONVENTION

1883

In the third quarter of the nineteenth century, exports of patented products of the two major industrial powers—the United States and Great Britain—encountered barriers in other countries, namely in relation to the following factors: difficulties in maintaining a strict notion of novelty (many English and American inventors would apply for patents and test their inventions in their countries of origin before applying abroad, thus making it impossible to meet the requirement of novelty); obligation to manufacture the products incorporating the new techniques in the countries where they obtained a patent; in addition, the French statute of 1844 provided for the lapse of any patent granted in France if objects covered by the patent or similar to them were made abroad and imported (*see* Text 1.45).

The internationalization of the protection of inventions occurred, therefore, as a reaction to free riding. And that reaction would take place, as the French Minister for Foreign Affairs pointed out in his opening speech of the 1883 Conference, through the adoption of the principle of national treatment—according to which foreigners (citizens or residents of the other contracting countries) would be treated in exactly the same way as the nationals of those countries. This principle was imposed internationally after 1883. Along with its adoption, some protectionist and opportunist rules were eliminated, such as the possibility of forfeiting a patent when its object was imported. The question of the obligation of local exploitation was not resolved, however, because the countries that imposed it continued seeing patents as tools of national policies of industrialization—it made no sense to grant patents only to protect imports, therefore.

In spite of not having established a complete set of harmonizing rules in the field of patents, the Paris Convention had the desired effect of reducing the levels of opportunistic practices.

Opening speech by Mr. Challemel-Lagour, Minister of Foreign Affairs, of France, at the first session of the 1883 Diplomatic Conference on the adoption of a convention on the protection of industrial property.

Gentlemen,

I congratulate myself on the honor I have been given to welcome you and to inaugurate the works of this Conference on behalf of the Government of the Republic. I am pleased to see, together with several members of the diplomatic corps, some of the eminent experts who, three years ago, in this same room, laid the first foundations of international legislation for the protection of industrial property.

In spite of the difficulties of such work, the Conference of 1880 had, if not completed, at least prepared it very fortunately. From its deliberations came a draft Convention which, if adopted, would have the effect of ensuring in all Contracting States, and without distinction as to nationality, an effective guarantee to industrial property, in its various forms, patents of invention, designs, trade names and trademarks.

This project, communicated to the other States by the Government of the Republic, has been the object of a careful and benevolent examination on the part of all; it has already obtained the approval of several of them, and the information as a whole that has come to us allows us to hope for the formation of an international Union, which would give as of now to industrial interests, within a very wide scope, the satisfactions they claim. It will be up to you, Gentlemen, to inquire into the form in which this Union can be organized under the most favorable conditions and to gather the greatest number of accessions: the time and experience gained will complete your work.

You will thus have, in this century, which is essentially the century of industry and scientific inventions, powerfully contributed to encourage the industry, by protecting their creations against imitations in bad faith, and to stimulate the ingenuity of the inventors, securing to them the enjoyment of the fruits of their discoveries. You will have extended and fortified, in the most fortunate way, this league of civilization and morality, this international league that affirms the principle of the protection due to private property, in all its forms.

Allow me, therefore, to convey to you the wishes of the Government of the Republic for the success of your work and the testimony of its gratitude for the eagerness with which the various States you represent have responded to its invitation. . . .

§1.50 THE PATENT WARS IN THE UNITED STATES IN THE SECOND HALF OF THE NINETEENTH CENTURY

1887

In the second half of the nineteenth century, the US patent system was under strict scrutiny by society at large. The reason was the abusive enforcement of frivolous patents. Farmers, in particular, would be harassed by patent owners—and, in many cases, by persons falsely claiming the ownership of patents—to pay small amounts of money as royalties for the licensing of their patents. Some patents became notorious not only because of the commercial success of the inventions they protected but also because of the abundant litigation they have given rise to. Examples are the so called "driven well" patent and the "barbed wire fence" patent. These two patents ended up being invalidated in court, but not before having generated large controversies and, indeed, having served as the pretext for the large collection of royalties.

The texts that follow illustrate the discussions involving the action of patent trolls in agriculture and the reactions that they provoked.

Earl W. Hayter on the abuse of patent enforcement against farmers

Farmers, especially in the Middle West, experienced no end of trouble. Deluged with circulars from manufacturers and patentees, they were threatened and harassed by royalty collectors on such articles as sliding gates, milk cans, barbed wire, clover hulls, plows, sewing machines, grain binders, and drive-wells. [note omitted] In purchasing one of these commodities they were seldom certain that it was properly patented, and when two or more patents had been granted on the same article they did not know which was void and which was valid. One western writer summarized the situation when he wrote: "How is a farmer to know to whom to pay the royalty, even if it was legal, with three or four applicants swarming around him, all claiming to be the legal patentees, as in the case with both the drive well and barbed wire." [note omitted] In a number of instances a person was sued upon something that he had developed himself or had seen in use among his friends and neighbors before any patent had been granted. [note omitted] Such anxiety arose among the farmers that general protest was heard against the entire patent system.

This wide use of these patented articles soon created a series of problems that in time threated the existence of the whole patent system. These problems fall into three main divisions. First was the tendency found in the patent system itself to encourage the development of monopolies by allowing patents on various essential articles to be controlled by a single patentee, but most generally by a group of manufacturers called a patent "ring." This, the farmers observed, was brought about through the weaknesses of the patent law, whose provisions were somewhat lenient and not too definite. . . .

The farmers were also irritated by the indiscriminate issuing of so many patents to different people on the same article, as well as granting patents on the most insignificant things. [note omitted] Such multiplicity placed too many on the market and it was difficult for the purchaser or user to keep from infringing someone's patent. . . .

A Michigan farmer commented on this same problem in a somewhat more colorful manner by saying that no matter how or what one did he could not escape the patent system. It is "in our boots, it is in our clothes, it is in the tools we work with, in the buggy we ride in, in the harness of the horse, in the whip we strike him with. It is to be found in our fences, in our gates, in our pumps, in our kitchen, in our food, and finally in our coffin." [note omitted] . . .

The Scientific American in defense of the patent system

The annual attack upon our patent laws

It is with a feeling of genuine regret that we announce the commencement of the annual attack upon our patent laws in the House of Representatives. It is in no idle spirit that we make this statement. Our duty in the matter extends far beyond the noticing or chronicling of the event. The remedy and antidote is to be provided. Let our readers take individual action in the matter; let every Congressman hear from his constituents in unmistakable tones that the patent system of America is not to be disturbed, and the work will be done. Whatever bills menacing the rights of inventors shall be brought forward, a single warning will apply to all.

The bill we particularly allude to is one that was introduced during the last session in the House of Representatives by Mr. R. W. Townshend, of Illinois. Its number is 4,458. This year it has been again brought forward, and it was the subject of debate on the 20th of December in the House.

Its provisions are in brief that the United States courts shall have no jurisdiction in patent cases where the damages do not exceed $200, and that purchasers of a patent right for actual use shall not be liable for its value or for infringement in any way if, at the time of its purchase, they had no knowledge of the claims of any third party.

By one provision, infringement of the multitude of small patents is legalized. Anyone could use patented churns, sewing machines, mowers, reapers, minor improvements in steam engines and general machinery, without reference to the inventor. It is well within the truth to say that a vast majority of cases of infringement could be brought within the operation of such a law.

In its second clause, the innocent purchaser of patent right is upheld in his bargain. He may buy what another has no right to sell, playing the part really of a receiver of stolen goods, and in this transaction he is to be protected by a congressional enactment.

With the constitutionality of this act we have no affair. It is enough to say that in the debate concerning it, its unconstitutionality, its want of clearness, and its surplusage were all subjects of attack. Our concern is for the interests of the country at large. The industries of America have been built up on and repose upon patents. Every factory large or small uses in its machinery numerous patents. Every individual workman has patent tools that expedite his labors. The farmer is perhaps more directly benefited by patents than anyone else. Instead of swinging a scythe of unimproved construction through a long eleven or twelve hour day, with the result of one acre mown at the end of it, he sits at ease upon the seat of a patented harvester, and with a team of horses reaps and binds, without other help, thirteen acres of wheat a day. Reapers, self-binders, and harvesters do the work of the West, on the great prairies. In the East, where smaller farms are the rule, the hand tools used are all subjects of patents. Without the patent system, none of these implements, large or small, would have been invented. The Townshend bill professes to be aimed at the protection of this particular class, the farmers, from some mysterious "blackmailers." The existence of the latter is quite doubtful. But if such do exist, and work detriment to the agriculturists, their measure of harmfulness is nothing compared to the evils threatened by this bill. Even more than the manufacturers, the farmers should oppose it. The very class for whose protection it is professedly introduced are attacked by it. . . .

Revival of Patent Nullification.

It will be remembered in 1884 an attempt was made in Congress to pass laws in the interest of certain infringers of patents, such as railway corporations, barb fence makers, drive well infringers, and others, to prohibit patentees from recovering damages for violation of their patents, and making it lawful for any person to make and use a patented invention without responsibility to the inventor or his assigns. By some unaccountable folly, two of these hostile bills passed the House of Representatives by very large majorities; they were rushed through without sufficient opportunity for debate, and before their full purport could be understood by the friends of the patent system. The passage of the bills in the House raised a storm of indignation in all parts of the country, especially in manufacturing districts, and among the great body of working people, who depend for their livelihood upon the success of home industries.

To exempt infringers of new inventions from penalty was regarded as tantamount to nullifying the patent laws and wounding all the vast industries that rest upon patents.

The most energetic means were taken to defeat this unprecedented action of the House. Meetings of citizens were held, conventions were called, boards of trade convened, legislatures of States passed resolutions condemning the act, floods of protests were sent to members of Congress, and to crown all, the press of the country discussed the matter thoroughly, and gave unanimous voice against the consummation of a measure so suicidal and unjust. These combined efforts were successful. The bill was disapproved in the Senate, where it was elaborately discussed, and the impression or expectation has prevailed that its revival would not be attempted. But this expectation has proved vain. On the 20th ult. the obnoxious measure, in a new form of words, was brought forward in the House, and its passage urgently demanded.

[the text of the Bill follows]

A bill like this, which overthrows an industrial policy that has been successfully carried on almost since the foundation of the government, which cannot be otherwise than disastrous to all manufacturing interests and to the property rights of patentees, is deserving of the most deliberate consideration and the fullest discussion. But its advocates took good care to prevent this.

Under the rules, only thirty minutes were allowed for debate—fifteen in support of the bill, and fifteen against it. Mr. Townshend of Illinois, Mr. Henderson of Iowa, Mr. Morgan from Mississippi, and Mr. O'Donnell from Michigan were the chief supporters. The principal advocate was Mr. Townshend, and from his remarks we gather that his most pressing reason for wanting to pass the bill is that a few farmers among his constituents have been victimized to a small extent by parties who pretended to be the proprietors of the drive well patent; and when the rightful owner of the patent appeared and claimed ten dollars each for use of his invention they refused to pay, denounced the demand as an outrage, and have gone to the Supreme Court about it. To prevent the recurrence of such claims, the advocates of the bill ask that the laws be emasculated. But if we take away from the patentee the right to compel infringers to stop piracy and pay for use, we nullify the law, and patents cease to have value. . . .

§1.51 THE USE OF PATENT RIGHTS IS NOT IMMUNE TO THE SCRUTINY OF ANTITRUST LAW

1909

Not long after the passing of the first United States antitrust statute—the Sherman Act, of 1890—one US court established that the right of exclusivity generated by a patent is not immune to its provisions.

The case involved manufacturers of liquid door checks, who entered into agreements regulating the manufacture and sale of their patented inventions. The agreements included a plan on the maintenance of prices, the elimination of competition, and the restraint of technical improvements. The main point was the reduction of the output in the exploitation of patents (suppression), to the extent that the manufacturers agreed to manufacture and sell only one type of the patented devices—thus leaving some patents unexploited. Upon disagreement on the accounting of profits, one of the parties sued, and the other alleged that the agreements infringed the Sherman Act.

The court stated the well-established (in the United States) doctrine that the patent owner may suppress the exploitation of his own invention, but that right does not comprise the possibility of a combination with other patentees so as to reduce competition and increase profits. This opinion, more than one-hundred years later, still stands.

Blount Mfg. Co. v. Towne Mfg. Co.

District of Massachusetts, 1909

166 F. 555 (D. Mass. 1909)

. . . It seems self-evident that a contract which is only coextensive with the monopoly conferred by letters patent, and which creates no additional restraint of trade or monopoly, does not conflict with the Sherman act. The monopoly granted by letters patent is of a particular invention. Devices thus protected by patents are as a matter of fact in commercial competition with both patented and unpatented devices. A contract whereby the manufacturers of two independent patented inventions agree not to compete in the same commercial field deprives the public of the benefits of competition, and creates a restraint of trade which results, not from granting of letters patent, but from agreement. While the monopoly of the patented articles is not increased, the monopoly of the commercial field is increased by the *unified tactics* as to prices. . .

Whether a patentee may not lawfully make such a license agreement in consideration of the making of a like license agreement by another patentee is a somewhat interesting question. If, as a result of mutual licenses, there is put upon the market an article embodying the inventions of both patentees, so that as the effect of exchange of licenses a new article of commerce is developed, it is doubtful if the public is thereby unlawfully deprived of any of its rights or expectations of free competition. Where, however, each patentee continues to make his own goods under his own patents, and seeks to enhance his profits by an agreement with competitors, who make either patented or unpatented articles, then it seems to follow that the agreement of each to restrain his own trade cannot be regarded merely as an incident to the assignment of patent rights. The patentee then restrains his own trade, not for the purpose of enhancing the value of the license which he grants, but for the purpose of enhancing the value of his trade by removing competition. . . .

The right of a patentee to suppress his own rests upon ordinary considerations of property right. The public has no right to compel the use of patented devices or of unpatented devices, when that is inconsistent with fundamental rules of property. When a patentee agrees, however, to restrain his own trade in the article of his own invention, not as an incident to a granting of rights, but for the purpose of enhancing his price by the removal of competitors, he is then quite outside the sphere of any right granted him by the government. . . .

It is a fact, familiar in commercial history, that patent rights have a commercial value for purposes of extinction; that many patents are purchased in order to prevent the competition of new inventions and of new machines with old machines already installed. The equitable status of an owner of a patent who has purchased and held it in nonuse for this purpose is still an open question, ... An attempt to make profit out of letters patent by suppressing the invention covered thereby is outside the patent grant, and is so far removed from the spirit and intent of the patent law that the mere fact that an inventor may make a profit by suppressing his invention is not a sufficient reason for holding the Sherman act inapplicable to agreements affecting patented articles. If there is secured to the patentee all profits legitimately arising from the manufacture, use, and sale of his invention, this is all that is within the terms of the grant. To prohibit contracts for the suppression or restraint of his own trade by the application of the Sherman anti-trust act is not inconsistent with his right to manufacture, use, and vend. That the Sherman act interferes with some supposed right, granted by the patent, to suppress an invention, is an unsound proposition, for the reason that letters patent grant no such rights, either in terms or by reasonable implication. When no question of the value of the right of excluding others is involved, I am unable to find in the patent law any reason for unfolding an agreement for the suppression or restraint of trade in a patented article against the provisions of the Sherman act.

Granting that nonuse of an invention is fully within the right of the owner of a patent, it does not follow that he may by agreement bind himself to nonuse, save in connection with an assignment of his letters patent. Ownership of a patent involves no obligation to use, nor does ownership of other property. That the Sherman act interferes with some supposed right, granted by the patent, to suppress an invention, is an unsound proposition, for the reason that letters patent grant no such rights, either in terms or by reasonable implication. . . .

Non-use ordinarily violates no law; but contracting with another, putting it in the power of another to compel one not to use, is a contract in restraint of trade, designed for the purpose of suppressing competition. . . .

The Sherman act is not inconsistent with any rights acquired by the patentee when it prevents agreements in restraint of trade which are not designed to make valuable the right to use. There is no inconsistency between the grant of an exclusive and assignable right to make, use, and vend, and the prohibition of an agreement restraining or suppressing the sale of the article in interstate commerce, because any profit from such an agreement does not arise from the value of making, using, and vending. There is no inconsistency between the proposition that an inventor may withhold his invention from use as he sees fit, and the proposition that he may not make an agreement whereby, for the advantage of a competitor, trade in his patented article is restrained or suppressed.

Though an invention may be suppressed by the patentee or his assignee, yet the fact that there are now two ways of suppressing a patent is no reason for disregarding a statute designed to prevent a third way.

In the consideration of this case I have dwelt principally upon the broad contention that the Sherman antitrust act has no application to patented articles. It seems quite clear that an agreement in restraint of trade, though it relates to patented articles, may tend to create a monopoly which is different from that conferred by grants of letters patent.

Combinations between owners of independent patents, whereby, as part of a plan to monopolize the commercial field, competition is eliminated, are within the Sherman act, for the reason that the restraint of trade or monopoly arises from combination, and not from the exercise of rights granted by letters patent. As by the terms of the contracts under consideration the owners of distinct patents each agreed to restrain its own interstate trade, I am of the opinion that the contracts are in these particulars obnoxious to the Sherman anti-trust act. . . .

§1.52 PATENT TROLLS AS CHARACTERS OF A SCIENCE-FICTION NOVEL

1936

The notion of patent trolls does not reside in the mind of judges or government officials, only: here we have a candid, literary appraisal, by the hand of the Czech writer, Karel Čapek, of a scheme to use patent rights to take control over the market (and, as the novel goes, over the world).

Excerpt from The War with the Newts, 1936, by Karel Čapek

Translator: David Wyllie

President G.H. Bondy rang the bell and stood up.

"Gentlemen," he began, "I have the honour of opening this extraordinary general meeting of the Pacific Export Company. I would like to welcome everyone here and thank them for the contribution they make." . . .

Kurt von Frisch asks whether the newts could not be employed in some other way that might be more profitable than pearl fishing. Their natural, one could say beaver-like, talent for building weirs and other underwater constructions should be taken into account. They could perhaps be put to use in deepening harbours, building piers and performing other technical tasks underwater.

G.H. Bondy states that management is actively engaged in this consideration; there are some great possibilities in this respect. He states that the company now owns nearly six million newts; if we consider that one pair of newts might have a hundred tadpoles in any given year the company could well have three hundred million newts at its disposal by this time next year; in ten years the number would be astronomical. G.H. Bondy asks what the company intends to do with this enormous number of newts, when the newt farms are already overpopulated and, because of a lack of natural foodstuffs, it has been found necessary to feed the newts with copra, potatoes, maize and similar.

K. von Frisch asks whether the newts are edible.

J. Gilbert: not at all. Nor do their hides have any use.

M. Bonenfant asks management what they now intend to do.

G.H. Bondy (standing): "Gentlemen, we convened this extraordinary general meeting in order publicly to draw your attention to the extremely unfavourable prospects of our company which--I hope you will allow me to remind you of this--has proudly paid returns of twenty to twenty-three percent over recent years as well as having well-funded reserves and low costs. We stand now at a turning point; the way of doing business which has proved itself so well over recent years is now practically at an end; we have no choice but to find new ways." (Loud applause).

G.H. Bondy: "Gentlemen, we have, from now on, to abandon any idea of having a monopoly on newts. Unfortunately, under current regulations, we are not able to take out a patent on them." (Laughter.) "We can and must do business with newts in a way that's fundamentally different from the way we have been up till now; and it is essential that our approach to business is fundamentally different and on a far bigger scale." (Hear hear!) "And there are many things, gentlemen, that need to be agreed beforehand. Management suggest the creation of a new, vertically organised trust under the name Salamander Syndicate. Besides our company, the members of the newt syndicate would consist of certain major companies and strong financial groups; there is one company, for instance, that would be engaged in manufacturing special, patented metal tools for the newts ..." (MEAS, you mean?) "Yes, that's right, MEAS is the company I have in mind. There will also be a cartel of companies in the field of chemicals and foodstuffs, manufacturing cheap, patented feed for the newts; there will be a group of transport companies, making use of experience already gained to patent special hygienic tanks for transporting the newts; a block of insurance companies to cover the newts against risk of death or injury during transportation or at the workplace; other interested concerns in the fields of industry, export and finance which, for legal reasons, we are not able to mention by name at this stage. Suffice it to say, gentlemen, that at the start of business the syndicate would have four hundred millions pounds sterling at its disposal." (Excitement) "This file, my friends, is already full of contracts and all they need now is a signature for the creation of one of the biggest commercial organisations of modern times. All that is asked of you by the management, gentlemen is that you give them the authority to establish this gigantic concern whose task will be to cultivate and employ the newts in the best possible way." (Applause and voices of protest).

"Gentlemen, please bear in mind the advantages a collaboration of this sort could bring. The Newt Syndicate would provide more than just newts, it would also provide equipment and food for the newts such as maize, carbohydrates, beef fat and sugar for thousands of millions of well-fed animals; then there would be transport, insurance, veterinary needs and everything at the lowest rate guaranteed for us if not by a monopoly then at least by being in a dominant position over any other potential rival that might want to deal in newts. Just let them try it, gentlemen; they won't be in competition with us for long." (Bravo!)

§1.53 THE GENERAL ASSEMBLY OF THE UNITED NATIONS DECIDES TO SCRUTINISE THE ROLE OF PATENTS IN THE TRANSFER OF TECHNOLOGY TO DEVELOPING COUNTRIES

December 19, 1961

The twentieth century brought great changes to the balance of political and economic power across the world. With the movement towards independence of

European colonies in Asia and Africa, a significant number of countries gained access to (and the right to vote in) international organizations. The relative equilibrium concerning the protection of patents and copyrights across the globe has been lost due to the fact that it was exclusively based on national treatment. Sentiments of protectionism and opportunism encouraged those new countries to refuse protection to their own nationals so that they would not be obliged to grant the same protection to foreigners. This was easy to achieve as regards certain aspects of protection that those new countries could live without, such as patents for pharmaceutical inventions. However, as they were acceding to international conventions as a form of asserting their sovereignty, such as the Paris Convention, those countries could not avoid to accept some obligations towards ensuring some minimum aspects of protection to foreign inventors.

So, in the 1960s, as the number of newly independent (and poor) countries grew, the concerns with a perceived imbalance in world economic power and, in particular, the fear that foreign patent ownership was an unsurpassable barrier to acquiring technology and enabling national development, Brazil (a developing country that, in spite of its dimensions, and of its historic precedence in protecting inventions through patents) led a movement of developing countries that, in international fora, questioned the value of patents.

The text that follows is the Resolution of the General Assembly of the UN that opened the debates (proposed by Brazil) on patents and technology transfer. Its recommendation for an international meeting on the value of the patent system was rejected by the specialized organization that had a specific mandate to take care of patents, copyrights, and other intellectual property rights—the Bureaux Réunis pour la Protection de la Propriété Intellectuelle (BIRPI)—and never took place.

Some of these debates and concerns would resurface in WIPO, some forty years later, under the so-called Agenda for Development (*see* Text 1.59).

1713 (XVI). The role of patents in the transfer of technology to under-developed countries

The General Assembly,

Recalling its resolution 1429 (XIV) of 5 December 1959 on the possibilities of a further expansion of international contacts, as well as an increased exchange of knowledge and experience in the field of applied science and technology, . . .

Bearing in mind that access to knowledge and experience in the field of applied science and technology is essential to accelerate the economic development of under-developed countries and to enlarge the over-all productivity of their economies,

Realizing that the protection of the rights of the patent-holders in their country of origin and in foreign countries has contributed to technical research and, therefore, to international and national industrial progress,

Affirming that it is in the best interest of all countries that the international patent system should be applied in such a way as to take fully into account the special needs and requirements of the economic development of under-developed countries, as well as the legitimate claims of patentees,

Requests the Secretary-General, in consultation with appropriate international and national institutions and with the concurrence of the Governments concerned, to prepare for the Committee for Industrial Development, the Economic and Social Council, and the General Assembly at its eighteenth session, taking into consideration any pertinent discussions which might take place in the

United Nations Conference on the Application of Science and Technology for the Benefit of the Less Developed Areas, a report containing:

(a) A study of the effects of patents on the economy of under-developed countries;
(b) A survey of patent legislation in selected developed and under-developed countries, with primary emphasis on the treatment given to foreign patents;
(c) An analysis of the characteristics of the patent legislation of under-developed countries in the light of economic development objectives, taking into account the need for the rapid absorption of new products and technology, and the rise in the productivity level of their economies;
(d) A recommendation on the advisability of holding an international conference in order to examine the problems regarding the granting, protection, and use of patents, taking into consideration the provisions of existing international conventions and the special needs of developing countries, and utilizing the existing machinery of the International Union for the Protection of Industrial Property.

1084th plenary meeting, 19 December 1961.

§1.54 THE PATENT SYSTEM ENTERS THE ERA OF GLOBALIZATION

1970

The particular features of protection of copyright and trade secrets make these areas inherently adequate for an era of globalization. Their protection being informal to a great extent, there is no need of anything else than political will for granting them protection beyond national borders. Things are different for most of industrial property rights, whose protection within national borders requires compliance with formal requirements—if, and only if, these are made available. As far as trademarks, industrial designs, and geographical indications are concerned, that major obstacle has been overcome by means of international agreements that permit their registration with effects in all contracting parties. But patents have been left out of that approach.

Since the 1960s, with the advance of the delocalization of centers of industrial production and the attendant use of new technologies in developing countries, some countries put in their diplomatic agendas the establishing of a global patent system, this meaning a system through which one central agency is in charge of examining and granting patents with validity and enforceability in all the participating countries. But such a deal has never been reached. Those countries, therefore, have accepted a second best solution: instead of having a centralized body for the examination and granting of global patents, a system of circulation of international applications (with moderately harmonized standards for the search of prior art and the examination of the patentability of inventions), has been put in place. This was the Patent Cooperation Treaty (known by the acronym PCT), of 1970.

The text that follows gives a candid account of the origins of the PCT in the words of a former WIPO Director General, Arpad Bogsch.

. . . Having briefly described the PCT and its usefulness, I shall recount its origins.

They reach back to the mid-1960s. In those years, national patent Offices were particularly worried about the rapidly increasing number of patent applications they had to deal with. The numbers were so high that examination backlogs grew alarmingly and pendencies were so long that by the time a decision was made by the patent office on whether or not to grant a patent, the applicant's economic interest in his invention may have faded. The whole patent system was in crisis.

Also, very long pendencies kept the public, particularly potential competitors, in the dark since during such pendency the applications were kept secret (e.g., in the United States of America) or, even if published, they were published without data which may have helped competitors in formulating opinions on the claimed invention's chances of obtaining patent protection.

Thus, those who advocated a system that became the PCT system thought that the interest of the public would, to a great extent, be served if the application were made public within a relatively short period of time after filing and if it were accompanied by a report which, without being conclusive, went far in allowing the assessment of the application's failure or success in obtaining a patent. The PCT achieved that, as I have already indicated above.

Another and at least equally important complaint in the 1960s was that when an invention sought protection in several countries, the applicant had to file several applications, with the patent offices effecting the same examination work. In other words, the same work was repeated several times, and no patent office had access to the work of the other patent offices.

A complete solution to this problem existed then and continues to exist today, only in theory. It would consist of creating a patent valid in all countries. Although partial solutions have been found in the meantime, a complete solution was not possible then and, I believe, will not be possible in the foreseeable future. For two main reasons. One is that countries want patents valid in their territories to be in their own language. The other is that—subject to certain exceptions—a country usually does not trust the judgment on patentability of a patent office other than its own. This lack of trust is also partly connected with the problem created by the multiplicity of languages, since the examiners of—say—the German Patent Office are less likely to understand already granted patents (to be searched) in the Japanese language than those in the German language, and vice versa. I said that there were exceptions to this lack of confidence in the work of another office. The most outstanding example so far is the European Patent Office [EPO], which grants patents valid in many countries. But there, too, the other—the language—question remains since a European patent granted in one language must be translated (generally, within three months from the mention of the decision to grant a patent in the EPO *Bulletin)* into that country's language, failing which, the patent shall be deemed to be void *ab initio* in that country.

The creators of the PCT knew that they would not be able to solve those problems completely. But they tried—and, I believe, succeeded—in reducing the practical burdens caused by repetitive searches and examinations, and the multiplicity of the required translations. The first was solved—partially, I repeat—through the introduction of search reports and preliminary examination reports. Rules were established as to what patent documents—from which countries and for which periods—and what non-patent literature (scientific articles, etc.) must be taken into consideration by all International Searching and Preliminary Examining Authorities in respect of all and any international application. These documents—they total many millions and currently grow every year by at least a million—constitute the "PCT minimum documentation."

Each Authority must have at least 100 examiners. These requirements are steps towards arriving at comparable search and examination results.

The difficulties caused by the multiplicity of languages were also, if not solved, at least very substantially reduced by the creators of the PCT. This was done by providing that the international application is to be filed in one language and in most cases, it is to be internationally searched, preliminarily examined and published in that same language. Thus, the international application has the effect of a national or regional application, in many countries having different languages, without any translation. Translations are necessary only 20 or 30 months after the priority date when the international application enters into what is called the "national phase." As can be seen, the creators of the PCT system were satisfied with a compromise: a midway between a single procedure for the whole world (a utopia) and as many procedures as there are countries (the situation in 1970).

I am convinced that the compromise was indispensable for the success of the PCT. It is, indeed, the explanation of its success. In the second half of the 1960s (when the plans for a PCT were under discussion) and in 1970 (when the PCT was adopted and signed), this compromise was the maximum of simplification that could be agreed upon. It still seems to be the maximum 25 years later. But I do not believe that it will remain the maximum also in the twenty-first century. On the contrary, I believe that further streamlining the procedures and a higher degree of relying on the results of the international search and examination can and will be realized. They should remain on the agenda of WIPO and should be vigorously pursued by the governments and the patent offices as well as by the International Bureau of WIPO.

§1.55 THE IDEA OF AN INTERNATIONAL AGREEMENT INCORPORATING INTELLECTUAL PROPERTY INTO TRADE-RELATED NEGOTIATIONS GAINS STRENGTH: THE ORIGINS OF THE TRIPS AGREEMENT

July 8, 1986

The negotiations of the Uruguay Round that, in 1994, led to the approval of the Agreement on Trade-Related Aspects of Intellectual Property Rights (the TRIPS Agreement), as part of the agreement that established the World Trade Organization (WTO), were inserted in two scenarios.

The first scenario was the gridlock in WIPO in respect of negotiations on harmonization of patent provisions. There had been an attempt in 1986, under the pretext of introducing the grace period (an exception to the novelty requirement), of raising the standards of protection, including by prohibiting the discriminatory treatment of inventions as regards their field of technology. Developing countries opposed that attempt, and 1991, the Diplomatic Conference that was convened to celebrate a treaty supplementing the Paris Convention, was suspended—significantly, in that same year most of those same developing countries would accept higher standards of protection in the negotiations that led to the establishment of the WTO.

The second scenario was the increase of global trade and the intensification of delocalization of manufacturing centers. The perception of differences in the levels of protection of intellectual property as a barrier to trade led major exporting trade partners to insist on the harmonization of rules. Such a harmonization would equalize opportunities, level the field, and, in most cases, discourage free riding. But there was also a different sort of pressure of promoting higher standards of intellectual property in developing countries. That was the pressure derived from the delocalization of manufacturing centers from developed to developing countries. Delocalization started as a way of reducing production costs but later, as a result of the income growth in those developing countries (partly due to that very delocalization), multinational companies started seeking to attend increasing local demand. Soon foreign investors would request from the authorities of host countries that they adopted rules in conformity with the legal regimes they had in their home countries. In many cases they were successful—and not only in the field of intellectual property.

The intellectual property rules in developing countries started, in this way, to converge in the direction of the standards adopted in developed countries even before the adoption of the TRIPS Agreement, as a form of attracting (or of maintaining) foreign direct investment.

Against these two scenarios, in 1994 GATT Contracting Parties adopted the TRIPS Agreement, which was drafted in a manner that aimed at responding to the need for the harmonization of norms, most of which aimed at eliminating free riding—as the major trading partners wished. It contained, on the other hand, a guarantee of fair treatment of developing countries in the case of trade-related disputes. It contained also language that expressed the positions of developing countries as regards their expectations on the use of intellectual property to promote national policies.

In 1986, a delegation of the United States submitted a statement to a preparatory meeting of the GATT proposing the negotiation and adoption of a treaty that raised the standards of international protection of intellectual property. In the background, worries with discriminatory treatment of pharmaceutical inventions were predominant, and explain the attention the future agreement would dedicate to their protection.

As a whole, the section of the TRIPS Agreement on patents is the area that has raised more controversies, especially those provisions that require that pharmaceutical inventions receive the same treatment under national laws as all other inventions. Debates on the difficulties of access to medicines in poor countries due to the high prices that patents might generate (an assertion that is based more on fear than on real facts) have led to strong reactions against the implementation of patent-related rules in those countries. That fear is behind rules on compulsory licenses (art. 31), special transitional periods (art. 65.4), and, more recently, the conditioned permission for issuing compulsory licenses for the purposes of exporting medicines (art. 31*bis*).

PREP.COM(86)W/46, July 8, 1986, Preparatory Committee

Trade and Intellectual Property Rights

The following communication, dated 7 July 1986, has been received from the delegation of the United States with the request that it be circulated to all members of the Preparatory Committee.

Trade and Intellectual Property Rights

Intellectual property protection is critically important to international trade and the world economy. Infringement of intellectual property rights (e.g., patents and copyrights) can severely distort and impede international trade by depriving innovators, creators and inventors of rewards and opportunities generated by innovations that enhance production and export capacity and demand for traded goods and services.

Adequate and effective protection fosters creativity and know-how, encouraging investment research and development and new facilities for international trade purposes. Innovation stimulates economic growth, employment and demand for traded goods and services. Technological progress is an increasingly important aspect of international competitiveness. In all countries, improved intellectual property protection can foster domestic technologies and attract foreign know-how and investment.

Trade distortions and impediments arise when a country's sales of products of innovation and creation are lost to foreign infringement activities which result in sales of duplicated or similar products in the country's home market, sales in the market where the infringing activities take place, or sales in third markets. Trade distortions occur disproportionately in technology intensive products (e.g., chemicals, transport equipment parts) and in products of artistic creation or expression (e.g., books, motion pictures).

Infringement activities can distort international trade to the detriment of all Contracting Parties' exports and foreign remittances. Certain countries fail to enforce intellectual property laws adequately. Further, some countries have adopted practices that have the effect of sanctioning abuse of intellectual property rights.

The provisions of some international intellectual property conventions are too weak to prevent trade distortions and impediments. The international intellectual property conventions were established before the development of the extensive international network of trade that exists today in products dependent on patents, copyrights and trademarks. For example, the dispute settlement and enforcement mechanisms of existing international intellectual property conventions are ineffective or are non-existent. Farther, the product coverage and terms of patents may be too restricted and subject to unreasonable working requirements and licensing policies, while they are still consistent with these conventions. . . .

§1.56 THE IDEA OF A GLOBAL PATENT HAS NOT VANISHED: IT RESURFACED IN WIPO, IN 2000

May 4 and 5, 2000

During the General Assemblies of September, 2000, the WIPO Director General presented to the Member States a proposal for resuming work on the establishment of a global patent system, under the pretext of submitting to Member States a report prepared by his Industry Advisory Commission.

In the text that follows, the reference to a treaty on the "harmonization of substantive patent law, with a view to facilitating greater mutual recognition of search and examination results by patent offices" led to the debates, for a few years, on the adoption of a Substantive Patent Law Treaty (SPLT), which were interrupted in 2008.

WIPO Industry Advisory Commission, Report of the Third Meeting

Geneva, May 4 and 5, 2000

1. The World Intellectual Property Organization (WIPO) Industry Advisory Commission (IAC) held its third meeting at WIPO Headquarters in Geneva on May 4 and 5, 2000. . . .
3. The discussion on the cost of obtaining and maintaining patent protection was opened by Mr. François Curchod, Deputy Director General, Global Protection Systems. Mr. Curchod reviewed the complaints of users of the patent system in terms of costs and the various international fora in which the issue had been discussed in recent years. He discussed the internal costs to applicants, official fees, agent's fees and enforcement costs as being the principal elements of costs to users of the patent system. He then reviewed the work that had been done at the national and international levels to address the problem of costs. Mr. Curchod concluded by indicating what WIPO could do in this regard, including further reduction of fees under the Patent Cooperation Treaty (PCT) system, resumption of discussions on substantive harmonization of patent laws, and increasing automation of systems for the application, examination and grant of patents.
4. Following its discussions, the IAC adopted the following resolution:
   Recognizing that the effectiveness of intellectual property as a stimulant to social and economic development is dependent upon the availability of protection at reasonable cost, the Industry Advisory Commission of the World Intellectual Property Organization (WIPO).
   Urges the Member States of WIPO to adopt a work program for the development of a more comprehensive approach to the reduction of the costs of obtaining and maintaining intellectual property protection in multiple countries, particularly through:

   (i) work, in the medium term, on a treaty on the harmonization of substantive patent law, with a view to facilitating greater mutual recognition of search and examination results by patent offices;
   (ii) further exploratory work on the possible introduction of a PCT certificate of patentability and work, in the long term, on the development of the legal framework for a world patent;
   (iii) the adoption of a general principle against barriers, *inter alia*, through fees, unreasonable delays and burdensome procedures, to obtaining and maintaining intellectual property protection at a reasonable cost.

§1.57 THE TRIPS COUNCIL HOSTS DEBATES ON ACCESS TO PHARMACEUTICAL PRODUCTS

June 12, 2001

When implementing their obligations under the TRIPS Agreement, once the transitional period they received was exhausted, a significant number of developing countries have been led to believe that they had made excessive concessions in the field of intellectual property, and in particular of patents for pharmaceutical inventions, as compared to those they had received as regards tariffs on agricultural and industrialized products. Even before such transitional period had finished, some countries had already started raising concerns over the impact of patent protection for pharmaceuticals in their territories and the access of their poor populations to health. The European Union (then the European Communities) has lent a sympathetic ear to those concerns (in spite of the major business interests of France, Germany and the United Kingdom on the patent protection of innovative medicines), and produced a paper that was the origin of long debates in the TRIPS Council (and around the world). Ultimately, that paper, excerpts from which follow, led to the adoption of the 2003 Decision of the WTO General Council, setting a mechanism of compulsory licenses for exporting pharmaceutical products to WTO Members that meet certain criteria, and to the 2015 adoption of an amendment to the Agreement, with the inclusion of its Article 31*bis*.

Communication from the European Communities and Their Member States

IP/C/W/280, of June 12, 2001

The following communication, dated 11 June 2001, has been received from the European Communities and their member States with the request that it be circulated to Members.

The Relationship between the Provisions pf the TRIPS Agreement and Access to Medicines

Background

1. At the last session of the TRIPS Council (2-5 April 2001), the Africa Group proposed that one day be set aside at the June session to clarify the interpretation and/or application of certain provisions of the TRIPS Agreement. The discussion is intended to examine the relationship between intellectual property and access to medicines and will seek to bring clarity regarding the interpretation and the application of the provisions of the Agreement which provide scope for Members to address public health concerns. The European Communities (EC) and their member States, together with most other delegations, welcomed and supported this initiative. It is an important development, since it will be the first time that the TRIPS Council discusses intellectual property issues in the context of public health. . . .
6. The EC and their member States recognize that the lack of affordable pharmaceuticals is a serious problem in many developing countries and especially for the poorest people.

Relevance of Intellectual Property

7. The EC and their member States consider that intellectual property rights provide an essential stimulus for creativity and innovation. These rights need to be adequately protected in order to encourage, for example, investment in research and development of new medicines, and particularly those targeted at the major communicable diseases.
8. The Agreement on Trade-Related Aspects of Intellectual Property Rights (TRIPS), which emerged from the Uruguay Round negotiations has, however, sometimes been criticized as limiting policy options in relation to public health concerns. In the view of the EC and their member States, the Agreement's objectives, principles and purpose (set out in Articles 7 and 8), special transitional arrangements and other provisions give these countries a sufficiently wide margin of discretion in implementing it. This margin enables

them to set up an intellectual property regime that meets their policy needs and is capable of responding to public health concerns. The EC and their member States have declared their willingness—most notably in the Programme for Action—to promote discussions, within the WTO, WIPO and WHO, to address the link between the Agreement and public health protection issues.

This Communication summarises the views of the EC and their member States on some of the relevant provisions of the Agreement.

Compulsory Licensing . . .

13. Article 31 has been further criticized for requiring that goods manufactured under a compulsory licence be 'predominantly for the supply of the domestic market of the Member authorizing such use.' This provision is sometimes said to prevent a small country that has no production facilities of its own from obtaining cheap medicines from abroad under a compulsory licence. This is an important argument as the Agreement does not appear to offer any legal certainty on the issue. What can be said is that a WTO Member is free to grant a compulsory licence for the importation of goods which are under patent in its own territory, as long as the imported goods have been produced in a country where they are not patented, or where the term of protection has expired. However, the EC and their member States also point to another possible interpretation of the Agreement . . . that would allow a Member to issue a compulsory licence to a manufacturer in another country, provided the government of that other country recognized the licence (which it would not be obliged to do under the Agreement), and provided that all the goods manufactured under the licence were exported to the country granting the licence. It should be noted, however, that it is far from certain whether such a 'permissive' reading of the Agreement would stand scrutiny by a panel or the Appellate Body. The EC and their member States are ready to discuss this matter in order to reach consensus on this issue among all WTO Members. . . .

Conclusion

17. The TRIPS Agreement represents a delicate balance between the interests of right-holders and consumers. The EC and their member States stand ready to contribute constructively to any debate concerning the interpretation of its provisions.
18. Moreover, the spiralling health crisis in the developing world has underlined the need for rapid action. The TRIPS Agreement has increasingly come under fire for allegedly standing in the way of developing countries' efforts to implement an effective public health policy. The EC and their member States take such criticisms seriously and stand ready to engage in a positive manner in the discussion, leading where necessary to clarification, of certain of the Agreement's provisions. This paper has focused on Articles 7, 8, 30, 31 and 39, but Members may wish to discuss other provisions they consider to be relevant. The EC and their member States are also ready to discuss to what extent technical assistance can take into account health concerns.
19. Improving health at the same time as combating poverty requires a mix of complementary social, economic and health policies and practices. Health gains largely depend on using available resources in productive and efficient ways, as shown by the great strides made by some middle and low-income countries. Intellectual property rights play a role with regard to access to medicines. However, the TRIPS Agreement cannot be held responsible for the health crisis in developing countries, while it must not stand in the way for

action to combat the crisis. The EC and their member States will continue to constructively and positively take part in the expanding global effort to develop a coherent and effective response to the health problems of the developing world.

§1.58 WIPO'S AGENDA FOR DEVELOPMENT

August 27, 2004

In the last years, the role of WIPO in conducting the international intellectual property regime has been revisited in the context of a movement called "the Agenda for Development" (AD). This movement was triggered by a proposal tabled by Argentina and Brazil at the WIPO General Assembly of 2004, for the establishment of a "Development Agenda for WIPO." This proposal was later expanded and re-submitted by a group of 14 countries self-designated as "Group of Friends of Development:" Argentina, Bolivia, Brazil, Cuba, Dominican Republic, Ecuador, Egypt, Iran, Kenya, Peru, Sierra Leone, South Africa, Tanzania and Venezuela.

The basic proposal of those countries is reflected in the text that follows. It was elaborated around four major clusters of principles and concerns, but in reality the main target of its proponents was the work on harmonization of patentability requirements. Those discussions were understood by some WIPO Member States as a step towards a global patent (*see* Text 1.56). Between 2004 and 2007 a vast number of proposals and recommendations on the future work of WIPO were discussed, 45 of which were approved. Moreover, the WIPO General Assembly of 2007 established a new committee with the objective of implementing the approved AD recommendations (the Committee on Development and Intellectual Property (CDIP)). Since 2008 the CDIP has taken a significant number of initiatives aiming at implementing the AD recommendations.

WIPO GENERAL ASSEMBLY

Thirty-First (15th Extraordinary) Session

Geneva, September 27 to October 5, 2004

PROPOSAL FOR THE ESTABLISHMENT OF A DEVELOPMENT AGENDA FOR WIPO

Document prepared by the Secretariat

WO/GA/31/11, of August 27, 2004

I. Development, the most important challenge facing the International community

At the dawn of a new Millennium, development undoubtedly remains one of the most daunting challenges facing the international community. The importance of facing up to this challenge has been widely acknowledged in many international fora at the highest level. The United Nations adopted the Millennium Development Goals, which established a firm commitment by the international community to address the significant problems that affect developing countries and LDCs. The Programme of Action for the Least Developed Countries for the Decade 2001-2010, the Monterey Consensus, the Johannesburg Declaration on Sustainable Development and the Plan of Implementation agreed at the World Summit on Sustainable Development, the Declaration of Principles and the Plan of Action of the first phase of the World Summit on the Information Society, and most recently the Sao Paulo Consensus adopted at UNCTAD [United Nations Conference on Trade and Development] XI, have all placed development at the heart of their concerns and actions. This has also been the case in the context of the current Doha round of multilateral trade negotiations of the World Trade Organization (the "Doha Development Agenda"), which was launched at the WTO's 4th Ministerial Conference, in November 2001.

II. The development dimension and intellectual property protection

Technological innovation, science and creative activity in general are rightly recognized as important sources of material progress and welfare. However, despite the important scientific and technological advances and promises of the 20th and early 21st centuries, in many areas a significant "knowledge gap" as well as a "digital divide" continue to separate the wealthy nations from the poor.

In this context, the impact of intellectual property has been widely debated in past years. Intellectual property protection is intended as an instrument to promote technological innovation, as well as the transfer and dissemination of technology. Intellectual property protection cannot be seen as an end in itself, nor can the harmonization of intellectual property laws leading to higher protection standards in all countries, irrespective of their levels of development.

The role of intellectual property and its impact on development must be carefully assessed on a case-by-case basis. IP protection is a policy instrument the operation of which may, in actual practice, produce benefits as well as costs, which may vary in accordance with a country's level of development. Action is therefore needed to ensure, in all countries, that the costs do not outweigh the benefits of IP protection.

In this regard, the adoption of the Doha Declaration on the TRIPS Agreement and Public Health at the 4th Ministerial Conference of the WTO represented an important milestone. It recognized that the TRIPS Agreement, as an international instrument for the protection of intellectual property, should operate in a manner that is supportive of and does not run counter to the public health objectives of all countries.

The need to integrate the "development dimension" into policy making on intellectual property protection has received increased recognition at the international level. Also in the framework of the WTO, paragraph 19 of the WTO's Doha Ministerial Declaration, in setting a mandate for the TRIPS Council in the context of the Doha Development Agenda, refers explicitly to the need to take fully into account the development dimension.

III. Integrating the development dimension into WIPO's activities

As a member of the United Nations system, it is incumbent upon the World Intellectual Property Organization (WIPO) to be fully guided by the broad development goals that the UN has set for itself, in particular in the Millennium Development Goals. Development concerns should be fully incorporated into all WIPO activities. WIPO's role, therefore, is not to be limited to the promotion of intellectual property protection.

WIPO is accordingly already mandated to take into account the broader development-related commitments and resolutions of the UN system as a whole.

However, one could also consider the possibility of amending the WIPO Convention (1967) to ensure that the "development dimension" is unequivocally determined to constitute an essential element of the Organization's work program. We therefore call upon WIPO General Assembly to take immediate action in providing for the incorporation of a "Development Agenda" in the Organization's work program.

IV. The development dimension and intellectual property norm-setting: safeguarding public interest flexibilities

WIPO is currently engaged in norm–setting activities in various technical Committees. Some of these activities would have developing countries and LDCs agree to IP protection standards that largely exceed existing obligations under the WTO's TRIPS Agreement, while these countries are still struggling with the costly process of implementing TRIPS itself.

The current discussions on a draft Substantive Patent Law Treaty (SPLT) in the Standing Committee on the Law of Patents (SCP) are of particular concern. The proposed Treaty would considerably raise patent protection standards, creating new obligations that developing countries will hardly be able to implement. In the course of discussions, developing countries have proposed amendments to improve the draft SPLT by making it more responsive to public interest concerns and the specific development needs of developing countries.

A consideration of the development dimension of intellectual property must be quickly brought to bear on discussions in the SCP. If discussions on the SPLT are to proceed, these should be based on the draft treaty as a whole, including all of the amendments that have been tabled by developing countries. Moreover, Members should strive for an outcome that unequivocally acknowledges and seeks to preserve public interest flexibilities and the policy space of Member States. Provisions on "objectives and principles", reflecting the content of Articles 7 and 8 of the TRIPS Agreement, should be included in the SPLT and other treaties under discussion in WIPO.

While access to information and knowledge sharing are regarded as essential elements in fostering innovation and creativity in the information economy, adding new layers of intellectual property protection to the digital environment would obstruct the free flow of information and scuttle efforts to set up new arrangements for promoting innovation and creativity, through initiatives such as the 'Creative Commons'. The ongoing controversy surrounding the use of technological protection measures in the digital environment is also of great concern.

The provisions of any treaties in this field must be balanced and clearly take on board the interests of consumers and the public at large. It is important to safeguard the exceptions and limitations existing in the domestic laws of Member States.

In order to tap into the development potential offered by the digital environment, it is important to bear in mind the relevance of open access models for the promotion of innovation and creativity. In this regard, WIPO should consider undertaking activities with a view to exploring the promise held by open collaborative projects to develop public goods, as exemplified by the Human Genome Project and Open Source Software.

Finally, the potential development implications of several of the provisions of the proposed Treaty on the Protection of Broadcasting Organizations that the Standing Committee on Copyright and Related Rights is currently discussing should be examined taking into consideration the interests of consumers and of the public at large.

V. The development dimension and the transfer of technology

The transfer of technology has been identified as an objective that intellectual property protection should be supportive of and not run counter to, as stated in Articles 7 and 8 of the TRIPS Agreement. Yet, many of the developing countries and LDCs that have taken up higher IP obligations in recent years simply lack the necessary infrastructure and institutional capacity to absorb such technology.

Even in developing countries that may have a degree of absorptive technological capacity, higher standards of intellectual property protection have failed to foster the transfer of technology through foreign direct investment and licensing. In effect, corrective measures are needed to address the inability of existing IP agreements and treaties to promote a real transfer of technology to developing countries and LDCs.

In this regard, a new subsidiary body within WIPO could be established to look at what measures within the IP system could be undertaken to ensure an effective transfer of technology to developing countries, similarly to what has already been done in other fora such as the WTO and the UNCTAD. Among these measures, we note with particular interest the idea of establishing an international regime that would promote access by the developing countries to the results of publicly funded research in the developed countries. Such a regime could take the form of a Treaty on Access to Knowledge and Technology. It is also important that clear provisions on transfer of technology be included in the treaties currently under negotiation in WIPO. . . .

IX. Conclusion

A vision that promotes the absolute benefits of intellectual property protection without acknowledging public policy concerns undermines the very credibility of the IP system. Integrating the development dimension into the IP system and WIPO's activities, on the other hand, will strengthen the credibility of the IP system and encourage its wider acceptance as an important tool for the promotion of innovation, creativity and development.

§1.59 THE UNITED STATES SUPREME COURT REJECTS PATENTS FOR PURELY ABSTRACT INVENTIONS

2014

As a reminiscence of the discussions that, in 1792, led the French National Assembly to reject patents for investment and saving plans (*see* Text 1.38), in this opinion, of 2014, the Supreme Court of the United States reaffirmed their antipathy against the patentability of purely abstract inventions.

Alice Corporation Pty. Ltd. v. CLS Bank Int'l

Supreme Court of the United States

573 U.S. 208 (2014)

Justice Thomas delivered the opinion of the Court.

The patents at issue in this case disclose a computer implemented scheme for mitigating "settlement risk" (i.e., the risk that only one party to a financial transaction will pay what it owes) by using a third-party intermediary. The question presented is whether these claims are patent eligible under 35 U. S. C.

§101, or are instead drawn to a patent-ineligible abstract idea. We hold that the claims at issue are drawn to the abstract idea of intermediated settlement, and that merely requiring generic computer implementation fails to transform that abstract idea into a patent-eligible invention. We therefore affirm the judgment of the United States Court of Appeals for the Federal Circuit. . . .

Section 101 of the Patent Act defines the subject matter eligible for patent protection. It provides:

> "Whoever invents or discovers any new and useful process, machine, manufacture, or composition of matter, or any new and useful improvement thereof, may obtain a patent therefor, subject to the conditions and requirements of this title." 35 U. S. C. §101.

We have long held that this provision contains an important implicit exception: Laws of nature, natural phenomena, and abstract ideas are not patentable. . . . We have interpreted §101 and its predecessors in light of this exception for more than 150 years. . . . We have described the concern that drives this exclusionary principle as one of pre-emption. . . . *See*, e.g., *Bilski*, *supra*, . . . (upholding the patent "would pre-empt use of this approach in all fields, and would effectively grant a monopoly over an abstract idea"). Laws of nature, natural phenomena, and abstract ideas are "the basic tools of scientific and technological work." . . . "[M]onopolization of those tools through the grant of a patent might tend to impede innovation more than it would tend to promote it," thereby thwarting the primary object of the patent laws. . . . We have "repeatedly emphasized this . . . concern that patent law not inhibit further discovery by improperly tying up the future use of " these building blocks of human ingenuity. . . .

§1.60 THE UNITED STATES PLANTS THE SEED OF THE GLOBAL PATENT SYSTEM

October 2, 2014

After introducing a major reform to their patent laws, through the passing of the American Invents Act (AIA), in 2011, the United States embraced themselves for strengthening their leadership of a movement towards the adoption of the global patent system. The AIA brought many changes to law until then in force, but its major feature was the adoption of a first-to-file system, accompanied by a publication of patent applications 18 months after the filing date. Thereby, from a procedural perspective, the United States eliminated the major feature that opposed its national mechanism of patent prosecution to the mechanisms adopted by practically all other countries of the world.

Even if the PCT was a first step towards a global system for obtaining patents, that was an insufficient one, given that Contracting Parties are not bound to follow the reports issued by the various international authorities involved.

So the United States in the last years has promoted the so-called Patent Prosecution Highway (PPH)—a mechanism established through bilateral agreements between national patent offices. According to that mechanism, participating offices share the results of searches and examinations of patent applications, thus enabling fast-tracking examinations in the case of applications with identical claims. The PPH has worked well so far, with a growing number of countries adhering. Perhaps this is a sign that, albeit hesitantly, the resistance against a global mechanism is fading away.

The text that follows, signed by Michelle K. Lee, Deputy Under Secretary of Commerce for Intellectual Property and Deputy Director of the United States Patent and Trademark Office, gives an account of the success of the PPH, which is undoubtedly associated with the ideas exposed by the WIPO Industry Advisory Commission, in 2000 (*see* Text 1.56).

Implementation of the Global and IPS PPH Pilot Programs with Participating Offices

I. Background

Beginning in July 2006, the United States Patent and Trademark Office (USPTO) has partnered with several other offices in Patent Prosecution Highway (PPH) programs. The PPH enables an applicant who receives a positive ruling on patent claims from one participating office to request accelerated prosecution of corresponding claims in another participating office, which allows the applicant to obtain a patentability decision in the second office more quickly. Furthermore, the PPH promotes patent application processing efficiency by allowing the examiner in the office of later examination (OLE) to reuse the search and examination results from the office of earlier examination (OEE), thereby reducing workload and duplication of effort.

Since its inception, various enhancements to the original PPH program have been introduced. . . .

As the work sharing benefits provided by the PPH have become apparent, participation in the PPH program in its various forms has grown rapidly. However, because the above-described modifications to the PPH program have not been universally implemented by the different participating offices, the administration of multiple PPH programs, each having particular requirements, has become increasingly cumbersome. Recognizing the need and opportunity for greater efficiency, the USPTO and several other offices seek to consolidate and replace existing PPH programs, with the goal of streamlining the PPH process for both offices and applicants. To this end, the USPTO and other offices have established the Global PPH pilot program and the IPS PPH pilot program.

The Global PPH and IPS PPH pilot programs are running concurrently and are substantially identical, differing only with regard to their respective participating offices. The USPTO is participating in both the Global PPH pilot program and the IPS PPH pilot program. A list of the other offices currently participating in the Global PPH pilot program is available at *http://www.uspto.gov/patents/init_events/pphl.* The European Patent Office (EPO), Japan Patent Office (JPO), Korean Intellectual Property Office (KIPO), and State Intellectual Property Office of the People's Republic of China (SIPO) are participating in the IPS PPH pilot program.
. . .

§1.61 PATENTS FOR INVENTIONS MADE BY INTELLIGENT MACHINES?

October 29, 2019

The text that follows concerns a patent issued in 2019 by the USPTO for a computer-enabled method of assisting in the generation of certain innovations. The method consists in combining searches of existing techniques so as to identify unexploited technical solutions for some technical problems. The patent specifications do not refer to the making of inventions, but rather of "innovations," because the concept of invention requires nonobviousness or a certain level of inventiveness. This, in patent terms, implies the achieving of unexpected results by the application of the new method found. It is possible that machines may never be able to "invent," in the sense of resorting to inspiration and creativity, but advances in artificial intelligence are coming close to that, to the point that a patent examiner might very well understand that an innovation made as a consequence of this invention would qualify as a patentable invention.

Let us suppose that the invention claimed in this patent works and computers operating the method start making inventions. To whom or what should patents for those inventions be granted? To the machine? To its owner? To the machine software's owner?

In 2019, the European Patent Office refused to recognize the inventorship of a machine (named by its owner as DABUS AI) in the context of two patent applications. In the same year, a patent application filed on behalf of the same machine was received by the UK Patent Office, but the inventor, at the time of this writing, appears in the corresponding official publication designated as "yet to be decided."

In 1954, British writer Roald Dahl wrote a superb short story that raises the same problem in connection with copyright: The Great Automatic Grammatizator. It is a very funny story, which raises very serious considerations about fraud in authorship. But Dahl did not go as far as claiming copyright for the machine. In the field of copyright, the problem of attributing authorship to creative machines does not raise serious issues, at least while it continues associated with the human spirit (which explains the strict enforcement of authors' moral rights in certain jurisdictions). But that problem does not exist in the context of patents—their only acknowledged moral right being that of their being designated as such in the patent letter (which right may be waived).

The text that follows provides for two excerpts from the patent mentioned above: the abstract and the first claim.

The United States Patent 10,459,925

Computer-enabled method of assisting to generate an innovation

Inventors: Debmalya Biswas; Julian C. Nolan; and Matthew J. Lawrenson

Patent owner (assignee): Ipprova Sarl (Lausanne, Switzerland)

Abstract

According to the present invention there is provided a computer-enabled method of assisting to generate an innovation, the method comprising the steps of: retrieving from a database a first set of more than two documents belonging to a first domain (D.sub.1); retrieving from said database a second set of more than two documents belonging to a second domain (D.sub.2); selecting all possible combinations of documents from the first set with all documents in said second set, and for each combination of documents: determining a composite novelty score, a composite proximity score and a composite impact score; and based on all of the determined composite novelty scores and/or composite proximity scores and/or composite impact scores, providing a recommendation which can assist to generate an innovation.

The invention claimed is:

1. A method comprising: retrieving a first set of more than two documents belonging to a first domain (D.sub.1); retrieving a second set of more than two documents belonging to a second domain (D.sub.2); defining one or more ontologies; generating all possible combinations of documents from the first set (d.sub.x) with documents in said second set (d.sub.y); determining respective composite novelty scores for said combinations of documents (d.sub.x, d.sub.y), wherein the composite novelty score for one of the combinations of documents (d.sub.x, d.sub.y) represents a likelihood that a merging of solutions in said combination of documents (d.sub.x, d.sub.y) will provide a novel solution, and wherein determining the composite novelty score for said combination of documents (d.sub.x, d.sub.y) includes: identifying sets of words and/or terms c(d.sub.x) and c(d.sub.y) included in the documents (d.sub.x, d.sub.y) which are not included in one or more other documents which belong to a same one of the first domain (D.sub.1) or second domain (D2) to which the document (d.sub.x, d.sub.y) belongs; and determining the composite novelty score based on a number of words and/or terms which are common to the sets of words and/or terms for the documents (|c(d.sub.x).andgate.c(d.sub.y)|); determining composite proximity scores for said combinations of documents (d.sub.x, d.sub.y), wherein the composite proximity score for one of the combinations of documents (d.sub.x, d.sub.y) represents a proximity of each of said documents to the one or more defined ontologies; determining composite impact scores for said combinations of documents (d.sub.x, d.sub.y), wherein the composite impact score for one of the combinations of documents (d.sub.x, d.sub.y) represents a feasibility of combining the solutions in said two or more documents; and selecting one or more of the combinations of documents (d.sub.x, d.sub.y) based on the composite novelty scores, the composite proximity scores, and the composite impact scores, and providing a recommendation related to generating an innovation based on the selected one or more of the combinations of documents, wherein providing the recommendation includes presenting a solution template S.sub.xy in which the respective solutions in the selected combination of documents are merged to provide a new solution which differs from the respective solutions in the selected combination of documents.

CHAPTER 2

Business Identifiers (Trademarks, Geographical Indications, Certification Marks, Trade Names, Shop Signs, Awards, Slogans)

§2.01 IN OLD ASSYRIA COURTS RECOGNIZED THE LEGAL VALUE OF PERSONAL SEALS

Nineteenth Century BC

The systematic practice of acts of trade requires a registration system, with two main purposes: accounting, i.e. recording the quantities and the nature of goods exchanged; and the identification of those who assumed the obligations in the event the need for claiming their liability in the case of non-compliance would arise. This second element imposes the setting of mechanisms of merchants' identification and differentiation, particularly when trade is carried out by private individuals, in pursuit of their own gain.

In Mesopotamia merchants would store grain and other goods in sacks and close them with a knot, to which they attached a clay tablet. On this tablet, they would print their seal—a pictogram that would identify them. Usually the tablets would be inserted into clay envelopes, on which the seal would also be printed. In this manner, the owner did not need to travel with the goods he would send away—his signature, in the form of a seal, would accompany the goods, thereby indicating his ownership as well as his liability for any commercial commitments made to the distant buyers. Commercial contracts would be formalized in a similar way.

This text is the report of a court dispute involving an unsettled obligation of a deceased merchant and the commitment by his son of settling it, on the recognition of his father's seal.

Ashurtab empaneled us (as judges) against Ashurlamassi, and thus (spoke) Ashurtab to Ashurlamassi: "This tablet—(does it bear) the seal of your father, or (does it) not (bear) the seal of your father?" Thus (spoke) Ashurlamassi: "(It does bear) the seal of my father; I shall bring you evidence of satisfaction (of the obligation) within six months. If I do not produce for you (this evidence within six months), I assume the debt." Month of the Sha-sarate, eponymate of a subordinate of Enna-Su'in. Witness (i.e., the judges): Abuziya son of Ashu-Su'in, [...] son of Ashur-Shamshi, Anina son of Shu-Erra.

§2.02 CODE OF HAMMURABI, LAWS 226 AND 227

Circa 1,750 BC

As insensitive and inhumane it may seem, the signs that were marked on the skin of slaves, in Babylon, were trademarks to the same extent as those signs that several centuries later would be printed on brood swans (*see* Text 2.11). They had the double purpose of designating ownership and of distinguish goods destined to be traded. The Code of Hammurabi had rules that prevented what today we would call of "passing off" of slaves.

226. If a barber, without the knowledge of his master, cut the sign of a slave on a slave not to be sold, the hands of this barber shall be cut off.
227. If any one deceive a barber, and have him mark a slave not for sale with the sign of a slave, he shall be put to death, and buried in his house. The barber shall swear: "I did not mark him wittingly," and shall be guiltless.

§2.03 IN ANCIENT GREECE, FIERCE COMMERCIAL COMPETITION LED TO THE INTENSIVE USE OF BUSINESS IDENTIFIERS

Seventh–Fifth Centuries BC

This text is a description by a French historian, Gustave Glotz, of the fierce competition among potters and other entrepreneurs that prevailed in Ancient Greece, between the seventh and the fifth centuries BC. Greek potters would resort to various differentiating strategies to lure clients, including a variety of business identifiers, such as trademarks, geographical indications, and slogans.

In flourishing industries, competition becomes strong and fierce. The sculptor proudly puts his name on his work; by becoming aware of his talent, he intends to distinguish himself from his rivals. The potter and the painter of vases do the same: is not the signature a certificate of origin that must spread the trademark? First, the manufacturer signs alone, because customers are interested only in the company name; then, he associates with his name the name of the painter; finally, more often the artist alone recommends himself to the public. Pride and publicity. . . .

But the struggle is not always very fair: a certain Pamphaios unscrupulously copies the manner of Hysclos or Nicosthenes. A little hype does not mess, and so much better if one can discredit the workshop across the street. On a mediocre amphora, Euthymides writes beside his signature: "Euphranios will never do so well."

Competition is no longer confined to private entrepreneurs and extends to the cities. It becomes international, at the same time as the division of labor. The reputation gained by the products of a city benefits all those who make them. When a figurine modeler signs Sicon of Cyprus, when obscure potters add to their name the Athenian toponym, they give their address and recommend their merchandise. Moreover, a fierce rivalry involves the ports able to compete for the universal market. As long as Milesians are the masters, they prohibit the access from Asia Minor to Samian pottery and do not let more than rare loads to arrive in the Black Sea; they exclude Corinthian pottery, so much so that we have not found the least bit of it in the ruins of their city; they manage a long time to remove it from Naucratis. When Corinth triumphs, in spite of the copying of its shapes and emulation of its industrial processes by the competitors it ousted, it retains its commercial superiority and, in some areas, such as in Delphi, does not tolerate other products than their own. At this time, the economic struggle is so fierce that it leads to acts of violence and bloody fights.

§2.04 GREEK AND ROMAN SLOGANS

Sixth Century BC to First Century AD

One of the instruments to which Greek and Roman merchants and artisans would resort so as to differentiate and exalt their products was slogans. They are particularly abundant on archeological remnants of pottery.

"I am a pretty vase."

Slogan printed on a Greek kylix (a shallow bowl), sixth century BC (found in Medellin, Badajoz, Spain), under the portrait of Zeus throwing rays. On display at the Museum of Archeology, Madrid, Spain.

LIQVAMEN / OPTIMVM / EX OFFICI [n] / A. SCAVRI

("Excellent *liquamen* made in the workshop of Scaurus")

In the ruins of the house of Aulus Umbricius Scaurus, the most renowned maker of *garum* (a fermented fish sauce), in Pompeii, archeologists have found mosaics reproducing some of the amphorae that the manufacturer used to export his famous product. Several of those amphorae display slogans.

EMITE LUCERNAS COLATAS AB ASSE(NE)

("Buy lamps made by Assen")

An oil lamp made by Essen, and found in Cadiz, Spain, had the inscription above. Essen was a potter in the second century AD. Archeologists believe he had a workshop at Cesarea (today Cherchell, in Algeria). Lamps made by Essen (or their imitations), with similar slogans, were found in Lausanne, Rome, and Lyon.

§2.05 IN OLD EGYPT EXCLUSIVITY IN PRIVATE SEALS WAS ENFORCEABLE

First Century BC

The Egyptian economy was essentially centralized and, therefore, by contrast with Sumer, differentiation among entrepreneurs was not of crucial importance. However, some vestiges of Egyptian private entrepreneurs have reached us, such as artisans' marks stamped on bricks and potteries. Private contracts would also be sealed with private signs. Diodorus of Sicily (first century BC) reports that those seals, either publicly or privately owned and used, were protected. In this text, Diodorus also refers to the (strict) enforcement of laws concerning weights and measures, which is a topic with old and deep morale roots (both the Bible and the Quran refer to compliance with those laws as a manner of pleasing God). Today the observation of weights and measures is, besides a matter of administrative law, a theme of unfair competition and certification marks.

In the case of those who had disclosed military secrets to the enemy, the law [of Egypt] prescribed that their tongues should be cut out, while in the case of counterfeiters or falsifiers of measures and weights or imitators of seals, and of official scribes who made false entries or erased items, and of any who adduced false documents, it ordered that both their hands should be cut off, to the end that the offender, being punished in respect of those members of his body that were the instruments of his wrongdoing, should himself keep until death his irreparable misfortune, and at the same time, by serving as a warning example to others, should turn them from the commission of similar offenses.

§2.06 PLATO ON SELF-REGULATION OF COMMERCE

First Century BC

In Book IV of one of his most famous dialogs, The Republic (written circa 380 BC), Plato asserts that certain practices in commerce should be self-regulated. Eventually this may be an explanation for the fact that in Antiquity trademarks and other business identifiers, which were used profusely by merchants and artisans, were not the matter of written statutes. Their observation, therefore, would be a matter of courtesy of the trade.

[Socrates] And again: in Heaven's name, as to these transactions relating to contracts which men of different classes make with one another in the marketplace, or, if you please, the contracts of builders, or insults, unprovoked assaults, the bringing of lawsuits, the impaneling of jurors, the exactions or payments of customs that may be necessary either in the markets or in the harbors, and, in general, whatever concerns the market, the city or the port, or the like, shall we venture to legislate about any of them?

[Adeimantus] There is no need to impose laws about these matters on good and noble men; for they will easily discover themselves whatever legislation is necessary.

§2.07 IN ROME, MARKS OF ORIGIN (EARLY GEOGRAPHICAL INDICATIONS) WERE COMMONLY USED

First Century AD

The texts that follow illustrate the early use of geographical indications. (i) In one of his Epigrams, Marcus Martial, the Roman poet, mocks the size of cheese made at Luna, in northwest Italy. Every piece of cheese was marked with the figurative sign of the crescent moon, designating its geographical origin. Pliny the Elder, in his Natural History (Book XI, chapter 97), informs that each cheese from Luna could weigh up to 1,000 pounds. (ii) In another passage of his Natural History, Pliny resorts to geographical names to identify pottery that was deemed in high esteem by Roman consumers.

Martial, on the size of cheese from Luna

XXX. Cheese, stamped with the crest of Etruscan Luna, will afford your slaves a thousand lunches.

Pliny the Elder, on various sorts of cheese and pottery

The pastures of the Alps recommend themselves by two sorts of cheese; the Dalmatic Alps send us the Docleatian cheese, and the Centronian Alps the Vatusican. The kinds produced in the Apennines are more numerous; from Liguria we have the cheese of Ceba, which is mostly made from the milk of sheep; from Timbria we have that of Aesina, and from the frontiers of Etruria and Liguria those of Luna, remarkable for their vast size, a single cheese weighing as much as a thousand pounds.

For the service of the table, the Samian pottery is even yet held in higher esteem; that, too, of Arretium in Italy, still maintains its high character; while for their cups, and, for those only, the manufactories of Surrentum, Asta, Pollentia, Saguntum in Spain, and Pergamus in Asia, are greatly esteemed. The city of Tralles, too, in Asia, and that of Mutina in Italy, have their respective manufactures of earthenware, and even by this branch of art are localities rendered famous; their productions, by the aid of the potter's wheel, becoming known to all countries, and conveyed by sea and by land to every quarter of the earth.

§2.08 CERTAIN TRADEMARKS WERE WELL-KNOWN AND HAD INFLUENCE IN ROMANS' DAILY LIFE

First Century AD

Greece and Rome based their vastly economic power and cultural influence on very broad commercial networks. The largest Greek cities established colonies on the shores of the eastern Mediterranean, and Rome extended its dominion from the Middle East to the Atlantic gates, from Africa to the Swiss Alps and England. Roman products were traded throughout the Mediterranean basin, including natural extracts such as olive oil, wine, and grain, as well as industrialized products such as oil lamps, ceramics, elaborated fish sauce, and medicines. The setting of wide commercial networks led naturally to the intense use of signs with the purpose of designating the goods by associating them with a specific manufacturer and, eventually, to a certain quality standard. As it happens today, trademarks in Rome acquired the power to influence consumption habits. A passage of the Natural History, of Pliny the Elder (first century AD), while criticizing the taste for luxury consumption of silver plate that the Roman well-off families had developed, gives us an illustration of such influence.

The caprice of the human mind is marvelously exemplified in the varying fashions of silver plate; the work of no individual manufactory being for any long time in vogue. At one period, the Furnian plate, at another the Clodian, and at another the Gratian, is all the rage—for we borrow the shop even at our tables. Now again, it is embossed plate that we are in search of, and silver deeply chiselled around the marginal lines of the figures painted upon it; and now we are building up on our sideboards fresh tiers of tables for supporting the various dishes.

§2.09 A MEDIEVAL JURIST EXPLAINS THE FUNDAMENTAL PRINCIPLE THAT BUTTRESSES TRADEMARK LAW: DISTINCTIVENESS

1358

After the demise of the Roman empire, intellectual property ceased to be useful to promote commercial rivalry, as long-distance trade practically vanished. Intellectual property resurfaced several centuries later, when Europe awakened to a new economic environment, after the turn of the first millennium. And that awakening was caused by the introduction of one invention: the stirrup. The stirrup permitted horse riders to carry heavier gear, thus giving rise to professional warriors—the knights, who would put their skills at the services of the newly emerging lords. As per the teaching of Lynn White, the rise of professional armies, besides serving as the basis for the new economic regime that prevailed through the low Middle Ages—feudalism—gave rise to a minimum of political security and stability that encouraged trade and specialized labor. At the same time, improvements in hygiene and increased availability of food led the European populations to grow, and small settlements, frequently annexed to monasteries, became burghs, villages, towns.

The increased military efficiency of knights was supported by their heavy armory, which would protect them in combat but, at the same time, would make them indistinguishable by their own soldiers. The need to acquire distinctiveness in war (and in tournaments) led the nobility to develop heraldry, and with it the corresponding legal principles of distinctiveness and veracity.

The principles (based on customary law) of heraldry are two: distinctiveness and veracity. Distinctiveness was (and is) fundamental, because it ensured that warriors, with their bodies fully covered by armors and their faces hidden beneath helmets, would be recognized by their allies (as well as by their enemies). For medieval warriors, distinctiveness, as Bartolo da Sassoferrato, in his work (published posthumously, in 1358) *De Insigniis et Armis*, explained, was a matter of life and death. And so it is today, figuratively speaking, for entrepreneurs.

. . . If a judge, by virtue of his office, sees that such [improper use of the coat of arms] may cause public scandal and confusion among the subjects, he can prohibit it lest the people be deceived. . . .

Sometimes it may happen that the use of a coat of arms or insignia by one individual may impinge on another who uses the same insignia. If a person who has many enemies and against whose life many are plotting assumes the coat of arms and insignia of another peaceful or quiet person, certainly it matters much to the latter, and he can see to it that the former is prohibited. Just as a complaint can be lodged against someone who bears a coat of arms or insignia contemptuously, all the more can a complaint be lodged to prevent one from being mistakenly killed or injured in place of another who has adopted the identical coat of arms. . . .

Sometimes it may happen that the use of the same coat of arms or insignia may impinge on many members of the community. Let us provide an example of insignia other than those which are borne for coats of arms. Suppose that there is a very skilled craftsman—a smith—who places certain marks on his swords and other products he makes, by which one recognizes that those products are made by that master. And therefore such merchandise sells well and is in high demand. In this case, I think that if another smith uses the same mark, he can be prohibited because when the work of one is in fact taken as the work of another it damages the people. . . .

Some trademarks are proper to a particular craft or skill, and here it should be noted that sometimes they are connected to the nature of the place in which the product is made. For example, in the March of Ancona, there is a certain renowned town named Fabriano, where the manufacture of paper is the main business. Here there are many paper mills, and some of them produce better paper, although even here the skill of the worker is of considerable importance. And here each sheet of paper has its own watermark by which one can recognize the paper mill. Therefore, in this case the watermark should belong to the one to whom the mill itself belongs, no matter whether it remains in his possession by right of ownership or lease, or by any other title, wholly or in part, or even in bad faith. . . .

§2.10 AN EARLY STATUTE SETTING THE DESIGNATION OF ORIGIN

October 1261

The text that follows is an excerpt from a statute enacted by the municipality of Douai, France, adopting the city's seal as a mark of origin for cloths. As medieval economy grew—the cloth industry and trade being the main economic activities—and corporations were established both as institutions for the social protection of workers and as structures of organization of labor and regulation of the industry, marks were initially adopted as signs of differentiation of cities. The reason was that, because of the way corporations were organized, there was no commercial rivalry within the city. Rivalry would be exercised against the articles (and their manufacturers) of other cities, either in the trade halls of each city or in local or regional fairs. Only as a second step, as trade continued to grow, and with the main purpose of certifying compliance with the technical standards imposed by the guilds, collective (guilds') marks and individual (artisans') marks were introduced.

Weavers of canvas.

In the beams of the VIII men [the eight eswards of the profession]

. . .

2. And that there be no weaver so bold in all this city who dare to weave cloth that is not marked with the mark of the cloth of the city of Douai, under the penalty of L pounds and his banishment for one year from the city and the loss of the cloth. . . .

§2.11 MARKS OF OWNERSHIP AND TRADE

November 16, 1276

In their early origins, trademarks would not only serve as signs of differentiation for the purpose of supporting trade, but also as signs of ownership—like today's companies' logos that are apposed to every piece of office furniture. In Classical Antiquity, as well as in the Middle Ages, when the tools for organizing inventories were rudimentary, trademarks were essential for identifying the owners of cargo in ships. As we have seen, trademarks would identify slaves in Babylon, when they were considered as a commodity. In the text that follows, a 1276 letter patent mentions William de Saham's marks printed on brood swans, which had been removed by a thief. The word "brood" indicates that these swans had commercial value, so we may very well be in the presence of trademarks with a double function: of distinguishing goods in trade and of indicating ownership.

This same idea would be flagged six centuries later. In the diplomatic conference of 1880 that led to the adoption of the Paris Convention for the Protection of Industrial Property (in 1883), there was a discussion about this topic. The delegate of Portugal, Mr. de Barros, had proposed to include the terms "agricultural products" in the provision that qualified the (broad) scope of industrial property. In response, a member of the Commission of Redaction, Mr. Jagerschmidt, of France, said that "After hearing Mr. de Barro's explanations, [the Commission] found it difficult to introduce in the Convention the words 'agricultural products,' and that the term 'industrial property' applied to everything, even to those trademarks with which the beasts are marked." Ministère des Affaires Étrangères, Conférence Internationale pour la Protection de la Propriété Industrielle, at 59 (Imprimerie Nationale, 1880).

The like [Commission of oyer and terminer] to Richard de Holebrok, touching the persons who by night took two brood swans and four cygnets of William de Saham at Be ... co. Norfolk, removed the mark of the said William with which the said swans had been marked, and extracted the chief quills from their wings and still detain the cygnets.

§2.12 CERTIFICATION MARKS FOR GOLD AND SILVERSMITHS

1300

The certification of quality in the industry of gold and silversmithing has always been a concern of authorities. In England, under Edward I, a statute was passed requiring smiths to submit the vessels of gold and silver they produced to the visit of the wardens of the craft, who would mark the articles with a certification mark (the Leopard's Head). These were not trademarks, strictly speaking, as we understand them today, but they were collective or certification signs that were used in trade to distinguish legitimate works from illicit ones. This Statute would be revised in 1477, under Edward IV, when, in addition to the collective mark of the Leopard's Head (crowned), reference was made to the smiths' individual marks (*see* Text 2.27).

It is ordained that no Goldsmith of England, nor none otherwhere in the King's Dominion, shall from henceforth [make or cause to be made] any Manner of Vessel, Jewel, or any other Thing of Gold or Silver, except if be of good and true Alloy, that is to say, Gold of a certain touch, and Silver of the sterling Alloy, or of better, at the Pleasure of him to whom the Work belongth; and that none work worse Silver than Money; and that no Manner of Vessel of Silver depart out of the Hands of the Workers, until it be essayed by the Wardens of the Craft; and further, that it be marked with the Leopard's Head; and that they work no worse Gold than of the Touch of Paris; and that the Wardens of the Craft shall go from Shop to Shop among the Goldsmiths, to essay if their Gold be of the same Touch that is spoken of before; and if they find any other than of the Touch aforesaid, the [Gold] shall be forfeit to the King; . . . And that all the good Towns of England, where any Goldsmiths be dwelling, shall be ordered according to [this Statute] as they of London be; and that one shall come from [every good Town for all the residue that will be dwelling in the same] unto London, for he to be ascertained of their Touch. And if any Goldsmith be attainted hereafter, because that he hath done otherwise than before is ordained, he shall be punished by Imprisonment, and by Ransom at the King's Pleasure. . . .

§2.13 A PATENT LETTER AUTHORIZING THE WOOL CLOTH MAKERS AND MERCHANTS OF CHÂLONS TO ADOPT A SEAL CERTIFYING THE ORIGIN OF THEIR PRODUCTS

April 1339

Philippe [VI], by the grace of God, King of France, make known to all, present and future,

That as by our loved guardians of the cloth industry of Châlons, we had been formerly informed on their behalf as well as on behalf of the cloth makers of the said city, that the cloth industry of this city being older than all others and having introduced a certain pattern and great beauty, which caused the cloths to be usually sold better than the cloths from other common cloth industries; and that after a short time, many of our kingdom and outside undertook to counterfeit their cloths, and sold them for cloths made at Châlons, of which fraud and malice the people and the good persons who bought them for their uses and believed to have real cloths from Châlons, were badly damaged and fooled, when they found the falseness of short duration in those false and counterfeited cloths, and that for this the cloth industry was very swallowed and defamed, and that so few cloths were made presently, because it was found who bought them, for the said counterfeit and defamation, and that it was convenient for the said cloth industry to come to naught, if remedy was not properly put in soon; and we were required by those named above that we should give them leave and license to put some seal of lead in their cloths.

So that the malice and deceit of the people were removed, and the cloth industry were retained in its good and first state, which seal was taken and held by the hand of the said guardians to whom belonged the guard and the government of the cloth industry, so that everyone may know henceforth the true cloths of Châlons against counterfeits and those falsely made; . . .

Let them have a seal of lead, as it pleases them, to hold forever and perpetually, to put in their cloths, which seal will be taken and held by the hand of the said guardians to whom the guard and the government of the cloth industry belongs, as said. . . .

Given at Maubuisson lès Pontoise, the year of grace of 1339, in the month of April.

§2.14 FRANCE SETS THE MANDATORY AND EXCLUSIVE USE OF A MARK OF ORIGIN FOR THE CLOTH INDUSTRY OF ABBEVILLE

June 1352

This text concerns an act granting the exclusive right to the commercial use of Abbeville mark and strings, which would be attached to the cloth made in that city and its suburbs. These particular regulations provided for an exception in the case the cloths were made for being used by the artisan and his family—i.e., without a commercial purpose. In this case, there was no obligation to use the city's seal and strings.

Strings in particular shapes and colors, as well as the borders of some works, such as carpets and bed sheets, have also been used as signs of differentiation.

The fact that this text employs the term etc. several times, thus suppressing language of a legal nature, indicates that in the fourteenth century France had already developed a template for granting this sort of privileges. The applicants of the privilege themselves make reference to similar acts granted in favor of the draperies of other cities, like Rouen.

June 1352.

Charles etc. we make known etc. We have received the humble request of our beloved makers and weavers of the drapery of our city of Abbeville containing that for a long time, for the preservation of said drapery, which is one of the beautiful and good of our kingdom and to obviate the faults and abuses that might have been caused to them, they had been given by our predecessors, kings and counts of Ponthieu, several fine privileges, formerly advised and concluded by the mayor and aldermen and those [enforcers] of the law of our said city, which privileges they have always enjoyed and still do, but they doubt that without having confirmation from us, others may wish to prevent them, requesting for this reason our provision, and with it, in amplifying their privileges, that henceforth no other people of the trade having good style and way of life, may use the said manufacture of drapery, unless it is for dressing them and their family only, or commercialize it as do those supplicants who live only from said drapery, and moreover that the city and suburbs of Abbeville be not and cannot be sold any cloths from towns, cities and neighboring places which do not bear or have a different mark or strings, so that they may not be surreptitiously countermarked, taken out, or sold in the city in retail or in any other way by concealment under the sign of the supplicants, under pain of confiscation of those cloths, corporal punishment and arbitrary fine, and all this as it is used to do in our city of Rouen and other good and great draperies of our kingdom etc. because etc. to the supplicants we have confirmed, ratified and approved, confirm . . . etc. their privileges as they were granted to them by our predecessors and that are contained in the letters on this [matter] granted to them and which are registered in the book of the law of the city of Abbeville and that they and their successors enjoy them from now on in the same manner as their [predecessors] have well and duly enjoyed and used them. And with this, of our greater grace, amplifying their privileges, we accord and grant that they enjoy the two points and articles said above, namely that no other than the supplicants, having other way of living, residing in the city and suburbs of Abbeville will engage in the trade of drapery from now on and for the time the manufacture of the commodity of drapery remains, unless it is for the dressing of them and their family, and also that in that city and its suburbs cloths from the surrounding cities and places may not be sold unless they display or have different marks or strings, so that they are not surreptitiously countermarked for and instead of the cloths of that city, under the penalty of confiscation of the cloths and of punishment of prison and arbitrary fine, and all this in the form and manner that it is above provided for, and that is contained and provided for by the ordinances of the city of Abbeville. Therefore we command the municipality of Ponthieu and all our other etc. who, by our grace, make confirmation and ampliation, obey and permit the supplicants and their successors to enjoy and use, without doing to them etc. and in doing and obeying this they oblige all those who for this will be compelled etc. And therefore etc. And so that etc. Except etc. Given in Paris, in the month of June of the year one thousand and one thousand CCC IIII and twelve, and of our reign the ninth. Thus signed by the king. . .

§2.15 TRADEMARKS ACQUIRE THE NATURE OF BUSINESS ASSETS

January 1364

The text that follows concerns the French king's approval to the transfer of ownership of a trademark that belonged to a merchant who has passed away without heirs or successors. The text does not say it, but it is not impossible that the assignee of the trademark had been an associate of the deceased, because reference is made to the fact that the assignee, Evard de Boessay, "is long accustomed to make knife blades under the sign of the stag horn [which is owned] by the heirs of Jean de Saint Denis."

Charles . . . we inform all present and those to come that, as Evrard de Boessay, knife merchant, is long accustomed to make knife blades under the sign of the stag horn [which is owned] by the heirs of Jean de Saint Denis, otherwise Saint Germain in our city of Paris, for the time that he lived, which sign no one else [could use], other than his people or by his command, under the penalty of a fine of XL Parisian pounds, to be paid for our profit, and to have forfeited his commodities in the case someone dared to counterfeit it, and now has remained no heir or successor of the said Jean who must or may use the mentioned sign, as it is said, and for this Evrard, who has always accustomed to make knife blades under the sign of the stag horn, as it is said, has begged us that we graciously please to grant him and his heirs that he may have forged by any good worker in our kingdom knife blades under the sign of the stag horn in the way Jean and his predecessors did and had done at the time they lived. We incline to the supplication of Evrard, and to Evrard, to him and to his heirs born and to be born from his body in loyal marriage, and who, like him, will seem to become merchants of knife blades, [We] gave and granted to inheritance and by these present [letters] of our certain science, special grace, and royal authority, give and grant the sign of the stag horn, in the event that there would be no heirs from Jean, to whom that sign should belong by reason, and We please and wish that Evrard and his heirs can have forged under that sign by any good worker in our kingdom, so as that other workers or cutlerymen cannot forge under that sign nor contradict him or forge in any way, except those to whom he will command, under the penalty above said.

Thus We determine, in accordance with the content of the present [letters] to the Provost of Paris and all our other justices, officers, and subjects . . . that by Our present grace and grant they make and let Evrard and his heirs and successors enjoy and use perpetually and under heritage . . . . And that this be firm and stable thing . . . . Given in Paris on the year of grace of one thousand CCC sixty four in the month of January.

§2.16 AN EARLY EXAMPLE OF INDIVIDUAL MARKS AND THEIR PUBLIC RECORDING (AMIENS, FRANCE)

April 24, 1374

Because of the particular concerns with the quality of certain products of higher value, the statutes of some guilds would include rules on the adoption of individual marks and their registration. Only later that practice would extend to other guilds and become a generalized practice. The text that follows is an excerpt from the by-laws of the guild of metallurgists (*fèvres*) of Amiens, as adopted by the aldermen of Amiens, on April 24, 1374.

15. Item any workman who works on an expensive article, be it white or black, each of them will have his mark different from the other, of which he will mark the work that he will have done, so that if any mischief or affliction is found in it, one may know by whom it has been made, for the application of the fine.
16. Item, the mark of each worker will be imprinted on a piece of lead, which will be placed in the safe of the guild of the profession, so that they are better known.

§2.17 ANOTHER EXAMPLE OF THE IMPOSITION AND REGISTRATION OF INDIVIDUAL MARKS FOR GOLDSMITHS OF AMIENS

June 30, 1376

4. The said goldsmiths, each in his place, henceforth is and shall be required to have a countersign or countermark, and each one different from the other, whose print will be placed and printed on two lead boards, of which one will be delivered to the said mayor and magistrates, and the other to the jurors of the guild.
5. Each goldsmith shall sign or mark with his countersign or mark the work he will make, as properly made with good fine gold or silver, and not before the jurors put the city's sign or mark, [...] so that anyone who has made work in a different manner be punished, and that bad works may be acknowledged.

§2.18 ANOTHER EXAMPLE OF THE ADOPTION OF MARKS OF ORIGIN AS WELL AS INDIVIDUAL TRADE MARKS IN AMIENS

1383

As trade increased and competition became more intense in the Middle Ages, the adoption of formal mechanisms of protection of business identifiers expanded—not only of marks as designations of origin and quality, but also as tokens of direct differentiation and commercial rivalry. The text that follows consists of excerpts from the by-laws of the guild of cobblers of Amiens, of 1383, approved by the city's aldermen in 1407.

The instructions and ordinances for the shoemakers, leatherworkers, and tanners follow.

. . .

21. Item, any shoemakers, leatherworkers of old or new, tanners, saddlers, glove makers or any other, outside of the city of Amiens, who purchase or order the purchase and bring to Amiens any pieces of tanned leather, notwithstanding that they are marked with the sign or mark of the city from which they will be brought, the person who has purchased them, as soon as he brings them to Amiens, shall be required to bring them to the place of the Pont de Baudri, and there they shall be controlled by the controllers of the tanners of Amiens; and if they are found well made, they shall be marked with the sign of the tanners of the said city of Amiens, and, if they are not controlled and marked, they cannot be sold, bought, neither transformed, nor resold afterwards. And if it happened that, in any of the said trades, the leathers that would be purchased and brought from outside the city, and which would not be controlled or marked with the sign of the city, were found for sale or for transformation, . . . they shall be sanctioned with a XX sols fine. And all this shall be brought before the mayor and the aldermen, and by judgment shall be condemned to burn before the house of the one who made this mischief. . . .
23. Item, it is ordered and forbidden to all the tanners of leather of the said city, that they do not dare to put in black or to make any pieces or whole leathers, hides and prepared leathers, pieces which will belong to them neatly or which will be brought to them, if, first and before any work is done, they do not send them to be marked with the sign of the city of Amiens and with the countermark of the shoemaker, and leatherworker of Amiens to whom the leathers will belong, upon the said fine. And the inspectors of the shoemaking trade shall be required to visit the leathers in the house of the leatherworkers and shoemakers aforesaid, and those that they will find badly tanned shall be brought to the mayor and the aldermen, to take such punishment as above is declared.
24. Item, that the leatherworkers may be leatherworkers and merchants at the same time, among which, in the ten trades, there will be good controllers of the tanners, shoemakers and leatherworkers, that is to say two for each of the said trades, and there will be an iron determined for such marking as the mayor and the aldermen will see fit. Which iron the controllers of the shoemakers will control, and will not be able to sell or deliver any leathers whatsoever, if that have not passed by the said controllers and marked with the ordered iron as said above, on the fine of xl sol parisis. . . .

25. Item, and with that, if any shoemaker wants to buy any leathers tanned in Paris, at Compiegne, Beauvais, Noyon, Arras, Lille, Abbeville, they may do it; but they will not be allowed to put them in their houses, unless they are controlled and marked with the previously mentioned mark and brought in the place determined for that purpose, on the fine of XX sols parisis. . . .

§2.19 ANOTHER EXAMPLE OF TRADEMARKS BEING DISPOSED OF AS BUSINESS ASSETS

June 10, 1383

On 10 June of the year 1383, Pietro de Preda, son of the late Gaspare, residing in the parish of St. Simpliciano, assigns to Petrolo Tanzio, son of the late Nicola, residing at St. Cipriano, at Porta Comasina, the signs copied below approved for use by the guild of the trade of wool of Milan, recorded in the book by the provosts of the society and community of the Art of wool trade of Milan, and they are sketched and designed below [the designs of 5 trademarks follow, representing a buffoon], with the right and the possibility of using the said marks, or any of them, or similar ones, and marking wool cloths or similar with them, at the will of Petrolo Tanzio himself. And likewise [he sells] all rights, suits, and advantages in and from these marks, and on account or by reason of them, which belong to the seller, Pietro himself. . . .

And for the sale, for the price and the agreed payment of the price and transaction concerning all and each of the aforesaid signs, the seller has acknowledged and acknowledges, and gives receipt that he has received form the said Ser Petrolo, buyer, 100 florins in silver coins of the Milanese currency in course, . . .

Done in the Broletto Nuovo of the Commune of Milan, . . .

§2.20 DISPUTES OVER TRADEMARKS AND SHOP SIGNS REACH THE COURTS

1402

Shop signs (or signboards) are signs that are placed at the entrance of commercial and industrial establishments with the purpose of designating the places where businesses are conducted. They have been used since Antiquity. But it was in the Middle Ages, with the Commercial Revolution and the consequent growth of cities, that the use of shop signs increased as artisans and traders began to concentrate in urban conglomerates. To better monitor compliance with their technical standards, and thus making the job of inspectors easier, guilds and municipalities required artisans to establish in the same neighborhood or in the same street of the borough. Numbers had not yet been introduced to help locate houses and commercial businesses.

The text that follows is a somewhat truncated description of a court dispute, occurred in 1402, between members of the same family involving a trademark and shop sign—the crescent moon—in Auxerre, France, and the attempts to secure rights in it through its registration with the municipality of Paris (the Châtelet).

1402, 3 April. National Archives, Parliament Registry. Between J. Chantepinot, defendant, and J. Coulon, appellant [...] of the bailiff of Auxerre. The appellant says that Renaud Chantepinot was a cutler in Auxerre and took the shop sign of the crescent, died, left two sons and one daughter, the two sons were cutlers and took the crescent, the mother married a man who was not of the profession at all. J. Coulon, who was her son, joined the profession of cutlery and took the crescent, adding a dot for a difference and kept this for seven years; and because his uncle Pierre was old and had no male son, he assigned him his crescent shop sign without a difference, and Enault, Pierre's brother, also gave it to Coulon [...], and thereby he has possessed and used it. Notwithstanding J. Chantepinot, who is Pierre's son, obtained letters by which he ordered Coulon to cease [the use of] the said crescent. He opposed and submitted to the bailiff that he had the crescent upon his uncles' advice, and that they came from the Chantepinot, and that in Auxerre the enforcement of every right is limited to a period of ten years *inter praesentes*, but he had possessed the crescent for thirteen years, in the presence of his uncles [...] The opposing party says [...] that he casted his sign at Châtelet, and therefore no one could take that sign [...] notwithstanding Coulon took the crescent and has used it with several differences [...] several times printing a comma, other times adding three dots [...]. Decided that the parties shall appear before the prevost of Paris [...]. [It has been] decided that the Court will examine what the parties will show to the Council.

§2.21 THE CLOTHMAKERS OF CHARTRES COMPLAIN OF COUNTERFEITING AND OBTAIN THE RIGHT TO USE THE CITY'S MARK AS A SIGN OF AUTHENTICITY

September 16, 1418

The regulation on the adoption and use of marks of origin and certification in France, originally aimed at fighting counterfeiting, soon became tangled with fiscal policies. The clothmakers of Chartres, harmed by dishonest practices, requested the King the passing of a regulation that, following the example of other cities in France and in Flandres, imposed sanctions on counterfeiting. The text that follows confirms such regulation, imposes sanctions on counterfeiting, and sets a fee for each piece of cloth that, upon inspection, is marked with the city's seal of quality and origin.

Charles, by the grace of God, King of France: We make known to all present and future, and see the Letters containing the form that follows.

To all those who see the present Letters, Etienne Deprez, Esquire, cupbearer of the King our Lord, his Bailiff at Chartres, and Esquire of the Stall of Monseigneur the Duke of Burgundy: Greetings.

As the Masters and Jurors of the trade and work of drapery of the city of Chartres, called Drapery's trade, had come before us a long time ago in Judgment, and had exposed to us that among the other trades of the city, the trade of Drapery was one of the most remarkable, ancient, and chief trades of the city, and by which more people of this city were supported and had their lives; and in the course of which trade the city of Chartres was renowned at the [fair of] Lendit, at the fairs of Châlon and other fairs of this Kingdom, one of the seventeen sworn cities of this Kingdom, where the trade is carried out; and preserving this in good policy, upon the antiquity of several statutes, ordinances and impositions that exist on the manners of cloth, which the Jurors and Workers of that trade are obliged to hold and to observe, for whose compliance the cloth industry of Chartres has been and is well renowned at the fairs and places above mentioned and others of this

Kingdom, and the cloth that in its manner have come, reputed as good, fair and of trade value, and all foreign Merchants are well pleased with it when they know that they come from the manner and drapery of Chartres; nevertheless, in other towns of smaller authority, and in several villages of the country of Chartain, the making of several fabrics of the same kind or similar manner, like that of Chartres, had become usual for some time, and that their vendors, or some of them, at fairs and markets, affirmed they were made in the manner of Chartres, or at least occasionally the buyers thought they were so; in regard of which cloth the visitation and compliance with the Statutes that existed and applied in the city of Chartres had not been observed, and the buyers could not notice in good faith, because the cloth made in the manner of that city did not have a mark or a public sign, by which it is possible to discern with certainty the cloth that had passed by the visitation and approval of the city, in what the buyers had been several times defrauded, and the drapery of the city blamed; for these reasons the said Masters and Jurors said that, to obviate the frauds and inconveniences that by the means above mentioned as well as other means could happen to the manufacture of the drapery of Chartres, for keeping it under good governance, for increasing its reputation, and for removing all suspicions that foreign merchants might have in its regard, it was expedient that the merchants of the cloth that from now on came out in that manner, and work of Chartres, had a mark and sign of lead, to be printed and attached after the cloth is visited and approved by the Jurors commanded to do so, and passed by the sworn cloth inspection of the King, which is in that city, put in the pulley, and signed by the Jurors, of a wax imprint to this specially ordered; and that no cloth be made in the city, nor delivered to the party to which it would belong, until after its visitation and approval, the printing of the mark and public sign of lead in the manner that is described; and that for the trouble of doing so, and for the interest on the lead to make the mark, there be certain fees that the Clerks may, in this regard, charge and levy on each piece of cloth thus passed, approved and signed; about which fees the Masters and Jurors said to be quite adequate and without grievance to any, in the sum of two deniers tournois for each mark thus attached; and furthermore the Masters and Jurors said that that was the practice in several good cities of this Kingdom, such as Rouen, Evreux, Saint-Lo, Bernay, Monsliervillier, the good cities of Flanders, and several others of this Kingdom; and that in order to better reinforce the Ordinance and its good compliance, and to retreat the bad intentions of those who would fraudulently remove their cloths from that approval, it was expedient to impose a penalty by way of a fine, on each person doing the opposite, that is to say, that for each cloth made in that manner that would have been found folded and prepared, the person with whom it would have been found, would be obliged to pay a fine of ten sols tournois to the King our Lord and suffer the penalty of the seizure of the cloth and otherwise; . . . For the causes and reasons above mentioned, and also taking into consideration the reports and the agreement of the Prosecutor of the King, and all that is worth of consideration and that can persuade us to move in this direction; by leaning on the request of the Masters and Jurors, and particularly on the public favor, we have ordered and determined, order and determine by way of perpetual Statutes and Ordinance:

(1) That all the cloths that will henceforth be made in the said city, for being put in commerce, in the manner and the work of that city, shall have a mark and public sign of lead; which mark shall have on one side of its imprint, the image of Notre-Dame, and below it shall have written Chartres, and on the other hand of that mark, it shall have an imprint of a Chartain containing the arms of the city; which mark and piece of lead shall be printed and fastened to such piece of cloth, after the cloth is visited and approved by the Jurors commanded

to do so, and passed by the sworn cloth inspection of the King, which is in that city, put in the pulley, and signed by the said Jurors, of a wax imprint to this specially ordered;

(2) Item. We order that from now on in the city of Chartres, no such cloth will be passed or delivered to the party to whom it will belong, until after its visitation and approval, the mark and public piece of lead be printed and attached, in the manner that is said.

(3) Item. We order that for the trouble of making and placing and attaching the lead, and for interest on the lead and other that the Jurors may have, by those Jurors or whoever will be committed by them to do so, may take and levy on each cloth thus passed, approved and signed, the fee of two denier tournois for each mark and lead thus attached.

(4) Item. We order that whoever passes or carries cloth of that manner and type, and which will be found or that one may show to have been folded or finished without having the said mark and lead, will be held to pay to the King a fine of ten sols tournois for each piece of cloth thus found or shown; and the Jurors of that trade and others to whom it will concern may take and cease all such cloths that they will find or will be able to prove or show to have been passed without that approval and without lead; and their task is to constrain those who have them to pay the mentioned fine, as well as to visit those cloths to check whether they are bad, and, as regards those cloths and the persons to whom they belong, to punish them according to the by-laws of the art; and if they are good, according to the said by-laws, to mark them with the mark and lead, according to what is said; and where, as the case may be, those pieces of cloths passed without the lead may not be found so that the fine can be exacted for the King, through the seizure of the cloth, those to whom such pieces of cloth belong, and who shall be guilty of having them passed, may be fined before us at the request of the Jurors. . . .

Given in testimony of this, under the Seal of Affairs of the Municipality of Chartres, Friday the xvith day of September, the year of grace of one thousand cccc & eighteen. Signed Cadou.

Approved by patent letters of Charles VI, in Paris, June 1419.

§2.22 ANOTHER COURT DISPUTE CONCERNING A SHOP SIGN

August 26, 1423

Between Colot de Toussy, appellant, on the one hand, and Guiot Angelin, defendant, on the other hand. The appellant says that his father was engaged in paper making and . . . once again, since he has returned to Troies, he has been trying to engage in such art and merchandise of his late father, and to take back the sign that he used, which is said to be a sea eel, but the opposing party, alleging to have married the second wife of his late father, has wished to prevent him and to argue over [the ownership of] the said sign and on this he brought a procedure before the bailiff of Troies . . . and . . . the said de Toussy was dismissed of the lawsuit and the sign. The defendant responds and says that Lorena de Toussy, the father of the appellant had a number of paper mills and was married to a woman named Thevenote who remarried to Angelin, who enjoyed that sign for a long time and for what Colot de Toussy, after he had been absent for a long time, had returned to Troies, and had wished to engage in making paper and take the shop sign of the unicorn, Giles le Pévrier had sued him and had won and he [Colot] was deprived of the shop sign of the unicorn and thereafter Colot had wished to take the shop sign of the sea eel, to which Angelin had opposed, who. . . used the shop sign the right in which was shared with his said woman, after the death of the late Lorent. . . .

Decided that the court will see what the parties will to show to the council.

§2.23 TWO GOLDSMITHS ARE GRANTED EXCLUSIVITY IN CERTIFICATION MARKS BY HENRY VI, OF ENGLAND

October 12, 1423

The boundaries between exclusive trademarks and administrative certification marks were not clear until specific regulations were passed that established the public nature of the latter. This text is a good example of that confusion: two goldsmiths are authorized to use two certification signs, but are granted exclusivity in those signs.

Appointment by assent of the council, of John Bernes of London, 'goldsmith,' south of Trent, and Robert Curteys of York, 'mercer,' north of Trent, to make steelyards (*stateras*) and good and lawful weights of the noble, half noble and farthing of gold with 'les rates' necessary thereto, and to mark them with a fleur de lys and a crown, to be graven in the manner ordained in the Parliament held at Westminster in 9 Henry V. Any other persons found making such steelyards or weights will be subject to a penalty to be ordained by the council, but the said John and Robert are not to take more than *4d.* for each pair of steelyards, and *2d.* for each weight of the noble, half noble and farthingof gold with 'les rates,' necessary thereto.

Appointment by assent of the council, of John Bernes of London, 'goldsmith,' south of Trent, and Robert Curteys of York, 'mercer,' north of Trent, to make steelyards (stateras) and good and lawful weights of the noble, half noble and farthing of gold with 'les rates' necessary thereto, and to mark them with a fleur de lys and a crown, to be graven in the manner ordained in the Parliament held at Westminster in 9 Henry V. Any other persons found making such steelyards or weights will be subject to a penalty to be ordained by the council, but the said John and Robert are not to take more than 4d. for each pair of steelyards, and 2d. for each weight of the noble, half noble and farthing of gold with 'les rates,' necessary thereto.

§2.24 A MEDIEVAL CHRONICLER INVOKES THE PRINCIPLE OF VERACITY IN THE CONTEXT OF HERALDRY LAW

Fifteenth–Sixteenth Centuries

Veracity, the second principle of the law of heraldry, was essentially a matter of ethics. The text that follows explains its practical dimension. No arms bearer should claim the glory of a feat represented in his/her arms and crest in which he/she (or his/her) ancestors would not have actually participated. So, in heraldry, veracity was of the essence to ascertain nobility.

In this text, a Portuguese medieval chronicler, Ruy de Pina (1440-1522), justifies the arms of Afonso III, king of Portugal (1210-1279), and assures their veracity.

. . . Because afterwards, along with the said Queen Dona Beatriz, to him [D. Afonso III] the Villages and Castles of the Kingdom of Algarve were given, he was the first to be named King of Portugal and Algarve, and placed on the border of the said Shield and Fifths ["Quinas," each of the five small shields in the center of the main shield of the arms of the Portuguese king] the golden Castles in a red field, which he, and then the other Kings of Portugal, who descended from him, always have brought until now, and this I affirm by clarifying the question that by many I heard being raised about the said Castles, namely whether they are Castles for this reason, which I said, or those of Riba de Côa, which to this Kingdom were added, or if they were with banners, or flags, which are said to be the arms of the County of Bologna, and thus questioning the number of said Castles, to which I respond and affirm that they cannot be Castles by those of Riba de Côa, because King Dom Diniz, son of King Dom Afonso acquired them, and afterwards he reigned, [...] that either out of respect for the Arms of Bologna, or because of his marriage, even if in his life he brought them, they would not stay, nor after his death could they stay with the Royal Crown of the Kingdom of Portugal, even more so because honesty and reason would prevent him from bringing to Portugal the Arms of Bologna, for the memory of the Countess, his wife, [...], and therefore it is very certain that they [the five *quinas*] are only by the said Castles of the Kingdom of the Algarve, as I said.

§2.25 SEVERAL BY-LAWS OF THE GUILDS OF ROUEN, FRANCE, WITH PROVISIONS ON INDIVIDUAL TRADEMARKS

1456 Onwards

This text shows trademark-related clauses of several by-laws, from 1456 through 1646, concerning guilds of the city of Rouen, no longer requiring the use of the city's seal, as it was the custom beforehand, but rather the use of individual marks. This was an indication that the collective responsibility of guilds was diminishing, and being replaced by the individual liability of artisans.

By-laws of the Brewers, 1456.

Art. XIV.—All masters before beginning their work will bring to the bailiff or his deputy their mark to be imprinted on a skin leather so that those to whom the recipients belong will be known.

By-laws of the Papermakers, 1544

Art. XIII.—All masters and merchants who work on paper will have a special mark, on which the first two letters of their names and nicknames will be printed, which they will apply on each sheet of their work, under the penalty of a fine of one thousand pounds.

By-laws of the makers of carding machines, 1597

Art. VIII.—No master can mark his work other than with one mark only, and make a false mark, and counterfeit any, under the penalty of a fine of . . . sols.

By-laws of the Apothecaries-Wax makers-Grocers, written at the Hotel-de-Ville of Rouen, by three medical doctors and by three Apothecaries-Wax makers-Grocers in 1508. Followed by an Ordinance against the Magicians, Wizards and Poisoners, in 1632

Art. LIII.—In order that the said barbers, etc., have visible marks of their art, for the cleanliness and ornament of the human body, they will be allowed to have shops painted in blue, closed with frames with large glass tiles, without any resemblance to the shop windows of the surgeon-masters, and to put on their signboards white basins as a mark of their profession, and to differentiate from of those of the master surgeons, with this inscription: "Barbers-Hairdressers-Bathers-Bath house owners; here hair is cared for properly, and baths and heaters are available." The Master surgeons and all others are prohibited to put frames similar to those of the barbers, hairdressers, and the barber-hairdressers to have them similar to those of the surgeons, under the penalty of a fine of three hundred pounds against each of the offenders.

By-laws of the Founders in earth, sand, stone, wax and brick, in 1646

Art. XXV.—Item, and in order to be able to recognize the works of the masters, each one will be required to have his mark in particular, and to mark all his works, which mark will be imprinted on the table which, for this purpose, has been made at the said trade, and will be affixed in the presence of the guards, assisted by four elders, under the penalty of the fine.

§2.26 LOUIS XI, OF FRANCE, ESTABLISHES A MANUFACTURE OF CLOTH IN MONTPELLIER

January 23, 1475

Louis, by the grace of God, King of France, to all those who will see these letters, greetings.

We have received the humble request of our dear and well-loved consuls, bourgeois, residents, and inhabitants of our city of Montpellier, containing that our city, which sits in very good and fertile country, used to be very populous and inhabited by several remarkable merchants, and other people of various states, abundant in wealth and goods, and presently, and since some time, on the occasion of mortalities that have taken place in our kingdom and especially in our country of Languedoc, and of the wars, divisions, and passages of men-at-arms who have been in the said country, and also of the great burdens that they have agreed upon, and that each one agrees to bear, in order to provide for the very great and urgent business of ours of and our kingdom, such city is so diminished and impoverished, both of people and of means of subsistence, that half of its houses are not inhabited, and which each day diminishes and impoverishes greatly; and for which it cannot be comfortably reassured or repopulated without a large attendance of people, which they could not reach without having any new art or profession in the said city, those supplicants have advised among them to have established in our said city of Montpellier the manufacture and the art of drapery, which seems to them the most suitable to help and restore that city, with the intention to order and conduct in it the manufacture and art of drapery, and to keep in it the police, justice and other matters, as those that are kept by the draperies of our cities of Rouen and Bourges, but they would not dare to do it, nor to proceed without having our leave and license in that regard, as they say, by humbly requesting us that, since the surrounding country is furnished with good and fine wools in great abundance, and that near and joining the said city there is a small river where there is water very clean and good for said profession and art of drapery and that, by the means of that art, the inhabitants of this city, among which there are many idle people, will exercise and occupy themselves to make it, and others will come, by whom our city will be able in any way to populate and enrich, for the good of us and the public thing of it and its surroundings, it pleases us to grant them our leave and license, and on this we shall give them our grace.

It is because of this that we, these things considered, wishing the good and growth of our said city, to the said consuls, residents and inhabitants of Montpellier, for these causes and considerations, and other motivations, we have given and granted, give and grant, by special grace, by the present [letters] leave and license that they can and decide to erect and establish in it the manufacture and the art of sworn drapery in our city of Montpellier, to be used and exercised, both in police and justice and in other way and manner of doing, exactly in the same manner it is used and exercised and it will be used and exercised from now on in our said cities of Rouen and Bourges. And to better conduct and maintain the said policy and in order, we have granted and accorded that they can make and write articles and chapters, in which shall be contained and written the form and order of how the work shall be performed in the manufacture and exercise of drapery, and which seals or marks, edges, length and width the cloth must have, so that the cloths that will be there made and crafted may be known, as [it is done] in the other good sworn cities of our kingdom, where the manufacture and exercise of drapery had its course; and also that they may designate and authorize a certain number of remarkable and knowledgeable men in that art, as many and who as they will see fit, who have the authority to visit the cloths that will be made and crafted in the said drapery, and to correct the defects that they will find in them, either by burning the cloths that will not be good and as they should be, or otherwise, and sentencing the offenders. . . .

Given at Plessis du Parc les Tours, the XXIIIth day of January, the year of grace one thousand IIIIth seventy five, and of our reign the fifteenth.

On behalf of the king, master Guillaume Picart, . . .

§2.27 EDWARD IV, OF ENGLAND, APPROVES A STATUTE ON CERTIFICATION AND INDIVIDUAL MARKS FOR GOLD AND SILVERSMITHS

1477

It is ordained by Authority of this present Parliament, for the better Execution of the said Statute, and for to eschew the deceit daily done by the said Goldsmiths and Workers of Gold and Silver in the said City of London and elsewhere, within this Realm and Wales, that no Goldsmith nor other worker of Gold and Silver, or either of the same Metals, from the said Feast of Easter, shall work, sell, or [set] to sale any manner base Gold under the Fineness of xviii Carats otherwise called Crates, nor no Silver unless it be as fine as the Sterling, except such Thing as requireth Solder in making of the same, which shall be allowed according to the Solder necessary to the making of the same, upon Pain of Forfeiture of the Double Value of any such Gold or Silver wrought or sold to the contrary. Nor that no Goldsmith, Jeweller, nor other Worker of Harness of Silver, [shall set no Harness of Silver Plate, nor Jewel of Silver to sell,] from the said Feast of Easter, within the said City of London, or within Two Miles of London, before it be touched with a Touch of the Leopard's Head crowned, such as may bear the same Touch, and also with a

> Mark or Sign of the Worker of the same so wrought within [the City of] London, or Two Miles of the same, upon Pain of Forfeiture of the Double Value of any such Silver wrought and sold to the contrary. And that the Mark or Sign of every Goldsmith be [committed] to the Wardens of the same Mystery; and if it may be found that the said [Keeper] of the Touch of the Leopard's Head crowned, aforesaid, do mark or touch any such Harness with the Leopard's Head, if it be not as fine in Allay as the Sterling, then the said [Keeper] of the said Touch, for every Thing proved not of as good Allay as the Sterling, shall forfeit the Double Value; . . .

§2.28 CHARLES VIII, OF FRANCE, COMPLEMENTS AND DETAILS THE REGULATIONS OF DRAPERY OF MONTPELLIER

July 1493

> The text that follows complements the privilege granted by Louis XI to Montpellier (*see* Text 2.26).

We, Charles, by the grace of God, King of France, make known to all present and to come, having received the humble supplication of our dear and well beloved consuls, bourgeois, residents and inhabitants of Montpellier, containing that, both by our late dear lord and father, may God absolve, and by us, license, and permission has been given to the said supplicants to establish in the said city the profession, art, and sworn exercise of drapery, as well as in some of the other good cities of our kingdom, as it appears more plainly by the letters of donation to them on this granted by us as well as by our said late lord and father, by means of which, among other things, we have given them leave and license to make certain by-laws, articles and ordinances, for the good, profit and utility of the said city and the said profession, as well as of the public affairs of the country, and to prevent the faults, frauds and abuses, which, in the absence of establishing and ensuring order and compliance, could be practiced and perpetrated. For these reasons, the said supplicants, in pursuance of our leave, license and permission, and by the advice of several remarkable cloth merchants, and other persons knowledgeable of the matter, both of the city of Montpellier, and of our city of Paris, as well as others, have advised, deliberated among them, and put in writing the said by-laws, articles and ordinances, in the form and manner that follows: . . .

> Item, it has been ordered that, after the cloth is woven, it will be duly refined and cleaned; and, once this is done, it will be brought to the house of those who will be committed to the inspection of the cloths, by whom those will be inspected, before they are sold and delivered to the fuller or miller. And, if it is found that they are well woven and cleaned, two small stamps of green and red wax will be placed in the middle of the top of the said cloth. And the fuller or miller shall not dare to take the said cloth for strengthening it if it has not been previously sealed, under the penalty of a fine of sixty sols tournois, the third party [to be paid] to the king, the other third party to the offenders' charity and fraternity, and the other third party to the said clerks' pension fund, to be received by their clerks as well as for the measuring, as it is provided next. And the sealed cloth will be brought by the fuller

or miller, for completing his duty; and it will be brought by the fuller or miller to the house of the designated persons or jurors; and the cloth shall be sealed with a seal of lead at the end of the top of the said cloth, which seal shall be on one side the majesty of the king, and on the other the arms of the said lord. . . .

Item, and after the cloth is set and finished well and duly by the master, as it belongs and is the custom of the city of Perpignan, the master shall be required, before he brings the cloth to the controller, to bring the cloth again to the house of the clerks and jurors; and it will be visited by them, and at least by three clerks, provided that one of them is a master, a weaver, a citizen or a merchant, who will pass the cloth by the perch, in the place for this determined; and if it is acknowledged to be of good quality, well woven and finished to their knowledge, it shall be ordered that a small sign be placed on the city's arms, which lead will have, as a mark, the city's arms on one side, and Our Lady on the other side, for which seal one denier tournai shall be paid, which seal will be named Seal of license, and afterwards, when it will please to the cloth owner to have it sealed with another seal of square lead, there it will have Fy as sign, and on the other side it will be Our Lady, having at her feet the coat of arms of the city, for which he will pay nothing. And if it happens that the cloth is found to be of not enough quality or poorly woven, instead of the seal of license [it will be sealed] with another small seal of lead, which on one side will be Our Lady and on the other side will have no impression; and, instead of the Fy sign, it will be sealed, under the city arms, with another small seal of lead, which will be named Seal of megem, which will have on one side for sign L., which will mean Loyal, and on the other side Our Lady. . . .

And if the cloth owner feels grieved, he may appeal to the eight counselors, so that they decide what in accordance to God and their consciences should be done. . . .

Item, it has been ordered that no cloth, no matter how good it is, shall not be sealed in the city, if it is not woven and finished by the masters of that city, and bearing theirs marks. . . .

Given at Paris, in the month of July, the year of grace, one thousand IIII ninety-three, and of our reign, the tenth.

By the king, the lords of Tremoille, Grimault, seneschal of Beaucaire, masters Jehan Trousselier and Jehan Michiel of Pierre Vives, ordinary doctors, and several others, present.

§2.29 LOUIS XII, OF FRANCE, APPROVES REGULATIONS FOR THE ENTIRE TERRITORY OF FRANCE, CONCERNING GOLDSMITHS' MARKS

1506

As an evidence of the special care that the profession of goldsmiths received from French authorities, in 1506 Louis XII signed an Ordinance confirming previous norms (the first one enacted in 1345) that required that goldsmiths used special marks and countermarks that enabled their identification in the event of defective works. The ordinance also reiterated the practice—then already common to other industries as well—of establishing a registry for those marks.

Louis, by the grace of God, King of France, to all those who will see these letters, greetings; . . .

Item, That all Goldsmiths have new Marks and countermarks, both for the faults they make in their works, and also to know the new work, because many Masters have illegally gone to foreign countries, taking the Marks with which they mark each day, and that the Goldsmiths of Paris bring the other Marks to the Chamber of Coins, and the other Goldsmiths to the ordinary Jurisdictions to which they belong.

Item, That there be another countermark in the hands of the Masters of the said Trade, where there will be a sworn Master of Goldsmiths, with which they will mark the works of the said Goldsmiths before they are delivered, after they have been tested, and that they have been marked by the particular Goldsmith.

Item, When the Masters change, that the mark of the Masters be changed, so that each responds to the work of his time, and that the Marks and Countermarks be registered in the Chamber of Coins, and printed on the Copper table, as to those of Paris; as to the others, in the ordinary Jurisdiction of places.

§2.30 BY-LAWS ON THE USE OF TRADEMARKS BY FRENCH CLOCKMAKERS

1544 and 1599

Until the Huguenots of France were subject to religious prosecution, which culminated in the massacre of St. Bartholomew, in 1572, and their escape to Geneva and London, a number of masters of that creed were behind the prosperous industry of clockmaking. They were required to have their individual marks, which would be communicated to (i.e., registered with) the eswards.

Those masters would later give origin to the Swiss and British clockmaking industries.

By-laws of the Master Clockmakers of the City and Suburbs of Paris, 1544.

Art. XI. The Masters of the clockmaking profession, will be required to take a mark, which they will declare to the aforesaid Inspector Guards, and of this mark thus taken and declared, to mark the works that they will make, and not others, under the penalty of confiscation of Works which will not have been marked, according to what is above contained and declared, and of an arbitrary Fine.

Ordinance of Henri IV, at Fontainebleau, May 1599.

Art. III. All the Masters of the said State [of clockmaking] will be held responsible for the wrongdoings, faults and abuses that will be found in the works marked with their mark; and they shall not lend or license it to any person of any quality or condition whatsoever, under the penalty of a fine of 50 écus: Nor will the said masters be allowed to excuse themselves under any pretext whatsoever that they will have only lent their mark, and have neither done nor ordered the said work; thus they will pay the said Fine, in addition to the Civil Compensation, in regard of which they will be held liable jointly with those who would have made and manufactured the Work, &c. . . .

§2.31 ON THE CONTROL OF QUALITY AND ORTHODOXY IN BOOKS: PRINTERS' AND BOOKSELLERS' MANDATORY MARKS AND SHOP SIGNS

1547

Once the business of printing and selling books strengthened and consolidated in the late fifteenth century, fierce competition led printers and booksellers to adopt trademarks, whose protection was gradually recognized by courts, on the basis of the principle "first in time, first in right" (which still prevails today). Some of those marks were adopted even before the granting of printing privileges became an administrative practice. The following texts are a selection of provisions on trademarks extracted from the CODE DE LA LIBRAIRIE ET IMPRIMERIE DE PARIS, a compilation of various Ordinances and Patent Letters of Henry II, 1547 and 1551; of Charles IX, 1571; of Henry III, 1586; and of Louis XII, 1618.

The purpose of the use of trademarks by the printing industry, however, was not confined to the need for differentiating commercial rivals. The use of distinctive signs was required by authorities as a way of identifying printers and booksellers for the purposes of ensuring quality (as to the selection of texts, their translation, and their revision) as well as of conformity with prevailing social and religious canons.

That the name and family name of the one who did it, be expressed or affixed at the beginning of the Book, and also that of the printer, with the shop sign of his address.

It is also forbidden for all Printers, to carry the exercise and profession of printing, if not in good cities and houses organized and accustomed to do so, and not in secret places, and that it be under a Master Printer, whose name, address and mark shall be put in the Books by them printed, the time of the printing and the name of the Author: which Master Printer will answer for faults and errors that, both by him and under his name and by his command, will have been made and committed.

The Printers will not be allowed to print any Books, except in their names, and in their Workshops and Addresses.

Master Printers, Booksellers, shall not take the marks of each other, so everyone will have one separated, different from each other.

The Authors of the books or Correctors will not be allowed to have a printing press, nor presses in their houses, or anywhere else, for printing or having their books printed, nor sell them, nor have them displayed under their names or otherwise: thus they will be allowed to have them printed to be sold by Booksellers, Printers and Bookbinders, and not by others, under penalty of confiscation and fines to the infringers.

The Master Printers and Booksellers shall be required to choose and have a particular mark, which they will put in, or cause to be placed in the books they will print, or have printed, without them being allowed to take the marks of one another. And the said Booksellers shall place and affix their marks at the front and at the beginning of the said books which they will have printed: the Printers shall also be obliged to place their marks at the end of the said books, which cannot be sold anywhere else but in the shops and workshops of the said Printers and Booksellers, according to what has been ordered and observed.

§2.32 CERTIFICATION AND TRADE MARKS FOR LOCKSMITHING PRODUCTS

July 7, 1557

The text that follows concerns an excerpt from the Patent Letters on the Visiting and the Marking of Locksmithing Products, approved by Henry II, of France, determining the registration of individual marks, and their recordal in a public office (the Châtelet, in Paris), with a dual purpose: to ensure the publicity of those marks and to permit their verification (as to ownership).

And because, due to the counterfeiting of keys and locks, several abuses are committed, we also wish, rule and order that all persons, both locksmiths and ironmongers as well as merchants, who engage in selling products of said specialty, shall have distinct and separate marks, all locksmithing products being required to display a mark, chiefly the keys and locks that each one will sell, so that other keys, locks and other similar works, which are often counterfeited, to the loss of the house masters, can be more easily verified against the workers and merchants who have made and sold them, and this under an arbitrary fine in the first time, and prohibition to carry the trade in a second one, against counterfeiters.

And so that the mentioned marks may be more easily known, and that they can be verified when there is the need, they shall all be engraved on a lead board, which will remain in the chambers of our attorney, at the Châtelet, and until the said marks are engraved on the said board, we prohibit and interdict all persons to engage in the said business, as a locksmith, haberdasher or ironmonger or any similar [profession], before he has had his mark engraved on the said board, under a fine of ten livres parisis to be paid to us.

§2.33 CERTIFICATION MARKS FOR ENGLISH CLOTHWORKERS

November 29, 1567

This text, extracted from the London Clothworkers' Court Book (1537-1627) shows that the practice of requiring artisans to adopt individual marks as tools of certification was not confined to France. England also resorted to that commercial and administrative practice with frequency.

November 29, 1567

. . . Item, that there shall be eight or ten persons elected and chosen by the wardens and assistants to have the view of all the merchants' cloths hereafter to be wrought within the company, and that no person of this company to fold, take, or press or to deliver to the owner any merchant's cloth before the same cloth be viewed and seen by two of the said persons so appointed. And the said cloths so by them seen and found truly wrought, that is to say rowed, barbed, first-coursed and shorn from the one end to the other according to the statute last made, they to set the common seal of the house to every such cloth in token of true workmanship done upon the same. And every such cloth as shall be by the said searchers or any of them found faulty in workmanship, or that shall be folded, tacked, pressed, or delivered to the owner before it be viewed and sealed in form aforesaid, every workman of such cloth or cloths to pay for a fine of every such cloth xxs.

§2.34 A FRENCH STATUTE ON TECHNICAL STANDARDS FOR WOOL CLOTH, AND THEIR MARKS OF ORIGIN AND CERTIFICATION

March 19, 1571

This French statute sets technical standards for wool cloth, and imposes the use of marks of origin and certification. Those standards would vary, depending on the specific geographical origin of each piece of cloth. In that manner a new mechanism of differentiation has been introduced, which merchants would be able to recognize.

Decree (Edict) of the King for a reform, police, and regulation on the ways and dyes of the cloth, small wool cloths [*estamets, sarges*], and other fabrics of wool, which are made in this Kingdom.

And for compelling the weavers, workers and clothiers to do their duty in the manufacture of said cloths, small wool cloths [*sarges et estamets*], and in order to punish those who will contravene it, and also to prevent the abuse of the names of the places where the best cloths are made:

We have ordered and order that in each piece of cloth, small wool cloths [*estamet, sarge, camelot de laine*], and other draperies that will henceforth be dyed in our Kingdom, country and lands of our obedience, of any color whatsoever, on its top and first end, after it is dyed, a mark or seal of lead will be printed, containing the place where the dying is made.

Likewise, all the woolen cloths and small cloths in wool, and the cloths, all together, that are whitened so as to be used and left white, will be sealed on its top and first end, when they leave the hand of the fuller.

Making express prohibitions and inhibitions to all dyers, fullers, and shearers, to give, lease or deliver any cloths, small wool cloths or other cloths and any product of wool of any kind, to the merchants and other persons who would have leased it to them for dyeing, finish or whitening respectively, unless firstly the said seal in the manner that is said has been put on and affixed to each piece, under the penalty of a fine of twenty pounds for each piece: prohibiting also all merchants of whatever quality they are, to buy, put on or display for sale the aforesaid cloths, unless they are previously sealed, as it is said, on the similar penalty of a fine of twenty pounds for each counterfeit and of confiscation of the piece sold or purchased. . . .

Done at the King's Council, held in Paris on the nineteenth day of March, the year M. D. LXXI.

§2.35 A LAWSUIT ON THE OWNERSHIP AND IMITATION OF TRADEMARKS, RENNES, FRANCE

September 12,1578

This text is a report of the judgment of the Parliament of Bretagne settling a dispute involving similar trademarks owned by two wool carders of Rennes, France.

There was a dispute between Guillaume Jolif, one of the master carders of Rennes, and Pierre Baimer, also master carder, which Baimer had as his mark a rampant lion, he complained that Jolif, who should have in his mark a Greyhound, had ordered one that resembled a lion, which disguise caused him serious damage. He concluded by pleading the reform of the mentioned Greyhound trademark.

The parties were taken out of the court and procedure, and nevertheless, it was decided that the mentioned mark of the mentioned greyhound should be reformed and that it will be engraved lying down, the feet together & the tail lowered.

§2.36 THE SANDFORTH'S CASE

1584-1585

The texts that follow are abstracts of an English lawsuit (known as the *Sandforth's case*), which appears to be the first reported case in England involving a dispute over the infringement of a trademark.

(i) J.S., being a clothier who made good cloth, used a mark; and J.D., being also a clothier but who made bad cloth, used another mark; then J.D. set J.S.'s mark on his [own cloth], and by means thereof obtained good business (utterance), but [J.D.'s] cloth was found upon trial to be bad, and by reason, thereof J.S's cloth was discredited, and he could not have as good business afterwards as he had before. Upon all this matter, J.S. brought an action on the case against J.D. Anderson C.J. said it seems the action lies because J.S. is damaged by J.D. using his mark. Peryam J. said there was no law against anyone using whatever mark he wished; and when J.D. used the mark which J.S. used, he did no wrong to J.S., it being a lawful act. And even though J.S. was thereby damaged, he shall not have an action on the case for it, because it is *damnum absque injuria*. Anderson C.J. said if someone has a house, he may lawfully burn it if he wishes; but if by its being burned someone else's house is burned, the latter shall have an action on the case; and yet it was a lawful act.

(ii) Note, by Fletewoode, that an action on the case lies by the custom of London for counterfeiting another's mark. And he put this case when the following matter was moved by Fenner: "a clothier did give the mark of another clothier, but with a little difference hardly to be perceived, and set that on bad and false cloths, whereby the cloths of the other (which made good) were after discredited." And it was demanded whether an action on the case lay. Anderson C.J. said it did. Wyndham J. agreed if the statute enacted that no clothier shall give the mark of another. Fletewoode. In 5 Mar., it was adjudged in one Longe's case accordingly in parliament, and the counterfeiter was [a member] of the house and for this reason, was put out and paid the other 300 pounds. Peryam and Mead JJ. said that anyone may give what mark he will, and it is *damnum absque injuria* to the other, and deceit does not lie against him who does a wholly lawful act for his own profit. *Id.* at 617-18 (citing manuscript HLS MS. 5048, fo. 118v. (formerly HLS MS. Acc. 704755, fo. 118v.)).

§2.37 SEVERAL COURT DISPUTES OVER THE OWNERSHIP OF SHOPSIGNS, IN FRANCE

1587 Onwards

The texts that follow are excerpts from reports, collected by Joseph Garnier, on several court disputes that took place in France from the second half of the sixteenth century onwards, concerning ownership and imitation of shopsigns—whose importance for the retail commerce in that period should not be underestimated. Of particular interest is a letter that the magistrates of Dijon, Bourgogne, France, have sent to their feudal lord, requesting his advice on a legal dispute involving the ownership of an inn shopsign, the Pan. The issue also involved the religion of choice of one of the parties involved (probably, he was a Huguenot), which may have been the reason for the aldermen of Dijon to seek their supervisor's advice.

At the beginning of the seventeenth century French jurisprudence had already set the fundamental principles of law concerning ownership of shop signs as differentiating elements: priority in use, and proximity of location. Interestingly, in another case, a rule of unfair competition was invoked by a court: the (apparently implied) covenant not to compete between a former employee and his/her former employer.

(i) A merchant cannot take as a shop sign the same sign that serves as the shop sign of another merchant, carrying out the same profession on the same street. Two court opinions, of March 20, 1612, and February 25, 1629, [...] condemned merchants who had engaged in such an usurpation to change their shop signs. The Journal du Palais, [...] mentions a similar decision against a hosier. Another similar decision, of August 12, 1648, was issued against a grocer [...]. It is worth noticing that, in several of those opinions, the shop signs that were ordered to be modified did not have a perfect similarity with the shop signs that were intended to be imitated. By an opinion delivered on March 17, 1745, [...] the court confirmed a police decision of September 11, 1744, which ordered Nicolas Guérin, merchant-grocer, to change his shop sign, which was almost identical to Mr. Brouet's, also merchant-grocer, his neighbor [...]. The same decision orders Mr. Guérin to leave his shop, on Rue Dauphine, near Sant Jean, and to retreat to a distance of six streets. The reason for this last determination was that Mr. Guérin had stayed, as an apprentice, with Mr. Brouet for almost twelve years, and he had established himself in the vicinity of his former master, shortly after leaving his service.

(ii) The Aldermen of Dijon to the Earl of Chabot-Charny.

Dijon, 1587, 27 mars.

. . . We have an innkeeper in this city named Antoine Bergier, who formerly held the whole inn of Pan. Since the death of his wife the inn has been shared between him and the children of her first marriage. It was necessary to know who would hold the name and sign of the Pan. This difficulty having been brought to us, it seemed to us for several reasons that the sign was to remain with the inn which had come to the children, because more than thirty years had passed since the sign and entrance of the Pan had been there. In addition, Bergier has always been of the party contrary to the Catholic religion, and if there is a suspect man who comes to this city, he retires to his inn. Furthermore, he made a door in his [wine] press to enter his neighbor's garden, from which he can access the walls of the city, on which the said garden ends. In the same garden there is a view so high that it overlooks the said wall and discovers very far in the countryside. He was the appellant of our judgment, the lieutenant of the bailiff reversed it and ordered that the sign would remain in the inn of Bergier, instead of him and her wife being expelled from the city or detained during these disorders. This, Monseigneur, and many other things, take away from us the means of doing what we would like for the safety of the city, of which we are obliged to alert you. We confide in the subject of your letters, because all men of judgment will consider it to be very perilous, especially as there are enough people in this city who favor the party of those of bad opinion. We beg you very humbly, Monseigneur, to order us what pleases you that we do as regards such perplexity, and want to interest your authority if you find the best thing, so that you are obeyed and the city ensured under the obedience of His Majesty, so much that afterwards we cannot be blamed of anything. Kissing your hands very humbly. We will pray to God, Monseigneur, that it please Him to keep you in happy prosperity and health.

§2.38 CERTIFICATION MARKS OF THE PEWTERERS IN SALISBURY

March 6, 1612

These by-laws elucidate the purpose of the marking of pewterers' crafts: to certify the quality of products and the conformity with the guild's standards.

Constitutions of the Company of Smiths of Salisbury, as ratified by the mayor on March 6, 1612

Article 1. Previous orders confirmed.

. . .

21. Order against deceitful workmanship. Item, It is further ordered that if any default shall be presented to the Wardens of this Company for the time being, of any untrue, unlawful or deceitful workmanship in any of the crafts or mysteries of Smiths, Armorers, Cutlers, Pewterers, Brayzers, Iremongers, Bellfounders, Plumbers, Saddlers, Wyredrawers or Cardmakers and the same shall be duly proved before the Wardens and the greatest number of this Company for the time being at any assembly. That then the party so found in such default shall be censured and fined for the same a sum not exceeding ten shillings for every offence and in default of obeying and abiding such censure and paying such fine every person so offending shall be from thenceforth

disfranchised for ever from this Company unless he shall pay the said fine and conforme himself thereunto . . . .

26. Pewterers to mingle their Metal . . . every pewterer being a freeman of this Company shall mingle their metal and make and mark their wares to be allowable according to the Sayes (assaye) of London, and according to the Statute in such case made and provided, upon pain that he shall forfeit the moyetie or half part of the penalty and forfeiture mentioned in the said Statute.

§2.39 THE FIRST PROVISION ON THE INTERNATIONAL PROTECTION OF MARKS

November 14, 1604

The first clause dealing with the international protection of intellectual property was part of the bilateral treaty that restored trade between the various powers directly and indirectly engaged in the Anglo-Spanish War (1565-1604), including Spain, France and Burgundy. That treaty eliminated the trade boycott as well as the 30 percent fine imposed by Spain on goods originated from or destined to France that eventually broke the reciprocal blockade. Because trade concessions were directed only at the goods exported from the signatory countries—as it happens with any treaty on trade—it was necessary to lay down rules concerning the recognition of the origin of those goods. It should be noted that the bilateral treaty refers only to French marks. The reason may be that France in 1604 already had a well settled practice of using city seals as trademarks, which, as seen above, served to distinguish products at fairs and trade halls.

Treaty made in England on the restoration of trade.

As by the persuasion and admonition of the King of England, Lord Christofle de Harlay, Earl of Beaulmont, Ambassador of the Most-Christian King in England, and Sieur Iean de Taxis, Earl of Villemediane, Ambassador of the Catholic King to said country of England, sieurs Earl of Aremberg, President Richardot and Louis Verreyhen, Ambassadors of the Archdukes of Austria and Burgundy, having often discussed and conferred about the means of putting an end to the divergences which occurred because of the publication of the tariff tables: recognizing also and deeming appropriate that this business could be composed according to the articles inserted hereafter. . . .

And First

It has been set that on both sides, and at the same time, the tariff tables published for the imposition of the thirty percent, and prohibition of the Trade, will be put aside and removed and raised by the said King and Archdukes. . . .

III

And in order to prevent the frauds which could ensue because of the resemblance of the goods, it has been set by the present article that the goods from France, which will be transported and carried to the Kingdoms and countries of the Catholic King and country of the Catholic King and Archdukes, will be registered and sealed with the seal of the city from which they will be removed, and thus registered and marked will be held and reputed as French goods, and as such approved and admitted, except if fraud is proved, without delaying or preventing, however, the course of goods and vessels. And as for the goods that will not be registered and marked, they will be confiscated, and declared of fair seizure. Similarly all Hollanders and Zelanders, who will be found in the said ships, can be caught and arrested.

§2.40 ADMINISTRATIVE PROVISIONS PUTTING AN END TO THE COUNTERFEITING OF TRADEMARKS IN THE COMMERCE OF BORDEAUX WINE AND OF LORAGNES PASTEL

August 5, 1614

This text, extracted from a commentary elaborated by the famous French jurist Antoine de Mornac, is about the counterfeiting of French wine and pastel (blue dye). It is worth of notice that, as far as wine is concerned, the reference to trademarks is only indirect—the prohibition is against copying the same methods of placing the hoops on barrels of Bordeaux wine. It seems, therefore, that the visual appearance of barrels used to load and transport wine from Bordeaux was characteristic of that region. Therefore, we are here in the presence of a measure of protection of the package itself—a sort of trade dress protection.

On August 5, 1614, prohibitions were imposed on certain inhabitants in the north of Orleans, to have their barrels hooped like those of the said city of Orleans; which is likewise followed at Bordeaux, for it is not possible to hoop the barrels in the manner of Bordeaux. It is also the same for the pastel of Loragnes; for it is forbidden for all other than those who are of the said country, to put pastel in bags which are of the mark of those of the said country of Loragnes.

The reason for all this is that one does not sell under such disguises wine as if it were from Orleans or Bordeaux, and yet they are not; nor of pastel as if it were of the said country of Loragnes, and yet it is not.

§2.41 SOUTHERN V. HOW

1618

In Southern v. How (a case heard in 1618, involving the counterfeiting of jewels) Judge Doddridge made a reference to another court dispute (unreported) concerning the counterfeiting of a trademark. For some time, this was thought to be the first court dispute over a trademark in England, but it was not (*see* Text 2.35, on the Sandforth case).

. . . Doddridge cited a case to be adjudged 33. Eliz. in the common Bench: A clothier of Gloucestshire sold very good cloth, so that in London if they saw any cloth of his mark, they would buy it without searching thereof; and another who made ill cloth put his mark upon it without his privity; and an action upon the case was brought by him who bought the cloth, for his deceit; and adjudged maintainable.

§2.42 CERTIFICATION MARKS OF THE BAKERS' GUILD, OF ABERDEEN, SCOTLAND

November 6, 1634

The text that follows is an excerpt from the by-laws of the bakers' guild of Aberdeen, Scotland. It concerns the mandatory use of certification marks (to be stamped on breads), so as to confirm (and establish the respective liability) that breads have been well baked (naturally, according to the industry standards).

Anent [concerning] the weight and stamping of bread.

6th November, 1634. The said day it is ordained that ilk twelf penny quheat loaf sail contain ten ounces of sufficient weall bakin bread and the twa shilling loaf to be conform, and in the meantime ordains every neighbour of the calling to have his stamp on his bread, and that the sufficiency or insufficiency of the said bread or lacking of the stamp be tried by the deacon or ony of his maisters whom he pleases with him until Candlemas next 1635, and who contravenes this present ordnance sail pay six shillings money toties quoties to the craft.

§2.43 A CLAUSE PROHIBITING THE LICENSING AND THE ASSIGNMENT OF TRADEMARKS WITHIN THE INDUSTRY

September 9, 1661

The regulations of the guilds would frequently contain clauses discouraging competition. However, on the other hand, they would also include clauses aiming at suppressing some inconveniences that could result from monopolist trade. In this sense, clauses prohibiting the association of masters and the hoarding of raw materials were frequent. Price controls were also frequent. Those concerns would sometimes have an impact on trademark regulations. In some guilds, the licensing and assignment of trademarks would not be allowed, unless in the case of the death of the master. This text, extracted from the by-laws of the haberdashers, candle makers, grocers and spice sellers of Amiens, prohibits the licensing and assignment of trademarks, as well as the use of foreign marks, unless that was necessary in times of war.

By-laws of the haberdashers, candle makers, grocers and spice sellers of Amiens

Louis [XIV], by the grace of God, King of France and Navarre, to all present and future, greetings. . . .

Given at said Amiens, the ninth day of September one thousand six hundred and sixty-one. Which articles follow. . . .

44 —Item, that no merchant of the mentioned status shall make or contract association with anyone if [the latter] is not merchant and master approved to that status, nor lend their names or marks for the effect of the goods dependent on that status and trade, under the penalty of the loss of the mastery and a fine of sixty sols, and use foreign names and marks, except if that [use] is for passing the strait [the English Channel] and the danger of the enemy, if they are constrained to do so, in which case they will be required to advert the

masters in charge, prior to arrival of said goods, under the penalty of [the goods] being declared foreign.

§2.44 A SELF-SERVING EXCEPTION TO THE OBLIGATION OF USING TRADEMARKS

April 6, 1662

This text concerns a municipal decree of Dundee, Scotland, requesting the masters of the coupar craft to appose individual marks on barrels. An exception is admitted, to the benefit of a certain Bot Salkirk, who, with the Bailees' approval, exempted himself from such mark. From the text one may conclude that Bot Salkrik was the industry's esward, which suggests that we are here in the face of a self-serving provision.

On which day the foresaid Bailee Counsel and Deacons of crafts and committee at this present holding court stated and ordained the acts after following for the common well of this burgh.

Anent [in regard to] the Coupar Craft—In the first, it is stated and ordained that from this day further all the masters of the coupar craft within this burgh make yr Salmond barrels good and sufficient and their own mark brunt thereupon. And that they contain eleven gallons and one half at the least and that the Herring and kylling [cod-fish] Trees be In like manner brunt with their own mark contain nine gallons under pain of escheating of all barrels to be made by them other ways nor is before specified. And Bot Salkirk affirms this present act and acts himself conform thereto except the burning of his marks which the said Bailees have exempted him from doing under the pain foresaid.

§2.45 A JUDGMENT OF THE PARLIAMENT OF AIX-EN-PROVENCE CONCERNING THE USE OF A MEDICINE NAME (ORVIETAN) AND TRADEMARK (THE SUN)

May 20, 1678

The text that follows is a report of the judgment of the Parliament of Aix-en-Provence that, acting as a court, settled a dispute between two medicine makers and sellers concerning the common name (Orvietan) and trademark (the Sun). The decision is based on principles of Roman law as well as on the case law set by a number of French Courts and Parliaments. It is of great significance, not only because of the breadth of its arguments and analysis, but also because it touches upon several areas of intellectual property, namely copyright, patents, trade names and trademarks. Its main conclusion is based on the fundamental principle of honesty, which cuts across the whole spectrum of intellectual property, and buttresses the meaning and the purpose of differentiation. As far as trademark law is concerned, this opinion reiterates the principle of first in time, first in right.

Initially, Orvietan had been used as a trademark. It was a derivation from the name of the city where the inventor was born: Orvieto, in Italy. However, the huge popularity of the medicine (an antidote, basically) through Europe in the seventeenth century led to the trademark's *genericide*. This explains the need for the use of the trademark "the Sun" by the allegedly descendant of Orvietan's inventor.

Antoine Levantin, known as the Orvietan, Roman physician, claimed to have descended from Horace Levantin of the City of Rome, inventor of the Orvietan. For distributing this medicine alone, he obtained a bull from Pope Urban VIII, in the year of 1629, giving [him] permission to sell and distribute the Orvietan in the whole territory of the Lands of the Holy *See*, with prohibitions to all other persons of selling it, under the penalty of one thousand ducats of gold, and of excommunication.

He comes to France; he has also obtained various judgments, both from the Parliament of Grenoble and from the Parliament of Provence, which authorize him to sell this medicine, and prohibit all others to distribute it under the name of Orvietan, and under the mark of the Sun, under the penalty of a fine of three thousand pounds, and of confiscation.

After several years the named Charles Beaulieu Operator presents himself, who had a Patent from the King granting the authorization of carrying his manual operations throughout France, together with the distribution of his medicines in theaters, and carry there his comical performances; he has this Patent registered at the Court; the Decision of registration forbids any other person to compose and distribute an Antidote, named Orvietan of France, under the mark of the Name of Jesus, on the penalty of a fine of five hundred pounds.

These conflicting privileges formed the dispute between Levantin and Beaulieu, two famous Operators. Levantin has opposed the execution of the Decision of registration of the Patent that the King had accorded to Beaulieu, and the case was brought to the Hearing of the Great Chamber.

Decoris, Antoine Levantin's lawyer, said he had four grounds of opposition. The first [was] based on the registration being groundless. The second, that at its bottom, Beaulieu's claim was contrary to common Law. The third, that it was contrary to the policy principles for the culture of the Arts. The fourth and last, that his party had for him the possession of particular titles of family, and Decisions in a contrary sense.

With regard to the groundlessness of the registration, it is entirely obvious. The King's Patent gives only permission to Beaulieu to carry out his manual operations, and his comic performances throughout the kingdom, as regards which the plaintiff does not envy him whatever.

Thus the decision of registration that authorizes the distribution of an antidote under the name of Orvietan of France is not in conformity with the Patent, which does not mention it; and this Order could not be issued to the detriment of the precedents, which had forbidden all persons, except Levantin, to distribute the Orvietan, under the penalty of a fine of three thousand pounds, and the confiscation of the medicines.

Even if we would agree that no, that the King's patent had allowed the plaintiff to sell his antidote under the name of Orvietan of France, it is always understood that, in the absence of another's right, that is the ordinary clause of the Royal Letters of Grant. Now, as there can be no doubt that this Privilege supersedes that of the plaintiff, it will always be necessary to return to the main question of knowing whether any other Operator, other than one of the descendants of the Inventors of Orvietan, and who by the way is grounded on [Court] Decisions, can publicly sell this medicine under the name of Orvietan.

Not only did Beaulieu surprise the Court, by alleging [the existence] in the King's Patent of a Privilege that this Patent does not mention at all, but also because its claim is based on common law.

No one doubts that all the authors of works have the right to impose upon them whatever name they please, without any other author being permitted to take it. Law 2. *ff. de operibus publicis* [of the Code of Theodosius] is formal in that regard, where the jurisconsult decides that if someone has had a public work made, he has the right to have his name engraved on it, and that if another person wishes to erase it so as to put his own, the President of the Province must interpose his authority to restore the name of the Inventor or of the benefactor.

It is true that by law 7. of the same title *de operibus publicis*, it is said that if another adds something to the work, and if that is done with the consent of the People, he will be also permitted to engrave his name on it, and without erasing the first one, *manentibus priorum titulis*.

But Beaulieu has not added anything to Levantin's medicines, he does not know the drugs, he does not know their secret, he does not know their virtue; and so he can add nothing to the name that Levantin's Ancestors have given to this medicine.

Indeed, the name designates the Master, it is not allowed to impose names or marks on the things of others; there is in the Code one precise title in the following terms: *Nemini liceat judicis autoritate signa rebus imponere alienis*. This is what made St. Augustine say about Psalm 21, that when a person has put his name on something, that is an ordinary mark that belongs to him: *titulos meos posui, mea res est, ubi nomen meum invenio, meo est.*

It does not follow that it is not regularly allowed to take the name of others. *L. 1. Cod. de mutations nominis*, but it must be *sine fraud & captione*; these are the terms of Mr. Cujas, interpreting law 13. *ff. ad L. Cornelian of falsis*. In this case, everyone can take the so-called Orvietan of France for the real Orvietan of Italy. One may believe Beaulieu to be the Inventor or descended from the Inventors of this excellent medicine. He will deceive the Public, he will even make Levantin's secret useless and fruitless. There is fraud; there is public deceit, and that kind of crime of falsehood that one wants to commit.

Moreover, and this is the third ground of opposition, the public requires that the Arts be not confused, that a craftsman does not counterfeit the works of another Artisan, *ne promiscuis artibus rerum turbentur officia. L. consulta. Cod. de testamentis*. That is why as soon as a craftsman has found in his art a new secret, and of which no one had yet been aware, he is easily given the privilege to profit from it alone, and of not being counterfeited, *munera alunt artes*, if it were otherwise used, it would take away the honor and the reward from those who excel in the Arts.

It is contested that there are here are two Operators who plead against each other; that one wants to obtain by the path of the Judiciary what the other does not want to owe other than to the reputation of his medicine; and that, on the contrary, as both appear on the theater's stage, there would be no need for other Judges than those who hear them, and from whom they seek approval, not only by their speeches, but particularly by the trials of their medicines.

It is answered that the functions of these two Operators are very different, they have their particular secrets, and their medicines that are peculiar to them. All they have in common is that they both appear on the stage: but while Levantin does so to exalt and explain in public the virtue of his medicine, Beaulieu does the same thing, but it pretends to give pleasure to the people, mingling among the Actors of the farce, of which he is the main character. As far as the Levantin who appears on Theater's stage is concerned, he does not derogate whatsoever from the honor due to the Doctors and practitioners, he does not make the fool and the joker, he practices Medicine, as it was formerly done. . . .

With regard to the quality of the medicines that these two Operators distribute, Beaulieu wished to distinguish his own with the Arms of France, giving it the name and the sign of Orvietan of France; but that is a ruse to ruin the commerce of Levantin, to the extent that the people will not be able to distinguish which Orvietan is best—that of Rome, or that of France; it will be enough for them that it be the Orvietan, they pay attention to the name only, which is nothing else than the shell, without looking in depth to its quality, which is its kernell, and they do not take the trouble, and are not even able to apprehend it. Yet it is upon this that Beaulieu call the Judges, he does not want any others, because he knows how to distract them by his tricks of street acrobat, and his jokes of comedian; which can only proceed from an unjust jealousy that Beaulieu has developed against the reputation of Levantin, and which has always been condemned by the Judgments of the sovereign Courts among those of the same profession.

Mornac on the law 14. *ff. de periculo and commodo reivendita*, speaks of two neighboring apothecaries, both of whom had a well-stocked shop, and which were only separated by a party wall. The oldest had the red cross as his shop sign. The other had put the same sign, with the single difference that the cross of this last sign was smaller than that of the other, and bore the following title: *at the small red cross*. The ancient apothecary had complained about it, and the claim, having been brought to the Hearing of the Grand Chamber of the Parliament of Paris, led to an Order, which enjoined [the new apothecary] to take this new shop sign down, with the prohibition to take that of the ancient apothecary. This is reported by the Author of the *Journal des audiences du Parlement de Paris*. [Antoine Mornac, In Senatu Parisiensi Patroni Observaciones, vol. 1, at 1073 (Franc Montalant, 1721). Source: <gallica.BnF.fr>].

The same author mentions another Judgment, delivered between two sword makers of the town of Moulins, one of whom had a very strong reputation for his trade, and had the Heart as the sign for his shop. The other, less skillful, took the Wounded Heart as a sign. The newcomer was forbidden to take this sign of the Wounded Heart, by the judgment of the twenty-fifth of February, 1619, *atque id ex conjectura emulationis, ac invidia, que novo illi operi causam dedisse visa est.*

We can add a third example. Two merchant hosiers from Paris, neighbors of one another, had the Pavilion as a shop sign. He who had taken this sign first having caused the other to take away his own, the latter, decided to have painted in his sign, instead of a Pavilion, a large butterfly, with wings wide spread, so that he represented, or at least imitated, the figure of a Pavilion. By a second judgment this hosier was ordered to change the sign.

All these examples persuade us that if [on the one hand] there is a good emulation between the persons of the same state to improve in their profession, there is [on the other] a bad envy, full of fraud, and which proposes to harm, which has always been repressed in Justice.

Lastly, it was said that Levantin was founded in titles, that he succeeded Horace Levantin, author of the Orvietan, and to which he has given that name because of the City of Orviette, in Italy, where he comes from. That Pope Urban the eighth has allowed this Horace Levantin's successor, by a special Bull, to sell the Orvietan in all the lands of his obedience, with prohibitions to all others of distributing it, under the penalty of a fine of one thousand ducats of gold.

He also has Letters Patent of the King who give him the same permission as regards France, and although he has not proved that he is from the family of the Levantines, Beaulieu is definitely not able to challenge his condition. He has always been recognized as such by the family, both in Italy, where he has distributed his medicine for a long time, and in France, where he has since established himself under the name of Levantin. . . .

Ultimately, this matter has been decided by a contradictory judgment of the Court, and by another of the Parliament of Grenoble against Operators similar to Beaulieu, which have forbidden them to sell their antidotes under the name of Orvietan.

These were Levantin's reasons.

Differing, Gaillar, on Beaulieu's behalf, said that he admitted that the inventors of medicines deserve special praise. There is no need for another example than that of Asclepiades, of whom Pliny the Naturalist speaks, book 26. chapter 3., who, having promised health by abstinence from meat, by massages, by walks, was looked at favorably by everyone as a man sent from heaven for the salvation of mankind.

But this medicine that is called Orvietan is not a new invention, it is a sort of Theriac [an antidote invented by the Greeks] and of Mtiridate [a medical concoction containing a number of ingredients, including opium, likewise invented by the Greeks]. Theriac is its main ingredient, to which sarsaparilla is added.

It is, therefore, a great temerity for Levantin to call himself the author of this medicine. Mr. Charras, Artist of the King, in his Jardin des Plantes, in his Royal Pharmacopoeia, fol. 325, made it public. He explains there the composition of the Orvietan, and reveals its authors. There he decides the cause of Levantin and similar products, and shows clearly their imposture.

Meissonnier, Doctor of Montpellier, in the Treatise on Poisonous Diseases, fol. 6, also show us the impostures that these Quacks do on the theater stage, to give authority to their Orvietan, and said that some have called it Athavan, and others, Orvietan. He describes its composition, and adds that it was Cardinal de Mantoile who has given it to Brother Jean Germain Minime. That is how it has become fashionable among us. He says that the Turks use it in Asia and Africa, where Levantin certainly has not brought it, and that it is not more than a medicine subsidiary to Theriac and Mitridate.

It is not out of place to note also that a lady of quality of this Province, excited by a principle of charity, makes the Orvietan herself, and has added to her composition some ingredients that render this medicine still more assured, and that therefore she has made it public and common to everyone.

Here is a medicine that has no true author, which is called sometimes Athavan, sometimes Orvietan, to which everyone adds what art and experience teach him/her. And after that how can one say that Levantin has the sole right to distribute it?—unless one wishes to say he has descended from Cardinal Mantoile, or from Brother Germain Minime, or, finally, that he should prohibit the use of this medicine to the Turks and Barbarians—which must be regarded as a misguidance of spirit, and as one of his jokes that he can dispense on the stage, but not at this August Hearing of the Court.

Moreover, it has been proved by the posters of those who have sold the Orvietan, that the named Jean Pierre Mazari Venitien had sold it under the sign of the Sun; that the named Lis, who claimed to be the son of the Orvietan, a native of Rome, has sold and distributed it under the same mark of the Sun; and according to Cristophle Contugi Romain, who lives in Paris, isn't it sold on the Quai des Augustins, at the corner of Rue Dauphine, under the name of the real Orvietan of Rome, and with the sign of the Sun?

All these Operators are not called Levantin, like this one. They do not claim to descend from the God Aesculapius, any more than from the Italian Ptolomei, Master of this Levantin; they have learned the composition of the Orvietan, they have made it, they have distributed it, and no one has found any fault in that. . . .

There really would be something to say if Beaulieu pretended to distribute the Orvietan of Rome. But he loves his Nation too much to take this medicine from the Italians, he distributes it as Orvietan of France, that is to say, with the corrections and the ingredients that France has added. And if the Turks distribute it under the name Atavan, why should not the defendant distribute it under the name of Orvietan of France, for it is composed in a manner different than that of Rome, and that all sorts of manufactures by foreigners are distributed in France with more approval than the original ones from which they have been taken?

In a word, privileges and works of art are common to everyone, and their exercise cannot be forbidden to people who use them well. . . .

If Beaulieu usurped the sign of Levantin, [the latter] would have some reason to complain about it, and to use the examples that Mornac brings about the law 14. *ff. of periculo & commodo rei vendita*, between two apothecaries jealous of each other.

But in this particular case, there is neither jealousy nor imitation between Beaulieu & Levantin; one sells the Orvietan of Rome, the other that of France; one takes the sign of the Sun, Beaulieu has one more illustrious and more salutary, for it is the name of Jesus, by which the Apostles have cured all the sick.

As to the judgments that Levantin has invoked, they do not deserve consideration. That of the Parliament of Grenoble, of the fifth of July 1668, is not against Beaulieu, but against the daughter of François Fosse and others, calling themselves Operators, who have been prohibited to give their medicine the name of Orvietan, and to take the sign of the Sun. But this has no impact on Beaulieu, who thirty years before sold the Orvietan of France under the sign of the Name of Jesus, and not the Sun.

The same can be said of the other Judgments, which are rendered against other parties who wanted to sell their antidote under the mark of the Sun.

Finally, Levantine lacks the permission of the king, *opus novum sine Principis authoritate fieri non licet*, says the law 3 *ff. of operibus publicis*. By contrast, Beaulieu has a Patent from the King of the last March 1662, which allows him to distribute his medicines all over France. It is registered by Judgment of this Court of the sixth of October, 1676. He has a Contract with the City of Narbonne of the thirteenth October, 1651, and a certificate of his Consuls. He served with success in this city of Aix, in Toulouse, in Marseille, where he resides, in Montpellier, Ufez, Beziers, Montauban, and other Cities of the Kingdom, where he has made his Orvietan of France to be esteemed, and obtained miraculous cures.

Thus a Tramp who deals with astrology and all those trifles, of which the Nation boasts, must not prevail over a subject of the King, Operator of his Naval Armies, which has the approval of the Naval Medical Officer, and all the Kingdom; This is what must not be done, if one reflects on what the Roman Orator says in his Oration *pro Cluentio*, of a Quack of his time named Lucius, whom he calls *Pharmacopolam circunsoraneum*: i.e., an Operator of this quality, *qui casu tum Lorinum Venum*, and had as many certificates as Levantin, and was of the same Nation. Opianicus promised him a sum of money to get rid of Dinea; he sold her his medicine, and as soon as this woman took it, she died of it, *simul atque introductus est, eam confecit prima potione mulierem*. This means that one should not trust these Italian Operators, who are either unfaithful or ignorant, and all quacks by profession.

The Attorney General of Saint Martin, after having gathered all the reasons of the parties, has shown that the Question had been settled in proper terms by the judgment of the Parliament of Grenoble, rendered with a great deal of knowledge in favor of Levantin, and that on the same restraints, said that the same judgment should be followed; and that consequently, he concluded that, as regards Levantin's Request, without considering the registration of the fifth of November, 1676, obtained by Beaulieu, prohibitions and inhibitions should be made against [the latter], and to all others to whom it concerned, to sell and distribute antidotes under the name of Orvietan, under the penalty of a fine of one thousand pounds, costs, damages and interest; and in the event of infringement, [it should be] ordered that it be informed by the first Royal Judge, or Bailiff of the Court; and nevertheless that Beaulieu were allowed to give his antidote such other name as he would see fit: which conclusions were followed by the Judgment of May 20, 1678.

§2.46 THE CONCEPT OF TRADEMARK REGISTRIES EXPANDS THROUGH EUROPE: ONE EXAMPLE FROM PORTUGAL

1690

The use of trademarks, mandatory or spontaneous, as tools of certification, or of origin, or of mere differentiation, became a normal practice in almost every business through the Middle Ages and onwards. Gradually, some by-laws of guilds added another requirement: that of inscribing the trademarks that were assigned to (or chosen by) the masters in a public, centralized registry, so that those signs could be publicly known and consulted, in case of disputes over product quality and trademark ownership.

This new requirement rapidly spread through Europe. The text that follows concerns a provision of the Regulation of the Cloth Industry (*Regimento da Fábrica dos Pannos*), of Portugal, in that sense.

Regulation of the Manufacture of Cloth of Portugal 1690

Chapter LXXXV

Let there be two Books, where signs and irons be printed.

I also order and command that in each of the Cities, or Villages, where cloths are made, there shall be two bound Books, on which the signs and irons of the fullers and ragmen shall be printed, so that one may see who has fulled and woven the cloths; of which two books one will always remain in the Notary of the Municipality, so that all the signs of the Officers who come anew will be placed on it, and from it they will pass to the other Book, which will have an Inspector, to whom it will be delivered at the time of his election; and the sign and mark of each Ragman and Officer who will come anew shall be different from the others; no other person shall be able to take the sign of that who dies, nor his son, with suspension from his office, until my mercy; and for this very reason, the sign and seal of each City, Town, or Locality, be also different from the signs and seals of the other Localities, so that through such signs and seals one may see and know in what Locality the cloths have been made, because the cloths of some Localities have advantage over those from others.

§2.47 A FRENCH JURIST STATES THE LAW OF BUSINESS IDENTIFIERS

1698

In this text a celebrated French jurist and practicing attorney of the 16th and 17th centuries, Gabriel-François du Pineau describes the law of business identifiers that prevailed in France at that time. Besides stating the general status of that law, he makes some points implying that, at that time, an understanding had already evolved towards distinguishing trademarks from shop signs as separate categories of business identifiers. The foundation of the protection of business identifiers in general was—and continues being—the protection of the consumer. Interestingly, du Pineau sets some parallels between trademarks and coats of arms (as Sassoferrato, whose authority he quotes, did, in the fourteenth century—*see* Text 2.9).

The text, it seems, was prepared as a supporting piece of his arguments in representation of a client in a lawsuit involving the ownership of a hotel's shop sign, which is mentioned at the end. The text says that the judge had dismissed the case, on the argument that the prevailing law on shop signs did not apply to hotels and pubs, and that an appeal had been filed, but not yet adjudged.

On the shop signs and marks of Merchants and Artisans:

This is not where I want to deal with Signs, Arms, Coats of Arms, Escutcheons, Pennons, and Guidons of Princes, Grand Lords, Knights, Gentlemen and other illustrious persons, about whom one must understand the texts. . . .

I go deeper down, to speak of the shop signs and marks of the Merchants and Artisans, which our Doctors call *signa, insignia.* I said, *shop signs,* meaning the signs that the Merchants and Artisans hang from their houses, and affix on the bags and packages of their goods, or on the chests, vessels, wagons, boats and ships in which they put them for keeping, carrying and transporting them; I said *marks,* to express the signs that the Artisans, and those who work and toil with the hands, print on their works.

The question is whether such kinds of people can take the signs and marks of each other, Ulpian. *m. l. 3. Dig. of solut.* said *"inter artifices longa differentia est, & nature, & ingenii, & doctrina, & institutionis"* ["among artisans, there is a great difference of intelligence, and of nature, and of instruction, and of science"]; so much so that if any Artisan has acquired perfection in his Art, or by inclination or goodness of mind, or by experience, and if a Merchant has decided to sell and distribute good articles only, and at a reasonable price, and both have acquired a reputation in their professions, so that he is sought after even by those who do not know his name, the usual expedient to preserve this reputation, to maintain his commerce, and to give confidence to those who wish to buy their articles or works, is that the Merchant hangs a signboard at his shop, and the Artisan marks his works with a mark of his own. And it is asked whether in the same City, in the same town, very closely established, another Merchant, or another Artisan of his profession can take and usurp the same shop sign or mark.

On which it will be noted that when any of the Doctors has wished to infer that it is permissible to take the shop sign, the mark, or even the coat of arms of another, since it is permitted to take his name, this argument is not acceptable, reasonable or probable, because there is quite a difference between changing the name (which is lawful, provided it is done without fraud, *l. un. Cod. de mutat. nom.*) and take the name of another, which is still tolerated, even ordinary and necessary as far as the first name is concerned. But as for the subname, *cognomen,* which is the name of a family and a race, it is not allowed to take it, because to affirm [falsely] to be part of the family is seen as an usurpation, and a sort of falsehood sanctionable, Paul. *lib. 5. sent. tit. 25. § si quis. l. falsi, Dig. ad L. Cornel. de fals. Benedict. ad cap. Rainutius, verbo, Rainutius, num. 57.* Moreover the Texts ordinarily cited are not appropriate. In *l. cum filius, §. pater. Dig. of leg. 2* it is an ancestor who charges his daughter to give to his nephew Sempronius more than to his other children in honor of his name; or if these words, *in honorem nominis mei*, mean "because it bears my name," it is not that he has usurped it, nor that *genus, parente sue sinxerit*, as Paul. says in the place above, since he has the name by the consent of his ancestor; and that being of the family, he is well founded to wear it: in *l. facta, § if vero nominis, Dig. ad S.C. Trebell.*, it does not matter that it is the usurpation of another's name, or that, to the contrary, the testator charges the heir to take his name. It follows that this argument *a simili* does not proceed; but the considerations of the Doctors are judicious and relevant, and the conclusion is that one cannot take the mark, or the shop sign of an Artisan or of a Merchant, if this usurpation is prejudicial to the one on which it is carried on, or to the public. As for the mark of the Artisan that he prints on his works, it cannot be taken or usurped by another, says Bartole. *Tract. insignii. § arm. num. 7. & 8.* where he quotes *cap. in nonnullis, de Judais, ap. Greg.*, which in its true intelligence would better apply to the signs of the houses than to the marks of the works: for, on this matter, the Council of Latran, held under Innocent III, not only forbids the Jews to wear clothes similar to those of the Christians, but also enjoins them from wearing such [clothes] that *publice ab aliis populis distinguantur*. Bald. *ad l. 1. Cod. qua res vendi not poss.* deals with the shop signs of the Merchants and the marks of the Artisans, and says that when someone has taken them *pro libito sue voluntatis*, another can also take them, provided that it be without fraud; otherwise he could not [do it], and adds this remarkable decision that this concerns who have them *per usum longi temporis*; after which, for a long time, *alius talia signa accipere non potest, quia jus ea habem di qualitum est primo*; unless it does not harm anybody, on what there is the need for weighing in the first place these words *longi temporis*, from which it follows that the possession for ten years suffices.

In the second place, that is a right, *jus*, and not a simple faculty. The same Balde, *ad cap. quanto. de jurejurando, ap. Gregor. num. 3*, after saying that one cannot carry another's coats of arms, if one does it by deception and circumvention with the intent of deceiving someone; he adds that it is the same for the marks affixed on the Merchants' bags, because by usurping them, it turns to the detriment of others; and gives as a conclusion that in those things that concern the public utility, *Melior is conditio occupantis*; and of whom has the right to have them *ex consuetudine, vel ex privilegio, Panormit. ad cap. dilecta de except Pralat. ap. Gregor. num. 4* says that if a good Artisan or a Merchant has some mark, and another wants to use it *ut habeat concursum, and sic decipere populum*, the Judge can forbid him to do so; but that each individual may take such coats of arms or signs as he sees fit, even those of another, provided that it is not to his detriment nor of the public.

Benedict. *ad cap. Rainutius, verbo, Rainutius, num. 59*, dealing with this matter, and speaking of the injunctions of the Judge against the usurper, says that the Judge can and must order them on his own initiative, in the absence of a party's request, especially since the public good is involved, *ne populis decipiatur*. The author of the Songe du Vergier, chap. 127, is of this opinion, because not only the Artisan or the Merchant would be interested, but the people deceived, because the individuals would buy the works of one for the works of the other.

Of the same opinion are Sains. *in Cons. Turon, tit. des droits de Chastelenie, article. 6.* Ming. *in Cons. Andegav. article. 49. num. 7.* Rat. *in Cons. ictav. article. 1. gl. ult. in fine.* Chassan, *in Catal. glor. mundi, part 1 considerat. 38. conclus. 31*

& seqq. deals extensively with this matter of the marks of the Artisans and the shop signs of the Merchants, and says in *conclusion 32.* that an Artisan cannot take the sign or mark of another Artisan; which he repeats in *conclusion 34.* and extends to the shop sign of a hotel (as Benedict. had done, at the place mentioned above *d. num. 59.*) and to the sign that the Merchant or the Artisan has in front of his house by usucaption, as his predecessors and himself have used, for the usucaption of which the very long period of thirty years is required, although it is based on the excerpt from Balde *ad. l. I. Cod. qua res vendi not poss.* who only speaks of long periods, i.e., of ten years, as I have noted above.

But by our use, especially as these signs are taken *pro libito voluntatis*, says Balde, it is enough to have given notice; for in this case those who wish to take the same sign, could do it only by fraud, envy, and jealousy; which must be understood with this caveat of Chassanée, when the usurpation would occur between neighbors; because if the houses are far from each other, and in different streets, the case for prohibition would cease, especially when the second would add some difference between his shop sign and that of the first; which I believe to be unquestionable as far as the signboards that hotel and tavern keepers hang in their houses; but, as regards the marks of the Artisans, my opinion is that there must be more severity, and that in the same town or village no Artisan must be allowed to take the mark of another Artisan; this has been thus decided by two judgments of the Court that Mornac cites, *ad. l. quod si neque, Dig. of peric. & comm. rei vend.*, because between two grocers the judgment there mentioned is grounded on the neighborhood of the two houses; and it seems to me that as regards the marks of two cutlers (which are in conformity with the shop signs) the fact of the neighborhood has not been accorded such weight, given that the distance and diversity of the places would be of little consideration in cities and boroughs of the Kingdom other than Paris, where the Artisans are all neighbors.

As for the Merchants and Artisans, the doctrine is confident that they cannot take the signs or the marks of each other, even if artificially disguised by some addition, the main body remaining. Thus it was judged, says Mornac, for the benefit of the one who had the heart as a shop sign against the one who took the wounded heart, having added an arrow. And from this, as far as Merchants and Artisans are concerned, all the Doctors offer this reason—the public interest, so that the people are not deceived by the usurpation of the shop sign or the mark, buying dearly bad articles, instead of the good ones, which are sold by those who had the first shop sign or mark; because this norm is of a political nature and has been introduced for the public good among those who have Masterships, By-laws and Masterpieces, and who make public proof to the Prince's authority and justice, of their ability in their profession.

Doubt remains if the rule is the same for hotel and tavern keepers, as Benedicti and Chassanée say: and it can be said that, in their profession there having no Mastery of seniority, nor Masterpieces or by-laws, our fathers did not consider that their profession concerns the public interest, and did not care whether those people would have good wine and good cooks for passers-by, given moreover that their houses are not supposed to receive those from the Province, as well as foreigners, and eventually many strangers, tramps, vagrants, and some derelicts who are taken care by the places in which they arrive. We can nevertheless say that we must reject all emulation, and that Justice must not accept that an individual does to others what he would not like to be done to him, since in this usurpation there is an obvious presumption of a purpose of doing harm to that of the same profession, having chosen his shop sign in the neighborhood, having been lawful to take that of someone who exercises another trade.

This question was pleaded in our Hearing of Monday, December 13, 1638, between the hotel keeper who holds the old house and hotel of Notre-Dame du Fauxbourg, through which one goes to Chateau-Gontier, and the new hotel keeper who took a house on the other side of the street, on which he put the same sign of Notre-Dame in a bigger board. The hotel keeper who exploits the house of the old Image called on the keeper of the house so that he took his shop sign out and put another. In this dispute the parties were dismissed from the court and the procedure. The judge did not consider that the opinion of the Doctors concerning the Merchants and Artisans should be extended to the hotel and tavern keepers, notwithstanding the expansion by Benedict. and Chassan. This opinion is under appeal, on which we await the judgment of the Court.

§2.48 ANOTHER FRENCH LAW DICTIONARY DIGRESSES ON THE LAW OF TRADEMARKS AND SHOP SIGNS

1711

Pierre Jacques Brillon, in his very popular, often cited dictionary of case law (entry "Enseigne") cites a few decisions applying the law on shop signs/trademarks. Of particular interest are the following three summaries that link the protection of shop signs to their geographical scope. The cases mentioned were already cited in the previous texts, which indicates that they had become jurisprudence.

. . . A Cutler from Moulins had the mark of the Heart; another took the same mark of the heart, and put an arrow in the middle to mean the wounded heart; the latter said that, having bought a house where this mark had always been, he could have taken it and changed his own. Judgment of the Parliament of Paris of February 10, 1610, which decides it in this manner: *Plaidoyers de Corbin, chap. 114.*

Two hotel keepers may not have in the same street two similar shop signs. Judgment of the same Parliament of February 16, 1647. *See* the facts of the case in *Soëfve, to. l. Cent. 1. ch. 100.*

Judged on the 12th of August 1648, that two merchants of the same profession, living near each other in the same street, cannot each have a similar shop sign. *Idem, Cent. 2. ch. 92.*

§2.49 IN ENGLAND TRADEMARK LAW CONTINUES EVOLVING

May 28, 1739

Another English Statute on the professions of silver and goldsmithing, but now with detailed rules on the ascertaining of marks, both of certification and of trade.

An act for the better preventing frauds and abuses in gold and silver wares.

. . . V. And be it further enacted by the authority aforesaid, that from and after the said twenty eighth day of May, one thousand seven hundred and thirty nine, no goldsmith, silversmith, or other person whatsoever, making or selling, trading or dealing in gold or silver wares, shall sell, exchange or expose to sale, within that part of Great Britain called England, any gold or silver vessel, plate or manufacture of gold or silver whatsoever, made after the said twenty-eighth day of May, one thousand seven hundred and thirty nine, or export the same out of this kingdom, until such time as such vessel, plate, or manufacture of gold, (being of the standard of twenty two carats of fine gold *per* pound troy) and such vessel, plate or manufacture of silver (being of the standard of eleven ounces two-penny weight of fine silver *per* pound troy) shall be marked as followeth; that is to say, with the mark of the worker or maker thereof, which shall be the first letters of his christian and surname, and with these marks of the said company of goldsmiths in *London*, *viz.*, the leopard's head, the lion passant, and a distinct variable mark orletter to denote the year in which such plate shall be made; or with the mark of the worker or maker, and with the marks appointed to be used by the assayers at *York*, *Exeter*, *Bristol*, *Chester*, *Norwich*, or *Newcastle upon Tyne*; or plate (being of the standard of eleven ounces ten-penny weight of fine silver *per* pound weight troy) with the mark of the worker or maker thereof, which shall be the first letters of his christian and surname, as aforesaid, and with these marks of the said company, *viz.*, the lion's head erased, the figure of a woman, commonly called *Britannia*, and the said mark or letter to denote the year as aforesaid; or with the mark of the worker or maker, and the marks of one of the said cities or towns; upon pain that every such goldsmith, silversmith, and other person, for every such offence shall forfeit and pay the sum of ten pounds, to be recovered and disposed of as herein after is mentioned; and for default of payment, shall be committed by the court in which judgment shall be given thereon, to the house of correction for the county, city or liberty, where convicted, there to remain and be kept to hard labour for any time not exceeding the space of six months, or until payment be made of the said forfeiture.

§2.50 IN ENGLAND, THE RIGHT TO EXCLUSIVITY OVER A TRADEMARK WAS NOT UNCONDITIONAL

December 18, 1742

An English court decision that would not stand the test of time: Lord Hardwick refused to issue an injunction to protect the exclusivity in the right of using a trademark in the absence of fraudulent intent.

In this particular aspect, French common law (if we can say so, in the absence of a written, general, and abstract statute) had moved further already, as seen in previous texts.

Blanchard v. Hill.

December 18, 1742. Lord Hardwicke, C. 2 Alk. 484; R. Cox, 633.

Motion for injunction, to restrain the use of the Great Mogul stamp on cards, refused.

Every particular trader has some particular mark or stamp; but I do not know of any instance of granting an injunction here to restrain one trader from using the same mark with another, and I think it would be of mischievous consequence to do it. Mr. Attorney General has mentioned a case where an action at law was brought by a clothworker against another of the same trade for using the same mark, and a judgment was given that the action would lie. But it was not the single act of making use of the mark that was sufficient to maintain the action, but doing it with a fraudulent design, to put off bad clothes by this means, or to draw away customers from the other clothier; and there is no difference between a tradesman's putting up the same sign, and making use of the same mark, with another of the same trade. An objection has been made that the defendant, in using this mark, prejudices the plaintiff by taking away his customers. But there is no more weight in this than there would be in an objection to one innkeeper setting up the same sign with another.

§2.51 A FRENCH COURT JUDGMENT RECOGNIZING EXCLUSIVITY IN A TRADEMARK

September 6, 1743

As noted before, French courts would recognize exclusive rights in trademarks before English courts. The text that follows concerns a judgment entered in favor of a trademark owner's widow ordering the seizure of a counterfeited skillet and other articles.

Judgment pronounced against Mr. François and his mother the widow François, merchants haberdashers, which, without paying consideration to the intervention of the Guards of Haberdashery, declares to be valid the seizure on them made of a new Skillet marked with a mark of a false Worker, and other iron goods engraved, pronounces their confiscation, and condemns them to pay the costs, September 6, 1743.

To all those who will see these Letters, Gabriel Jerome of Bullion, Knight Count of Esclimont, Prevôt of Paris, greetings. We make known,. . .

We, after it has been deliberated on the parts and records of the Parties put in our hands, without paying consideration to the intervention of the Parties of Regnard, nor to the means of nullity and claims of the Parties of Bruley the elder, whom we have dismissed, declare the seizure of the mentioned new yellow copper skillet marked with a crowned J., the great pot and the little old skillet also of yellow copper bordered with good and valid iron, with confiscation for the benefit of the Parties of Perrot the Elder. We say that according to the offers of the said Parties of Perrot the elder, the surplus of the seized Goods will be returned to the widow François . . . . On the surplus of the respective demands of the Parties, we have dismissed them from the court; . . . Signed and given a copy to Master Bruley the elder and Regnard Prosecutor at the Châtelet. . . October 1743.

§2.52 UPPER DOURO REGION, PORTUGAL: FOR THE FIRST TIME, A PARTICULAR, SPECIFIC GEOGRAPHICAL AREA IS DEMARCATED FOR THE PURPOSES OF THE PROTECTION OF A GEOGRAPHICAL INDICATION

1756, September

Excerpt from a Decree signed by José I, of Portugal, in September of 1756, formally recognizing the company for the production and distribution of Port wine, established by Portuguese wine makers and traders, and requiring (for the first time) the demarcation of the territory that serves as a geographical indication.

. . .

§ XXIX

The wines of the Coasts of the Upper Douro and of their territory to be shipped to America and the Foreign Kingdoms shall be separated completely and absolutely from all other wines of the places that only produce them capable of being consumed locally, so that the inferiority of these wines will not ruin the reputation that those deserve for their natural goodness. His Majesty is served that as soon as possible a Map and general record be made of the two Northern and Southern Coasts of the Douro River, that demarcates the whole territory that produces the true wines to be loaded, which are able to leave by the bar of the same River: and specifying each large and small farm of this sort, and declaring through a common estimate, or average calculated upon the productions of the five years that each of those farms usually delivers, so that their owners cannot sell without disclosing to the Company what they sell, nor a greater number of barrels be admitted to be sold to the Company, or to Foreigners, than the number that in said registration is attributed to them, under the penalty that, if they sell in excess of the said quantities, they will pay the excess nine fold, and will be prohibited to sell wines outside the Kingdom.

§ XXX

From the lands that remain outside the said demarcation no wine can be transported into its territory without bringing letters of guide issued by the whole body of the Town Halls of the places from which the such wines depart, ...

And this so that it does not happen that bad wines are bundled with the good ones in order to increase their quantity to the detriment of their reputation and the Company's, and of Foreigners who will buy them. . . .

Decree through which Your Majesty manifests his pleasure with the fifty three chapters and conditions contained in the thirty six half leaves above written, that the main farmers of High Douro, and Good Men of the City of Porto, have made and ordered, with the Royal consent of Your Majesty, so as to form a Company, which, sustaining the culture of vineyards, maintains their production in its natural purity, to the benefit of agriculture, of trade, and of public health.

§2.53 LIMITATIONS ON THE USE OF BUSINESS IDENTIFIERS: CURTAILING THE EXCESSES OF SIGNBOARDS IN PARIS

December 1761

Possibly inspired by a similar order enacted by the English Parliament in 1760, one year later the Lieutenant of Police of Paris issued an administrative order imposing some order in the use of signboards. Indeed, in Paris (and in London, as well) merchants and artisans had gone to extreme ways of advertising their businesses and shops, by hanging enormous, heavy and dangerous signboards over their shops' doors. It was not rare that signboards collapsed under their own size, eventually hurting inattentive pedestrians.

Ordinance of police concerning the shop signs. December 1761.

All merchants and artisans, of whatever status and condition, and generally all persons who use shop signs for the exercise and the designation of their commerce in this city and suburbs of Paris, will be obliged to place their signs in the form of a board against the wall of the shops or houses by them occupied, which signs cannot have more than four inches of projection or thickness from the bare wall, including the borders or such other ornaments that the owner will judge convenient to add to it, both for the decoration of the said sign or board, and for the designation of his trade or profession: we order likewise that all displays used to designate such trade or profession, and which will be placed above the awnings, or above the ground-floor of the houses that have no awnings, will also be removed and reduced to an advance of four inches from the bare wall, as well as all clumps and all figures in relief serving as signs, will be suppressed, except individuals, merchants or artisans who have them, to reduce said figures and clumps to a board that they will likewise apply to the facades of the shops and houses by them occupied; the costs for observing the form and reduction above prescribed for the other shop signs or boards shall be borne by the said individuals, merchants or craftsmen; we order moreover that the said boards used as signs, as well as the clumps, displays and figures in relief, of which we have ordered to be suppressed and reduced to boards, will be attached with iron clamps, high and low, sealed in plaster to the wall, and covering the edges of the board of the aforesaid displays, and not simply hanging or suspended; that all individuals will be required, in the period by us prescribed, to lift and remove in their entirety the iron gallows that served to suspend their signs or to support their clumps and figures in relief, and that our present ordinance will apply to all signs that are hanging in all the places that serve as a public way or passage, under the penalty of the violators being assigned and sentenced to the fine, if that is the case.

§2.54 TWO FRENCH CITIES DISPUTE THE OWNERSHIP AND USE OF FIGURATIVE TRADEMARKS

December 5, 1782

Louis XI, in 1782, settled a dispute between the manufacturers of cloth of Louviers and Elbeuf concerning the misguiding use of a colored pattern (the border of cloths). Today this would correspond to a figurative trademark, something like the well-known trademark of National Geographic (a yellow rectangle following the edges of its magazine's cover).

Interestingly, when, in England, the Industrial Revolution was already in full swing, in France, whose industry's competitiveness was left behind, and was about to engage in its own (political) Revolution, the industries were still using the city's seals and trademarks, in the old medieval way. This does not reveal, however, tardiness in the evolution of trademark law, but rather the strictness of French law in protecting geographical indications as differentiating signs of quality and certification.

Judgment of the council concerning the yellow border of the cloths of Louviers, and the red border of the cloths of Elbeuf

Versailles, December 5, 1782.

On what has been represented to the king, being in his council, by the manufacturers of Louviers and those of Elbeuf, that under Article 6 of the letters patent of March 1st 1781, regulating the manufacture of woolen cloths in Rouen, it would have been allowed to all manufacturers to make all kinds of woolen cloths, yarn and wool or floss silk, included in the boards of manufacture that would be prepared for the other factories of the kingdom, complying with what would be prescribed by the said boards; that the same provision is found in the letters patent that have been issued to regulate the manufacture of woolen cloths of the other places; that this faculty, granted indiscriminately to all manufacturers of cloths wherever their manufactures may be situated, would doubtless have had for main object the greatest perfection in the manufacture, but that it would become disastrous to the manufacturers of Louviers and Elbeuf, which have always distinguished themselves by the delicacy of their cloths, by their beauty and by the manner in which they are made, if [other] factories that employ only inferior wools, or whose production is less perfect, had the liberty of circulating in trade and export their cloths abroad as if they had been made at Louviers or at Elbeuf, placing on them the characteristic marks assigned to these two manufactures; that it would be easy, by hiding the true place of manufacture, to mislead the merchant, and still more the consumer; that there were already several examples of this abuse; that finally, the borders assigned to the main manufactures of the kingdom form in some way their patrimony, and are guarantors towards the public of the kind, the nature and the quality of the cloths or stuffs. And H. M. being informed that difficulties would have arisen between the said manufacturers of Louviers and Elbeuf, as to the color of the borders that must distinguish the fine cloths of these two manufactures; that at all times, and even since the new regulations, the manufacturers of Elbeuf would have claimed that the red border should belong to their manufacture, as being the oldest; that, on the other hand, the manufacturers of Louviers contested this claim, and maintained that they were in possession of [the right] of finishing their cloths with the said red border; that, moreover, this color was attributed to their manufacture by the board of manufacture annexed to the letters patent of March 1st, 1781; that, however, in order to put an end to these difficulties, they were determined to abandon the said red border to the Elbeuf factory, and to adopt for theirs the yellow border, provided that the said Elbeuf factory could not, in any case, use the yellow border, and that it would not begin until two years later to cover its cloths with the red border, so as to give the Louviers cloths made with a red color border the time to dispose of the stock. . . .

The king being in his council, has ordered and orders that in the future the cloths of Louviers will be finished with a yellow border, having four or six blue threads, either inside the cloth's border, or outside the said border, at the choice of the manufacturers of the said manufactory, according to the color of those cloths; and that with regard to the fine cloths that will be made at Elbeuf, they will be finished with a red border; derogating, in favor of the said manufactures, from the provision of Article 6 of the Letters Patent of March 1st 1781: as a result, H. M. makes very express prohibitions and inhibitions to all manufacturers of the other cloth factories of the kingdom to finish their cloths with the mentioned borders, on penalty of seizure and confiscation of said cloths, and yet, to give to the cloths of Louviers that are already manufactured and that will be made with red borders until the day of the publication of the present judgment, the time necessary to be sold by the merchants who will buy them, H. M. orders that the manufacturers of Elbeuf will not start to put the red border in their cloths before one year from the day of publication of that judgment. Moreover, it is the wish of H. M. that the said letters patent of March 1st, 1781 be fully and entirely executed, in what it has not been derogated from by the present judgment, concerning which all necessary letters patent will be issued.

§2.55 SPAIN ESTABLISHES A NATIONAL TRADEMARK REGISTRY

November 20, 1850

At the end of the Renaissance, there was not much more to invent about trademarks and their protection. The legal regime that applied to them at that time was already appropriate to support the ever expanding trade, both internally and internationally. Eventually, there was one element still missing, so as to add security to those distinctive signs: the setting of one national centralized registry for all trademarks, in all classes, and the corresponding publicity.

Spain was one of the first countries to introduce this new element, through a statute of 1850. The Conservatory of Arts, a public agency in charge of promoting trade and industry, was put in charge of examining, registering and publicizing trademarks. The statute included a system of preliminary registrations, which could be useful in the case of the urgent need of suing a competitor engaged in counterfeiting.

Royal Decree of November 20, 1850

Royal Decree establishing the rules for the granting of Trademarks in Spain. Provision for the use of the Marks in products of the Industry.

When the Spanish industry receives a powerful impulse from the spirit of association and of enterprise, [arising] from the general tendencies of the time and from the interests already created, an abuse, if not very frequent, at least against the law of property, and more than once object of very just claims, cannot be tolerated any longer. Such is the usurpation of the brands with which manufacturers in good faith distinguish the products of their industrial establishments. In this manner a factory without a name and without credit sells its products, at the expense of what has fairly earned a reputation among the public. Unfortunately, such odious trickery grows with the increase of production and traffic; directly attacks the property right; deceives the inexperienced buyer; grants an undeserved value to industrial production, serving as a false guarantee so as to accredit the merit of which they lack and to give them a false origin. Our legislation rightly condemns this fraud, recognizes all its awfulness and dictates convenient provisions against its perpetrators. Article 217 of the Penal Code determines with wise foresight the penalties incurred, but its application would be impossible if in a legal way the means of legitimizing the use and ownership of the marks were not established beforehand. For this purpose, and to avoid as far as possible that a condemned greed falsify and employ them against the will of their true owners, attending to the reasons that the Minister of Commerce, Industry and Public Works has exposed to me, I come to decree the following:

Article 1. In order that the manufacturers may establish the responsibility of the usurpers of the trademarks and signs of their factories, they shall beforehand request from the governors of their respective provinces that a trademark certificate be issued. . . .

Art. 4. By the provincial governors, the applicants will be issued certificates of the presentation of their instances, and under their responsibility they will send them to the Ministry of Commerce, Industry and Public Works with the other documents presented.

Art. 5. Upon a previous report of the director of the Conservatory of Arts on whether the trademark has already been used in artifacts of the same class, the manufacturer shall obtain a certificate that proves that he has presented and displayed his distinctive mark, expressing with all precision its form and other circumstances . . . .

Art. 7. The manufacturers may adopt for the products of their factories the sign that they deem convenient, excepting only:

1. The Royal coat of arms and the insignia and Spanish awards, if not competently authorized for that purpose.
2. The signs for which others have previously obtained a certificate of existence.

Art. 8. Manufacturers who lack the certificate referred to in art. 1 will not be able to pursue in court those who use the trademark they employ in the products of their factories; but if they have obtained it, not only will they be authorized to claim before the Courts against the usurpers the penalty prescribed in art. 217 of the Criminal Code, but also to request compensation for all damages and losses suffered. As far as the statute of limitations is concerned, this right shall follow the rules that apply to movable property. . . .

Art. 10. The authorized and recognized trademarks whose certification is granted to those interested shall be archived at the Conservatory of Arts; every quarter those granted in this period will be published in the Gazette, and, at the end of the year, the general status of all those granted in this period. . . .

Given at the Palace on November 20, 1850. From the Royal Hand to Minister of Commerce, Industry and Public Works.

§2.56 SECOND HALF OF THE NINETEENTH CENTURY: FRANCE SIGNS A MYRIAD OF BILATERAL AGREEMENTS CONTAINING CLAUSES ON TRADEMARKS AND DESIGNS

1850 Onwards

In the second half of the nineteenth century international trade increased significantly, because of the necessity of the great economy powers to export the surpluses of production that manufactures were producing. This led to the major economic powers to engage in bilateral negotiations on free trade with the purpose of easing tariff and technical barriers to exports.

France signed agreements on the reciprocal protection of trademarks with a large number of its trading partners, such as Sardinia (1850), Portugal (1851), the Kingdom of Saxony (1856), the Great-Duchness of Bade (1857), the Canton of Geneva (1858), Belgium (1861, 1874 and 1881), Italy (1862), Prussia and the Zolverein (1862), the United States (1869), Russia (1870), Brazil (1876), Venezuela (1879), Luxemburg (1880), Denmark (1880), Switzerland (1882) and Great Britain (1882). However, not all those agreements would deal specifically with free trade. Many of them were “literary conventions” or agreements on the protection of "works of art and the spirit." The obligation to protect trademarks would be added to those agreements as an additional or complementary clause. In this manner, generally speaking, those agreements would assimilate trademarks with literary and artistic works, and their infringement was to be sanctioned in the same manner as pirated works.

Imperial Decree that prescribes the promulgation of the Treaty of Commerce concluded on January 23, 1860, between France and the United Kingdom of Great Britain and Ireland.

Napoleon [III], By the grace of God and the national will, Emperor of the French, To all present and to come, greetings:

On the report of our Minister Secretary of State, Department of Foreign Affairs, we have decreed and decree the following:

Article 1. A Treaty of Commerce having been signed at Paris, January 23, 1860, between France and the United Kingdom of Great Britain and Ireland, and the ratifications of this Act having been exchanged on February 4, 1860, the said Treaty, whose content follows, will be published wherever needed and inserted in the Journal of Laws.

Treaty.

His Majesty the Emperor of the French and Her Majesty the Queen of the United Kingdom of Great Britain and Ireland, equally animated by the desire to strengthen the bonds of friendship that unite the two peoples, and wanting to improve and extend the commercial relations between their respective States, have decided to conclude a Treaty for this purpose, and have appointed as their plenipotentiaries: . . .

Who, having communicated their respective full powers, found in good and due form, have agreed on the following Articles: . . .

Art. 12. The subjects of one of the High Contracting Powers shall enjoy, in the States of the other, the same protection as nationals in respect of the property of trade marks and industrial designs of every kind. . . .

Imperial Decree that which prescribes the promulgation of the Convention concluded on May 1st, 1861, between France and Belgium, for the reciprocal guarantee of literary, artistic and industrial property.

Napoleon [III], By the grace of God and the national will, Emperor of the French, To all, present and future, greetings.

On the report of our Minister Secretary of State at the Department of Foreign Affairs, we have decreed and decree the following:

Article 1.

A convention having been concluded on May 1st, 1861, between France and Belgium for the reciprocal guarantee of the property of the works of spirit and art, and of marks, industrial models and designs; and the ratifications of this act having been exchanged at Paris, May 27th, 1861, the said convention, the content of which follows, will receive its full and entire execution.

His Majesty the Emperor of the French and His Majesty the King of the Belgians, equally animated by the desire to protect the sciences, arts and letters, and to encourage their application to the industry, have, for these purposes, decided to adopt, by common accord, the measures which appeared to them most suitable to assure reciprocally in the two countries, to the authors, to the manufacturers or to their successors, the property of the works of literature or art, and the marks, industrial models or designs, and have, for this purpose, appointed as their plenipotentiaries, . . .

Who, having exchanged their full powers, found in good and due form, have agreed on the following articles: . . .

Art. 15. The subjects of one of the Contracting Parties shall enjoy, in the States of the other, the same protection as nationals, for all matters relating to the ownership of trademarks, as well as of industrial designs and models of any kind.

The exclusive right to exploit an industrial model or design may not have, at the profit of the French in Belgium, and, reciprocally, for the benefit of the Belgians in France, a term of protection longer than that fixed by the law of the country with regard to the nationals.

If the industrial design or model belongs to the public domain in the country of origin, it cannot be the object of exclusive enjoyment in the other country.

The provisions of the preceding two paragraphs are applicable to trademarks. . . .

Art. 16. The French may not claim in Belgium the exclusive ownership of a mark, a model or a design, unless they have filed two copies of it at the secretariat of the Commercial Court in Brussels.

Reciprocally, the Belgians will not be able to claim in France the exclusive property of a mark, a model or a design, if they have not filed two copies of it in Paris, at the secretariat of the Commercial Court of the Seine.

§2.57 AN EARLY MODERN TRADEMARK STATUTE: THE FRENCH TRADEMARK LAW OF 1857

June 23-27, 1857

The French Trademark Statute of 1857 presents the most important features of contemporary trademark law: definition of the rights and the manner to acquire them, rules on enforcement, including border measures, and the destruction of the counterfeited goods. However, the French Act kept certain dated aspects, namely that it provided for nationwide protection, but registration was still local.

Law of 23-27 June 1757

On trademarks.

Title 1.—Trademarks

Art. 1. [The use of] Trademarks is optional.

However, decrees issued in the form of regulations of public administration may, exceptionally, declare it compulsory for the products they determine.

The names in a distinctive form, such as denominations, emblems, prints, stamps, casts, seals, imprints, letters, figures, envelopes and any other signs used to distinguish the products of a factory or the objects of a trade are considered trademarks.

Art. 2. No one may claim the exclusive ownership of a mark unless he has deposited two copies of the model of this mark at the secretariat of the commercial court of his domicile.

Art. 3. The deposit has effect for fifteen years only.

The ownership of the trademark can be retained for a new term of fifteen years, through a new deposit.

Art. 4. A fixed fee of one franc shall be charged for the preparation of the records of the deposit of each mark and for the cost of issuance, not including the stamp and registration expenses.

Title II.—Provisions relating to foreigners.

Art. 5. Foreigners who have industrial or commercial establishments in France shall enjoy, for the products of their establishments, the benefit of this Act, by fulfilling the formalities prescribed by it.

Art. 6. Foreigners and French nationals whose establishments are situated outside France shall also enjoy the benefit of this Act in respect of the products of such establishments if, in the countries in which they are situated, diplomatic conventions establish have established reciprocity for French trademarks.

In this case, the deposit of foreign trademarks takes place at the secretariat of the Commercial Court of the Department of Seine.

Title III.—Penalties.

Art. 7.

1° Those who have counterfeited a trademark or used a counterfeited trademark;

2° Those who have fraudulently affixed on a trademark belonging to others;

3° Those who have knowingly sold or offered for sale one or more products bearing a counterfeited or fraudulently affixed trademark;—

are punished by a fine of 50 francs to 3000 francs and imprisonment from three months to three years, or by only one of these penalties.

Art. 8.

1° Those who, without counterfeiting a trademark, have made a fraudulent imitation of it so as to deceive the buyer, or have made use of a trademark fraudulently imitated;

2° Those who have made use of a trademark bearing indications capable of deceiving the buyer as to the nature of the product;

3° Those who knowingly have sold or offered for sale one or more products bearing a fraudulently imitated trademark or containing indications capable of misleading the buyer as to the nature of the product;—

are punished by a fine of 50 francs to 2000 francs and imprisonment from one month to one year, or one of these penalties only

Art. 9.

1° Those who have not affixed on their products a trademark declared obligatory;

2° Those who have sold or offered for sale one or more products not bearing the trademark declared mandatory for that species of products;

3° Those who have contravened the provisions of the decrees issued pursuant to Article 1 of this law. . . .—

are punished by a fine of 50 francs to 1000 francs and imprisonment of fifteen days to six months, or by one of these penalties only:

Art. 13. Offenders may also be deprived of the right to participate in elections of courts and chambers of commerce, of advisory chambers of arts and manufactures, and of councils of prud'hommes, for a period not exceeding ten years.

The court may order the publication of the judgment in the places it determines, and its insertion in full or by extract in the newspapers it designates, all at the expense of the convicted person.Art. 14. The confiscation of products whose trademark is found to be contrary to the provisions of Articles 7 and 8 may, even in the event of acquittal, be decided by the court, as well as that of tools and devices specially used to commit the offense.The court may order the confiscated goods to be returned to the owner of the counterfeited or fraudulently affixed or imitated mark, irrespective of further damages, if any.It shall prescribe, in all cases, the destruction of trademarks recognized contrary to the provisions of Articles 7 and 8.Art. 15. In the case mentioned in the first two paragraphs of Article 9, the court shall always prescribe that the marks declared obligatory be affixed to the goods which are subject to it.The court may order the confiscation of the products, if the defendant, within the five previous years, has been convicted for one of the offenses covered by the first two paragraphs of article 9. . . .

Title V. General or transitional provisions.

Art. 19. All foreign products bearing either the trademark or the name of a manufacturer resident in France, or the designation of the name or place of a French factory, are prohibited at the entry [in the country] and excluded from transit and from warehousing, and may be seized at any place whatsoever, either by the initiative of the customs administration or at the request of the public prosecutor or the injured party. . . .

§2.58 FAIRS AND EXHIBITIONS AND THEIR INTELLECTUAL PROPERTY BY-PRODUCT: INDUSTRIAL AWARDS

May 28, 1862

The text that follows concerns industrial awards, which are business identifiers in their own right. Industrial awards are the product of their time. Between the late 1700s and the early 1900s, when the Industrial Revolution was pushing production and invention to unprecedented levels, entrepreneurs had several ways of advertising the excellence of their articles, such as the press, with its limited geographical coverage, and public events, such as theater and circus shows (*see* Text 2.45). Another effective means of advertisement was participation in regional, national, and international exhibitions. Exhibitions were organized with great care and expense. The most important ones would be preceded by the adoption of rules on the admission of exhibitors, the granting of awards and the selection of juries.

The medals and awards granted by certain well reputed exhibitions were coveted by entrepreneurs as powerful weapons of advertisement of their articles. Soon, those indications of excellency started being the object of abuses by dishonest competitors, who would falsely claim having received awards for their products. In some cases, those competitors had actually being distinguished, but for products different than those in regard of which they asserted the awards.

The text that follows is an illustration of the convoluted manner in which the institutions of intellectual property evolve. In spite of Great Britain's leading role in putting the Industrial Revolution in march and the seriousness of its efforts in organizing and participating in international exhibitions and fairs, English courts would at first hesitate in acknowledging industrial awards as signs of differentiation that were of protection. In the first case where the abuse of an award was alleged (*Batty v. Hill*, 1862) the court refused to issue an order against the defendant, on the ground that the plaintiff had not been able to show an association by his customers between the designated products and the reference to the award. In other words, in the court's view, the award had not (yet) become a trademark. The court acknowledged the fraudulent intent of the defendant, but in the absence of harm, it would not interfere.

Batty v. Hill

May 28, 1862

This was a motion to restrain the defendant Hill from placing on his goods the words "prize medal, 1862," and from in any manner representing or inducing persons to believe, or endeavouring so to do, that he had gained in respect of his goods a prize medal from the International Exhibition, 1862, and from in any other way infringing the plaintiff's trade mark, or depriving, &c., the plaintiff of the benefit of the grant of the medal to him.

The plaintiff, who was an oil and Italian warehouseman in the city, obtained in July last one of the two prize medals awarded by the jurors of the International Exhibition for "pickles and preserved fruits." The defendant, who had formerly been in the plaintiff's employment, but now carried on business as an "export oilman and confectioner," in Bury-street, Aldgate, had supplied the refreshment department at the exhibition with pickles, but had not exhibited and had not obtained a prize medal. In June last, before the awards were made, the defendant Hill stamped his labels with the words "prize medal, 1862," and also placed these words in a prominent form upon the packing goods, in which he exported pickles, &c., to Australia and elsewhere. Under these circumstances the plaintiff had filed his bill to restrain the use of the words "prize medal, 1862," alleging that the representation contained in these words was altogether false, and calculated and intended by the defendant to obtain for his goods the benefit of the reputation attached to the medal and to the plaintiff's goods, which are extensively known in this country and abroad in connexion therewith. The plaintiff also alleged injury to himself from the use by the defendant of these words, and from his inducing persons (especially in the colonies where the facts as to the grant of medals were not so well known) to mistake his goods for those which were known in connexion with the medal, and in particular for the plaintiff's goods. . . .

The plaintiff, in an affidavit in support of the motion, stated that the words "prize medal, 1862," had become his trade mark, and was an important means of identifying his goods, especially in the colonies and abroad; "and I believe that my goods have become and are extensively known and distinguished in the colonies and abroad, and also in this country, by means of and in connection with the said statement of the said medal; and I believe that my goods have acquired and now enjoy a great additional reputation by reason and means of such medal, especially by reason of my being (except Partridge) the only person who received such medal for pickles."

The defendant in his affidavit denied having imitated the plaintiff's label, as he had adopted the words "prize medal, 1862," for at least a month before the plaintiff had done so; showed the difference between the labels and trade marks, and denied that the plaintiff had acquired any greater reputation than himself for the manufacture and sale of mixed pickles. He also stated that his goods commanded higher prices than those of the plaintiff, and were in greater demand; so that any attempt to pass off his goods as those of the plaintiff would be no advantage, but a positive detriment. . . .

Wood, V.C., regretted that he could not interfere. Upon the balance of convenience and inconvenience, it had been rightly put, that by granting the injunction the defendant would only suffer the inconvenience of having to tell the truth. His principle would seem to have been, as was too often the case,

"Rem facias, rem, Si possis, recte, si non, quocunque modo rem;"

and he was admittedly guilty of a deliberate and bare-faced falsehood. But the case did not rest there. If it had turned upon a deliberate imitation of the plaintiff's trade marks, or there had been any previous attempt to do so, and the defendant had added to his imitation this falsehood, that would have been a very strong ingredient in the consideration of the whole case. But there was no appearance of an attempt to copy, the labels being totally different in shape, colour, and arrangement. The only thing, therefore, was this deliberate falsehood. The pleader had evidently felt the difficulty, and the bill halted between two views. If a person chose to put a false statement upon his goods, provided it did not interfere with the property of the person entitled to that which was falsely asserted by the other to belong to him, this Court could not interfere. Was it alleged that the plaintiff's goods had acquired such a reputation abroad by the term "prize medal," and were so connected with it that anyone asking for prize medal pickles would mean those manufactured by the plaintiff, and those only? If proved, that would have been a very important circumstance. But the averment in the plaintiff's affidavit (to which his Honour referred) did not go to that extent. Further than this, the defendant had taken this very immoral course of affixing the words "prize medal" to his goods, and issuing them under that title, before the plaintiff obtained his medal. Upon this ground it was very difficult for this Court to interfere in favour of the plaintiff. There was this further difficulty, that the plaintiff had erroneously made the other prize medallist, Partridge, a defendant to the suit. If the prize medal had become so identified with the plaintiff's goods as to constitute a trade-mark, then, on that theory, Partridge, or any other person, would have to be enjoined. His Honour, after referring to the case of Dent's business, where the firm became split into two upon the testator's death (*see Dent v. Turpin*, *Tucker v. Turpin*, 9 W. R. 548), and to the circumstance that for some articles—oil, for instance—no less than thirty or forty prize medals had been awarded, where no such exclusive right as had been claimed by the plaintiff could possibly be asserted, said that no order could be made upon the present motion, and the costs would be costs in the cause.

§2.59 GREAT BRITAIN PASSES THE FIRST STATUTE ON THE REGISTRATION AND PROTECTION OF INDUSTRIAL AWARDS

1863

As a reaction to a court's refusal to acknowledge industrial awards as elements of differentiation in their own right, in *Batty v. Hill* (*see* Text 2.58), the British Parliament enacted the statute of 1863, establishing the protection of industrial awards, and, importantly, making it clear that protection would apply even in the absence of proof of damages. The English statute added a rule on false claims of the use of patented inventions. This rule stemmed from an interesting aspect of exhibitions at that time: many exhibitors would claim the novelty of their products, and many would also sustain their claims based on patent letters.

The Exhibition Medals Act, 1863—26 § 27 Vict. c. 119

§ 1. If any trader commits any of the offences following; that is to say—
(1) Falsely represents that he has obtained a medal or certificate from the Exhibition Commissioners in respect of any article or process for which a medal or certificate has been awarded by the Commissioners;
(2) Falsely represents (knowing such representation to be false) that any other trader has obtained a medal or certificate from the Exhibition Commissioners;
(3) Falsely represents (knowing such representation to be false) that any article sold or expected for sale has been made by, or by any process invented by, a person who has obtained in respect of such article or process a medal or certification from the Exhibition Commissioners:

He shall incur the following penalties, that is to say:
(1) For the first offence he shall forfeit to her Majesty a sum not exceeding five pounds;
(2) For any subsequent offence he shall forfeit to her Majesty a sum not exceeding twenty pounds, or be imprisoned for a period not exceeding six months. . . .

By § 2, in proceedings under this Act, it is not necessary to prove that any person has sustained damage by the false representation. . . .

By § 5, no provision of this Act is to affect any right or civil remedy.

§2.60 IN THE UNITED STATES, COURTS CONSOLIDATE TRADEMARK LAW

1867

The text that follows is a landmark United States trademark case. In this case, the New York Supreme Court drew the line defining the boundaries of exclusivity in a distinctive sign, and the reasons for such boundaries.

Burnett v. Phalon

N. Y. Super. Ct. 22 Monthly L. R. (12 N. 5.) 220, June, 1867.

The plaintiffs being manufacturers of a hair-oil which they sold under the name of "Cocoaine" the defendants began to sell an oil of their own under the name of "Cocoïne." Injunction granted to restrain the defendants from selling their oil under that name, or any other name imitated from the name applied by the plaintiffs to their oil, that name being held to be a valid trade-mark and the property of the plaintiff.

Per Pierrepont, J.: "Every man has a right to the reward of his skill, his energy, and his honest enterprise; and when he has appropriated, as his trade-mark, letters combined into a word before unknown, and has used that word, and has long published it to the world as his adopted trade-mark, he has acquired rights in it which the courts will protect."

§2.61 PERVASIVE TRADEMARK COUNTERFEITING IN FRANCE AND A STRANGE PROPOSITION: THE OFFICIAL AUTHENTICATION OF TRADEMARKS

November 26, 1873

This text shows a strange proposition: the setting of an official seal certifying the authenticity of trademarks. The idea was to add the nature of administrative violation to the private enforcement of trademarks. Therefore, the infringement of those trademarks certified with the public seal could be addressed both by the trademark owner and the State.

Apparently, this proposition was motivated by rampant counterfeiting, to the point that consumers might have lost confidence in all trademarks, including those that were legitimate.

Law of November 26, 1873 on the establishment of a stamp or special sign intended to be affixed on trademarks.

Article 1.—Any owner of a trademark registered under the law of June 23, 1857, may be admitted, on his written requisition, to be affixed by the State, either on the labels, paper strips or envelopes, or on metal labels or seals bearing his trademark, a special stamp or hallmark intended to confirm the authenticity of that mark.

The hallmark may be affixed to the mark that is embedded in the objects themselves, if the administration deems them to be susceptible of such.

Art. 2—It will be perceived for the benefit of the State, by the apposition of each stamp, a fee that can vary from 1 centime to 1 fr. . . .

Art. 7—The stamp or hallmark of the State affixed to a trademark is an integral part of this mark.

If the State fails to pursue, in France or abroad, the counterfeiting or forgery of said stamp or hallmark, the enforcement may be exercised by the owner of the mark. . . .

§2.62 GREAT BRITAIN ALSO SIGNS BILATERAL AGREEMENTS CONTAINING CLAUSES ON TRADEMARKS AND DESIGNS

December 5, 1876

Like France, Great Britain also signed bilateral agreements with a significant number of their trading partners, such as Austria-Hungary (1876), the United States (1877), Denmark (1879), Switzerland (1880) and France (1882). All these agreements ensured the reciprocal protection of trademarks under the national treatment principle. With the exception of the agreements made with Switzerland and the United States, Great Britain's bilateral treaties included "patterns and designs for manufactures." Two of those (signed with Denmark and the United States) also included commercial labels, thus covering trade names.

Treaty of Commerce between Great Britain and Austria-Hungary

December 5, 1876

. . .

Article VI.

Trade-Marks, &c. —National Treatment.

The subjects of one of the two High Contracting Parties shall enjoy in the territories of the other the same protection as native subjects with regard to rights of ownership over trade and manufacture marks, and other distinctive marks of goods or their packages, as well as over patterns and designs for manufactures.

The subjects of Her Britannic Majesty will not, however, be able to claim in Austria-Hungary the exclusive right to a mark or other indication on a pattern or design unless they have filed two specimens of it in the Chambers of Commerce at Vienna and Buda-Pesth. . . .

§2.63 FRANCE PASSES A STATUTE PROTECTING INDUSTRIAL AWARDS

April 30, 1886

In France, where the first international exhibition was organized (in 1798, in Paris), soon courts would accord industrial awards and medals the same protection they granted to entrepreneurs against acts of unfair competition. The text that follows is the first French statute dealing with awards, of 1886, which was a consolidation of jurisprudence. A new element was the extension of protection to awards granted by scientific entities—hence, without a trade connection.

Law concerning the usurpation of industrial medals and awards

April 30, 1886

Article 1—The use of any medals, diplomas, mentions, awards or honorary distinctions awarded in exhibitions or competitions, either in France or abroad, is permitted only to those who have obtained them personally and to the trading house in consideration of which they were awarded.

He who uses it must make known its date and its nature, the exhibition or competition where it was obtained and the object rewarded.

Art. 2—(1) Those who, without right and fraudulently, have publicly attributed to themselves the rewards or distinctions mentioned in the preceding article; (2) those who, under the same conditions, have applied them to objects other than those for which they had been obtained, or which have been attributed imaginary; (3) those who have falsely indicated them on their signboards, advertisements, prospectuses, invoices, letters or commercial papers; (4) those who have unduly prevailed before exhibition or competition juries—

will be punished with a fine of 50 to 600 francs and imprisonment of three months to two years, or with one of those two penalties only

Art. 3—Those who, without right and fraudulently, have publicly availed themselves of awards, distinctions or approvals granted by learned bodies or scientific societies, will be punished with the same penalties.

Art. 4—The omission of the indications listed in the second paragraph of Article 1 shall be punished with a fine of 25 to 3,000 francs.

Art. 5—The courts may order the destruction or the confiscation, for the benefit of the injured parties, of the objects on which the false indications have been applied. They may order the publication and the insertion of their judgments.

Art. 6—Article 463 of the Penal Code is applicable to offenses provided for and punished by this Law. . . .

§2.64 THE TREATY OF VERSAILLES: FOR THE FIRST TIME BUSINESS IDENTIFIERS ARE PROTECTED THROUGH THE REPRESSION OF UNFAIR COMPETITION

1919

The text that follows is an excerpt from the Treaty of Versailles (Treaty of Peace with Germany), of 1919, signed between the Principal Powers (United States of America, the British Empire, France, Italy and Japan), and the Allied and Associated Powers (22 countries), on the one part, and Germany, on the other part), which put an end to the First World War (1914-1918). Influenced by the growing attention paid to the repression of unfair competition and its broad scope as a more flexible and effective way of repressing the infringement of business identifiers in general, the allied and associated powers included in the Treaty a clause that obliged Germany to repress "all forms of unfair competition" in commercial transactions. Thus, the Treaty of Versailles preceded the Paris Convention by 6 years, because the clause on the repression of unfair competition of that Convention was introduced only in 1925, in the Diplomatic Conference that took place at The Hague.

Part X (Economic Clauses), Section I (Commercial Relations), Chapter III (Unfair Competition)

Article 274

Germany undertakes to adopt all the necessary legislative and administrative measures to protect goods the produce or manufacture of anyone of the Allied and Associated Powers from all forms of unfair competition in commercial transactions. Germany undertakes to prohibit and repress by seizure and by other appropriate remedies the importation, exportation, manufacture, distribution, sale or offering for sale in its territory of all goods bearing upon themselves or their usual get-up or wrappings any marks, names, devices, or description whatsoever which are calculated to convey directly or indirectly a false indication of the origin, type, nature, or special characteristics of such goods.

Article 275

Germany undertakes on condition that reciprocity is accorded in these matters to respect any law, or any administrative or judicial decision given in conformity with such law, in force in any Allied or Associated State and duly communicated to her by the proper authorities, defining or regulating the right to any regional appellation in respect of wine or spirits produced in the State to which the region belongs, or the conditions under which the use of any such appellation may be permitted; and the importation, exportation, manufacture, distribution, sale or offering for sale of products or articles bearing regional appellations inconsistent with such law or order shall be prohibited by the German Government and repressed by the measures prescribed in the preceding Article.

§2.65 AN AUSTRALIAN COURT DEFINES THE ESSENCE OF TRADEMARKS: ESTABLISHING EMPATHY BETWEEN THE CONSUMER AND THE ARTICLE (OR SERVICE) THEY DESIGNATE

August 9, 1956

The significant importance of the *Mark Foy's* opinion lies in two elements: the careful analysis of the distinctive effect of words that are part of the common vocabulary; and the conclusion that trademarks do not need to transmit a define idea. It is enough that they create in consumers a pleasant feeling that lead them to purchase, i.e., that they originate in consumers empathy towards the product (or service) they designate. In other words, it is consumers who make the marks, not the merchants. This corresponds to the concept of the social construction of marks, which also applies in the field of patents—for the commercial success of an invention, it does not matter that it be covered by a patent, what matters is that society approves and uses it.

Mark Foy's Ltd v Davies Coop & Co Ltd ("Tub Happy case")

[1956] HCA 41; (1956) 95 CLR 190

August 9, 1956

High Court of Australia

1. Dixon C.J. I have had the advantage of reading the judgment prepared by considerations which Kitto J. has marshalled with so much force against the view that the words "tub happy" are words having no direct reference to the character or quality of the goods within the meaning of par. (d) of s. 16 (1) of the Trade Marks Act 1905-1948. But nevertheless I am unable to adopt the conclusion that these words are disqualified from forming a registrable trade mark under s. 16 (1) (d) because they directly refer to the character or quality of the goods.
2. It is, I think, a mistake first to assume that words like "Tub Happy" do convey a meaning either to people in general or to a particular class of persons and then on that assumption to inquire what exactly the meaning is. Indeed to institute a search for a meaning almost necessarily implies that in ordinary English speech the words do not possess a connotation sufficiently definite to

amount to a direct reference to the character or quality of the goods. And that is true even when to standard English usage is added all the figurative idiomatic and slang phraseology that may be currently in use. Once, however, the question is asked what do the words mean and there is started a search for a meaning, a process of analysis and of reasoning by exclusion of alternatives is begun. No doubt such a search may, without any sacrifice of logic, end in construing the words as meaning that the garments will emerge happily from the washtub. But if they are so interpreted, the interpretation is chiefly the consequence of failure to find another meaning. I venture to think, however, that a man, or for that matter a woman, hearing for the first time the words used in combination and in connection with cotton garments, would not so understand the words at once. Certainly such a person would not so understand them intuitively and without stopping to reflect and ask himself or herself what meaning the words could really possess.

3. The fallacy of asking what is the meaning of the phrase lies in the basal assumption that the words are intended to convey some definite meaning and perhaps the further assumption that the meaning has reference to the garments or the cottons. The assumption is fallacious because it overlooks the fact that language is not always used to convey an idea. Many uses of words are purely emotive. A word or words are often employed for no purpose but to evoke in the reader or hearer some feeling, some mood, some mental attitude. This is true of much advertising, which common experience shows to be full of meaningless but emotive expressions supposedly capable of inducing a generally favourable inclination in the almost subconscious thought of the passing auditor or hasty reader. Words put forward as trademarks are very likely indeed to be chosen in the same way.
4. Though Mr. Holmes for the respondent did of course put forward the claim that "tub happy" means washable, it was a meaning it was necessary to suggest. It was not a meaning that had sprung unaided to the mind and it was not one which he was able to establish by reference to instances of known usage. . . .
7. I cannot think that the words now in question go further than, if as far as, suggesting in a vague and indefinable way a gladsome carelessness a propos of the tub. They may have an emotive tendency, but they do not appear to me to convey any meaning or idea sufficiently tangible to amount to a direct reference to the character or quality of the goods.
8. I agree in the judgment of Williams J. and I have added the foregoing only in an endeavour to make clear why I remain unconvinced by the judgment of Kitto J.
   1. Williams J. This is an appeal by the plaintiff company from a decree of the Supreme Court of New South Wales in Equity (McLelland J.) dismissing with costs a suit brought by the plaintiff appellant against the defendants-respondents to restrain the alleged infringement by the defendants of its registered trade mark No. 103308. This trade mark was registered under the provisions of the Trade Marks Act 1905-1948 on 25th July 1950 in class 38 in respect of articles of clothing and consists of the words "tub happy". The plaintiff owns a large retail store at 143-147 Liverpool Street, Sydney where it has for more than forty years carried on an extensive retail business. This business consists principally of retailing clothing for men, women and children, materials for such clothing and draper's manchester and household requisites. The plaintiff also owns and operates in the vicinity woollen mills, a knitting mill and shirt factory and a clothing factory. Since the date of registration the plaintiff has used and advertised

the trade mark extensively upon and in connection with articles of clothing, particularly cotton frocks of various designs and good quality, manufactured by itself for which there is a ready sale. Each frock has attached to it by sewing a label bearing in bright colours the words "Tub Happy Cottons by Mark Foy's Limited, Sydney". The plaintiff has also extensively advertised its cotton frocks under the trade mark in newspapers published in Sydney and has, in each summer since 1950, exclusively displayed "Tub Happy" frocks in one of its largest show windows and has used show cards in such windows and in its departments carrying these words in large type.

2. The defendant Davies Coop (N.S.W.) Pty. Ltd., a New South Wales company which carries on business at Marrickville, is a subsidiary of the defendant Davies Coop & Co. Ltd., a Victorian company which carries on business at Swanston Street, Melbourne. In August or September 1953 the plaintiff received a letter from the Victorian company advising it of a projected 1954 sales promotion campaign of "Exacto Cotton Garments—Tub Happy Cotton Fresh Budget Wise" manufactured by this defendant. The circular stated that the weight of advertising would tell the public the story of "Exacto Cotton Garments—Tub Happy Cotton Fresh Budget Wise" and would ensure an immediate demand for Exacto products. One suggested advertisement was "Buy Tub Happy Windcheaters Skimps etc." The plaintiff immediately drew this defendant's attention to the existence of its trade mark "Tub Happy" and claimed that any use by the defendant or any of its traders of these words in connection with any line of clothing would be an infringement. But the defendants through their patent attorney replied that they were not using the words "Tub Happy" as a trade mark and that the words "Tub Happy Cotton Fresh and Budget Wise" were being used "in a modern descriptive sense", whatever this may mean, and that these words when used in relation to Exacto garments referred to their good washing properties, freshness and economy. The defendants pointed out that their garments were in every instance prominently branded as Exacto goods, that this was their trade mark, and that it was this mark that was distinctive of their goods. Considerable correspondence followed, the plaintiff being desirous of avoiding litigation in the trade and hoping that the defendants would abandon the use of the controversial words. But they refused to do so, continuing to claim that the words "tub happy" were merely descriptive of a quality of their cotton goods and finally, in October 1954, the plaintiff commenced this suit. . . .

4. The plaintiff filed a statement of claim and moved for an interlocutory injunction and by consent the motion was turned into a motion for a decree. His Honour dismissed the suit on the ground that the words were being used by the defendant as a bona fide description of the character or quality of the goods within the meaning of s. 53A of the Trade Marks Act. He said: "In my opinion, the facts in this case bring the defendants within s. 53A, assuming otherwise a valid trade mark and facts showing an infringement. I have examined all the advertisements very carefully, but, in my opinion, each must be read as a whole, even bearing in mind the various elements to which Mr. Hardie directed my attention, and all must be read, I think, in the light of the evidence of Mr. Furphey, which I accept. Reading the advertisements in the manner I have indicated, I am of opinion that the use up to this point of time by the defendants of the words "Tub Happy" has been a use by the defendants of a bona fide description of the

character or quality of the goods of the defendants." We were informed by counsel for the defendants that his Honour said that he was prepared to dismiss the motion either on this ground or on the ground that the defendants had not used the words "tub happy" as a trade mark, that it was only if they were so doing that the plaintiff's rights in the trade mark would be infringed, and that his Honour only adopted the former ground after he had given counsel for the plaintiff the option to choose between them. . . .

6. The first question is whether the words "tub happy" are registrable as a trade mark under s. 16 (1) (d) of the Trade Marks Act. To qualify they must be words having no direct reference to the character or quality of articles of clothing. In his speech in Eastman Photographic Materials Co. Ltd. v. Comptroller-General of Patents, Designs and Trade Marks ("Solio" Case) (1898) AC 571 Lord Herschell explained the meaning of this qualification. He said: "any word in the English language may serve as a trade-mark—the commonest word in the language might be employed. In these circumstances it would obviously have been out of the question to permit a person by registering a trade-mark in respect of a particular class of goods to obtain a monopoly of the use of a word having reference to the character or quality of those goods. The vocabulary of the English language is common property: it belongs alike to all; and no one ought to be permitted to prevent the other members of the community from using for purposes of description a word which has reference to the character or quality of goods" (1898) AC, at p 580. . . . Any reference that the words "Tub Happy" have to the character or quality of articles of clothing is very remote. They are in the nature of a coined phrase. Inanimate objects including articles of clothing cannot have the character or quality of happiness whether they are in a tub or not. But the defendants' case is that the common metaphorical use of the adjective would convey to prospective buyers of the fabrics that the cotton emerged from the wash tub more attractive than ever in appearance with fibres and colours as good if not better than ever. Therefore, so it is said, the words are a description of the character or quality of the goods and moreover are not entitled to registration. This claim gives far too specific a meaning to the vague figurative use of the word "happy" in connection with "tub". Like so many expressions used in advertisements no definite or actual meaning seems to belong to the combination "Tub Happy". There is a cloudy suggestion only about it that all will be well in a wash tub but that is all. The attitude of mind of those who glance at such advertisements may be affected favourably by some sort of vague association of ideas but it falls a long way short of conveying any meaning to them. To say that articles of clothing are tub happy is in the ordinary use of English meaningless. The words contain at most a "covert and skillful allusion" to the quality of washability which is characteristic of articles of clothing made of some kinds of material including cotton. At most they create an impression that this is what they are intended to convey. They do not trespass upon the rights of other traders to use any ordinary English words or phrases referring to the washable qualities of their goods. They do not attempt to "enclose and appropriate as private property certain little strips of the great open common of the English language". No doubt the words are intended to "contain a meaning—a meaning is wrapped up in them if you can only find it out." . . . And it may not be hard to find out that meaning but the words do not refer in any

ordinary sense, laudatory or otherwise, to any character or quality of articles of clothing, still less do they do so directly.

7. The conclusion that the words "Tub Happy" are registrable under s. 16 (1) (d) of the Trade Marks Act because they have no direct reference to the character or quality of articles of clothing goes a long way towards deciding the ground on which his Honour ruled against the defendants. There is nothing in the registration of these words to prevent the defendants describing their cotton goods as having the qualities of washability, freshness and cheapness, and in particular the first of these qualities. The whole English language is open to them, even the most up to date English, if the defendants wish to refer to these qualities "in a modern descriptive sense". In *J. B. Stone & Co. Ltd. v. Steelace Manufacturing Co. Ltd.* (1929) 46 RPC 406 Lawrence L.J. said: "In my opinion the object of s. 44" (of the English Trade Marks Act 1905 which corresponds to s. 53A of the Commonwealth Act) "was to safeguard traders in cases where the registered trade mark consisted of more or less descriptive words forming part of the ordinary English language, without the use of which other traders would find some difficulty in describing certain qualities of their goods; but was never intended and does not operate to enable a trader to make use of a rival trader's registered trade mark consisting of a fancy word having no reference to the character and quality of the goods in order more readily to sell his own goods" (1929) 46 RPC, at p 417. . . . Section 53A of the Trade Marks Act protects the use by any person of any bona fide description of the character or quality of his goods. But that means a description and not a mere suggestion in fanciful language. It does not protect an attempt by the defendants to usurp a metaphorical phrase like "Tub Happy" however magnetic the force of its public appeal may be. . . .

§2.66 A BRAZILIAN COURT DEFINES THE ESSENCE OF INTELLECTUAL PROPERTY'S ROLE: TO SERVE HONESTY IN TRADE

June 29, 1982

The text that follows, although it speaks to trademark law only, states the essence of intellectual property: all merchants and manufacturers aim at differentiating themselves and their products or services from competitors' but society is not served when they do so through dishonest practices.

This opinion gains more in relevance when one realizes that Brazil is not a common law country. And yet, for the sake of the preservation of the fundamental value of fairness in competition, this court has not hesitated to put aside a written norm of administrative law (that of the presumption of validity of a title issued by the Trademark Office) and has given predominance to that value. In this manner, this court acted like an equity court.

Brazil—Court of Criminal Appeals of São Paulo (5th Chamber)

HC 114.846 ("*YKK Case*")

Judgment on June 29, 1982

Opinion delivered by Appellate Judge Adauto Suannes.

1. Attorney José Antonio Ivo Galli applies for a *habeas corpus* order, aiming at the dismissal of the criminal action moved by Metalúrgica Brasileira Ultra against Iwao Kamiichi, Yutaka Ikegami and Norio Miyaguchi, to whom the crime of art. 175 I, II and IV, (a), of Decree-Law 7.903/45 is attributed, arguing in brief that the crime of the defendants consisted of using the trademark YKK for the zippers they manufacture, trademark which had regularly been registered by the plaintiff. It happens, however, that the trademark YKK is registered in about 116 countries by its legitimate owner, the company Yoshida Kabushiki Kaisha, which exported those devices to Brazil for many years. On 29.12.1967 the defendants filed with the National Institute of Industrial Property an application for the registration of the said mark, which, once granted, led to registration 837,584. Because of a mistaken translation, the term slide fasteners, which refers to zippers and similar products, was registered in class 8, which concerns photo slides. Having noticed the mistake, the defendants are currently engaged in correcting it administratively. However, in the meantime the plaintiff, surreptitiously, registered, on 16.05.1969, under nr. 884,377, the same trademark YKK for designating slide fasteners. Alleging the lack of fair ground for the criminal action, given the doubt surrounding the right of the plaintiff, the defendants expect its dismissal.

Opinion by the Prosecutor. In a nutshell, it says that: (a) the allegation of lack of fair ground is unacceptable because [that is] a matter of civil law, given that the plaintiff is still the owner of the trademark; ...

This is the report in synthesis.

2. In the analysis of this case, one must bear in mind two superior principles: a) The Law does not exist to reward malice; b) mistakes do not give rise to rights.

...

It happened that Yoshida Brasileira Indústria e Comércio, of which the defendants are partners, in attempting to register the trademark YKK for zippers, by an obvious mistake of the firm in charge of that, obtained the registration as if it concerned photographic material.

Hence registration 837,584, of 19.11.74 (filed on 29.12.67). It refers to metal, cardboard and plastic frames for photo slides, an area of business to which YKK is absolutely strange.

But on 16.05.69, Metalúrgica Brasileira Ultra S/A, with the obvious and ineludible purpose of appropriating the fame that the products that bear that mark certainly enjoy, and having knowledge of the blatant mistake in the classification of the product, decided to apply for the global trademark YKK as if it were its own. And it got the registration, exactly because of the mentioned mistake.

One might even wonder how Ultra was informed of that mistake and who would have promised it the possibility of incorporating into its equity the reputation of a product it has never manufactured.

It is certain, however, that it will never be understood how a company with that name decides to have as a trademark that term formed by two letters that do not exist in the Portuguese alphabet. What relation could there be between Metalúrgica Brasileira Ultra S/A and YKK?

Obviously, none.

Therefore, the registration obtained by the plaintiff was animated by a completely immoral purpose, because a manufacturer of zippers could not ignore the existence of a worldwide known company, as Yoshida Kabushiki Kaisha is, or simply YKK.

To the surprise of Law lovers, however, to the dock of defendants does not come the company that, without any scruple, benefitted from another's mistake, waving as its own a worldwide known trademark, created so many decades ago. On the contrary, going further in its unfortunate adventure, under the cover of a stillborn acquired right, it brings a criminal action against no less than the representatives in Brazil of the legitimate YKK.

And it expects the support of the Judiciary for such an adventure.

For the solution of the present request of *habeas corpus* eventual considerations of a civil nature concerning the good or bad repercussions of the glaring and absolutely unacceptable malice of the plaintiff do not matter.

Here the issue is that it is more than evident that the defendants have not committed any crime whatsoever. The fault is on the side of the managers of Metalúrgica Ultra who, without any scruple, are imposing on consumers, with the usual blessing of our powerless authorities, a product to whose name they have not contributed anything that could justify its use.

That the plaintiff would not respect its competitor, one can understand. That it would not respect consumers, it would be blameful. But that it does not respect the Judiciary, inducing it to condone with an act of piracy, it is quite appalling.

If the minimum one expects from a criminal charge is that it is provided of *fumus boni juris*, how could we accept that a criminal action born from such a procedure, which is supported by Law only formally, can embarrass anyone?

It would lack what illustrious Luis Recaséns Siches called *logos del razonable* . . . And Justice Carlos Maximiliano recalled Cicero's praise to jurisconsult Caius Aquilius Gallus, because he "always interpreted laws in a way so that reprehensible maneuvers and flaws would never benefit their authors." . . .

3. In view of the above, defendants not having practiced any crime, the requested order is granted, so as to dismiss, definitively, the criminal action moved against them by Metalúrgica Brasileira Ultra S/A . . .

§2.67 THE URUGUAY ROUND AND ITS IMPACT ON THE LAW OF BUSINESS IDENTIFIERS

February 5, 1988

The text that follows is a compilation of trademark-related issues raised by the Contracting Parties at the opening of discussions on a future TRIPS Agreement that the Chair of the negotiating group has prepared. Such compilation reveals that there were no major problems as regards which the Paris Convention did not already provide for or at least permitted already a solution. At most, the Paris Convention needed some clarifications (e.g., as regards the definition of well-known marks) and some guarantees concerning transparency in the prosecution of registrations.

The other field of business identifiers covered by the TRIPS Agreement—geographical indications—did not add much to what the Treaty of

Versailles already provided for, although in a much narrower context (its provisions applied to the belligerent parties only and were of a temporary nature). The concern in not introducing significant changes to the laws then prevailing led to the adoption of a provision—Article 24—that admits that the Members of the WTO may continue using usurped geographical indications, provided that usurpation corresponds to long standing practices (10 years old, at least).

II. Issues in connection with the availability and scope of intellectual property rights

. . .

(a) Inadequacies in the availability and scope of intellectual property rights

. . .

(iii) Trademarks

41. The issues raised by some participants about inadequacies in the scope and availability of trademark rights are:

- the absence of effective systems for registering and recording rights in trademarks in some countries;
- the absence of protection for trademarks on single ingredient pharmaceutical and chemical products or for service marks in some countries;
- difficulties with obtaining trademark rights in a country where an application for registration is considered abandoned if the registration is opposed and is only pursued if the applicant reaches an agreement of reconciliation with the opponent or raises a suit of opposition within a year;
- lack of clarity in the validity of the trademark right in countries with no system of examination of applications for registration;
- difficulties in preventing the unrestricted use as generic words of well-known foreign trademarks in some countries, leading to rejection of applications for renewal of registration;
- the difficulty of meeting use requirements in some countries for the maintenance of trademark rights because of high tariffs and import restrictions;
- inadequate control of the registration of trademarks similar or identical to well-known foreign trademarks in some countries;
- insufficient duration of the period before the right lapses without use; in some countries, renewal of registration must be made after 5 years and is denied if commercialization has not taken place;
- difficulties in taking action against unauthorized use of a trademark in a country because of problems in meeting local use requirements due to delays in the registration of licensed users and in the consequent legal permission for the licensee to use the mark.

(iv) Appellations of origin and geographical indications

42. Some participants have referred to problems of imitation, counterfeiting and usurpation of appellations of origin and geographical indications arising in their view because of insufficient protection in many countries. A participant has said that the protection provided for in the Paris Convention in this connection was limited and that, while the Madrid Agreement for the Repression of False or Deceptive Indications of Source on Goods and the Lisbon Agreement for the Protection of Appellations of Origin and their International Registration provided

for more extensive protection, their membership was limited. Such protection as existed was, therefore, largely based on national provisions on unfair competition and bilateral arrangements offering recognition on a reciprocal basis. Some other participants have indicated that there are fundamental differences of view about basic rights in regard to geographical indications, particularly appellations of origin.

§2.68 REGISTERING AND PROTECTING NON-TRADITIONAL TRADEMARKS

December 12, 2002

National governments have for a long time struggled with the concept of registering and protecting the so-called non-traditional trademarks—those that are not susceptible of being visually reproduced, such as sounds, tastes, scents, and figures in movement, as well as isolated colours. The problem is not in the trademarks themselves, because the capacity of some of those to operate as elements of differentiation of articles and services is undeniable. The problem is in giving to the governmental agency in charge of registering trademarks proof of the existence and distinctiveness of the sign itself.

The text that follows consists of excerpts from a decision of the European Court of Justice in which it, in the context of an application for the registration of a scent trademark that had been rejected by the German Trademark Office, defined the lines to be followed in examining those applications. However, the refusal by the court of a chemical formula as the element describing the trademark as well as of a sample (because of its lack of stability) makes it virtually impossible for an entrepreneur to obtain the registration of an olfactory trademark unless it has been used and become well-known by consumers. This would be the case of the scent that customers perceive when they enter a store where famous brands are sold, such as Abercrombie & Fitch and Osklen. In the case of these two unique, distinctive scents, the respective owners should not be required to engage in complex descriptions—the mere reference to the fact that they have become well-known to their customers should suffice. While the scents are used to identify the stores, they are trademarks. The same, however, cannot be said of the perfumes that the stores sell with those same scents given that, as far as the perfumes are concerned, the scents are purely functional. By contrast, their scents are arbitrary elements of the stores' differentiation.

Sieckmann v. Deutsches Patent- und Markenamt

European Court of Justice

Judgment of December 12, 2002

1. By order of 14 April 2000, received at the Court on 10 July 2000, the Bundespatentgericht (Federal Patents Court) referred to the Court for a preliminary ruling under Article 234 EC two questions on the interpretation of

Article 2 of First Council Directive 89/104/EEC of 21 December 1988 to approximate the laws of the Member States relating to trade marks (OJ 1989 L 40, p. 1; 'the Directive"').

2. Those questions were raised in proceedings brought by Mr Sieckmann against the refusal of the *Deutsches Patent- und Markenamt* (German Patent and Trade Mark Office) to register an olfactory mark in respect of various services in Classes 35, 41 and 42 of the Nice Agreement on the International Classification of Goods and Services for the Purposes of the Registration of Marks of 15 June 1957, as revised and amended. . . .
10. Mr Sieckmann deposited with the *Deutsches Patent- und Markenamt* a trade mark in respect of various services in Classes 35, 41 and 42 of the Nice Agreement of 15 June 1957, as revised and amended, which include advertising, business management, business administration and office functions (Class 35), education, providing of training, entertainment and sporting and cultural activities (Class 41), providing of food and drink, temporary accommodation, medical, hygienic and beauty care, veterinary and agricultural services, legal services, scientific and industrial research, computer programming and services that cannot be placed in other classes (Class 42).
11. In the section of the application form headed 'Reproduction of the Trade Mark', required under Paragraph 8(1) of the Markengesetz and pursuant to Article 2 of the Directive, provisions under which, to be able to constitute a mark a sign must be capable of being represented graphically, Mr Sieckmann referred to a description attached as an annex to his registration application. That description reads as follows:

> Trade mark protection is sought for the olfactory mark deposited with the Deutsches Patent- und Markenamt of the pure chemical substance methyl cinnamate *(*= cinnamic acid methyl ester), whose structural formula is set out below. Samples of this olfactory mark can also be obtained via local laboratories listed in the Gelbe Seiten (Yellow Pages) of Deutsche Telekom AG or, for example, via the firm E. Merck in Darmstadt.
>
> C6H5-CH = CHCOOCH3.

12. In the event that the description set out in the previous paragraph was not sufficient to satisfy the application requirement under Paragraph 32(2) and (3) of the Markengesetz, the applicant in the main proceedings made the following addendum to that description:

> The trade mark applicant hereby declares his consent to an inspection of the files relating to the deposited olfactory mark 'methyl cinnamate' pursuant to Paragraph 62(1) of the Markengesetz and Paragraph 48(2) of the Markenverordnung (Trade Mark Regulation).

13. Mr Sieckmann also submitted with his registration application an odour sample of the sign in a container and stated that the scent was usually described as "balsamically fruity with a slight hint of cinnamon."
14. The *Deutsches Patent- und Markenamt* refused the application for registration on the ground that it was doubtful whether the trade mark applied for was capable of being registered under Paragraph 3(1) of the Markengesetz and of being represented graphically in accordance with Paragraph 8(1) thereof. Ultimately, it was not necessary to determine whether the sign was capable of being registered as a trade mark and of being represented graphically because,

under Paragraph 8(2) of the Markengesetz, that sign's lack of any distinctive character precluded its registration in any event. . . .

34. It should first be recalled that, as is stated in the 10th recital in the preamble to the Directive, the function of the protection afforded by a trade mark is in particular to guarantee the mark as an indication of origin.
35. It is also clear from the Court's case-law that the essential function of a trade mark is to guarantee the identity of the origin of the marked product or service to the consumer or end-user by enabling him, without any possibility of confusion, to distinguish that product or service from others which have another origin and that, for the trade mark to be able to fulfil its essential role in the system of undistorted competition which the EC Treaty seeks to establish, it must offer a guarantee that all the goods or services bearing it have been manufactured or supplied under the control of a single undertaking which is responsible for their quality . . . .
43. The purpose of Article 2 of the Directive is to define the types of signs of which a trade mark may consist. That provision states that a trade mark may consist of "particularly words, including personal names, designs, letters, numerals, the shape of goods or of their packaging . . . ." Admittedly, it mentions only signs which are capable of being perceived visually, are two-dimensional or three-dimensional and can thus be represented by means of letters or written characters or by a picture.
44. However, as is clear from the language of both Article 2 of the Directive and the seventh recital in the preamble thereto, which refers to a "list [of] examples" of signs which may constitute a trade mark, that list is not exhaustive. Consequently, that provision, although it does not mention signs which are not in themselves capable of being perceived visually, such as odours, does not, however, expressly exclude them.
45. In those circumstances, Article 2 of the Directive must be interpreted as meaning that a trade mark may consist of a sign which is not in itself capable of being perceived visually, provided that it can be represented graphically.
46. That graphic representation must enable the sign to be represented visually, particularly by means of images, lines or characters, so that it can be precisely identified.
47. Such an interpretation is required to allow for the sound operation of the trade mark registration system.
48. First, the function of the graphic representability requirement is, in particular, to define the mark itself in order to determine the precise subject of the protection afforded by the registered mark to its proprietor.
49. Next, the entry of the mark in a public register has the aim of making it accessible to the competent authorities and the public, particularly to economic operators.
50. On the one hand, the competent authorities must know with clarity and precision the nature of the signs of which a mark consists in order to be able to fulfil their obligations in relation to the prior examination of registration applications and to the publication and maintenance of an appropriate and precise register of trade marks.
51. On the other hand, economic operators must, with clarity and precision, be able to find out about registrations or applications for registration made by their current or potential competitors and thus to receive relevant information about the rights of third parties.
52. If the users of that register are to be able to determine the precise nature of a mark on the basis of its registration, its graphic representation in the register must be self-contained, easily accessible and intelligible.

53. Furthermore, in order to fulfil its role as a registered trade mark a sign must always be perceived unambiguously and in the same way so that the mark is guaranteed as an indication of origin. In the light of the duration of a mark's registration and the fact that, as the Directive provides, it can be renewed for varying periods, the representation must be durable.
54. Finally, the object of the representation is specifically to avoid any element of subjectivity in the process of identifying and perceiving the sign. Consequently, the means of graphic representation must be unequivocal and objective.
55. In the light of the foregoing observations, the answer to the first question must be that Article 2 of the Directive must be interpreted as meaning that a trade mark may consist of a sign which is not in itself capable of being perceived visually, provided that it can be represented graphically, particularly by means of images, lines or characters, and that the representation is clear, precise, self-contained, easily accessible, intelligible, durable and objective. . . .
69. As regards a chemical formula, as the United Kingdom Government has rightly noted, few people would recognise in such a formula the odour in question. Such a formula is not sufficiently intelligible. In addition, as that Government and the Commission stated, a chemical formula does not represent the odour of a substance, but the substance as such, and nor is it sufficiently clear and precise. It is therefore not a representation for the purposes of Article 2 of the Directive.
70. In respect of the description of an odour, although it is graphic, it is not sufficiently clear, precise and objective.
71. As to the deposit of an odour sample, it does not constitute a graphic representation for the purposes of Article 2 of the Directive. Moreover, an odour sample is not sufficiently stable or durable.
72. If, in respect of an olfactory sign, a chemical formula, a description in words or the deposit of an odour sample are not capable of satisfying, in themselves, the requirements of graphic representability, nor is a combination of those elements able to satisfy such requirements, in particular those relating to clarity and precision.
73. In the light of the foregoing considerations, the answer to the second question must be that, in respect of an olfactory sign, the requirements of graphic representability are not satisfied by a chemical formula, by a description in written words, by the deposit of an odour sample or by a combination of those elements. . . .

§2.69 REDUCING THE DISTINCTIVENESS OF BUSINESS IDENTIFIERS FOR THE SAKE OF PUBLIC POLICIES

June 28, 2018

Like patent rights, which have been under attack because of its allegedly negative effects on access to pharmaceuticals; like copyrights, which have been criticized because of the barrier they might generate for the poor who wish to access culture and education; and like industrial designs, which have been censored because of their monopolist effects on spare parts necessary for repairing complex products; trademarks also have been under siege. The main attack has focused on trademarks for tobacco products, but the same public health concerns also have inspired the assault on trademarks for other regulated products, such as foodstuffs, infant formulae, etc. The debate has developed around trademarks' potential capacity to lure consumers to the consumption of unhealthy products. In taking measures against that capacity, governments have introduced restrictive measures designated in general as "plain packaging," which restraint the colors, sizes and figurative presentation of trademarks, thus reducing—when not eliminating completely—their distinctive function.

Several bodies of the United Nations have encouraged Member States to actively engage in the fight against the alleged effect that those trademarks have in inducing the consumption of unhealthy products. In that sense, the World Health Organization (WHO) approved, in February 2005, the Framework Convention on Tobacco Control (FCTC) and, jointly with the United Nations' Children's Fund (UNICEF), in May 1981, the International Code of Marketing of Breast-milk Substitutes. In both texts there is language that recommends Member States to impose restrictions on, or even to eliminate, the use of certain trademarks used to differentiate those products.

Some countries have challenged one of those initiatives in regard of tobacco trademarks in the dispute settlement mechanism of the WTO. The arbitration panels, reunited in one single panel, issued a Report that concluded in favor of Australia, which in 2011 had passed a law requiring the plain packaging of tobacco. The appeal is pending at the time of this writing. The text that follows has been extracted from that Report.

Australia—Certain Measures Concerning Trademarks, Geographical Indications and Other Plain Packaging Requirements Applicable to Tobacco Products and Packaging

Reports of the Panels

WT/DS435/R, WT/DS441/R WT/DS458/R, WT/DS467/R

June 28, 2018

7.2604. Overall, we are not persuaded that the complainants have demonstrated that Australia has acted beyond the bounds of the latitude available to it under Article 20 to choose an appropriate policy intervention to address its public health concerns in relation to tobacco products, in imposing certain special requirements under the TPP [Tobacco Plain Packaging] measures that encumber the use of trademarks in the course of trade. While recognizing that trademarks have substantial economic value and that the special requirements are far-reaching in terms of the trademark owners' possibilities to extract economic value from the use of figurative or stylized features of trademarks, we note that the TPP measures, including their trademark restrictions, are an integral part of Australia's comprehensive tobacco control policies, and designed to complement the pre-existing measures. As noted above, the fact that the special requirements, as part of the overall TPP measures and in combination with other tobacco-control measures maintained by Australia, are capable of contributing, and do in fact contribute, to Australia's objective of improving public health by reducing the use of, and exposure to, tobacco products, suggests that the reasons for which these special requirements are applied provide sufficient support for the application of the resulting encumbrances on the use of trademarks. We further note that Australia, while having been the first country to implement tobacco plain packaging, has pursued its relevant domestic public health objective in line with the emerging multilateral public health policies in the area of tobacco control as reflected in the FCTC [United Nations Framework Convention on Tobacco Control] and the work under its auspices, including the Article 11 and Article 13 FCTC Guidelines.

CHAPTER 3

Trade Secrets

§3.01 IN BABYLON, AN INDIRECT METHOD OF KEEPING CONTROL OVER TRADE SECRETS

Circa 1,750 BC

The Code of Hammurabi is an early (but not the first) codification of rules that concern many aspects of the social life of Mesopotamia, including trade. The combination of two of its rulings (which have received the modern designation of "laws")—"Laws" 188 and 189—implies not only a sanction in the case the artisan would have breached the contract of apprenticeship he had entered with the apprentice's family (and failed to train the apprentice), but also, in the case he had trained him, that he could retain control over the apprentice and, consequently, over the transmitted knowledge. Therefore, the apprentice's family would not be able to transfer him (along with his acquired knowledge) to another artisan.

Here we have here a mix of elements of contract law, of family law, of prevention of unfair competition (prohibition of interference in contracts, known by the French term of "débauchage"), and of appropriation of technical knowledge.

In order to understand the social context of this rule, two considerations should be made. First, adoption was a mechanism commonly used in Babylon for master artisans to obtain cheap labor. Second, unlike artists, who usually were hosts in the royal palace and lived from royal patronage, a significant number of artisans owned their shops and tools, and would engage in private trade. They would sell their crafts in exchange of money or goods. They were, therefore, private businessmen, and would naturally face the competition of other artisans, likewise carrying out private businesses. Therefore, differentiating knowledge was a precious asset to them—as much as it is to today's manufacturers.

In 1994 the prohibition of interference in contracts was inserted in the TRIPS Agreement, through its note 10—a note to Article 39, which deals with confidential information, or trade secrets (*see* Text 3.25).

Paraphrasing Samuel Noah Kramer, we can affirm, without fear of error, that the Sumerians did not left us the legacy of a written codification of laws only—they also left us the first written norms on industrial property.

The Code of Hammurabi, "Laws" 188 and 189

§ 188. If an artisan has undertaken to rear a child and teaches him his craft, he cannot be demanded back.

§ 189. If he has not taught him his craft, this adopted son may return to his father's house.

§3.02 IN ANCIENT EGYPT, STATE SECRETS WERE PROTECTED

First Century BC

Laws protecting the owners of trade secrets from breach of confidence have taken a long time to emerge. In ancient times there was simply no social awareness on the importance of according to those persons in control of private commercial secrets the right to exercise such control against competitors. As in other fields of intellectual property, the passing of statutes dealing with that specific issue was preceded by the so-called "courtesy of the trade"—the practice of honest commercial rivals respecting each others' differentiating assets, under the Golden Rule, "Do not do unto others as you would not have them do unto you."

But as far as the protection of trade and military secrets as national assets was concerned, the scenario was different. Several sources inform us that since early times governments have had the concern to prevent other nations from having access to technical information, both of a commercial and military nature.

The text that follows, by Diodorus of Sicily, provides for an example of how state trade secrets were protected in Ancient Egypt.

In Egypt, the tongue would be severed of those who revealed some State secrets to enemies, and both hands of those who had made false coins or had used false weights and false measures or who had counterfeited the seals of the Prince or of private individuals.

§3.03 PROTECTION OF STATE SECRETS IN THE CODE OF JUSTINIAN

Sixth Century AD

Another example of the protection of state secrets by an early statute: the Corpus Juris Civilis (known as the Code of Justinian), Book IV. The Code was a collection of statutes, ordinances and jurisprudence, elaborated under Emperor Justinian I, of Byzantium, from 529 to 565.

The Code of our Lord the Most Sacred Emperor Justinian. Given at Constantinople, on the seventeenth day of the *Kalends* of December, during the Consulate of Our Lord Justinian, for the fourth time Consul, and of Paulus.

Book IV. Title LXIII. Concerning Commerce and Merchants.

3. [The Emperors Honorius and Theodosius] to Anthemius, Praetorian Prefect.

Not only merchants who owe allegiance to Our government, but also those who are subject to the King of the Persians, must not hold markets beyond the places agreed upon at the time of the treaty concluded with the above-mentioned nation, in order to prevent the secrets of either kingdom from being disclosed (which is improper). Therefore, no subject of Our Empire shall hereafter presume to travel for the purpose of selling merchandise beyond Nisibis, Callini-cum, and Artaxata, nor think that he can exchange merchandise anywhere beyond the above-mentioned cities. All persons are hereby notified that if one makes a contract under such circumstances, any merchandise which has been either sold or purchased beyond said cities shall be confiscated by Our Treasury, and, in addition to this, the price which was paid, or any articles given in exchange shall be surrendered, and the offender sentenced to the penalty of perpetual exile. [...]

§3.04 TRADE SECRETS AND ALCHEMY

April 3, 1337

The text that follows is an early account of a dispute over a trade secret that an alchemist alleged to have been forcefully taken from him. The mere existence of the dispute suggests that in the fourteenth century the control over trade secrets may have already been acknowledged as an enforceable right.

Calendar of Patent Rolls, Edward III, Part I, at 445.

Commission of oyer and terminer to John de Pulteneye, mayor of London, Robert de Scardeburgh and William Scot, on complaint by Thomas de Eboraco that, whereas he by the science of alchemy had forged silver plates and had them proved by goldsmiths and others of the city of London, one Thomas Corp of London, 'spicer,' and others plotting to disturb him maliciously took him by night at the said city and brought him to the house of the said Thomas Corp there, and made him bring with him an elixir (*quoddam elixerium*) and some other instruments wherewith he made such silver, and to compel him to teach them the art, imprisoned him there until through fear of death he forged silver by his art in their sight, and made two bonds to the said Thomas in 100*l.* each, and carried away the elixir and instruments with other goods, and that they afterwards, by pretext of the bonds, although he was never bailiff of the said Thomas Corp or receiver of any of his moneys, before the mayor and sheriffs of the city they called him to account before auditors appointed for this for the sums in the bonds and arrears and procured him to be adjudged to Newegate gaol until he satisfied him of these, whereby he had been long and still remains in the said gaol. By pet. of C., and by fine of 1/2 mark.

§3.05 EDWARD III AND HIS SECRET DEALINGS WITH THE BANKING SOCIETY OF THE PERUZZI

—August 18, 1337

Edward II and III would frequently resort to the financial help of two banking societies of Florence: the Bardi and the Peruzzi. The text that follows acknowledges the receipt by the bankers of the sum of 2,000 £ under the pretext of their having paid for some "great and secret business" on behalf of Edward III. Probably this sum corresponds—at least in part—to the payment of disguised interests, which at that time were prohibited under usury laws. But it is not impossible that the bankers may have also engaged in some secret business deals for the English king. There is an abundance of documents in the Calendar of Patent Rolls showing that English kings would hire the services of foreigners to do espionage for them. Conversely, English sovereigns would repress severely those who would take English secrets abroad.

Acquittance to the king's merchants, John Baronshel, John Stephani, Thomas de Peruchiis and the other merchants of the society of the Peruzzi, for 2,000*l.* lately received by them from William de la Pole, as appears by letters of receipt returned by him into the Exchequer, which they have paid for some great and secret business in foreign parts as the king gave them command by word of mouth.

Mandate to the treasurer and barons of the Exchequer to cancel the said letters of receipt.

§3.06 CONTRACT OF APPRENTICESHIP CONTAINING A SECRECY CLAUSE, ENGLAND, 1459

April 1, 1459

Very rarely the by-laws of guilds would contain clauses on the mandatory protection of the secrets of the trade. The probable reason was that those by-laws were mainly addressed to the masters, who did not need to be reminded of the importance of keeping those secrets for themselves. Next we will see one of the few exceptions to that (*see* Text 3.7).

However, in hiring the services of apprentices, some masters would be careful in including a clause requiring the apprentices to keep the secrets they would receive in the course of their training. The text that follows is an example of one of such clauses.

This indenture made between John Gibbs of Penzance in the county of Cornwall of the one part and John Goffe, Spaniard, of the other part, witnesses that the aforesaid John Goffe has put himself to the aforesaid John Gibbs to learn the craft of fishing, and to stay with him as apprentice and to serve from the feast of Philip and James next to come after the date of these presents until the end of eight years then next ensuing and fully complete; throughout which term the aforesaid John Goffe shall well and faithfully serve the aforesaid John Gibbs and Agnes his wife as his masters and lords, shall keep their secrets, shall everywhere willingly do their lawful and honourable commands, shall do his masters no injury nor see injury done to them by others, but prevent the same as far as he can, shall not waste his master's goods nor lend them to any man without his special command. And the aforesaid John Gibbs and Agnes his wife shall teach, train and inform or cause the aforesaid John Goffe, their apprentice, to be informed in the craft of fishing in the best way they know, chastising him duly and finding for the same John, their apprentice, food, clothing linen and woollen, and shoes, sufficiently, as befits such an apprentice to be found, during the term aforesaid. And at the end of the term aforesaid the aforesaid John Goffe shall have of the aforesaid John Gibbs and Agnes his wife 20s. sterling without any fraud. In witness whereof the parties aforesaid have interchangeably set their seals to the parts of this indenture. These witnesses: Richard Bascawen, Robert Martyn and Robert Cosyn and many others.

Given at Penzance, 1 April in the 37th year of the reign of King Henry the Sixth after the Conquest of England.

§3.07 THE TRADE SECRET OF MASONS

1459

In the Middle Ages, one of the most famous trade secrets was the secret of the masons. Masons organized in guilds (namely, that of Strasbourg) would swear not to disclose the secret of the elevation of a pinnacle from the measurement contained in the ground plan—in common terms, the circle's quadrature. That secret, however, was already known to some persons outside the guilds. One century earlier, Villard d'Honnecourt, the medieval itinerant architect, had disclosed it in his sketch book.

The text that follows is Article 13 of the by-laws of German mason lodges, approved in Regensburg, in 1459, and confirmed in 1498 by Emperor Maximilian I, compelling masons to keep their professional secret. This clause is, to some extent, exceptional. As said in the previous note, guilds' members did not need, in general, to be reminded of the importance of keeping their knowledge to themselves. The exception may be due to the particular nature of the associations of masons, which have kept a strong religious nature, in parallel with their professional conformation, as shown by the symbolism of many of the thousands of masons' marks inscribed on the stones of cathedrals and castles throughout Europe

Also no workman, nor master, nor parlier, nor journeyman shall teach anyone, whatever he may be called, not being one of our handicraft and never having done mason work, how to take the elevation from the ground plan.

§3.08 ANOTHER CONTRACT OF APPRENTICESHIP CONTAINING A SECRECY CLAUSE, FRANCE, 1535

June 8, 1535

In the name of God, it be done, Amen. To all be manifest that, in the year one thousand five hundred and thirty five and on the eighth day of June, in front of me, undersigned notary public and the witnesses hereunder named, existing and personally constituted Symon de Despit, alias Guilhomet, son of honest man Pierre of Despit, the elder, of the jurisdiction of Rochefort, who, in his good, pure and frank will, on behalf of himself and his heirs and any successors, under the license and authority of the mentioned Pierre the Elder, his father, servant, to master Pierre Gobert, clothmaker of the city of Romans, here present on behalf of himself and of his heirs and any successors, stipulating and accepting and Symond as apprentice for learning and practicing the art and craft of clothmaking, which the mentioned Gobert uses and that is by the term and period of three continuous years next already begun on the first day of May last and passed, during which, for three years, Symond de Despit, apprentice, will be held liable, up to his power and possibility, for duly and faithfully serving and obeying the master Pierre Gobert, his master, and his family in all lawful and honest things, and not revealing his secrets, escaping and avoiding his injury, treating his profile and honor, and Gobert similarly will be required to duly and honestly nourish and treat Symond, apprentice, and, up to his power and faculty, show and teach him the art and craft of clothmaking, . . . and thus promised and swore the masters Pierre Gobert, Pierre and Symond de Despit, Symond, under license of Peter, his father, and promises, by means of their oaths by them and each of them, touching the scriptures on the holy gospels of God made and ready and under obligation. . . and were made and publicly recited the things above said in the city of Romans and in my shop, notary, present Glaude Burel, master Glaude Bonardel, potter of the city of Romans, Glaude Falonnet of Saint John d'Alteveon, Sabastin Julhian of the place of Tein, residents, called as witnesses.

And I, Jehan de Aqua, notary, by apostolic and public dalphinal authorities of the city of Romans, on behalf of master Pierre Gobert undersigned. De Aqua.

§3.09 MEDICAL TRADE SECRETS

1550

The medical profession has for long been the subject of secrecy, as an informal but effective way of ensuring the competitive advantage of professionals often engaged in bitter commercial rivalry. Medical procedures and medicines' formulae were reserved as confidential information, sometimes with the blessing of authorities, which would not hesitate to grant privileges on their commercial exploitation. In the text that follows French historian Alfred Franklin briefly describes the facts involving a secret method of extracting stones from the gall bladder, which would have been invented in France.

In Paris, [the lithotomy] remained for a long time the specialty of a family whose members kept the secrets and passed on to one another certain chirurgical procedures. Laurent Collot or Colot, surgeon of Henry II and lithotomist of Hôtel-Dieu, taught his method to his son, who applied it successfully. He had a son, a third Laurent Colot, whose skills equaled that of his ancestors. This one gave birth to Philippe Colot, *peritissimus artifex*, . . . he himself afflicted by the stone, was operated his son, and his nephew, who was associated in his labors. Severin Pineau, his son-in-law, put in possession of the famous secret, thought his duty to divulge it; but the Colots did not for that reason ceased to practice their art, and two of them, Jerome and Francis, left a famous name.

§3.10 A FRENCH INDUSTRIAL PRIVILEGE FOR A TRADE SECRET: THE MANUFACTURE OF GLASS IN THE MANNER OF VENICE

June 15, 1551

For many years—until the disclosure requirement was incorporated into patent laws, in the seventeenth century—governments would not hesitate to award industrial privileges to inventors or introducers of new inventions that presented a particular interest, without requiring them to disclose and teach their techniques before the expiry of the privilege. Actually, in many cases those privileges, or the promise of their being granted, served as the bait that lured skilled foreign artisans to migrate and bring with them their coveted technical knowledge (as well as tools and apprentices).

Conceptually, this privilege does not differ significantly from those privileges granted in the fourteenth century to the Flemish artisans who brought to England their techniques of working on wool clothes (*see* Texts 1.9 to 1.11).

Letters patent that grant to an Italian the exclusive privilege of manufacturing, during 10 years, glassware in the manner of Venice, of which he had imported the Secret into France

Châteaubriant, June 15, 1551; recorded at the Parliament of Paris, on 3 February 1552.

HENRY, etc. We have received the humble supplication of our dear and well-loved Theses Mutio, an Italian gentleman, a native of Boulogne the Grace, stating that, under the persuasion of some noble persons of our kingdom, he would have departed from his country of Italy, and come to live in this kingdom to melt and make glasses, mirrors, units of measure [*canons*] and other kinds of glassware in the manner of Venice.

Whereas, in doing so, he could not bring with him the tools and other instruments necessary for his art, once arrived in our kingdom, so as to set up his furnaces, fonts, and other things fit for the art, before he could work in our kingdom, he would have been compelled to make and order new tools and other things necessary to that art, with enormous and significant costs and expenses.

And now that the whole thing is written in the required form and so much that the works that come out of it are commonly found with the same beauty and excellence as those one wanted to bring from the said Venice, he fears that some other glassmakers would attempt to counterfeit his said work in the manner of Venice, and by this means to frustrate him of the refund of the said costs and expenses [incurred] by him at his arrival and beginning sustained and done in our said kingdom, if by us this were not provided to him.

We make known that we, well advised of the causes that would have led the said Mutio to be transported to our kingdom to work and make there the mentioned glasses, mirrors, units of measure, and other sorts of glassware, in the said manner of Venice, and the honorable and useful convenience that results to our republic from it. For this reason, we wish to give him the means of repaying himself and rewarding of the mentioned costs and expenses.

To Theses Mutio we have given and granted, and of our certain science, full power and royal authority, give and grant faculty, permission and express privilege that during the term of the next ten years, he can, alone, make or order in our kingdom the mentioned glasses, mirrors, units of measure and other kinds of glassware in the said manner of Venice and to offer or have them offered for sale in our kingdom and elsewhere, wherever he sees fit: making inhibitions and prohibitions to all glassmakers, merchants and sellers of glasses of our kingdom, country, lands and lordships of our obedience that during the said term of ten years they make or order or offer for sale glasses, mirrors, units of measure or other kinds of glassware in the said manner of Venice, if they are not of those that would have been made by said Theses Mutio or by his command, and this under the penalty of confiscation of said glasses, mirrors, units of measure and other things and an arbitrary fine.

We thus order, etc. By the king, you (the Chancellor) present.

§3.11 ANOTHER FRENCH INDUSTRIAL PRIVILEGE FOR A TRADE SECRET

January 14, 1666

The text that follows concerns an industrial privilege for a trade secret (a method for tanning and currying leather). According to the text, it seems that the initial privilege did not satisfy the inventor entirely, for it covered the process of tanning only. Under the regime of corporatism then in force, and because the process of finishing leather and hides was the monopoly of curriers, the inventor feared that the privilege would not exempt him from sending his leathers and hides to the curriers. Thus, he asked the King for an extension of the privilege, in a way that it would also cover the acts of currying. Because, as mentioned before, medieval industrial privileges were primarily permissions to use, the required extension would imply a permission for the inventor to engage in that additional activity.

Patent Letters, interpreting those granted to Elie Bonnet, on November 6, 1666. Registered, in Parliament, on January 4, 1666; with modifications.
Louis [XIV], by the grace of God, King of France and of Navarra:

To our beloved and senior Councilors, the People holding our Court of Parliament in Metz, greetings. Having considered how much the manufacture of leather, and the preparation of all kinds of hides, is useful and necessary to our subjects, and having made our Council to examine the proposal of Elie Bonnet, a citizen of our good city of Paris, on tanning and preparing all kinds of leathers and hides of a new invention, and not yet used in our kingdom, more promptly and making the hides more beautiful and more perfect, because of their grain, color, strength and duration, We have, by our Patent Letters, addressed to you, of the 6th of November, 1666, upon the advice of the Lieutenant-Civil and Deputy to our Solicitor-General at the Châtelet of Paris, following the return to them on behalf of the said Bonnet, granted him the enjoyment, with the exclusion of all other persons, of the permission, grant, and privilege of practicing alone, in the extent of our Kingdom and the lands of our obedience, the mentioned new invention, by him proposed, to tan the hides and leathers of all kinds, and for this purpose, to establish the works and tanneries of the said invention in such cities and places of our Kingdom that he will see fit, during the time of twelve years.

But because the secret of the mentioned Bonnet is for the complete perfection of the leathers and hides, which consists in currying as well as tanning, and that, under the pretext that in our said letters the said privilege is not sufficiently extensive, it mentioning nothing else than tanning and preparing the leathers and hides, the Curriers might pretend to oblige the said Bonnet to pass through their hands, to have the leather and skins of his new factory curried, which would be of great consequence to him, and all the more so that, by this means, the secret of the said Bonnet would be imperfect, and said Curriers could alter and spoil the said leathers, to discredit the said factory and new invention, whereupon the said Bonnet would have required us to grant him our Letters to this necessary.

For these reasons, wishing that such a beautiful secret, so advantageous to our subjects, be given to the public, and not wanting it to remain without effect, under the pretext of the injuries that be made to the said Bonnet, we have declared and declare our intention to have been in granting, by our mentioned Letters of November 6th, 1666, the privilege of the said Bonnet, to tan and prepare all kinds of leathers and hides, to grant him likewise, as We grant him by these Present [letters], signed by our hand, the faculty and the privilege of currying or having curried, as well as tanning, all sorts of leathers and hides of his new manufactory and invention; and moreover we have discharged and exempted [him] from bringing to the leather markets those he will have manufactured, which he may sell in his shops and workbenches, provided he makes the necessary declarations at the offices of the control of the Revenue, and paying the corresponding fees.

And to prevent that frauds be committed and the new factory be counterfeited, we allow the mentioned Bonnet to affix his mark to the leathers and hides that he will have worked, and even to hold a clerk, if he thinks fit, at his own expense, in the mentioned leather markets, to prevent such abuses, and in the event of contravention, to order their seizure; to the charge by the said Bonnet to have apprentices, to make his secret public, after the expiry of the twelve years of his privilege, which apprentices will be received and admitted to the masterships of Tanners and Curriers, in the ordinary forms, in all the Cities of our Kingdom.

We order to all our Bailiffs, Senechals, their Lieutenants and other officials to whom it may concern, that they shall ensure that the said Bonnet and his representatives enjoy and use [the rights described] in our Letters of the 6th of November, 1666, the judgment of our Council of the last December, 1664, and these Present [Letters], fully and peacefully, ceasing and making to cease all disturbances and impediments to the contrary. We forbid all Tanners, Curriers and other persons, of whatever quality and condition they may be, to disturb them as to the effect and execution of the Present [Letters], under any pretext whatsoever, and to establish tanneries and curriers' shops of leathers and hides of the invention of the said Bonnet, to use totally or partly of the drugs, waters, liqueurs and preparations used in them, without his consent or of his associates, during the said time, under the penalty of disobedience, a fine of three thousand pounds, expenses, damages and interest; and to do this, to suffer, to obey and to compel all those to whom it may concern: for such is our pleasure. . . .

§3.12 KEEPING THE SECRETS OF TAILORS' TRADE IN ABERDEEN, SCOTLAND

February 18, 1678

Acts and Ordinances of the Tailor Trade of Aberdeen, ordained by John Forbes, deacon of the Trade

Anent [Concerning] Keeping the Secrets of the Craft.

18th February, 1678. In presence of Alexander Milne, deacon, it is strictlie statute and ordained unanimously be the haill traid that whatever entering freeman of the craft, or any other freeman thereof, shall anyways reveal or divulge to the Magistrates or any Burgess of Guild, directly or indirectly, any of the craft's secrets, especially anent their procedure when entering freemen of the traid, anent the composition or other expenses and debursements, that the person or persons so doing (being made out) shall never carry public charge amongst the said traid as deacon, maister, or boxmaster, until they give to the traid all satisfaction anent the said misdemeanour.

§3.13 ANOTHER MEDICAL TRADE SECRET: THE INVENTION OF THE FORCEPS

1762

Having invented the forceps, Dr. Peter Chamberlen kept it secret and only transmitted it to his brother and nephews, obstetricians like him. The family would go a long way in protecting the secret. The legend goes that when the Chamberlens were called for intervening in a difficult delivery, only those in possession of the secret would be allowed in the room. The forceps would be introduced in the room hidden inside an enormous wood box. The Chamberlens would then lock the doors, and while one of them would carry the medical procedure, the others would produce strange noises, including the ringing of bells. The secret would be sold by Hugh Chamberlen to a Dutch practitioner, Roonhuysen. But it would not be revealed until 1818, by means of a report submitted to the Royal Medical and Chirurgical Society of London by H.H. Cawardine, based on findings in the Chamberlen's estate.

The text that follows consists of excerpts from the preface by Hugh Chamberlen, Senior, to his translation into English of Dr. Mauriceau's textbook on midwifery (first edition published in 1762), making reference to his family's secret.

Courteous reader;

Having long observed the great Want of necessary Directions how to Govern Women with Child, and in Childbed, and also new-born Babes should be well ordered, I designed a small Manual to that purpose; but meeting sometime after in France with this Treatise of Mauriceau, (which, in my Opinion, far exceeds all former Authors, especially Culpeper, Sharp, Speculum Matricis, Sermon, &c., being less erroneous, and enriched with divers new Observations) I changed my Resolution into that of translating him; whom I need not such commend, because he is fortified with the Approbation of the Wardens of the Chirurgeons Company of Paris. . . .

In the 17th Chapter of the second Book, my Author justifies the fastening Hooks in the Head of a Child that comes right, and yet because of some Difficulty or Disproportion cannot pass; which I confess has been, and is yet the Practice of the most expert Artists in Midwifery, not only in England, but throughout Europe; and has much caused the Report, That where a Man comes, one or both must necessarily die; and is the reason of forbearing to send, till the Child is dead, or the Mother dying. But I can neither approve of that Practice, nor those Delays; because my Father, Brothers, and my Self (tho no one else in Europe as I know) have, by God's Blessing and our Industry, attained to, and long practiced a way to deliver Women in this Case, without any Prejudice to them or their Infans; tho all others (being obliged, for want of such an Expedient, to use the Common Way) do, and must endanger, if not destroy one or both with Hooks. By this manual Operation a Labour may be dispatched, (on the least Difficulty) with fewer Pains, and sonnoer, to the great Advantage, and Without Danger, both of Woman and Child. If therefore the use of Hooks by Physicians and Chirurgeons, be condemned, (without thereto necessitated through some monstruous Birth) we can much less approve of a Midwife's using them, as some here in England boast they do; with rash Presumption in France, would call them in Question for their Lives.

In the 15th Chapter of this Book, my Author proposes the Conveying sharp Instruments into the Womb; to extract a Head; which is a dangerous Operation, and may be much better done by our aforementioned Art, as also the Inconvenience and Hazard of a Child dying thereby prevented, which he supposes in the 27th Chapter of this second Book.

I will now take leave to offer an Apology for not publishing the Secret I mention we have to extract Children without Hooks, where other Artists use them, viz. there being my Father and two Brothers living, that practice this Art, I cannot esteem in my own to dispose of, nor publish it without Injury to them; and think I have not been unserviceable to my Country, although I do but inform them that the forementioned three Persons of our Family, and my Self, can serve them in these Extremities, with greater Safety than others. [...]

§3.14 THE KING OF FRANCE ACQUIRES A SECRET MEDICINE

January 15, 1681

Because in the seventeenth and eighteenth centuries the compositions of many medicines were kept secret—to the point that the term "secret" has become synonymous with medicine—, the king of France would with certain frequency buy the respective formulae of some of those that were deemed of particular interest and efficacy to treat common diseases, and submit them to the examination of the Palace's doctor. In the case the latter recommended its use, the formulae would be made public, along with recommendations on their use. The text that follows is an excerpt from a technical memory that discloses the secret formula and uses of an antipyretic medicine, known as the *remède de l'anglais*, mainly composed of an extract from quinine, which Louis XIV acquired in 1679 from a certain Talbot, Talbor or Tabor, for the sum of 48,000 pounds. In addition, the inventor received a knighthood and a pension for life in the amount of 2,000 pounds.

The practice of the acquisition and disclosure of medicine trade secrets would be regulated in 1810, through a Decree (mentioned above, *see* the note preceding Text 1.45).

Supplement of the Journal of Medicine, published by order of the King, on January 15, 1681.

I have spoken to you several times of the liberalities of the King towards a large number of individuals, from whom his Majesty has drawn the secrets of Medicine, with the intention of devoting them to the common utility of his subjects; and you have been so much less surprised that no one knows better than you the greatness of this incomparable Prince; but will you believe it Monsieur, all these rich presents, all his great rewards, this pension so considerable; in a word, all the good deeds that the English Doctor has received from him, have had for principle only the same paternal goodness of which we feel every day so many surprising effects.

Perhaps you have felt that he had bought so dearly the admirable Antipyretic of this Physician with the only purpose of reserving it for himself, and for the Princes and Princesses of His Royal Family; and I confess that any other Sovereign would have used it in this way; but such maxims are as much below the Character of the King, as he is above other men, by his virtue and glory; all these excellent medicines that he had published on different occasions, by the care and orders of his first Physician, are strong proofs of this; it is in this manner that this great Prince has found a sure means to spread over his subjects the most precious treasures of medicine, so that nothing is missing in their happiness; and it is on this same principle that he wishes to gratify the public of the English remedy, which I have just received by his order from the hands of Monsieur Daquin, his first physician, to deduce from it the nature and the properties, to justify its goodness, and to prescribe its adequate use. . . .

Thus to return to my own duty, and for the execution of the orders of which I have just been honored, I am going to confine myself in the character of simple Naturalist, to give you an exact description of the English Medicine, with the judicious observations of Monsieur the first Doctor on all his dependencies; to which I will add of my own the natural history of Quinquina, that of opium, several important remarks on fevers, and a new system on antipyretics, in which one will find some important reflections on the nature, on the proprieties and on the use of these kinds of medicines. . . .

§3.15 PROTECTION OF A TRADE SECRET THROUGH ADMINISTRATIVE MEASURES

February 10, 1681

Entrepreneurs frequently resort to their imagination to secure means for preserving their competitive advantages. This text is an example of that: an inventor, having invented a trick of magic, asked, first, for the king's authorization for showing his art to the public (in fairs and theaters, one can suppose). After securing it, he then requested the support of the police, so as to ensure order during the exhibitions, which only paying patrons could attend.

This is not intellectual property, of course. Nevertheless, it is a means for ensuring the extraction of revenue from a trade secret.

Permission to Philip Jouilliani Scotto, Roman, water-swallower, to be seen in public.

By the King.

His Majesty having regard to the very humble supplication that was made to him by the named Philippes Jouillani Scotto, Roman, to accept to grant him permission to show in public his invention of swallowing a large amount of water and to rejecting it immediately in different colors and smells, His Majesty has allowed him and allows him to be seen both in his good city of Paris and in all the other cities and places of his kingdom, and to take for this purpose the houses that will be indicated to him by the police officers, in payment of what it will be agreed. His Majesty commands and orders to all said officers and others to whom it will concern to permit that the said Jouilliani Scotto and his associates enjoy the present permission without giving him any trouble or impediment. Done at Saint-Germain-en-Laye, the tenth day of February, one thousand six hundred and eighty-one. Signed: Louis, and lower: Colbert.

Permission to Philippi Jouilliani Scotto to place guards in the places where he is seen.

By the King.

His Majesty wishing to prevent any disorder in the place where the name Philippes Jouillani Scotto, who found the invention of swallowing a large quantity of water and rejecting it at the same time, will be seen, He makes very express inhibitions and prohibitions to all persons, of whatever quality and condition they may be, even to the officers of his house, to enter without paying, allowing the said Scotto to put two archers at the gate of the said place, who will be given to him by the short-dress criminal lieutenant, for the execution of this order. Done at Saint-Germain-en-Laye, the twentieth day of March 1681. Signed: Louis; and lower: Colbert.

§3.16 THE KING OF FRANCE GRANTS AN INDUSTRIAL PRIVILEGE FOR THE SECRET OF MAKING PORCELAIN

May 16, 1702

The privilege granted by Louis XIV to the widow and heirs of Pierre Chicanneau, founder of the porcelain factory of Saint-Cloud, is of particular interest. It excluded one specific person (another manufacturer, who had secured a privilege for the making of earthenware in Rouen) from its exclusive effects, but was enforceable against everybody else. Moreover, the privilege prohibited that anyone, without the family's consent, approached the factory as well as any places where the manufactured goods would be displayed for sale. The privilege had a duration of ten years, but did not impose the condition of the secret's disclosure upon its expiry.

The Saint-Cloud factory operated between 1693 and 1766, manufacturing imitations of Chinese and Japanese porcelain. The factory was shut down because of its inability to compete with better quality porcelain made elsewhere in France.

Louis, by the grace of God, King of France and Navarre, to all those who will see these letters, greetings; the graces and privileges which we have granted in favor of various manufactures to promote their establishment in our kingdom, having excited our subjects to make inquiries and to reach, by their application, the knowledge of the most hidden arts, the appointed Barbe Coudray, widow of Pierre Chicanneau, Jean, Jean-Baptiste, Pierre and Geneviève Chicanneau, brothers and sisters, children of the said Coudray and of the said Pierre Chicanneau, and entrepreneurs of the factory of earthenware and porcelain established in Saint-Cloud, would have very humbly shown us that said Pierre Chicanneau father having applied himself several years to the factory of earthenware, and having arrived at a high point of perfection in this factory, would have liked to push his knowledge further and to find the secret of making real porcelain; for that he would have made several experiments of different materials, and tried different preparations that had produced works almost as perfect as the porcelains of China and the Indias. His children, whom he had brought up to the work of the factory, and to whom he had taught all that he had found, have, since his death, continued the same application, and have finally arrived, before the year six hundred and six hundred ninety-six, to the point of being able to make real porcelain of the same quality, more beautiful and also perfect and proper for the same purposes as the porcelain of China and the Indias, according to the testimony of the most skillful and the most capable persons of judging them, and that they were in a position to give to this factory, whose trade would be very advantageous to the kingdom, all the extent that it can have, if it pleased us to grant them the graces and privileges necessary to withdraw from the establishment of this manufactory, which they will do at their expense, all the profit that they can hope for, and to compensate themselves for the great expenses in which they have been obliged to incur to acquire the knowledge of the porcelain factory, and to put it in a position to make an enterprise from it and to succeed in it; that this manufacture would have already seemed to us so advantageous to our kingdom that we would have granted letters patent containing several privileges in favor of the named Saint-Etienne to make the factory at Rouen and in the other places of our obedience that he would have deemed appropriate, with prohibition to all persons to make factories of this manufacture; that for this the said Saint-Etienne has not done more than approaching this secret and never brought it to the same point of perfection or execution that the applicants have put it, and did not go beyond manufacturing earthenware, and since his death, which happened several years ago, neither his wife, who has always continued to make earthenware, nor anyone on his part did anything in porcelain and that therefore we could, without doing wrong to the said Saint-Etienne and his successors, grant the same privilege and the same general exclusion for the porcelain factory only, being certain that no one else executes it in the kingdom and never has executed the secret as they do. To these causes and others exposed to us, being well informed of the good quality, the beauty and the perfection of the porcelain manufactured by the said Chicanneaux and their capacity and skill in the art of making it, and the great expenses in which they have incurred to acquire the knowledge of this art to the point that they possess it, and that the establishment of this factory could be very advantageous to the kingdom, and desiring to treat the applicants favorably; on the advice of our council and our certain Science, full power and royal authority, we have by the present [letters] signed with our own hand, allowed and granted, allow and grant to Barbe Coudray, widow of Pierre Chicanneau, Jean, Jean-Baptiste, Pierre and Geneviève Chicanneau, both jointly and separately, their heirs and successors, that they establish in the borough of Saint-Cloud and in such cities and other places of our kingdom as they please, except the city and suburbs of Rouen, one or more factories for the making of fine porcelain of all colors, types, ways and sizes; we also allow the said Coudray and Chicanneau to continue the manufacture of earthenware in the said borough of Saint-Cloud and to work in earthenware of all colors, types, ways and sizes in all cities and places where they will establish porcelain factories, and to sell as wholesale and in retail in all cities and places of our kingdom the porcelain and earthenware of their manufacture. We prohibit any person of any quality whatsoever, except the mentioned Saint-Etienne, his heirs and successors, to undertake to make porcelain in any place of our kingdom, lands, lordships and countries of our obedience, whatever they are, even in the places deemed privileged, during the time and period of ten years, beginning on the first day of next October, under the penalty of seizure of the goods made, materials and tools used for the said manufacture and fine of three thousand pounds. We also expressly prohibit all persons, under the pretext of mastery, membership of a guild [*jurande*] or otherwise, to visit the premises of the factories of the said Coudray and Chicanneau or the places where the sale and delivery of their merchandise will be made, to disturb them in the making, selling and delivering of porcelain and earthenware of their factories, and to demand from them any sum for taxation or any other cause, except the charges of the community of masters enamels of the community, unless he joins the guild of the said community, if he so desires. We have exempted and exempt Barbe Coudray, widow of Pierre Chicanneau, Jean, Jean-Baptiste, Pierre and Geneviève Chicanneau, both jointly and separately, their heirs and successors of all taxes, exactions and ordinary and public charges of the borough of Saint-Cloud, ... Thus we instruct our beloved Councilors, the people holding our Court of Parliament, the Chamber of Accounts, the Paris Court of Assistants, and all our other officers of justice, that they register the present [letters], and its contents, so that the said Caudray and Chicanneau enjoy them fully and peacefully, for this is our pleasure. Given at Versailles on the sixteenth day of May, the year of grace one thousand seven hundred and two, of our reign the sixtieth. Signed Louis . . . .

§3.17 JUDGMENT BY THE STATE COUNCIL OF LOUIS XV, OF FRANCE, ACCORDING EXCLUSIVITY TO A SECRET RECIPE OF A MEDICINE AGAINST APOPLEXY

August 2,1748

In the eighteenth century, in France, exclusivity in trade secrets was a settled matter, as this judgment shows. No special arguments or justifications were necessary for the State Council to acknowledge exclusivity in the secret formula of a medicine—the verification of precedence was enough to persuade the Council to exclude the later comer from making and selling the medicine.

Since the early Middle Ages, attempts by pharmacists to secure exclusivity in new medicines have been subject to two lines of tension. One concerned the tension between the mandatory use of common names to designate medicines *versus* trademarks (early regulations enacted in Venice, in 1258, would oblige pharmacists to use common names; in France, by contrast with other professions, the by-laws of the guilds of apothecaries would not mention the use of marks, either of certification or of trade). The other line of tension concerned the private appropriation of knowledge, between the acknowledgement and protection of trade secrets and the granting of industrial privileges. In France, pharmacists would in general prefer trade secrets. In England, after the passing of the Statute of Monopolies, inventors of new medicines would frequently apply for (and obtain) patents.

Judgment of the State Council of the King,

Which keeps Mr. Arnoult Merchant Pharmacist, Cinq-Diamans Street, in Paris, with the right to compose, sell and distribute alone the Anti-Apopletic Medicine and Specific against Apoplexy, of which he and his late father have been in possession since almost 50 years. Prohibits Ms. Rhodès, widow Arnoult, and all others to compose, sell and distribute the same Medicine, under the pretext that they would have the Secret of said Mr. Arnoult, under the penalty of a fine of 1000 lbs., and abolishes the Printout in the form of Opinion of the said Ms. Rhodès, widow Arnoult.

Of August 2, 1748.

Extract from the Records of the Council of State.

On the Motion presented to the King, present in his Council, by Louis Arnoult, Merchant Grocer-Wholesaler-Pharmacist, containing that since the year 1701, he is by him and by Guillaume Arnoult his father, in the right and the possession of composing and selling alone the true Specific against Apoplexy. Guillaumme Arnoult himself received the Recipe from an Italian who had brought it to France, and who presented it to him as a token of gratitude, nevertheless under the seal of secrecy, promising by Sr. Arnoult never to make public the preparation of this medicine. Faithful to this commitment, Guillaume Arnoult alone composed and distributed the Specific in question, until, fearing death, and that the public was deprived of the great and inestimable advantages they derived from it, he confided it to the Plaintiff alone, who is the only person in France, and perhaps in Europe, who has the true secret of this Specific. The good effects it has produced in the Court and the City, in the Provinces of the Kingdom and among foreigners, are well-known and such that there is not one person who has used it that has not been cured or preserved from relapse of Apoplexy. The late Cardinal de Polignac has dedicated it the greatest of appraisals at the Academy, even citing a dozen Lords his relatives and friends who were healed by the use of the said Medicine; the late Dame Princess of Guise spoke of it with the same advantages; the late Cardinal of Fleury and the late Hérault know and protect it; Messrs. Dukes of the Force . . . and others are in a position to certify the same to His Majesty. The fact has been attested by non-suspicious testimonies of persons of every state and every country; in particular famous doctors both of His Majesty and of various Medical Schools, as well as skillful Surgeons who have seen the wonderful effects of the said Specific. The Gazettes and Newspapers have even mentioned it for several years; many people were very jealous of the progress of this Medicine, and spared nothing to take it from Mr. Arnoult, or to make him lose the high reputation he has acquired. The attacks he has suffered only served to strengthen this reputation. Among the false Imitators of this Specific, there is only one alleged widow of Mr. Arnoult who had the audacity to announce herself to the Public through printouts, as having the real secret, having received it from her Ancestors, and always having distributed it successfully. Everything in this proposition is tainted with falsity. There is no widow Arnoult; the one who adorns herself with this quality is the wife of Mr. Rhodès. She had actually for first husband a brother of the Plaintiff, but this brother has never had the secret of this anti-Apoplectic Specific: Mr. Arnoult father did not entrust it, as he declared on December 30, 1734, other than to the Plaintiff. Never his other son, let alone his widow, today Mr. Rhodès' wife, has had the said secret, hence she has not distributed it; it is therefore only to impose herself on the Public and to confront them that the wife of Mr. Rhodès announces herself as the widow of Mr. Arnoult, and attests to the Public that she has received from her Ancestors the anti-Apoplectic Medicine, and that she has always distributed it. [...] From such a bold action it follows not only that Ms. Rhodès does not possess the secret which she claims to have, but also that she makes a false Medicine capable of producing two dangerous effects: one of making the true secret, of which the Plaintiff is the only holder, to lose the Public reputation, which it has justly acquired; the other of causing much harm, either by not having the effect which is guaranteed on the part of the true Specific, or even by operating badly on those who would use it, who would never be compensated for the loss of their money, and moreover would run a clear risk of life. These misfortunes are more to be feared, that the Plaintiff, who has had one of her Sachets against Apoplexy collected in Ms. Rhodès' shop, dares to attest to His Majesty that at the only sight it is possible to judge the difference between this false Medicine and the true one. He speaks with all the more confidence, that in the end it is physically impossible for Ms. Rhodès to compose this Medicine in the same way as the Plaintiff, as well as the late Mr. Arnoult his father. The public interest does not allow such an attempt to be tolerated. . . . If it were true that Ms. Rhodès had always and successfully composed and distributed her anti-Apoplectic Medicine, she would have proofs of it; she is challenged to produce only one.

Pleading on these grounds, the plaintiff [requests] that it please to His Majesty to maintain him and retain in right and possession, such as he and his late father have been since almost fifty years, of composing, selling and distributing alone the anti-Apoplectic Medicine and the Specific against Apoplexy, taking all the precautions he deems appropriate for its safety and that of the Public; To prohibit Ms. Arnoult, and all others of whatever quality, to compose, sell, or distribute any Medicine of the same quality and as if it came from Mr. Arnoult, for whatever cause and under any pretext whatsoever, under such penalty as His Majesty deems fit; To order that the Printout by which the alleged widow of Mr. Arnoult gave notice that she has the secret of said Medicine, which she has received from her Ancestors, and which she has always distributed successfully, will be and will remain removed; To enjoin Ms. Rhodès, claiming to be widow Arnoult, to bring in twenty-four hours to the Police Court, at the Châtelet of Paris, all the copies she may have of the said Printout, to be destroyed; to prohibit her and all others, to have others printed, and to all the Printers to print them, also on such penalties as appropriate; Allow the supplicant to print, display, publish and distribute the Judgment that will be made on the Motion, together with such notice or instruction as he deems appropriate. [...]

Heard the Report, the King being in his Council, having regard to the Motion, has maintained and maintains the said Arnoult in the possession of which he and his Father have been for nearly fifty years of composing, selling and delivering alone the anti-Apoplectic medicine and Specific against Apoplexy; Prohibits Ms. Rhodès and all others, of whatever status and quality they are, to compose, sell and deliver the same Remedy on the pretext that they would have the secret of the said late Arnoult, under the penalty of a fine of one thousand pounds, half being due to the whistleblower, and the remaining to the said Arnoult, and all costs, damages and interests; Furthermore His Majesty orders that the Printout by which the said widow Arnoult gave notice that she has the secret of the said medicine and that she has received it from her Ancestors will be and will remain abolished; Enjoins the said Rhodès, widow Arnoult, to bring within twenty-four hours, from the date of the service of the present Judgment to the Police Court, at the Châtelet of Paris, all the copies she may have of said Printout to be destroyed; Prohibits her, and all others, to have it printed, sold, and distributed; His Majesty permits the said Arnoult to print, publish and display the present judgment wherever necessary, together with such advice and instruction that he will consider appropriate for the use of the said Anti-Apoplectic medicine. Done at the Council of State of the King, His Majesty being present, held at Compiegne on the 2nd of August, one thousand seven hundred and forty-eight. Signed [...]

§3.18 FRANCE ENACTS THE FIRST STATUTE EXPLICITLY PROTECTING TRADE SECRETS

1810

Although trade secrets have always been used by entrepreneurs as an informal, easy way of appropriating knowledge, the laws protecting them in a general and abstract manner started being adopted recently, and with a thrust that was much narrower than those French decisions mentioned above.

The example of France of defining the violation of trade secrets as a crime was followed by other countries, like Italy, which did the same in 1859 (but without the discriminatory element—against foreigners—of the French rule).

Article 418 of the French Penal Code, of 1810.

Every director, clerk or factory worker who has communicated to foreigners or to French persons residing abroad secrets of the factory in which he is employed, shall be punished with reclusion and a fine from 500 francs. to 2,00 francs.

If these secrets have been communicated to French nationals residing in France, the penalty shall be the imprisonment from three months to two years and a fine from 16 francs to 200 francs.

§3.19 AN ENGLISH COURT REFUSES TO ENFORCE EXCLUSIVITY IN A TRADE SECRET AGAINST A FORMER EMPLOYEE

June 23,1813

In 1813, in the UK confidentiality in the relationship between employer and employee was not yet protected, unlike France. The decision that follows expressed the understanding that, in the absence of a patent, there was no exclusivity in the formula of a secret medicine, and thus an injunction against the former employee who had been acquainted with the secret in reason of his job was not called for. Moreover, the employee had not assumed "the name and character of the original maker," which, in the court's view, eliminated the element of fraud.

Canham v. Jones

June 23, 1813. Plumer, V. C. of E. 2 V. B. 218.

The plaintiff being the proprietor of a secret medicine called "Velno's Vegetable Syrup," the defendant, who had been in the plaintiff's service, and had there become acquainted with a part of the secret, began to make and sell a spurious preparation under the same name. Demurrer to a bill for an injunction to restrain him from so doing allowed, on the ground that there was no exclusive right in a medicine, not protected by patent, such as to prevent the sale of a medicine under the same title by another person, the latter not assuming the name and character of the original maker.

§3.20 EARLY ENGLISH CASES INVOLVING TRADE SECRETS

1817 Onwards

As it happened with patent law, the law of trade secrets evolved gradually, step by step, as courts set the understanding that they should be protected against illicit access and use by others. At first, courts linked the protection of trade secrets to the existence of a relationship of confidence or, more broadly, of duty (which, besides confidence, includes contracts and other deals). Only later, when the illicit acquisition of trade secrets was associated with unfair competition, the link between them and confidence was diluted.

The following excerpts from English court judgments reveal that in the early nineteenth century the English society was already comfortable with the idea of enforcing rights in trade secrets, mostly based on the notion of breach of confidence or breach of duty. It is worth noticing that the majority of the judgments that follow concern medicines. As noted before, patenting new medicines was a common practice in England after the passing of the Statutes of Monopolies. But, as it happened in France, many English pharmacists would prefer the timewise indefinite duration of secrets.

Williams v. Williams

High Court of Chancery

March 14, 1817

This was a motion to dissolve an injunction which had been granted by the Vice-Chancellor to restrain the defendants and their agents "from divulging or exposing the secrets in the bill mentioned or either of them, and from making, preparing, vending, or selling the medicines or remedies therein mentioned, or either of them, or otherwise disposing thereof or interfering therein in any manner howsoever." The injunction had been obtained upon an affidavit stating that the plaintiff had for several years carried on an extensive practice in the cure of diseases of the eye, and was the sole inventor and owner of recipes for preparing medicines for those purposes; that, being desirous of promoting the success in life of his son Bramwell Williams, he acquainted him with the secret of making such medicines, and gave him the management of his dispensary with a view of taking him into partnership, if he should conduct the business from March 1817, to February 1818, (the day on which he would come of age) to the plaintiff's satisfaction; that he made a proposal to the defendant to such an effect, which the defendant accepted, and promised so to conduct himself with a view to its completion; that, having confidence in the defendant's integrity, he thereupon put him in possession of his floating stock of medicines and other things, and actually caused a draft of partnership articles to be prepared by his solicitor; that after the defendant had so taken upon himself the management of the business, instead of conducting himself according to his engagement with the plaintiff, he assumed the entire dominion over the concern, and endeavoured to exclude the plaintiff from all control therein, and, instead of keeping the secret communicated to him by the plaintiff for making the eye medicine, as he ought to have done, he communicated the same to his wife and to the defendant Harris, with a view to injure and ruin the plaintiff, and, upon his remonstrating with him, not only set him at defiance, but removed the various articles committed to his custody, and sold large quantities of such articles, and offered the medicines to sale, and threatened to prepare such medicines and to vend the same, and to sell and distribute various publications of the plaintiff relative thereto, and to divulge the secret; having, by such acts, deprived the plaintiff of the means of carrying on his business. . . .

The Lord Chancellor.

There can be no doubt that the Court was strictly regular in granting the injunction, except so far as it goes to restrain the defendant from divulging the secret.—If, on a treaty with the son, while an infant, for his becoming a partner when of age, the plaintiff had, in the confidence of a trust reposed in him, communicated to him this secret, and at the same time given him the possession of the articles mentioned in the bill; and, instead of acting according to his trust, the son had taken to himself the exclusive dominion over these articles, and begun to vend them without permission, it must be said that he had no right in any case so to act,—and that he was bound, either to abide by, or to waive, the agreement. If, then, he had intended to abide by the agreement, the injunction was so far right—and, if to waive it, he was bound to return the articles, and so far the injunction was also right in that case. Upon the plaintiff's affidavit, therefore, the injunction was properly granted as to this part of the case. But so far as the injunction goes to restrain the defendant from communicating the secret, upon general principles, I do not think that the Court ought to struggle to protect this sort of secrets in medicine. The Court is bound indeed to protect them in cases of patents, to the full extent of what was intended by the grant of the patent, because the patentee is a purchaser from the public, and bound to communicate his secret to the public at the expiration of the patent. Then, whether the principle can be extended to such a case as this—whether a contracting party is entitled to the protection of the Court in the exercise of its jurisdiction, to decree the specific performance of agreements, by restraining a party to the contract from divulging the secret he has promised to keep, that is a question which would require very great consideration. But the present case is not one which calls for the determination of it. If the defendant has already disclosed the secret, the injunction can be of no use. If he only threatens to disclose, it then becomes necessary to look at his affidavit; and by that he insists that what he has to disclose is no secret at all. Then how is the Court to try this question?—or what can the Court do with the case altogether? Upon the other part of the case there appears, by the defendant's affidavit, to be no ground for supporting the injunction.

Injunction dissolved.

Newbery v. James and Others

March 27, 1817

The Court will not interfere by Injunction to prevent the violation of an agreement, of which, from the nature of the subject, there could be no decree for a specific performance; as, for instance, to restrain the Defendant from imparting the secret of an invention which had been the subject of a patent long since expired. To support a patent, the specification should be so clear as to enable all the world to use the invention from the moment of the expiration of the patent.

The Bill stated that D. Robert James, deceased, "being the inventor and proprietor of certain pills for the gout, rheumatism, &c., and of a certain powder for the cure of fevers, &c., and being desirous to extend the circulation and use of the said medicines, and thereby to increase the profits to arise therefrom," applied to Newbery (the Plaintiff's father) to assist him in such design, which Newbery agreed to do upon the terms after-mentioned; and that thereupon certain articles of agreement were made and entered into between them, whereby James, for himself, his heirs, &c., covenanted with Newbery, his executors, &c., that he, James, his executors, &c., should, during the term of twenty-one years, prepare and make the aforesaid pills, and sell and deliver the same to Newbery at a certain rate therein mentioned, and should also prepare and make the aforesaid powder, and sell and deliver the same to Newbery at the rate therein mentioned, when and as often as he should have occasion to require the same respectively, to supply his customers; and should not sell or cause to be sold any of the said medicines, during the term, to any other person or persons (except in the course of his own private practice, and then not in the same form, or under the same title, nor at a lower rate than Newbery should sell the same to his customers); and, in order to protect the secret of preparing all or any of the said medicines from being lost, he thereby further covenanted to instruct Newbery in the true art and method of making and preparing the same, and to be at an equal expense with Newbery in obtaining a patent; Newbery on his part covenanting during the term to take the medicines from James as he should have occasion, and not to make or prepare, or cause or procure to be made or prepared, by any other person or persons, not to discover or make known to any person or persons the secret, art, or mystery of making or preparing, any of the said medicines, so long as James should continue to supply him; but to be at liberty to leave an account in writing, sealed up, how to prepare the same, to be opened by his representatives after his death, in order to instruct them therein.

By Indenture dated the 13th November 1747, between James and Newbery, reciting the articles of agreement, and letters patent of the same date, granted to James for the exercise of his invention during the term of fourteen years, and that Newbury and James had contributed in equal shares to the expense of procuring the same, it was witnessed that James, for the consideration therein mentioned, assigned to Newbery, his executors, &c., one moiety of the invention during the term of fourteen years mentioned in the patent; it being covenanted on the part of Newbery that nothing in the deed should be construed so as to alter or change the articles of the agreement, and that neither party should assign his respective interest in the patent without first offering the same to the other. . . .

The Bill (to which the executors, and the said R.G.G. James, and other parties interested in the will of R.H. James, were made parties), charging that the Defendants or some of them, had refused to supply the plaintiff as usual, according to the terms of the agreement, and that they threatened to communicate the secret of preparing the medicines, insisted on the indefinite continuance of the agreement so long as either party should desire, and prayed a specific performance, and an injunction to restrain the Defendants from disclosing or imparting the secret of making and preparing the medicines, other than and except to such persons, and in such manner, as in the several deeds and wills described; and also from selling or vending all or any of the said fever powders, pills, or medicines, to any persons, for sale or otherwise, other than and except to the Plaintiff, or with his consent or approbation.

Upon the filing of the bill, an application was made for an injunction only as to the sale of the medicines, which was granted, expressly without prejudice to any question that might be made as to the possibility of sustaining such an injunction. . . .

A motion was now made, on the part of the Defendants, to dissolve the injunction. . . .

March 27. The Lord Chancellor [Eldon] said, the difficulty in such a case was, how to decree the specific performance of the agreement. Either it was a secret, or it was none. If a secret, what means did the Court possess of interfering so as to enforce its own orders?—if none, there was no ground interfering. The Injunction being already granted *ex parte*, afforded no reason for its continuance, even though the answer had not materially varied the case made by the bill; it being granted without prejudice to any question that might be made in the cause. In this case, the medicines in question were the subject of a patent which had expired; and the agreement which the bill sought to enforce was an agreement, by which, independently of the patent, the proprietors had entered into covenants not to sell that which was the subject of the patent, except to each other. But, in order to support a patent, the specification should be so clear, as to enable all the world to use the invention as soon as the term for which it has been grated is at an end. Ten, with regard to the Analeptic Pills, for which no patent had been procured, if the art and method of preparing them were a secret, what signified an injunction, the Court possessing no means of determining on any occasion whether it had or had not been violated? This Court could do nothing but put the parties in a way to try their legal rights by an action. That was the utmost extent to which it would go, and he would not even order the Injunction to be continued in the meantime till an action should be tried. The only way by which a specific performance could be effected, would be by a perpetual injunction; but this would be of no avail, unless a disclosure were made to enable the Court to ascertain whether it was or was not infringed; for, if a party comes here to complain of a breach of an injunction, it is incumbent on him first to show that the injunction has been violated.

His Lordship concluded by saying, that he thought not to continue the injunction; and that, if he did not mention the case again, his opinion must be considered to be that the injunction must be dissolved,—the Defendants to keep an account of what they sell,—and the Court to give the parties the means of trying their rights in action, by removing out of their way the difficulty arising from the circumstance of the Plaintiff being one of Dr. James's executors.

Yowatt v. Winyard

High Court of Chancery

May 15, 1820

Mr. Wetherell moved, upon certificate of the bill filed and affidavit, to restrain the Defendant from making use of or communicating certain recipes for veterinary medicines, and from printing and publishing certain papers of directions for the mode of administering them, and of managing the animals while taking them.

The Plaintiff, who was the proprietor of the medicines, had employed the Defendant for some time as an assistant or journeyman, under an agreement, by which he was to have a salary, and to be instructed in the general knowledge of the business, but was not to be taught the mode of composing the medicines; he, some time since, left the Plaintiff, and entered into business for himself, and the Plaintiff had lately discovered that he had, while in his service, surreptitiously got access to his books of recipes, and copied them, and was now selling the medicines, with printed papers for administering them, which were almost literal copies of those composed by the Plaintiff. The Defendant had after wards offered, for a small salary, to agree not to divulge the recipes.

Mr. Wetherell, in support of the motion, distinguished the case from *Newberry v. James*, and *Williams v Williams*, as being an instance of breach of confidence towards an employer, in the manner of acquiring the knowledge, contending that though the Court might not protect a secret from disclosure by one to whom the proprietor had himself communicated it, yet it would, when the person sought to be restrained had clandestinely possessed himself of it. In those cases the knowledge was communicated for a particular purpose, and it was attempted to prevent the party from using it for any other; but here the first discovery was obtained by a breach of duty, and in violation of a positive agreement.

The Lord Chancellor granted the injunction, upon the ground of there having been a breach of trust and confidence; but confined it so as not to prevent the Defendant from administering the medicine to any animals then under a course, it being stated in the papers of directions that a sudden discontinuance would be prejudicial.

Bryson v Whitehead

High Court of Chancery

1822

This was a Bill for the specific Performance of an Agreement, for the sale of the Goodwill of a Trade, and of a Secret in Dying.

The Plaintiff had for many years carried on the trade of a Dyer in Spitalfields and had a particular mode of dying Bombazeens and Stuffs. None but himself and his Son-in-law, one Portlock, knew the secret of dying Stuffs in that mode; and this secret was esteemed of great value. In December 1820, Bryson being about to retire from Business, agreed to sell the Good-will of his trade, together with the Plant and Fixtures, to the Defendant for 1,500 /., and the exclusive benefit of the Secret for 1,000/. Heads of the Agreement in writing were signed by both Parties, and were expressed as follows: "Heads of Agreement between Mr. Bryson, of, &c. and Mr. John Whitehead, of, &c. Mr. Bryson possesses a Secret in the art of dying Bombazeens, Princes Stuffs, and other Goods, which is known to himself and Son-in-law, Samuel Portlock, only: Mr. Bryson is about to retire from his Business, and therefore he has agreed with Mr. Whitehead as follows: Mr. Whitehead is to pay him, for himself and Son, 1,000/. for the Secret, and 1,500/. for the Plant and Fixtures upon his Premises, and for the Goodwill of the Trade, and to have the Premises leased or assigned at the following Rents: [then followed a description of the Buildings, and the amount of the Rent]. Mr. Bryson to make the Secret known to Mr. Whitehead, and instruct him in the Art, and to make over the Trade and Goodwill, and use his endeavours to secure it to Mr. Whitehead, by circular Letters, and other usual means; and he is not himself to engage in the business of a Dyer for Twenty-years; and he is to engage that his Son-in-law will not divulge the Secret, or engage in the business of a Dyer for the same term as Mr. Bryson; and that neither of them shall do anything to prejudice Mr. Whitehead in the Trade of Mr. Bryson, and in securing and continuing the Business of the connections of Mr. Bryson; and he is to procure his Son-in-law to enter into an Engagement to the same effect to Mr. Whitehead: An Inventory of the Plant to be delivered, &c. Possession to be delivered to Mr. Whitehead on payment of the 1,000/., and a Circular immediately issued, so that the Trade may be continued in the usual manner, under the direction of Mr. W., with the assistance of Mr. Bryson, who is to divulge the Secret, and instruct Mr. W. there in immediately after the payment of the 1,000 /. . . .

Whitehead forthwith paid the 1,000/. and was put into Possession of the Trade, and had the Secret communicated to him.

Bryson and his Son-in-law soon afterwards executed a Bond to Whitehead in the common form, with a Penalty of 2,000/. reciting the Agreement, and with the condition, that they or either of them would not, for Twenty years, in any manner exercise the trade of Dyers within the distance of Fifty miles from Spitalfields, and would not, at any time, disclose the Secret.

Whitehead, however, thought that this Bond (which was prepared by Bryson's Solicitor) was not sufficiently restrictive, and that Bryson and his Son might, at any time, without incurring any Penalty, resume their trade at any place beyond the distance of Fifty miles from London; as at Kidderminster, Norwich, or in York shire, where Bombazeens and Stuffs are principally manufactured. For this reason he insisted on a Deed of Covenant more restrictive in its terms, and with Clauses for liquidated Damages in case of breach of the Agreement.

Disputes arose in consequence, as to the terms of the Deeds to be executed under the Agreement, . . . Mr. Heald, and Mr. Whitmarsh, for the Plaintiff.

Mr. Bell and Mr. Theobald, for the Defendant, submitted it to the judgment of the Court, whether the Agreement was of such a kind as could be carried into execution. It was the essence of the Agreement that neither Bryson nor his Son-in-law should, for Twenty years, carry on the Trade of Dyers. If, however, the Agreement was to be acted on so as to confine the Restriction on exercising the Trade to places within Fifty miles from London, then the Defendant would not have that Benefit which he had stipulated for by the Agreement; because the Plaintiff, or his Son-in-law, by removing to Norwich, or any other convenient Situation beyond the distance of Fifty miles, would come into direct competition with him. If considered as an Agreement not to exercise the trade of a Dyer anywhere for Twenty years, it was void by the policy of Law, Mitchell v. Reynolds. If, on the other hand, it was to be acted on so as to limit the Restraint on carrying on the trade to the distance of Fifty miles from London, the Defendant would lose the benefit for which he had contracted.

The Vice-Chancellor:—

Although the policy of the Law will not permit a general restraint of trade, yet a Trader may sell a Secret of Business, and restrain himself generally from using that Secret. Let the Master, in settling the Deed which is to give effect to this Agreement, introduce a general Covenant to restrain the use of the Secret for Twenty years, and a limited Covenant, in point of locality, as to carrying on the ordinary business of a Dyer, both Parties being willing that the Agreement should be so modified.

The Decree therefore referred it to the Master to settle a proper Deed.

Green and Others v. Folgham and Others

High Court of Chancery

1823

In 1791 William Singleton was possessed of a Recipe for making an Ointment called "Dr. Johnson's Ointment for the Eyes," the contents of which were known only to himself; and in the month of September in that year, upon the treaty for the Marriage of his Daughter Selina with Timothy Folgham, it was agreed that the Ownership Trust for her and of the Ointment, and the Recipe, should be settled, after the decease of Singleton and his Wife, for the benefit of Folgham and his intended Wife, and their Issue, in the manner after mentioned. Accordingly, by an Indenture dated the 12th of September, 1794, and made between Mr. and Mrs. Singleton of the first part, Mr. and Mrs. Folgham of the second part, and three Trustees, of whom the Defendant Church was the Survivor, of the third part, in pursuance of the Agreement, and in consideration of the Marriage which had then lately taken place, Singleton assigned to the Trustees the Proprietorship of the

Medicine, upon Trust for Singleton and his Wife, during their Lives, and the Life of the Survivor of them; and after the Survivor's decease, upon Trust for Selina Folgham, for her Life, for her separate use; and after her decease, upon Trust for Folgham for his Life: and it was declared, that if at the decease of the Survivor of these four persons there should be more than one Child of Folgham and his Wife, the Trustees should sell the Ownership of the Ointment, and the Money arising from the Sale should be laid out by the Trustees in their Names, on Government or Real Securities, for the benefit of such Children, in equal Shares, and to be transferred to them at the usual periods. And Mr. and Mrs. Folgham covenanted, that if any of their Children should survive them, they should discover to one or more of them the method of making the Ointment.

Mr. Singleton survived his Wife and Mr. Folgham; and on his death the Recipe was delivered to Mrs. Folgham. She, assisted by the Defendant, William Singleton Folgham, one of her Sons, made and vended the Ointment until about six months before her death; when, having previously communicated to him verbally the Secret of making the Ointment, she retired into the Country, and left him in the entire management of the Concern. In Jan. 1816 Mrs. Folgham died, leaving Issue the Plaintiff, Selina Elizabeth Green, (who afterwards married the Plaintiff Stephen Green,) the Defendant William Singleton Folgham, and three other Children, all of whom were then Infants. The Recipe was not found after Mrs. Folgham's death, and it was therefore believed that she had destroyed it. In March 1816, William Singleton Folgham came of Age; when Church, the surviving Trustee, conceiving that it would be more beneficial to the Parties interested, that W. S. Folgham should make up and vend the Ointment according to his Mother's instructions, for the benefit of himself and his Brothers and Sisters, than that the Secret should be sold, an Indenture, dated the 22nd day of June, 1816, was made between W. S. Folgham of the one part, and Church, and one Hall, of the other part; by which, after reciting that the Secret of making the Ointment had been communicated to W. S. Folgham by his Mother, for the benefit of himself and his Brothers and Sisters, W. S. Folgham covenanted to make up and sell the Ointment, and twice in every year to pay to Church and Hall four fifths of the clear profits, after deducting 25 percent, yearly from the gross Amount of the Sales, for his trouble. And it was declared that Church and Hall should stand possessed of the four fifths of the Profits, in Trust for Mr. and Mrs. Folgham's other Children.

W. S. Folgham made up and sold the Ointment, and disposed of the Profits according to the Provisions of this Deed. In March 1817, Mrs. Green came of Age; and on the 17th of September in that year, she, at W. S. Folgham's request, signed an Agreement to transfer to him all her Interest in the Ointment, in consideration of his paying an Annuity of 100 £. to her, and to the Plaintiff Stephen Green (to whom she was then about to be married) for their Lives; and on the 2nd of the same month she also, at W. S. Folgham's request, executed a Deed-Poll confirming the Indenture of the 22d of June, 1816. . . .

The Vice-Chancellor:—

It was stated, at the Bar, that the Defendant, W. S. Folgham, was a Purchaser of this Secret for a valuable Consideration, without notice of the Settlement; but no such case is made in his Answer. And, after the admission made by him in his Answer that he voluntarily considered himself as a Trustee for the Marriage Settlement, and after the execution of the Deed of June 1816, which is not impeached, he cannot successfully assert a personal Title to this Secret.

By the terms of the Marriage Settlement the Trustees were directed to sell this Secret upon the death of Selina Folgham; and, having no authority to deal with this subject as they have in fact dealt with it by the Deed of June 1816, that Deed is merely void against the younger Children, who were all then Infants. The subsequent Agreement of September 1817, by which Selina Green engaged to assign her Interest in the Secret to the Defendant for the Annuity therein stated, being abandoned at the Bar, is now out of the question. The Defendant, W. S. Folgham, being to be considered therefore as a Trustee of this Secret under the Settlement, the first relief to which the Plaintiffs are entitled is, that he should come to an Account for the Profits actually made by him since the death of his Mother, from the Sale of the Ointment, having a reasonable Allowance made to him for his time and trouble in preparing and vending the same. If this Secret could be made a subject of Sale, the Plaintiffs would be next entitled to ask from the Court that a Sale should be directed accordingly. But, inasmuch as the Court has no possible means either to communicate this Secret to a Purchaser with certainty, or to protect him in the enjoyment of it, a Sale becomes impracticable. But although the Court cannot direct a Sale, it has the power of taking a course which, in point of advantage, will be equivalent to the Plaintiffs. It can inquire what would be the Value of this Secret to sell, provided it could be made the subject of Sale; and the Annual Profits which have actually been made by the Sale of the Ointment from the death of the Mother will be a fair criterion by which that Value may be estimated.

I think that this Value is more fit for the consideration of a Jury than of the Master; and, after decreeing the Account of the Profits from the death of the Mother, in the manner which I have stated, I shall direct the Parties to proceed to an Issue at Law, in order to try what, at the date of this Decree, was the pecuniary Value of the Secret for the preparation of the Ointment in the Pleadings mentioned, called, "Dr. Johnson's Ointment for the Eyes, or the Golden Ointment." The circumstances, that the Plaintiff Selina Green's Interest in the Secret is made the subject of her Marriage Settlement, and that one or more of Mrs. Folgham's Children are still Infants, are not material for present consideration.

Let further Directions and Costs be reserved.

Morison v. Moat

House of Lords, Privy Council

August 5, 6, and 20, 1851

The facts, arguments, and authorities cited in this case are fully detailed in his honor's judgment. . . .

Sir George Turner, V.C. This was a motion for an injunction to restrain the defendant, William Crofton Moat, from making, compounding, or selling any medicine as "Morison's Universal Medicine," or as "Morison's Vegetable Universal Medicine," or from in any manner using the name of Morison in the manufacture or sale of any medicine; and from using the secret of compounding the said medicines, or any part thereof; and from communicating to any person or persons whomsoever the knowledge of the "ingredients whereof the said medicines are compounded, or the secret, or any part of the secret, of compounding the said medicines." The facts of the case, so far as they are undisputed, are these: James Morison was the inventor and sole proprietor of the medicine or medicines in question. By an indenture bearing date the 23rd of June, 1830, and made between James Morison of the one part, and Thomas Moat of the other part, reciting that James Morison was the inventor and sole proprietor of the medicine called or known by the name of "Morison's Vegetable Universal Medicine," the secret of making which he, Mr. Morison, had communicated to his son John; and then reciting "that James Morison, in consideration of the past services of the said Thomas Moat, and in further consideration that the said Thomas Moat should devote his whole time and attention to the conduct and promotion of the manufacture and sale of the said medicine or medicines, had agreed to take the said Thomas Moat into partnership with him in the manufacture and sale of such medicine or medicines upon the terms after mentioned;" it was witnessed that Morison and Moat were to be the partners in the profession and business of manufacturers and venders of the medicines for the term of twenty years and three quarters of a year, to commence and be computed from the 24th of June next ensuing, the day of the date of the indenture, upon the terms and under the provisions thereinafter contained; and the style of the firm was to be "Morison, Moat, & Co., Hygeists." The profession or business of the partnership was to be carried on certain terms, in certain premises, which are mentioned in the deed, where alone (save and except the foreign establishments) the medicines were to be compounded, and whence alone, save as aforesaid, the said medicines so made and compounded might be issued to any part of the world, through the respective agents of the copartnership; with a proviso that it should be lawful to and for the partners for the time being of the partnership to cause the establishment to be removed to and carried on at such other place or places as he or they should or might from time to time judge most convenient. The deed then witnessed that the premises in which the business was to be carried on were to be called "The British College of Health," and that Morison and Moat were to be considered to be entitled to the gains and profits of the business, and liable to the losses, in the proportion of two thirds to Morison and one third to Moat, and upon no account was any partner to draw more than two thirds of the share of the annual profits; and that if Moat should die before the 25th of March, 1851, then the interest, share, or proportion of Mr. Moat of and in the copartnership was not to devolve, as by law it would, upon the personal representatives of Moat, but it should go and belong to such person, not being a female, as Thomas Moat should by any instrument under seal, with or without power of revocation, to be by him sealed and delivered, and to be attested by James Morison, his appointee or appointees, direct or appoint; and in default of such direction or appointment, then the interest, share, or proportion of him, Moat, of and in the partnership, should devolve upon James Morison, his appointee or appointees, executors, administrators, or assigns.

Then the deed witnessed that Moat was to devote and employ his whole time and attention in the conduct and promotion of the manufacture and sale of the medicine or medicines, or in such other manner as should best conduce to the advantage or benefit of the partnership. Morison was not to be obliged to devote any more time or attention to the manufacture and sale of the medicine or medicines, or otherwise, in and about the premises, than he should think proper; and might, if he should think proper, introduce into the copartnership any person or persons whomsoever, such person or persons not being a female or females, upon the same terms and conditions as Moat was thereby subjected to. That James Morison should, on or before the commencement of the partnership, communicate to Thomas Moat a full and true knowledge of the mode of making and compounding the medicines, and should be at liberty to communicate such knowledge to such person or persons as he was thereby empowered to introduce into the partnership. That Morison, notwithstanding anything contained to the contrary, should be at liberty to form an establishment in any part of the world, except the United Kingdom of Great Britain, Ireland, and America, for the manufacture and sale of the medicines; and that all the medicines which he might order or receive from the partnership should be charged to him at a certain price. In case Thomas Moat should live to the expiration of the partnership, a new partnership for a further term of years was to be agreed upon between the parties before the expiration of the partnership, on terms similar to those in the in denture contained; but if Morison or Moat should happen to die before the expiration of the partnership, then an account in writing should be made and taken, under the signature of the partners for the time being, of the state of the partnership, and a balance struck between the partners and the representatives of the party so dying, for the purpose of ascertaining what then might be due from the partnership to the estate of Morison, or to the estate of Moat, as the case might be. . . .

On that part of the case it is sufficient, therefore, to observe that there might be difficulty in maintaining it; at all events, until the plaintiffs should have established their right at law. The true question is, whether, under the circumstances of this case, the court ought to interfere by injunction on the ground of breach of faith or of contract. That the court has exercised jurisdiction in cases of this nature does not, I think, admit of any question. Different grounds have been assigned for the exercise of that jurisdiction. In some cases it has been referred to property, in others to contract, and in others, again, it has been treated as founded upon trust or confidence; meaning, as I conceive, that the court fastens the obligation on the conscience of the party, and enforces it against him in the same manner as it enforces, against a party to whom a benefit is given, the obligation of performing a promise on the faith of which the benefit has been conferred. But upon whatever ground the jurisdiction is founded, the authorities leave no doubt as to the exercise of it. The case of *Green v. Folghamb*, 1 Sim. & S. 398, which was cited for the plaintiffs, and where the court decreed an account against a party to whom a secret of this nature had been entrusted, might perhaps be accounted for upon the ground that the defendant in the case had expressly admitted himself to be a trustee of the secret. But there are other cases in which the court has interfered without any such admission. In *Williams v. Williams*, 3 Mer. 159, Lord Ellon, dealing with a case in which a father had divulged a secret like the present to a son, and had delivered to him a stock of medicines upon the faith of a future partnership being formed between them when the son should come of age, puts the case, as to confidence, in these terms: "If, on a treaty with the son while an infant, for his becoming a partner when of age, the plaintiff had, in the confidence of a trust reposed in him, communicated to him this secret, and at the same time given him the possession of the articles mentioned in the bill; and, instead of acting according to his trust, the son had taken to himself the exclusive dominion over these articles, and begun to vend them without permission, it must be said that he had no right in any case so to act, and that he was bound either to abide by or to waive the agreement. If, then, he had intended to abide by the agreement, the injunction was so far right." That was an injunction that had been granted by the vice chancellor. "And if to waive it, he was bound to return the articles; and so far the injunction was also right in that case. Upon the plaintiff's affidavit, therefore, the injunction was properly granted as to this part of the case. But so far as the injunction goes to restrain the defendant from communicating the secret, upon general principles I do not think that the court ought to struggle to protect this sort of secrets in medicine. The court is bound, indeed, to protect them, in cases of patents, to the full extent of what was intended by the grant of the patent, because the patentee is a purchaser from the public, and bound to communicate his secret to the public at the expiration of the patent. Then, whether the principle can be extended to such a case as this—whether a contracting party is entitled to the protection of the court, in the exercise of its jurisdiction to decree the specific performance of agreements, by restraining a party to the contract from divulging the secret he has promised to keep—that is a question which would require very great consideration. But the present case is not one which calls for the determination of it. If the defendant has already disclosed the secret, the injunction can be of no use; if he only threatens to disclose, it then becomes necessary to look at his affidavit; and by that he insists that what he has to disclose is no secret at all." In that case, the son said he had a right otherwise than from the father, and that it came to him from his mother. "Then," continued his lordship, "how is the court to try this question?" Here Lord Eldon, I think, distinctly lays down the doctrine—it does not carry that case farther—it does not go very far— that articles delivered over upon the faith and in the confidence of a future arrangement cannot be used for a purpose different from that for which they were delivered over. The cases, however, do not stop here. In *Yovatt v. Winyard*, 1 Jac. & W. 395, Lord Eldon, upon the express ground of breach of trust and confidence, granted an injunction to restrain the defendant, who had been the plaintiff's assistant in his business, from using or communicating recipes which he had surreptitiously copied whilst in the plaintiff's service. There, there was a motion, "upon certificate of the bill filed, and affidavit, to restrain the defendant from making use of, or communicating, certain recipes for veterinary medicines, and from printing and publishing certain papers of directions for the mode of administering them, and of managing the animals while taking them."

The motion was put upon the ground of its being "a breach of confidence towards an employer, in the manner of acquiring the knowledge." Sir Charles Wetherell contended, "that though the court might not protect a secret from disclosure by one to whom the proprietor had himself communicated it, yet it would when the person sought to be restrained had clandestinely possessed himself of it." In those cases," (referring to *Newberry v. James*, 2 Mer. 447, and *Williams v. Williams*,) his lordship says, "in those cases the knowledge was communicated for a particular purpose, and it was attempted to prevent the party from using it for any other; but here the first discovery was obtained by a breach of duty, and in violation of a positive agreement."

The lord chancellor "granted the injunction on the ground of there having been a breach of trust and confidence; but confined it so as not to prevent the defendant from administering the medicine to any animals then under a course, it being stated in the papers of directions that a sudden discontinuance would be prejudicial." The question again came before Lord Eldon in Mr. Abernethy's case, (*Abernethy v. Hutchinson*, 3 L. J., Ch., 209.) in which Mr. Abernethy had filed a bill to restrain the publication of the lectures delivered by him at St. Bartholomew's Hospital, and I well remember that upon the first argument he refused to grant the injunction on the ground of copyright, Mr. Abernethy not being able to swear that the whole lecture was written; but that afterwards, on a second argument, he granted it on the ground of breach of confidence.

We have also Lord Eldon's opinion referred to by Lord Cottenham in *Prince Albert v. Strange*, as contained in a note, with which he had been furnished by Mr. Cooper, of the case of *Wyatt v. Wilson*, before Lord Eldon, in the year 1820, in which Lord Eldon is reported to have said, "If one of the late king's physicians had kept a diary of what he heard and saw, this court would not, in the king's lifetime, have permitted him to print and publish it." And in the case of *Prince Albert v. Strange*, Lord Cottenham very decidedly expresses his own opinion upon the subject. What he says, after going into the right of Prince Albert to the etchings,—the mode in which it came before Lord Cottenham being upon motion to dissolve an injunction which had been granted to restrain the publication of the catalogue of the etchings which had been prepared,—is this: His lordship, after dealing with the question as a subject of property, says, "But this case by no means depends solely upon the question of property; for a breach of trust, confidence, or contract would, of itself, entitle the plaintiff to an injunction." . . .

And upon the evidence on behalf of the plaintiff, and in the absence of any explanation on the part of the defendant, I am bound to assume that the possession of the etchings by the defendant or Judge has its foundation in a breach of trust, confidence, or contract, as Lord Eldon did in the case of Mr. Abernethy's lectures; and upon this ground, also, I think the plaintiff's title to the injunction sought to be discharged fully established. The observations of Vice Chancellor Wigram in *Tipping v. Clarke*, 2 Hare, 393, are applicable to this part of the case. He says, "Every clerk employed in a merchant's counting-house is under an implied contract that he will not make public that which he learns in the execution of his duty as clerk. If the defendant has obtained copies of books, it would very probably be by means of some clerk or agent of the plaintiff; and if he availed himself surreptitiously of the information, which he could not have had except from a person guilty of a breach of contract in communicating it, I think he could not be permitted to avail himself of that breach of contract." He approves, therefore, of what fell from Vice Chancellor Wigram in *Tipping v. Clarke*.

Vice Chancellor Knight Bruce appears also to have concurred in opinion with Lord Cottenham in *Prince Albert v. Strange*. There is, therefore the concurrent opinion of Lords Eldon and Cottenham and of Vice Chancellors Knight Bruce and Sir James Wigram upon the question. By those authorities, in which I most fully concur, and which appear to me to agree in principle with many other cases to be found in the books, I must hold myself to be bound. It was much pressed in argument on the part of the defendant, that the effect of granting an injunction in such a case as the present would be to give the plaintiffs a better right than that of a patentee; and the case of *Cunham v. Jones*, 2 W. & B. 218, was cited on the defendant's behalf. But what we have to deal with here is, not the right of the plaintiffs against the world, but their right against the defendant. It may well be that the plaintiffs have no title against the world in general, and may yet have a good title against this defendant; and the case of *Cunham v. Jones* does not appear to me to touch the question. In that case the allegation was, not that the defendant was compounding the sirup according to the recipe, but that he did not know the recipe, and was compounding and selling a spurious preparation, falsely describing it under the title by which the true preparation was known, and thereby damaging the character of that preparation. The case, therefore, did not depend on any breach of confidence, for there was no confidence reposed, but depended wholly upon a supposed right of property in the medicine; . . .

Such being the state of the authorities upon this subject, I have now to consider whether the circumstances of this case bring it within the range of those authorities, and whether the court ought not to interfere by injunction, for which purpose it is necessary to examine the case as it has stood at several different periods. . . .

The true effect of these instruments appears to me to be this: that Morison reserved to himself the secret against all the world except Thomas Moat. Morison had power to introduce partners into the concern; Moat had the like power, with the concurrence of Morison, but not otherwise. It was entirely at the option of Morison whether he would communicate the secret to any partner, introduced either by himself or by Moat. Moat was absolutely bound not to reveal the secret to any person whomsoever. At this stage of the case, therefore, there was, according to the authorities to which I have referred, a perfect right on the part of Morison, against Moat, to restrain him from divulging the secret. It is to be seen whether what has since passed has destroyed that right; and if not, whether the plaintiffs are entitled to enforce it against the defendant. The next stage in the case which we have to consider is the transaction of 1835.

. . . And in this state of the evidence I am bound, I think, to conclude, that if the defendant did, in fact, after he became a partner in the concern, acquire by practice the knowledge of the mode of mixing these medicines, (but which I do not believe he did,) he acquired that knowledge surreptitiously, and without the sanction of his partners. The case, then, in this stage stands thus: The defendant admits that the secret was communicated to him by Thomas Moat. His allegation, that he acquired a knowledge of it by acting as partner in the concern, is disproved; and it is shown that, if he did so, he did so surreptitiously. The question then is, whether there was an equity against him; and I am of opinion that there was. It was already a breach of faith and of contract on the part of Thomas Moat to communicate the secret. The defendant derives it under that breach of faith and of contract, and I think he can gain no title by it. . . .

The deeds were executed for carrying into effect this compromise, and each of those deeds recited the will of Morison, with the recital contained in it that he was the inventor and sole proprietor of the medicine, and with the trusts for sale of the secret declared by it, and by one of those deeds the annuity was secured in the manner above mentioned. The defendant was a party to each of those deeds; and it is clear, therefore, that he did not claim any right or interest in the secret adverse to the title under the will of Morison. . . . And besides, the defendant had clearly the right to sell the medicines and use the labels allotted to him at the termination of the partnership. Upon the whole, therefore, I am of opinion that the plaintiffs have made out their case for an injunction. I think, however, that the injunction cannot go to the extent which is asked for by the notice of motion. It should, I think, go to the extent of restraining the defendant from selling, under the title or signature of "Morison's Universal Medicine," any medicine made or manufactured by him—proceeding to this extent, not upon the mere use of the name, but because this is clearly the mode in which the defendant is availing himself of the breach of faith and contract. And upon the authorities, and particularly upon *Yovatt v. Winyard*, I think it should also go to the extent of restraining the defendant from making or compounding any medicines according to the secret in the bill named, and from in any manner using the secret of compounding the said medicines, or any part thereof; but I cannot grant it to restrain the defendant from in any way or manner using the name of Morison in the manufacture or sale of any medicine, as, in my view of the case, it would very much depend on the purpose for which, and the mode in which, the name may be used, whether the injunction would be due or not. Nor can I grant it to restrain the communication of the secret, there being no evidence, or even allegation, of an intention to communicate it. The order, therefore, that I shall make will be for an injunction to restrain the defendant, his agents, servants, and workmen from selling, or causing or procuring to be sold, under the title or designation of "Morison's Universal Medicine," any medicine made or manufactured by him, the said defendant, or by and under his order or direction; and also to restrain the defendant, his agents, servants, and workmen from making or compounding any medicines according to the secret in the said bill mentioned, and from in any manner using the secret of compounding the said medicines, or any part thereof.
. . .

§3.21 A SCOTTISH COURT CONDEMNS THE UNDUE INTERFERENCE IN A LABOR CONTRACT

March 19, 1836

The text that follows is one of the earliest cases dealing with trade secrets under common law in Scotland. The issue involved is interference in a labor contract, with the intention of luring a competitors' employee who was in possession of secrets of the trade (the so-called "débauchage").

John Rutherford, v. William Boak

Jury Cause.—Second Division.—(J.D.M.) Scotland

19 March, 1836

Master and Servant—Seduction of Workman–Action of damages for seduction of a workman—verdict for defender.

The pursuer of this action was a leather japanner in Edinburgh, and the defender a tanner, and also leather japanner. The issues were as follows:

> Whether one Charles Bryan was engaged by the pursuer for a year from 5th April 1834 until the 5th April 1835, to assist the pursuer in his trade as a leather japanner; and whether, on or about the month of May 1834, the defender, being in the knowledge of the said engagement, by himself or another, or others, wrongfully seduced the said Charles Bryan from his said service, and caused him to desert the same, whereby the pursuer was deprived of the service of the said Charles Bryan, from the 26th day of May 1834, until the 11th day of September 1834, or during any part of the said period, to the loss, injury, and damage of the pursuer? Damages laid at £1000.
>
> In defence, the seduction of Bryan was denied, or that he had been bribed, as alleged by the pursuer, to reveal any secrets of his trade; and though Bryan might have conversed with one of the defender's work men about his method of operation, Bryan was under no obligation to conceal any particular secret, and he was therefore not guilty of breach of contract or good faith.
>
> Mr. Graham Bell stated the case for the pursuer. If a workman desert his service, his master is entitled to have him brought before a magistrate and imprisoned until he find caution to complete his engagement. This step the pursuer had adopted, and it had been rendered necessary by the defender's conduct, and that of one of his workmen named Nisbet. It was not incumbent on the pursuer to aver that any express secret had been revealed, as he held no patent, nor had applied for any in regard to the preparation or composition of the materials employed in his trade, or that Bryan had contracted to conceal such. Damages were not therefore craved for injury, through a specific secret revealed, but upon the general issue here taken, the pursuer was entitled to the consequential damages arising from the loss of the services of his workman.
>
> The pursuer was then about to refer to certain English cases, as showing the amount of damages awarded in similar cases, when it was objected by the defender that this was incompetent.
>
> The evidence adduced established that the defender had not instructed his workman, Nisbet, to entice Bryan from his engagement, but that Nisbet and Bryan

had been formerly acquainted, and Nisbet had prevailed on Bryan to show him the preparation of the materials. That Bryan had been absent a whole day from the pursuer's work, and on that occasion was drunk, and that during that day he had been seen in the defender's premises looking over the preparation of the materials there. That Bryan was after this detained in prison for four months at the pursuer's instance. That he was a valuable workman to the pursuer, who, during this time, had several large orders to execute for japanning certain articles, of which he was considered the most skillful manufacturer in Scotland.

Rutherford, for the defender, declined leading evidence, but contended that the proof of enticing had failed, and that the loss of Bryan's services had been caused by the pursuer's own act.

The Lord Justice-Clerk summed up the evidence. Statements had been made of alleged secrets in the preparation of this japanning composition, yet the pursuer had taken no issue as to any engagement to keep any specific secret of trade, or that such had been learned from Bryan by any improper means on the defender's part. Before a verdict could be returned for the pursuer, the jury must be satisfied that this person had been induced to desert his service by the defender, or through the agency of others on his account. His Lordship did not think the issue had been proved, but if the jury thought otherwise, and that there was here seduction of the workman, then they would consider the amount of damages to be awarded. From the issue it might be supposed that Bryan's seduction had been the act of the defender throughout, but it appeared that the pursuer himself had thrown him into jail for four months; and even if it had been proved that Bryan had been seduced for a short period, damages for that period was all that could be found due.

The jury found a verdict for the defender.

Lord Justice-Clerk, Boyle.

§3.22 AT THE HAGUE, ONE PROPOSAL TO INSERT THE INTERFERENCE IN CONTRACTS WITH THE PURPOSE OF ACQUIRING TRADE SECRETS (DÉBAUCHAGE) WAS REJECTED—AND NEVER DISCUSSED AGAIN UNTIL THE URUGUAY ROUND

1925

The Paris Convention does not contain any express reference to the protection of trade secrets. This topic, in the course of the almost 150 years of existence of the Paris Convention, has been in the minds of delegations only once—at The Hague, in 1925, when a proposal from Italy and France to include the interference in labor contracts with the purpose of acquiring trade secrets was rejected by all other delegations. The reason for that apparent neglect is that the notion of *débauchage*—the hiring of a competitor's employee with the purpose of obtaining the secrets of that competitor's trade—did not gain international relevance until companies started to transfer their manufacturing facilities to other countries, in the 1960s. Until then, the repression of *débauchage* was purely a matter for national law.

The text that follows was extracted from the official records of the 1925 Paris Union Conference. It reports (very laconically) on the proposal to introduce the prohibition of interference in labor contracts (with the goal of obtaining trade secrets) and its rejection.

4. The *débauchage* [interference in labor contracts; diversion of competitors' employees]

France and Italy have proposed to insert in Article 10*bis* a clause concerning the case of inducing subordinates to the violation of obligations arising from the law or the contract. Several delegations having declared to the Study Committee that it was impossible for them to accept this proposal, the question has been dropped. It was not picked up at the meeting of the Sub-Commission.

§3.23 A UNITED STATES COURT EXPLAINS HOW FAR THE OWNER OF A SECRET IS OBLIGED TO GO TO KEEP IT SECRET

20 July, 1970

The opinion that follows raises two important topics. One is that the protection of trade secrets is not entirely unconditional as far as formalities are concerned. Actually, one requirement has always been imposed upon the owners of trade secrets: in the absence of a formal title of property, they need to prove that they believe they own them, and, accordingly, reasonable measures have been taken to keep the secrecy. Evidence of these measures is taken as proof of possession and property (in the same manner that evidence of a patent or of a trademark certificate is proof of their respective possession and property).

The other is that not every act of trade secret infringement has a connection with breach of confidence. It is possible for someone unrelated to the trade secret owner to unlawfully take control of a secret that belongs to another. Breach of confidence is only one example of improper means to take control of a secret that is legitimately in possession of its holder.

E. I. du Pont de Nemours & Co. v. Christopher

United States Court of Appeals for the Fifth Circuit

July 20, 1970

Goldberg, Circuit Judge:

This is a case of industrial espionage in which an airplane is the cloak and a camera the dagger. The defendants-appellants, Rolfe and Gary Christopher, are photographers in Beaumont, Texas. The Christophers were hired by an unknown third party to take aerial photographs of new construction at the Beaumont plant of E. I. du Pont de Nemours & Company, Inc. [hereinafter DuPont]. Sixteen photographs of the DuPont facility were taken from the air on March 19, 1969, and these photographs were later developed and delivered to the third party.

DuPont employees apparently noticed the airplane on March 19 and immediately began an investigation to determine why the craft was circling over the plant. By that afternoon the investigation had disclosed that the craft was involved in a photographic expedition and that the Christophers were the photographers. DuPont contacted the Christophers that same afternoon and asked them to reveal the name of the person or corporation requesting the photographs. The Christophers refused to disclose this information, giving as their reason the client's desire to remain anonymous.

Having reached a dead end in the investigation, DuPont subsequently filed suit against the Christophers, alleging that the Christophers had wrongfully obtained photographs revealing DuPont's trade secrets which they then sold to the undisclosed third party. DuPont contended that it had developed a highly secret but unpatented process for producing methanol, a process which gave DuPont a competitive advantage over other producers. This process, DuPont alleged, was a trade secret developed after much expensive and time-consuming research, and a secret which the company had taken special precautions to safeguard. The area photographed by the Christophers was the plant designed to produce methanol by this secret process, and because the plant was still under construction parts of the process were exposed to view from directly above the construction area. Photographs of that area, DuPont alleged, would enable a skilled person to deduce the secret process for making methanol. DuPont thus contended that the Christophers had wrongfully appropriated DuPont trade secrets by taking the photographs and delivering them to the undisclosed third party.

In its suit DuPont asked for damages to cover the loss it had already sustained as a result of the wrongful disclosure of the trade secret and sought temporary and permanent injunctions prohibiting any further circulation of the photographs already taken and prohibiting any additional photographing of the methanol plant. . . .

It is true, as the Christophers assert, that the previous trade secret cases have contained one or more of these elements. However, we do not think that the Texas courts would limit the trade secret protection exclusively to these elements. On the contrary, in *Hyde Corporation v. Huffines, 1958, 158 Tex. 566, 314 S.W.2d 763,* the Texas Supreme Court specifically adopted the rule found in the Restatement of Torts which provides:

> One who discloses or uses another's trade secret, without a privilege to do so, is liable to the other if
>
> (a) he discovered the secret by improper means, or
> (b) his disclosure or use constitutes a breach of confidence reposed in him by the other in disclosing the secret to him.
>
> *Restatement of Torts § 757* (1939).
>
> Thus, although the previous cases have dealt with a breach of a confidential relationship, a trespass, or other illegal conduct, the rule is much broader than the cases heretofore encountered. Not limiting itself to specific wrongs, Texas adopted subsection (a) of the Restatement which recognizes a cause of action for the discovery of a trade secret by any "improper" means. . . .
>
> The question remaining, therefore, is whether aerial photography of plant construction is an improper means of obtaining another's trade secret. We conclude that it is and that the Texas courts would so hold. The Supreme Court of that state has declared that "the undoubted tendency of the law has been to recognize and enforce higher standards of commercial morality in the business world." *Hyde Corporation v. Huffines, supra 314 S.W.2d at 773.* That court has quoted with approval articles indicating that the *proper* means of gaining possession of a competitor's secret process is "through inspection and analysis" of the product in order to create a duplicate. . . .

One may use his competitor's secret process if he discovers the process by reverse engineering applied to the finished product; one may use a competitor's process if he discovers it by his own independent research; but one may not avoid these labors by taking the process from the discoverer without his permission at a time when he is taking reasonable precautions to maintain its secrecy. To obtain knowledge of a process without spending the time and money to discover it independently is *improper* unless the holder voluntarily discloses it or fails to take reasonable precautions to ensure its secrecy.

In the instant case the Christophers deliberately flew over the DuPont plant to get pictures of a process which DuPont had attempted to keep secret. The Christophers delivered their pictures to a third party who was certainly aware of the means by which they had been acquired and who may be planning to use the information contained therein to manufacture methanol by the DuPont process. The third party has a right to use this process only if he obtains this knowledge through his own research efforts, but thus far all information indicates that the third party has gained this knowledge solely by taking it from DuPont at a time when DuPont was making reasonable efforts to preserve its secrecy. In such a situation DuPont has a valid cause of action to prohibit the Christophers from improperly discovering its trade secret and to prohibit the undisclosed third party from using the improperly obtained information. . . .

In taking this position we realize that industrial espionage of the sort here perpetrated has become a popular sport in some segments of our industrial community. However, our devotion to freewheeling industrial competition must not force us into accepting the law of the jungle as the standard of morality expected in our commercial relations. Our tolerance of the espionage game must cease when the protections required to prevent another's spying cost so much that the spirit of inventiveness is dampened. Commercial privacy must be protected from espionage which could not have been reasonably anticipated or prevented. We do not mean to imply, however, that everything not in plain view is within the protected vale, nor that all information obtained through every extra optical extension is forbidden. Indeed, for our industrial competition to remain healthy there must be breathing room for observing a competing industrialist. A competitor can and must shop his competition for pricing and examine his products for quality, components, and methods of manufacture. Perhaps ordinary fences and roofs must be built to shut out incursive eyes, but we need not require the discoverer of a trade secret to guard against the unanticipated, the undetectable, or the unpreventable methods of espionage now available.

In the instant case DuPont was in the midst of constructing a plant. Although after construction the finished plant would have protected much of the process from view, during the period of construction the trade secret was exposed to view from the air. To require DuPont to put a roof over the unfinished plant to guard its secret would impose an enormous expense to prevent nothing more than a school boy's trick. We introduce here no new or radical ethic since our ethos has never given moral sanction to piracy. The market place must not deviate far from our mores. We should not require a person or corporation to take unreasonable precautions to prevent another from doing that which he ought not do in the first place. Reasonable precautions against predatory eyes we may require, but an impenetrable fortress is an unreasonable requirement, and we are not disposed to burden industrial inventors with such a duty in order to protect the fruits of their efforts. "Improper" will always be a word of many nuances, determined by time, place, and circumstances. We therefore need not proclaim a catalogue of commercial improprieties. Clearly, however, one of its commandments does say "thou shall not appropriate a trade secret through deviousness under circumstances in which countervailing defenses are not reasonably available." . . .

§3.24 THE US SUPREME COURT EXTENDS THE PROTECTION OF TRADE SECRETS TO CONFIDENTIAL DATA THAT COMPANIES ARE REQUIRED TO SUBMIT TO GOVERNMENTS

1984

The text that follows is a groundbreaking opinion of the United States Supreme Court: acknowledging state (Missouri) law, under which commercial data submitted to governments in the process of obtaining the authorization for the commercialization of regulated products have a proprietary nature, the Court held that governments are obliged to protect them not only by refraining from disclosing them but also by avoiding the use of those data or the information extracted therefrom for approving the commercialization of similar products manufactured by competitors of the company that originated and submitted the data in question.

A few years later the foundational arguments of this ruling would be transposed to the TRIPS Agreement. They are reflected in its Article 39.3 (*see* Text 3.25). Thus, it has become the law of the Members of the World Trade Organization.

Ruckelshaus v. Monsanto Co.

United States Supreme Court

467 U.S. 986 (1984)

Justice Blackmun delivered the opinion of the Court.

In this case, we are asked to review a United States District Court's determination that several provisions of the Federal Insecticide, Fungicide, and Rodenticide Act (FIFRA), 61 Stat. 163, as amended, 7 U.S.C. § 136 et seq., are unconstitutional. The provisions at issue authorize the Environmental Protection Agency (EPA) to use data submitted by an applicant for registration of a pesticide (note omitted) evaluating the application of a subsequent applicant, and to disclose publicly some of the submitted data.

I

Over the past century, the use of pesticides to control weeds and minimize crop damage caused by insects, disease, and animals has become increasingly more important for American agriculture. . . . While pesticide use has led to improvements in productivity, it has also led to increased risk of harm to humans and the environment. . . . Although the Federal Government has regulated pesticide use for nearly 75 years, (note omitted) FIFRA was first adopted in 1947. . . .

As first enacted, FIFRA was primarily a licensing and labeling statute. It required that all pesticides be registered with the Secretary of Agriculture prior to their sale in interstate or foreign commerce. . . . The 1947 legislation also contained general standards setting forth the types of information necessary for proper labeling of a registered pesticide, including directions for use; warnings to prevent harm to people, animals, and plants; and claims made about the efficacy of the product. . . .

Upon request of the Secretary, an applicant was required to submit test data supporting the claims on the label, including the formula for the pesticide. . . . The 1947 version of FIFRA specifically prohibited disclosure of "any information relative to formulas of products," . . . but was silent with respect to the disclosure of any of the health and safety data submitted with an application. (note omitted)

In 1970, the Department of Agriculture's FIFRA responsibilities were transferred to the then newly created Environmental Protection Agency, whose Administrator is the appellant in this case. . . .

Because of mounting public concern about the safety of pesticides and their effect on the environment, and because of a growing perception that the existing legislation was not equal to the task of safeguarding the public interest, . . . Congress undertook a comprehensive revision of FIFRA through the adoption of the Federal Environmental Pesticide Control Act of 1972, 86 Stat. 973. The amendments transformed FIFRA from a labeling law into a comprehensive regulatory statute. . . . As amended, FIFRA regulated the use, as well as the sale and labeling, of pesticides; regulated pesticides produced and sold in both intrastate and interstate commerce; provided for review, cancellation, and suspension of registration; and gave EPA greater enforcement authority. Congress also added a new criterion for registration: that EPA determine that the pesticide will not cause "unreasonable adverse effects on the environment." . . .

For purposes of this litigation, the most significant of the 1972 amendments pertained to the pesticide registration procedure and the public disclosure of information learned through that procedure. Congress added to FIFRA a new section governing public disclosure of data submitted in support of an application for registration. Under that section, the submitter of data could designate any portions of the submitted material it believed to be "trade secrets or commercial or financial information." . . . Another section prohibited EPA from publicly disclosing information which, in its judgment, contained or related to "trade secrets or commercial or financial information." . . . In the event that EPA disagreed with a submitter's designation of certain information as "trade secrets or commercial or financial information" and proposed to disclose that information, the original submitter could institute a declaratory judgment action in federal district court. . . .

The 1972 amendments also included a provision that allowed EPA to consider data submitted by one applicant for registration in support of another application pertaining to a similar chemical, provided the subsequent applicant offered to compensate the applicant who originally submitted the data. . . . In effect, the provision instituted a mandatory data-licensing scheme. The amount of compensation was to be negotiated by the parties, or, in the event negotiations failed, was to be determined by EPA, subject to judicial review upon the instigation of the original data submitter. The scope of the 1972 data-consideration provision, however, was limited, for any data designated as "trade secrets or commercial or financial information" exempt from disclosure under §10 could not be considered at all by EPA to support another registration application unless the original submitter consented. . . .

The 1972 amendments did not specify standards for the designation of submitted data as "trade secrets or commercial or financial information." In addition, Congress failed to designate an effective date for the data-consideration and disclosure schemes. In 1975, Congress amended §3(c)(1)(D) to provide that the data-consideration and data-disclosure provisions applied only to data submitted on or after January 1, 1970, . . . but left the definitional question unanswered.

Much litigation centered around the definition of "trade secrets or commercial or financial information" for the purposes of the data-consideration and data-disclosure provisions of FIFRA. EPA maintained that the exemption from consideration or disclosure applied only to a narrow range of information, principally statements of formulae and manufacturing processes. In a series of lawsuits, however, data-submitting firms challenged EPA's interpretation and obtained several decisions to the effect that the term "trade secrets" applied to any data, including health, safety, and environmental data, that met the definition of trade secrets set forth in Restatement of Torts §757 (1939). . . . These decisions prevented EPA from disclosing much of the data on which it based its decision to register pesticides and from considering the data submitted by one applicant in reviewing the application of a later applicant. . . .

Because of these and other problems with the regulatory scheme embodied in FIFRA as amended in 1972, . . . Congress enacted other amendments to FIFRA in 1978. These were effected by the Federal Pesticide Act of 1978, ... The new amendments included a series of revisions in the data-consideration and data-disclosure provisions of FIFRA's §§3 and 10, ... Under FIFRA, as amended in 1978, applicants are granted a 10-year period of exclusive use for data on new active ingredients contained in pesticides registered after September 30, 1978. . . . All other data submitted after December 31, 1969, may be cited and considered in support of another application for 15 years after the original submission if the applicant offers to compensate the original submitter. . . . . [note omitted] If the parties cannot agree on the amount of compensation, either may initiate a binding arbitration proceeding. The results of the arbitration proceeding are not subject to judicial review, absent fraud or misrepresentation. The same statute provides that an original submitter who refuses to participate in negotiations or in the arbitration proceeding forfeits his claim for compensation. Data that do not qualify for either the 10-year period of exclusive use or the 15-year period of compensation may be considered by EPA without limitation. . . . .

Also in 1978, Congress added a new subsection, §10(d), . . . that provides for disclosure of all health, safety, and environmental data to qualified requesters, notwithstanding the prohibition against disclosure of trade secrets contained in §10(b). The provision, however, does not authorize disclosure of information that would reveal "manufacturing or quality control processes" or certain details about deliberately added inert ingredients unless "the Administrator has first determined that the disclosure is necessary to protect against an unreasonable risk of injury to health or the environment." . . . . [note omitted] EPA may not disclose data to representatives of foreign or multinational pesticide companies unless the original submitter of the data consents to the disclosure. . . . . Another subsection establishes a criminal penalty for wrongful disclosure by a Government employee or contractor of confidential or trade secret data. . . . .

II

Appellee Monsanto Company (Monsanto) is an inventor, developer, and producer of various kinds of chemical products, including pesticides. Monsanto, headquartered in St. Louis County, Mo., sells in both domestic and foreign markets. It is one of a relatively small group of companies that invent and develop new active ingredients for pesticides and conduct most of the research and testing with respect to those ingredients. [note omitted]

These active ingredients are sometimes referred to as "manufacturing-use products" because they are not generally sold directly to users of pesticides. Rather, they must first be combined with "inert ingredients"—chemicals that dissolve, dilute, or stabilize the active components. The results of this process are sometimes called "end-use products," and the firms that produce end-use products are called "formulators." . . . A firm that produces an active ingredient may use it for incorporation into its own end-use products, may sell it to formulators, or may do both. Monsanto produces both active ingredients and end-use products. . . . .

Monsanto, like any other applicant for registration of a pesticide, must present research and test data supporting its application. The District Court found that Monsanto had incurred costs in excess of $23.6 million in developing the health, safety, and environmental data submitted by it under FIFRA. . . . The information submitted with an application usually has value to Monsanto beyond its instrumentality in gaining that particular application. Monsanto uses this information to develop additional end-use products and to expand the uses of its registered products. The information would also be valuable to Monsanto's competitors. For that reason, Monsanto has instituted stringent security measures to ensure the secrecy of the data. . . .

It is this health, safety, and environmental data that Monsanto sought to protect by bringing this suit. The District Court found that much of these data "contai[n] or relat[e] to trade secrets as defined by the Restatement of Torts and Confidential, commercial information." . . .

Monsanto brought suit in District Court, seeking injunctive and declaratory relief from the operation of the data-consideration provisions of FIFRA's §3(c)(1)(D), and the data-disclosure provisions of FIFRA's §10 and the related §3(c)(2)(A). Monsanto alleged that all of the challenged provisions effected a "taking" of property without just compensation, in violation of the Fifth Amendment. In addition, Monsanto alleged that the data-consideration provisions violated the Amendment because they effected a taking of property for a private, rather than a public, purpose. Finally, Monsanto alleged that the arbitration scheme provided by §3(c)(1)(D)(ii) violates the original submitter's due process rights, and constitutes an unconstitutional delegation of judicial power. . . .

III

In deciding this case, we are faced with four questions: (1) Does Monsanto have a property interest protected by the Fifth Amendment's Taking Clause in the health, safety, and environmental data it has submitted to EPA? (2) If so, does EPA's use of the data to evaluate the applications of others or EPA's disclosure of the data to qualified members of the public effect a taking of that property interest? (3) If there is a taking, is it a taking for a public use? (4) If there is a taking for a public use, does the statute adequately provide for just compensation?

For purposes of this case, EPA has stipulated that

> Monsanto has certain property rights in its information, research and test data that it has submitted under FIFRA to EPA and its predecessor agencies which may be protected by the Fifth Amendment to the Constitution of the United States.

. . . Since the exact import of that stipulation is not clear, we address the question whether the data at issue here can be considered property for the purposes of the Taking Clause of the Fifth Amendment.

This Court never has squarely addressed the applicability of the protections of the Taking Clause of the Fifth Amendment to commercial data of the kind involved in this case. In answering the question now, we are mindful of the basic axiom that

> '[p]roperty interests . . . are not created by the Constitution. Rather, they are created and their dimensions are defined by existing rules or understandings that stem from an independent source such as state law.'

. . . Monsanto asserts that the health, safety, and environmental data it has submitted to EPA are property under Missouri law, which recognizes trade secrets, as defined in §757, Comment b, of the Restatement of Torts, as property. . . . The Restatement defines a trade secret as

> any formula, pattern, device or compilation of information which is used in one's business, and which gives him an opportunity to obtain an advantage over competitors who do not know or use it.

. . . . And the parties have stipulated that much of the information, research, and test data that Monsanto has submitted under FIFRA to EPA "contains or relates to trade secrets as defined by the Restatement of Torts." . . .

Because of the intangible nature of a trade secret, the extent of the property right therein is defined by the extent to which the owner of the secret protects his interest from disclosure to others. . . . Information that is public knowledge or that is generally known in an industry cannot be a trade secret. Restatement of Torts, *supra*. If an individual discloses his trade secret to others who are under no obligation to protect the confidentiality of the information, or otherwise publicly discloses the secret, his property right is extinguished. . . .

Trade secrets have many of the characteristics of more tangible forms of property. A trade secret is assignable. . . . A trade secret can form the *res* of a trust, . . . and it passes to a trustee in bankruptcy. . . .

Even the manner in which Congress referred to trade secrets in the legislative history of FIFRA supports the general perception of their property-like nature. In discussing the 1978 amendments to FIFRA, Congress recognized that data developers like Monsanto have a "proprietary interest" in their data. . . . Further, Congress reasoned that submitters of data are "entitled" to "compensation" because they "have legal ownership of the data." . . . . [note omitted] This general perception of trade secrets as property is consonant with a notion of "property" that extends beyond land and tangible goods and includes the products of an individual's "labour and invention." . . .

Although this Court never has squarely addressed the question whether a person can have a property interest in a trade secret, which is admittedly intangible, the Court has found other kinds of intangible interests to be property for purposes of the Fifth Amendment's Taking Clause. . . . That intangible property rights protected by state law are deserving of the protection of the Taking Clause has long been implicit in the thinking of this Court:

> It is conceivable that [the term 'property' in the Taking Clause] was used in its vulgar and untechnical sense of the physical thing with respect to which the citizen exercises rights recognized by law. On the other hand, it may have been employed in a more accurate sense to denote the group of rights inhering in the citizen's relation to the physical thing, as the right to possess, use and dispose of it. In point of fact, the construction given the phrase has been the latter. . . .

> We therefore hold that, to the extent that Monsanto has an interest in its health, safety, and environmental data cognizable as a trade secret property right under Missouri law, that property right is protected by the Taking Clause of the Fifth Amendment. [note omitted]

IV

Having determined that Monsanto has a property interest in the data it has submitted to EPA, we confront the difficult question whether a "taking" will occur when EPA discloses those data or considers the data in evaluating another application for registration. The question of what constitutes a "taking" is one with which this Court has wrestled on many occasions. It has never been the rule that only governmental acquisition or destruction of the property of an individual constitutes a taking, for courts have held that the deprivation of the former owner, rather than the accretion of a right or interest to the sovereign constitutes the taking. Governmental action short of acquisition of title or occupancy has been held, if its effects are so complete as to deprive the owner of all or most of his interest in the subject matter, to amount to a taking. . . .

As has been admitted on numerous occasions, this Court has generally "been unable to develop any set formula for determining when 'justice and fairness' require that economic injuries caused by public action" must be deemed a compensable taking. . . . The inquiry into whether a taking has occurred is essentially an "ad hoc, factual" inquiry. . . The Court, however, has identified several factors that should be taken into account when determining whether a governmental action has gone beyond "regulation" and effects a "taking." Among those factors are:

> the character of the governmental action, its economic impact, and its interference with reasonable investment-backed expectations.

. . . It is to the last of these three factors that we now direct our attention, for we find that the force of this factor is so overwhelming, at least with respect to certain of the data submitted by Monsanto to EPA, that it disposes of the taking question regarding those data.

A

> A "reasonable investment-backed expectation" must be more than a "unilateral expectation or an abstract need."
>
> . . . We find that, with respect to any health, safety, and environmental data that Monsanto submitted to EPA after the effective date of the 1978 FIFRA amendments -- that is, on or after October 1, 1978 (note omitted)—Monsanto could not have had a reasonable, investment-backed expectation that EPA would keep the data confidential beyond the limits prescribed in the amended statute itself. Monsanto was on notice of the manner in which EPA was authorized to use and disclose any data turned over to it by an applicant for registration.
>
> Thus, with respect to any data submitted to EPA on or after October 1, 1978, Monsanto knew that, for a period of 10 years from the date of submission, EPA would not consider those data in evaluating the application of another without Monsanto's permission. . . . It was also aware, however, that, once the 10-year period had expired, EPA could use the data without Monsanto's permission. . . .

Monsanto was further aware that it was entitled to an offer of compensation from the subsequent applicant only until the end of the 15th year from the date of submission. . . . In addition, Monsanto was aware that information relating to formulae of products could be revealed by EPA to "any Federal agency consulted and [could] be revealed at a public hearing or in findings of fact" issued by EPA "when necessary to carry out" EPA's duties under FIFRA. . . . The statute also gave Monsanto notice that much of the health, safety, and efficacy data provided by it could be disclosed to the general public at any time. . . . If, despite the data-consideration and data-disclosure provisions in the statute, Monsanto chose to submit the requisite data in order to receive a registration, it can hardly argue that its reasonable investment-backed expectations are disturbed when EPA acts to use or disclose the data in a manner that was authorized by law at the time of the submission.

Monsanto argues that the statute's requirement that a submitter give up its property interest in the data constitutes placing an unconstitutional condition on the right to a valuable Government benefit. . . . But Monsanto has not challenged the ability of the Federal Government to regulate the marketing and use of pesticides. Nor could Monsanto successfully make such a challenge, for such restrictions are the burdens we all must bear in exchange for "the advantage of living and doing business in a civilized community." . . . This is particularly true in an area, such as pesticide sale and use, that has long been the source of public concern and the subject of government regulation. That Monsanto is willing to bear this burden in exchange for the ability to market pesticides in this country is evidenced by the fact that it has continued to expand its research and development and to submit data to EPA despite the enactment of the 1978 amendments to FIFRA. [note omitted) . . .

Thus, as long as Monsanto is aware of the conditions under which the data are submitted, and the conditions are rationally related to a legitimate Government interest, a voluntary submission of data by an applicant in exchange for the economic advantages of a registration can hardly be called a taking. . . .

C

The situation may be different, however, with respect to data submitted by Monsanto to EPA during the period from October 22, 1972, through September 30, 1978. Under the statutory scheme then in effect, a submitter was given an opportunity to protect its trade secrets from disclosure by designating them as trade secrets at the time of submission. When Monsanto provided data to EPA during this period, it was with the understanding, embodied in FIFRA, that EPA was free to use any of the submitted data that were not trade secrets in considering the application of another, provided that EPA required the subsequent applicant to pay "reasonable compensation" to the original submitter. . . . But the statute also gave Monsanto explicit assurance that EPA was prohibited from disclosing publicly, or considering in connection with the application of another, any data submitted by an applicant if both the applicant and EPA determined the data to constitute trade secrets. . . . Thus, with respect to trade secrets submitted under the statutory regime in force between the time of the adoption of the 1972 amendments and the adoption of the 1978 amendments, the Federal Government had explicitly guaranteed to Monsanto and other registration applicants an extensive measure of confidentiality and exclusive use. This explicit governmental guarantee formed the basis of a reasonable investment-backed expectation. If EPA, consistent with the authority granted it by the 1978 FIFRA amendments, were now to disclose trade secret data or consider those data in evaluating the application of a subsequent applicant in a manner not authorized by the version of FIFRA in effect between 1972 and 1978, EPA's actions would frustrate Monsanto's reasonable investment-backed expectation with respect to its control over the use and dissemination of the data it had submitted.

The right to exclude others is generally "one of the most essential sticks in the bundle of rights that are commonly characterized as property." . . . With respect to a trade secret, the right to exclude others is central to the very definition of the property interest. Once the data that constitute a trade secret are disclosed to others, or others are allowed to use those data, the holder of the trade secret has lost his property interest in the data. [note omitted]

That the data retain usefulness for Monsanto even after they are disclosed—for example, as bases from which to develop new products or refine old products, as marketing and advertising tools, or as information necessary to obtain registration in foreign countries—is irrelevant to the determination of the economic impact of the EPA action on Monsanto's property right. The economic value of that property right lies in the competitive advantage over others that Monsanto enjoys by virtue of its exclusive access to the data, and disclosure or use by others of the data would destroy that competitive edge. . . .

We further hold that EPA consideration or disclosure of health, safety, and environmental data will constitute a taking if Monsanto submitted the data to EPA between October 22, 1972, and September 30, 1978; [note omitted] the data constituted trade secrets under Missouri law; Monsanto had designated the data as trade secrets at the time of its submission; the use or disclosure conflicts with the explicit assurance of confidentiality or exclusive use contained in the statute during that period; and the operation of the arbitration provision does not adequately compensate for the loss in market value of the data that Monsanto suffers because of EPA's use or disclosure of the trade secrets.

V

We must next consider whether any taking of private property that may occur by operation of the data-disclosure and data-consideration provisions of FIFRA is a taking for a "public use." . . .

We therefore hold that any taking of private property that may occur in connection with EPA's use or disclosure of data submitted to it by Monsanto between October 22, 1972, and September 30, 1978, is a taking for a public use. . . .

VIII

We find no constitutional infirmity in the challenged provisions of FIFRA. Operation of the provisions may effect a taking with respect to certain health, safety, and environmental data constituting trade secrets under state law and designated by Monsanto as trade secrets upon submission to EPA between October 22, 1972, and September 30, 1978. [note omitted] But whatever taking may occur is one for a public use, and a Tucker Act remedy is available to provide Monsanto with just compensation. Once a taking has occurred, the proper forum for Monsanto's claim is the Claims Court. Monsanto's challenges to the constitutionality of the arbitration procedure are not yet ripe for review. The judgment of the District Court is therefore vacated, and the case is remanded for further proceedings consistent with this opinion.

It is so ordered.

§3.25 THE FIRST MULTILATERAL RULE ON THE PROTECTION OF TRADE SECRETS: ARTICLE 39 OF THE TRIPS AGREEMENT

April 15, 1994

The silence of the Paris Convention in regard of trade secrets has given rise to the doubt whether its provision on the repression of unfair competition would extend to them. The opinion of some of its Contracting Parties was that it did. The opinion of others was that it did not. The Agreement on Trade-Related Aspects of Intellectual Property Rights (TRIPS Agreement), Annex 1C of the Marrakesh Agreement Establishing the World Trade Organization, signed in Marrakesh, Morocco, on 15 April 1994, overcame that doubt. Not only the repression of unfair competition under the Paris Convention extended to the protection of trade secrets, but the Agreement itself added a few important provisions: it defined trade secrets (on which definition the Restatement of Unfair Competition Law, of the American Law Institute, had significant influence) and included confidential test data of mandatory submission by companies to governments in that definition.

Agreement on Trade-Related Aspects of Intellectual Property (TRIPS Agreement)

Part II Standards concerning the Availability, Scope and Use of Intellectual Property Rights

Section 7: Protection of Undisclosed Information

Article 39

1. In the course of ensuring effective protection against unfair competition as provided in Article 10*bis* of the Paris Convention (1967), Members shall protect undisclosed information in accordance with paragraph 2 and data submitted to governments or governmental agencies in accordance with paragraph 3.
2. Natural and legal persons shall have the possibility of preventing information lawfully within their control from being disclosed to, acquired by, or used by others without their consent in a manner contrary to honest commercial practices (10) so long as such information:
   (a) is secret in the sense that it is not, as a body or in the precise configuration and assembly of its components, generally known among or readily accessible to persons within the circles that normally deal with the kind of information in question;
   (b) has commercial value because it is secret; and
   (c) has been subject to reasonable steps under the circumstances, by the person lawfully in control of the information, to keep it secret.
3. Members, when requiring, as a condition of approving the marketing of pharmaceutical or of agricultural chemical products which utilize new chemical entities, the submission of undisclosed test or other data, the origination of which involves a considerable effort, shall protect such data against unfair commercial use. In addition, Members shall protect such data against disclosure, except where necessary to protect the public, or unless steps are taken to ensure that the data are protected against unfair commercial use.

(10) For the purpose of this provision, "a manner contrary to honest commercial practices" shall mean at least practices such as breach of contract, breach of confidence and inducement to breach, and includes the acquisition of undisclosed

information by third parties who knew, or were grossly negligent in failing to know, that such practices were involved in the acquisition.

§3.26 RECENT APPROACHES TO THE ENFORCEMENT OF TRADE SECRET PROTECTION: THE US DEFEND TRADE SECRETS ACT

2016

In recent years, some of the largest world economies (the United States, the European Union, Japan) have strengthened the protection of trade secrets, thereby acknowledging their importance in global trade. In 2016 the United States approved the Defend Trade Secrets Act of 2016, which extended federal jurisdiction to civil cases involving violation and theft of trade secrets with an interstate or international impact (beforehand, that was a matter for the states) and included a number of rigorous enforcement measures, such as the *ex parte* seizure of property when necessary to prevent the dissemination of secrets (hence, of their value) and the imposition of exemplary damages. In addition, the new statute established a Report on the theft of U.S. trade secrets occurring abroad.

The first verdict applying the Defend Trade Secrets Act was issued in January 2017, in the civil action *Dalmatia Import Group v. Foodmatch, Inc.* (involving a secret recipe), under the supervision of Judge Smith, of the Eastern District Court of Pennsylvania. The plaintiff was awarded 2,5 million US dollars in damages.

Public Law 114-153 114th Congress

An Act To amend Chapter 90 of title 18, United States Code, to provide Federal jurisdiction for the theft of trade secrets, and for other purposes.

Be it enacted by the Senate and House of Representatives of the United States of America in Congress assembled,

Section 1.

Short Title. This Act may be cited as the "Defend Trade Secrets Act of 2016".

Section 2.

Federal Jurisdiction for Theft of Trade Secrets.

. . .

(b) Private Civil Actions.—

(1) In general.—An owner of a trade secret that is misappropriated may bring a civil action under this subsection if the trade secret is related to a product or service used in, or intended for use in, interstate or foreign commerce.

(2) Civil seizure.—

(A) In general.—

(i) Application.—Based on an affidavit or verified complaint satisfying the requirements of this paragraph, the court may, upon ex parte application but only in extraordinary circumstances, issue an order providing for the seizure of property necessary to prevent the propagation or dissemination of the trade secret that is the subject of the action.

(ii) Requirements for issuing order.—The court may not grant an application under clause (i) unless the court finds that it clearly appears from specific facts that—

(I) an order issued pursuant to Rule 65 of the Federal Rules of Civil Procedure or another form of equitable relief would be inadequate to achieve the purpose of this paragraph because the party to which the order would be issued would evade, avoid, or otherwise not comply with such an order;

(II) an immediate and irreparable injury will occur if such seizure is not ordered;

(III) the harm to the applicant of denying the application outweighs the harm to the legitimate interests of the person against whom seizure would be ordered of granting the application and substantially outweighs the harm to any third parties who may be harmed by such seizure;

(IV) the applicant is likely to succeed in showing that—

(aa) the information is a trade secret; and

(bb) the person against whom seizure would be ordered—

(AA) misappropriated the trade secret of the applicant by improper means; or

(BB) conspired to use improper means to misappropriate the trade secret of the applicant;

(V) the person against whom seizure would be ordered has actual possession of—

(aa) the trade secret; and

(bb) any property to be seized;

(VI) the application describes with reasonable particularity the matter to be seized and, to the extent reasonable under the circumstances, identifies the location where the matter is to be seized;

(VII) the person against whom seizure would be ordered, or persons acting in concert with such person, would destroy, move, hide, or otherwise make such matter inaccessible to the court, if the applicant were to proceed on notice to such person; and (VIII) the applicant has not publicized the requested seizure.

. . .

(3) Remedies.—In a civil action brought under this subsection with respect to the misappropriation of a trade secret, a court may—

(A) grant an injunction—

(i) to prevent any actual or threatened misappropriation described in paragraph (1) on such terms as the court deems reasonable, provided the order does not—

(I) prevent a person from entering into an employment relationship, and that conditions placed on such employment shall be based on evidence of threatened misappropriation and not merely on the information the person knows; or

(II) otherwise conflict with an applicable State law prohibiting restraints on the practice of a lawful profession, trade, or business;

(ii) if determined appropriate by the court, requiring affirmative actions to be taken to protect the trade secret; and

(iii) in exceptional circumstances that render an injunction inequitable, that conditions future use of the trade secret upon payment of a reasonable royalty for no longer than the period of time for which such use could have been prohibited;

(B) award—

(i) (I) damages for actual loss caused by the misappropriation of the trade secret; and

(II) damages for any unjust enrichment caused by the misappropriation of the trade secret that is not addressed in computing damages for actual loss; or

(ii) in lieu of damages measured by any other methods, the damages caused by the misappropriation measured by imposition of liability for a reasonable royalty for the misappropriator's unauthorized disclosure or use of the trade secret;

(C) if the trade secret is willfully and maliciously misappropriated, award exemplary damages in an amount not more than 2 times the amount of the damages awarded under subparagraph (B); and

(D) if a claim of the misappropriation is made in bad faith, which may be established by circumstantial evidence, a motion to terminate an injunction is made or opposed in bad faith, or the trade secret was willfully and maliciously misappropriated, award reasonable attorney's fees to the prevailing party.

(c) Jurisdiction.—The district courts of the United States shall have original jurisdiction of civil actions brought under this section. . . .

§3.27 THE EUROPEAN DIRECTIVE ON TRADE SECRETS

2016

The TRIPS Council, in its meeting of 8-9 November 2016, held a long discussion on trade secrets, with particular emphasis on new nationals laws that enhanced their protection. In that session, the European Union provided a detailed description of the Directive adopted in 2016, which required its Members to increase the protection of trade secrets. That description follows.

This valuable know-how and business information that is intended to remain confidential is what we know as a trade secret.

As the US mentioned, this covers a wide range of information, which extends beyond technological knowledge to commercial data such as information on customers and suppliers, business plans and market research and strategies.

Trade secrets play an important role in protecting the exchange of knowledge between businesses, in particular SMEs and research institutions in the EU in the context of research and development and innovation.

The ex-post evaluation of the 7th EU Research Framework Programme concluded that 64 % of the projects report no patenting activities and 60 % of the projects opted for secrecy as intellectual property avenue. This shows how often trade secrets are the tools that are used by small companies, companies who do not have extensive financial resources, that do not have lawyers at their disposal to protect their intellectual property and opt for a more economical and more effective model to keep some information confidential.

This is one of the main reasons why the EU considered it necessary to adopt the Trade Secrets Directive and harmonize the protection of undisclosed know-how and business information to the extent of civil litigation because that is the area for which we have clearly established competence. It was not possible at the current stage to adopt similar legislation for criminal infringement and criminal litigation regarding the theft of trade secrets. The Directive was adopted on June 8, 2016 and, as is often the case in Europe, is subject to an implementation period by national legislation, as it is not directly applicable. It requires each Member State to adopt its own laws that put in place the system; Member States will have until June 9, 2018 to do so.

Before the adoption of the Trade Secrets Directive there was great diversity of systems and definitions in European Union Member States as regards the treatment and the protection of trade secrets. This new Directive brings legal clarity and a level playing field to all European companies. It applies to all companies operating in Europe. It also helps to increase their interest in the development of research and innovation activities.

The recently adopted Directive sets out rules for the protection of trade secrets and confidential information of companies who are operating in the European Union. It lays down common measures against the unlawful acquisition, use and disclosure of trade secrets, and aims at ensuring the smooth functioning of the European Union's internal market.

It is also intended to have a deterrent effect against the illegal disclosure of trade secrets while at the same time fundamental rights and freedoms or the public interest, such as public safety, consumer protection, public health, environmental protection and mobility of workers are not undermined.

While the Directive provides for measures preventing the disclosure of information to protect the confidentiality of trade secrets, the new measures fully ensure that investigative journalism can be exercised without any new limitations, including with regard to the protection of journalistic sources. The directive is in compliance with the EU's Charter of Fundamental Rights, which preserves freedom and pluralism of the media.

There will also be no limitation to employees' use of the experience and skills honestly acquired in the normal course of their employment. Furthermore, the autonomy of social partners and their rights to enter into collective agreements is not affected by the implementation of the new mechanisms.

The new Directive introduces that persons acting in good faith that reveal trade secrets for the purpose of protecting the general public interest, commonly known as "whistle-blowers", enjoy adequate protection. Trade secrets protection does not apply in cases in which the objective was to reveal misconduct, wrongdoing or illegal activity, provided that the respondent acted for the purpose of protecting the general public interest.

In accordance with the new legal framework, EU Member States have to provide for the measures, procedures and remedies necessary to ensure the availability of civil redress against the illegal acquisition, use and disclosure of trade secrets. These have to be fair, effective and dissuasive. They must not be unnecessarily complicated or costly, nor may they entail unreasonable time-limits or unwarranted delays.

The Directive also set outs that trade secret holders are entitled to apply for remedies in case of damages following cases of illegal appropriation of documents, objects, materials, substances or electronic files containing a trade secret or from which a trade secret can be deduced.

Also the legislation introduces mechanisms for the removal from the market of goods manufactured on the basis of a trade secret that was illegally acquired. The Directive puts in place mechanisms to ensure that where necessary, confidentiality of trade secrets is preserved during the course of and after the legal proceedings. Actually, we found it was often the case that a company that had suffered the misappropriation of its trade secrets and then went to court to make its right prevail, the court was not equipped to address these kinds of cases and often the company had no option, but to reveal its trade secrets. This was fairly illogical and an unreasonable process. We have therefore introduced mechanisms that equip courts to judge these cases with the necessary level of confidentiality so that the company does not suffer twice this prejudice, first by some illegal means and then by court proceedings. That is a very important element of the Directive. . . .

CHAPTER 4

Copyright

§4.01 THE GREEKS WERE AWARE OF THE NEED FOR ORIGINALITY

First Century BC

In classical Greece, theater plays were a public matter. The authors who wished to have their works (plays, poems) represented in public, would submit the texts to a jury previously selected. That selection, as this text implies, was surrounded by some measures that ensured impartiality and honesty. In Vitruvius' example, the audience would have a saying in that selection, by expressing their preference for one author or another. The selected work would be performed on stage. The winner would be crowned and receive a money award, to be funded by the city. Therefore, the correct identification of the genuine author in Ancient Greece was of utmost importance. According to Diodorus of Sicily, Sophocles (fifth century BC), the most celebrated Greek playwright, during his life received eighteen prizes for his tragedies. The great jubilation that he had when he received the eighteenth prize was the cause of his death.

The story Vitruvius told may have taken place in the second century BC, when Ptolemy V Ephinas ruled over Egypt, then a center of classical Greek culture. The librarian that takes part in the story is Aristophanes of Byzantium, who directed the Library of Alexandria and was himself an author.

Vitruvius (circa 80-70—circa 15 BC), THE TEN BOOKS ON ARCHITECTURE

. . . So, while they deserve our thanks, those, on the contrary, deserve our reproaches, who steal the writings of such men and publish them as their own; and those also, who depend in their writings, not on their own ideas, but who enviously do wrong to the works of others and boast of it, deserve not merely to be blamed, but to be sentenced to actual punishment for their wicked course of life. With the ancients, however, it is said that such things did not pass without pretty strict chastisement. What the results of their judgments were, it may not be out of place to set forth as they are transmitted to us.

The kings of the house of Attalus having established, under the influence of the great charms of literature, an excellent library at Pergamus to give pleasure to the public, Ptolemy also was aroused with no end of enthusiasm and emulation into exertions to make a similar provision with no less diligence at Alexandria. Having done so with the greatest care, he felt that this was not enough without providing for its increase and development, for which he sowed the seed. He established public contests in honour of the Muses and Apollo, and appointed prizes and honours for victorious authors in general, as is done in the case of athletes.

These arrangements having been made, and the contests being at hand, it became necessary to select literary men as judges to decide them. The king soon selected six of the citizens, but could not so easily find a proper person to be the seventh. He therefore turned to those who presided over the library, and asked whether they knew anybody who was suitable for the purpose. Then they told him that there was one Aristophanes who was daily engaged in reading through all the books with the greatest enthusiasm and the greatest care. Hence, when the gathering for the contests took place, and separate seats were set apart for the judges, Aristophanes was summoned with the rest, and sat down in the place assigned to him.

A group of poets was first brought in to contend, and, as they recited their compositions, the whole audience by its applause showed the judges what it approved. So, when they were individually asked for their votes, the six agreed, and awarded the first prize to the poet who, as they observed, had most pleased the multitude, and the second to the one who came next. But Aristophanes, on being asked for his vote, urged that the poet who had least pleased the audience should be declared to be the first.

As the king and the entire assembly showed great indignation, he arose, and asked and received permission to speak. Silence being obtained, he stated that only one of them—his man—was a poet, and that the rest had recited things not their own; furthermore, that judges ought to give their approval, not to thefts, but to original compositions. The people were amazed, and the king hesitated, but Aristophanes, trusting to his memory, had a vast number of volumes brought out from bookcases which he specified, and, by comparing them with what had been recited, obliged the thieves themselves to make confession. So, the king gave orders that they should be accused of theft, and after condemnation sent them off in disgrace; but he honoured Aristophanes with the most generous gifts, and put him in charge of the library.

§4.02 MARTIAL, A VICTIM OF PLAGIARISM

First Century AD

In Rome, in spite of the absence of a copyright law as such, the notion of plagiarism was well settled. The following three Epigrams, by Martial (between 38 BC and 41 AD—between 102 and 104 AD), accusing Fidentinus of plagiarizing his poems, are a good illustration of this. Authors needed to be identified and authorship unequivocally attributed to them, so that they could reap the benefits then available—social reputation, patronizing, public prizes, and, to a minor extent, commercial success.

Book I, LII

To your charge I entrust, Quintianus, my works—if, after all, I can call those mine which that poet of yours recites. If they complain of their grievous servitude, come forward as their champion and give bail for them; and when that fellow calls himself their owner, say that they are mine, sent forth from my hand. If thrice and four times you shout this, you will shame the plagiarist.

Book I, LIII

There is one page of yours, Fidentinus, in a book of mine—a page, too, stamped by the distinct likeness of its master—which convicts your poems of palpable theft. So, when set among them, a Lingonian cowled cloak defiles with greasy wool the violet-purple robes of town; so crocks from Arrentium degrade crystal glass; so a black raven, perchance wandering on Cayster's banks, is laughed at among Leda's swans; so, when a sacred grove is afire with the varied notes of the Athenian nightingale, an impudent jay jars on those Attic notes of woe. My books need no title or judge to prove them; your page stares you in the face, and calls you "thief."

Book I, LXXII

Do you imagine, Fidentinus, that you are a poet by the aid of my verses, and do you wish to be thought so? Just so does Aegle think she has teeth from having purchased bone or ivory. Just so does Lycoris, who is blacker than the falling mulberry, seem fair in her own eyes, because she is painted. You too, in the same way that you are a poet, will have flowing locks when you are grown bald.

§4.03 THE REACTION OF PLINY THE YOUNGER TO THE INFORMATION THAT HIS BOOKS WERE BEING SOLD IN LYON

First Century AD

This text is an excerpt from a letter of Pliny the Younger (61—circa 113 AD) in which he shows surprise in learning that his books were being sold in Lyon. As it was customary in that business, in ancient Rome, book sellers would not inform him of any sales, let alone would pay him any dues. Books would be copied by hand on papyrus rolls by slaves. Authors would eventually, and very rarely, be paid a lump sum for their manuscripts.

Epistle XI, to Ducennius Geminus

. . . I did not think that any booksellers had settled in *Lugdunum* [Lyon]; and therefore your information of the sale of my books gave me the greater pleasure; being much rejoiced to know that they still support, in foreign parts, the same degree of applause, which they had acquired in Rome. I begin now to esteem them in reality, as they have met with approbation in a variety of countries, and among a variety of judgments. Adieu.

§4.04 MARTIAL, ON THE CONSEQUENCE OF THE ABSENCE OF THE PROTECTION OF AUTHORS' RIGHTS

First Century AD

In this Epigram, Martial complaints that in spite of his book being very popular in Britain among Roman officers, he did not receive any money. He wonders that if there were a Maecenas in Rome, he could have been much more inspired.

There is not city idleness alone that delights in my Muse, nor do I give these epigrams to vacant ears, but my book, amid Getic frosts, beside martial standards, is thumbed by the hardy centurion, and Britain is said to hum my verses. What profit is it? My money-bag knows nothing of that. But what immortal pages could I frame, and of wars how mighty could I blow my Pierian trump, if the kindly deities, now they have restored Augustus to earth, were also, Rome, to give you a Maecenas!

§4.05 THE IMPORTANCE OF PUBLIC PRIZES FOR LITERARY WORKS

First Century AD

Another illustration of the importance of contests and prizes to emulate artists and writers in Rome: the commemorative inscription of the tomb of Quintus Sulpicius Maximus, a boy who died before completing twelve years, and who in 94 AD, in spite of his young age, won the third of the quinquennial contests instituted by Domitian in honor of Jupiter Capitolinus.

Sacred to the Deified Shades of the Dead.

In memory of Quintus Sulpicius Maximus, the son of Quintus, of the Claudian tribe. His home was at Rome. He lived eleven years, five months, and twelve days. In the third lustrum of the contest, entering the competition as one among fifty-two Greek poets, he roused to admiration by his talent the favor he had won by his tender years, and came off with distinction. That his parents may not seem to have been unduly influenced by their affection for him, his extemporaneous verses have been inscribed below. Quintus Sulpicius Eugramus and Licinia Januaria, his unfortunate parents, erected this tomb for their devoted son, for themselves, and for their descendants.

§4.06 ON THE PUBLIC PATRONAGE OF LITERARY WORKS

First-Second Centuries AD

The following text, an excerpt from the Annals of Cornelius Tacitus (c. 56—c. 120 AD), explains the importance of patronage—both private and public—for playwrights.

Annals, Book XIV, XXI.

Licentious pleasure had a number of advocates, all of them the apologists of vice disguised under specious names. By these men it was argued, "that the citizens of Rome, in the earliest period, were addicted to public shows, and the expense kept pace with the wealth of the times. Pantomime players were brought from Tuscany, and horse-races from Thurium. When Greece and Asia were reduced to subjection, the public games were exhibited with greater pomp; though it must be acknowledged, that in two hundred years (the time that elapsed from the triumph of Lucius Mummius, who first introduced theatrical representations) not one Roman citizen of rank or family was known to degrade himself by listing in a troop of comedians. But it is also true that, by erecting a permanent theatre, a great annual expense was avoided. The magistrate is now no longer obliged to ruin his private fortune for the diversion of the public. The whole expenditure is transferred to the state, and, without encumbering a single individual, the people may enjoy the games of Greece. The contests between poets and orators would raise a spirit of emulation, and promote the cause of literature. Nor will the judge be disgraced, if he lends an ear to the productions of genius, and shares the pleasures of a liberal mind. In the quinquennial festival, lately instituted, a few nights, every fifth year, would be dedicated, not to criminal gratifications, but to social gaiety, in a place fitted for a large assembly, and illuminated with such a glare of light, that clandestine vice would by consequence be excluded.

§4.07 AN EARLY TALE OF COPYRIGHT INFRINGEMENT

Sixth Century AD

Has Saint Columba (521-596), the Irish apostle who took Christian faith to Scotland, in the early Middle Ages, been acknowledged as a counterfeiter? That is what an early medieval tale tells us.

It seems thus apparent that Columba was as much a bard as a monk during the first part of his life; he had the vagabond inclination, the ardent, agitated, even quarrelsome character of the race. Like most Irish saints and even monks whom history has kept in mind, he had a passionate love for travelling; and to that passion he added another which brought him more than one misadventure. Books, which were less rare in Ireland than everywhere else, were nevertheless much sought after, and guarded with jealous care in the monastic libraries, which were their sole depositories. Not only an excessive value was put upon them, but they were even supposed to possess the emotions and almost the passions of living beings. Columba had a passion for fine manuscripts, and one of his biographers attributes to him the laborious feat of having transcribed with his own hand three hundred copies of the Gospel or of the Psalter. He went everywhere in search of volumes, which he could borrow or copy, often experiencing refusals which he resented bitterly. . . .

While visiting his ancient master, Finnian, our saint found means to make a clandestine and hurried copy of the abbot's Psalter, by shutting himself up at night in the church where the Psalter was deposited, lighting his nocturnal work, as happened to I know not what Spanish saint, by the light which escaped from his left hand while he wrote with the right. The abbot Finnian discovered what was going on by means of a curious wanderer, who, attracted by that singular light, looked in through the keyhole, and while his face was pressed against the door had his eye suddenly torn out by a crane, one of those familiar birds who were permitted by the Irish monks to seek a home in their churches. Indignant at what he thought a theft, Finnian claimed the copy when it was finished, on the ground that a copy made without permission ought to belong to the master of the original, seeing that the transcription is the son of the original book. Columba refused to give up his work, and the question was referred to the king in his palace at Tara. . . .

This king might accordingly be regarded as a competent judge in a contest at once monastic and literary; he might even have been suspected of partiality for Columba, his kinsman—and yet he pronounced against him. His judgment was given in a rustic phrase which has passed into a proverb in Ireland—To every cow her calf, and, consequently, to every book its copy.

§4.08 VENICE GRANTS THE FIRST PRIVILEGE FOR THE EXCLUSIVE PRINTING OF BOOKS

1469

The invention by Johannes Gutenberg, assisted by his partner, Jean Fust, of the printing press (importing from the wine industry the idea of transferring the ink from individual, movable characters, to paper) opened the doors to the fast and wide dissemination of knowledge in Europe. Invented (actually, improving on a technique invented in China, in the ninth century) in the first half of the fifteenth century, at Mainz, the new technique was kept as a secret for a very short time. Soon other European States, eager to bring that industry to their territories, would send artisans to Mainz to learn the technique. In their turn, German printers and booksellers would export books as well as the techniques to print them.

Searching for genuine works of Greek and Roman authors, checking their conformity with the originals, and putting them in a readable form, demanded much work and skills. The costs of obtaining the originals, acquiring the paper and the presses, added to that of ensuring skilled expertise, were high. Therefore, soon printers and booksellers would ask for some sort of governmental protection that could guarantee the recouping of those costs, as well as allowing them to make a living. In the absence of a special regime, European authorities used a system that they already knew, for they had been using it for a few centuries already—industrial privileges.

Printing privileges were very different from today's copyright, even if they accorded the exclusivity of reproducing certain works. Unlike today's copyright, privileges were indifferently granted to authors, printers, and booksellers. They were instruments of commercial rivalry, and thus of support for business and trade, but they were also—and in some cases, mainly—administrative acts of industry regulation (hence the term "licence" with which many privileges started), as well of tax exaction, and of religious censorship. Frequently, the acquisition of the privilege was preceded by and depended on the prior grant of the printing authorization by religious authorities (*imprimatur*). Another important condition included in many privileges was the accuracy of the works (many of which would be reprints and translations of classical books). This explains the mention made in a number of privileges to the necessity of an errata and the possibility of their lapsing in the event too many errors were to be found.

Since the art of printing has been introduced into our famed city, and among others, the reputation, commitment and character of Master Joannis de Spire have been indicated to us, who among other cities elected ours for his residence with his wife and children, and so as to exercise the said art of printing books; and now that, having received all the recommendations, he printed the Epistles of Cicero and Pliny's noble work concerning the Natural History, in the largest and most beautiful literary forms, and wishes to continue printing other splendid works with diligence and by humane virtue, so the price of many volumes can enrich him.

And given that such is an invention of our time, unique and entirely unknown, any support and help to advance it is to be fomented, as well as the efforts of Master Joannis, who suffered the expenses of the art and therefore must be rewarded . . .

By the Counsel, upon the humble and devout supplication of the aforesaid master John, it is decreed that during the next five years, no one else, whoever it might be, would dare to practice the said art of printing books in this beautiful city of Venice and its dominions, apart from Master Joannis.

And if someone is found that, in spite of this order, dared to practice this art and print books, he shall be fined and condemned to lose his equipment and books. And, under the same penalty, no books printed in other lands and places shall be sold.

§4.09 LOUIS XI, OF FRANCE, ACCORDS A FISCAL PRIVILEGE TO TWO GERMAN BOOKSELLERS

April 21, 1475

Louis, etc. On the part of our dear and beloved Conrart Hanequis and Pierre Scheffre, bourgeois merchants of the city of Mainz in Germany, we have been informed that they have occupied much of their time in the industry, art and use of the printing of writing, of which, by their care and diligence, they have made several beautiful, singular and exquisite books, both of stories and of various sciences, which they have sent to several places, and even to our town and city of Paris, both because of the remarkable university that exists there, and also because it is the capital city of our kingdom, and have committed several persons for the sale and distribution of books, and, among others, since some time, for that purpose they have committed and instructed for them one named Herman of Stathoen, a native of the Diocese of Munster in Germany, to whom they have entrusted and sent a certain quantity of books for selling them where he would wish, for the profit of the mentioned Conrart Hanequis and Pierre Scheffre, to whom Stathoen was due to render account, and Stathoen having sold several of those, concerning which, at the time of his death, he had the money in his hands, and likewise had several books in his possession and others that he had kept in custody in our city of Paris, and at Angiers, and elsewhere in various places of our kingdom, and that Stathoen has gone from life to death in our city of Paris; and for that reason, by the general law of our kingdom, whenever any foreigner and not native of our kingdom goes from life to death, without letters of citizenship and residence and our authorization to make will, all the goods that he has in our kingdom, at the time of his death, are attributed and belong to us by the right of *aubaine*, and that Stathoen was of the above mentioned quality, and had no letters of citizenship nor the capacity to make will, our prosecutor and other officers or commissioners have taken, seized and arrested all the books and other goods which he had with him and elsewhere in our kingdom, at the time of his death, and since then, and before anybody came to ask for them, those books and goods, or most of them were sold and diverted, and the resulting money was distributed, after which the mentioned Conrart Hanequis and Pierre Scheffre have come before us and the people of our council, and have shown that, although the books were in possession of Stathoen at the time of his death, they did not belong to him, but actually belonged and belong to the applicants, and to prove and demonstrate this, they have exhibited the will of Stathoen with certain schedules and obligations, and produced some witnesses and other things making mention of this, asking us to have the books and other goods returned to them, or the value and estimation of these, which they have estimated at the sum of two thousand four hundred twenty-five écus of gold and three sols tournois.

For these reasons, taking the things above mentioned considered, and also in consideration of what the very high and very powerful prince, our very dear and beloved brother, cousin and ally, the King of the Romans, has written to us on this matter, also that Hanequis and Scheffre are subjects of the country of our very dear and much beloved cousin Archbishop of Mainz, who is our relative, friend, confederate, and ally, who likewise on this has written and requested us, and for the good love and affection that we have for him, having also consideration of the pain and toil that the applicants have taken for the art and the printing industry, and for the profit and utility that comes and may come to the public thing as a whole, both for the growth of science and otherwise, and that all the value and estimation of the books and other goods that have come to our knowledge of two thousand four hundred and twenty-five écus and three sols tournois are not of a great amount, of which the applicants have estimated them, nevertheless, persuaded by the foregoing and other considerations, we have liberally inclined to restore to Conrart Hanequis and Pierre Scheffre the sum of two thousand four hundred and twenty-five écus and three sols tournois, and have accorded and granted them, accord and grant hereby, that on the money of our finances they have and take the sum of eight hundred pounds for each year, the first year starting on the first day of next October coming, and to continue from year to year forward until they are fully paid in the sum of two thousand four hundred and twenty-five écus and three sols tournois. Thus we order, etc.

By the king, the bishop of Evreux and several others present.

§4.10 VENICE GRANTS ITS FIRST PRINTING PRIVILEGE TO AN AUTHOR

September 1, 1486

In 1486 the Senate of Venice granted the first privilege to an author—Marcum Antonium Sabellico, hired to write the city's History—so that he could chose a printer of his preference. The privilege concerns a history of Venice (*Historiae rerum Venetarum ab urbe condita decades*), which was published in 1487 by Andrem de Torresanis de Asula.

MCCCCLXXXVI, first day of September.—The learned gentleman Marcum Antonium Sabellico has produced a work on the administration of our city, which, because of its elegance and historical truth, deserves to be known by all. For that reason the undersigned councilors deliberated and decided that the work elaborated by the aforesaid Marcum Antonium may be given to any diligent printer so that he prints it at his own expense, and with the care that befits the elegance of the history, so that it becomes immortal, and it is lawful that only he may print it under the penalty of the indignation of the Serenissimi Lord and of five hundred ducats not only in Venice but also in any city and dominion of the Serenissimi Lord.

§4.11 A PRIVILEGE GRANTED BY MANOEL I, OF PORTUGAL, TO A GERMAN PRINTER

February 25, 1503

Exclusive privilege granted in 1503 by Manoel I of Portugal to Valentim Fernandes, a German printer who carried out the profession in Lisbon between 1495 and 1516, for the printing of his *Regimentos* (Regulations).

This file has been made by mandate of Brás Affonso Correa, Reviewer, at the request of Valentim Fernandez, Bookseller

Year of the birth of our Lord Jesus Christ of one thousand five hundred and three years on the twenty-fifth day of February in the city of Lisbon, before Brás Affonso Correa, of the council of the King our lord and his court of appeals and Reviewer by him [given] authority in the mentioned city, Valentine Fernandez, bookseller, has appeared and presented to the Reviewer this decree from the lord, which is as follows:

We the King, through this decree are pleased, as regards the work that Valentine Fernandez has done in printing the books of the Regulations that we now order to be made for all the Judges and officials of the Kingdom, that no other person in our Kingdoms can print or make them except him, the mentioned Valentim Fernandez, under the penalty that whoever does the opposite pays a fine of one hundred gold cruzados, half for those who accuse him and the other [half] for the works of our hospital. And it also pleases Us that, if by chance they are printed and made out of the Kingdom and to these kingdoms and lordships brought to be sold, that they may not be sold to them as soon as they arrive from outside, under the same penalty for who sells or buys them. Upon that we order this decree to be passed, and order that it be complied with and kept as it is contained in it. And order that it be proclaimed and notified so that ignorance cannot be claimed.

We are pleased that this is valid as if it were a letter signed by us and sealed with our seal and passed by our chancellery, notwithstanding our regulation to the contrary. Done at Lisbon, this twentieth day of February, 1503.

And yet he will give them at the price at which he now gives these and not more.

King.

§4.12 IN VENICE, ALBERT DÜRER FILES A COMPLAINT FOR THE INFRINGEMENT OF HIS ENGRAVINGS AND TRADEMARK

1506

The text that follows is a report by Giorgi Vasari on a lawsuit that Albert Dürer, the celebrated German engraver, filed against Marcantonio Raimandi, from Bologna, who unashamedly imitated a number of his engravings, including his trademark, and sold them in Venice. Dürer could not obtain full satisfaction from the Doge, because the latter only determined that Marcantonio could not imitate Dürer's sign.

Marcantonio, perceiving to what honour and profit the man might aspire who should attach himself that branch of art in Italy, determined to devote his own time thereto, and commenced his work with all possible zeal and diligence,. He first began by copying those engravings thus obtained of Albert Dürer's, carefully studying the method of each stroke, and every other particular of the prints he had purchased, and which had obtained so much reputation by their novelty, and beauty, that all were seeking to become possessors of them. Having thus imitated the wood-cuts with strong lines on copper-plate, which he rendered as similar as possible to the work of Albert Dürer, until he had copied all the said Life and Passion of Christ in thirty-six plates, and having added the signature used by Albert on his plates,—this A.D., namely—he produced the most faithful similitude of his subjects, insomuch that, as no one knew them to be done by Marcantonio, they were supposed to be by Albert Dürer himself, whose works they were accordingly bought and sold.

When intelligence of this thing was written to Flanders, and one of the counterfeit plates by Marcantonio was at the same time sent to Albert, the latter fell into a most violent rage, and leaving Flanders he at once departed to Venice. Here he had recourse to the Signoria, and made his complaint against Marcantonio, but could obtain nothing beyond the command that Marcantonio should no longer affix to his works the name or signature aforesaid of Albert Dürer. . . .

§4.13 A PRIVILEGE GRANTED BY MANOEL I, OF PORTUGAL, TO JACOB CROMBERGER, EXTENDED TO ALL PRINTERS ESTABLISHED IN THE COUNTRY

February 20, 1508

Privilege granted in 1508 by Manoel I, of Portugal, to the German Printer Jacob Cromberger, who had established in Seville a printing shop with great commercial success. The privilege was motivated by the need to have the *Ordenações* (an official compilation of laws organized by order of Manoel I—hence called *Ordenações Manuelinas*) printed. That compilation was printed partly in Lisbon, and partly in Seville. However, this privilege did not concern one book specifically, but the "art of printing" in general, and extended to all printers then carrying out the business in Portugal. Besides, there was no mention to exclusivity in the industry, but to nobility privileges, and a sum of money.

Later, Cromberger's grandson, Jacomo Cromberger, would obtain from the Spanish sovereign a privilege to print books in Mexico.

Dom Manoel, etc. To those who see this letter of ours, we make known that, as regards what in his petition says Yacobo Cromberger, a German book printer, and how by our command he has come to serve us in these Kingdoms and how necessary is the noble art of printing in them for the good governance, because more easily and with less expense the ministers of justice may use our laws and regulations, and the priests may administer the sacraments of the Mother Holy Church, and wishing to be gracious and merciful to him, we consider appropriate that Yacobo Cromberger and all other book printers who, in our Kingdoms and lordships, currently use the mentioned art of printing, possess and have those same graces, privileges, liberties and honors that have and must have the knights of our house, by us confirmed, although they have no horses or weapons according to the regulation and as such are held and regarded everywhere with such an understanding, and for the time being in these kingdoms and lordships, that of the mentioned privilege are supposed to receive as capital two thousand doubloons of gold.

And in addition that they be old Christians without a part of Moor or Jew, or suspected of any heresy, nor have they incurred in infamy or the crime of lèse-majesté and not otherwise, because in this way I will have him longer at the service of our Lord and ours and our Kingdoms' good, in view of the danger that there will be some heresies through the books that they print. And we order all the officers and persons of Kingdoms and lordships to whom this letter of ours is shown and their knowledge belong, that the mentioned printers have and use for the sake of our Kingdoms and lordships the capital and the other things by means of the privilege, honors, and liberties, in the way and as long as in this letter of ours is contained without any doubt or challenge being raised against it, because that is our mercy. Given in our town of Santarém, XX days of February. Álvaro da Maia has made it. Year of our Lord Jesus Christ, of one thousand and five hundred and eight years.

§4.14 A PRIVILEGE GRANTED BY HENRY VIII, OF ENGLAND, TO RICHARD PYNSON

1510

In England the first printing privileges were granted in the early 1500s, but there is divergence among copyright historians as to their exact dates. The text that follows concerns a privilege granted by Henry VIII to Richard Pynson, circa 1510, for the exclusive printing of a compilation of statutes for a two-year term. The text of the privilege itself has been lost but the colophon of that work reads:

Here ends the statutes holden at Westminster the xxii day of January in the first year of the most noble reign of king Henry the viii. Imprinted in London by his commandment in Fleet Street, at the sign of the George, by Richard Pynson, printer unto his noble grace. With the privilege of our most gracious Sovereign lord king Henry the viii, granted to his trusty and wellbeloved servant Richard Pynson, printer unto his most noble grace, that no man within this Realm of England print nor sell, but such as the said Richard shall thereunto think best by the space of two years.

§4.15 ON THE PROTECTION OF ALBERT DÜRER'S WORKS

1512

The text that follows is a description by publisher and writer George Haven Putnam of how, in Nuremberg, certain works by Albert Dürer would be protected against unauthorized copying. Interestingly, one of Dürer's works—a technical essay on proportion—would be protected as regards the idea of its organization, rather than in its literary expression.

The works of Albert Dürer, both in art and in literature, afford early examples of the attempts of local governments to secure protection for copyrights.

In 1512, complaint was made to the Magistracy of Nuremberg that a certain man was offering for sale some prints or drawings which pretended to be the work of Dürer and which bore Dürer's signature, but that both the designs and the signatures were counterfeits. . . . The decision of the magistrates was that the sale of these prints must be stopped, and that the copies remaining which bore the fraudulent signature must be confiscated. In 1532, sometime after the death of Dürer, a certain Hans Guldemund re-engraved the *Triomph-wagen* and began to sell impressions from this unauthorised plate. The magistrates, upon being appealed to by Dürer's widow, promptly forbade Guldemund to make any further sales. The latter evidently delayed giving obedience to the order, and this was accordingly re-affirmed two weeks later.

Dürer's *Instruction in Perspective*, first published in 1525, appeared in Paris in a Latin translation in 1532, and copies of this Paris edition shortly found their way into sale in Nuremberg and in other German cities. Dürer's widow, who had, in 1528, secured an imperial privilege for her husband's writings, made complaint of these unauthorised sales, and, in October, 1532, the magistrates of Nuremberg summoned all the booksellers of the town and cautioned them against keeping in stock or selling any copies of the unauthorised editions. On the same day, copies of this Nuremberg order were sent to the magistrates of Strasburg, Frankfort, Leipzig, and Antwerp, with the request that similar orders should be issued in those cities for the protection of Dürer's works. It does not appear for how long a term the widow succeeded in protecting these copyrights either in Nuremberg or elsewhere.

The last case in which the infringement of Dürer's works came into question presents an instance of a larger claim for the protection of an author's idea than would be accepted under modern copyright law. Dürer's treatise on *Proportion* was being put into print in Nuremberg by Hieronymus Andreä. It became known, however, that Andreä, in conjunction with a painter named Beham, himself had in preparation a work on the subject of *Proportion* and in July, 1528, the magistrates of Nuremberg issued an edict forbidding these two authors from proceeding with the publication of their volume (which must, he saw fit to assume, have been based upon the labours of Dürer) until the publication of the authentic work (*das rechte Werk*) had been completed. Beham protested that his volume was entirely original and quite distinct in its plan from that of Dürer. The magistrates, however, took the ground that the idea or plan of a treatise on this subject had originated with Dürer, and that Dürer's heirs were entitled to be protected against any attempt to diminish (by means of such advance competition) the commercial value of such plan. Beham was obliged to content himself by publishing at this time that part of his work only which had to do with the subject of *Proportion in Horses*. His chapters on *Proportion in the Human Figure* were held in manuscript until 1546, when they were printed in book form in Frankfort. The completion of his publication showed that he had been entirely correct in his contention that he had not borrowed in any way from the material left by Dürer. The magistrates themselves do not appear to have adhered to their original charge that Andrea and Beham were pirating Dürer's work, or they would, instead of simply prohibiting their publication until the Dürer's book was in the market, have enjoined its publication altogether as a plagiarism or infringement. They seem simply to have convinced themselves that Dürer's wife and other heirs were entitled to the first fruits of any profits that could be secured from the subject of *Proportion*, on the ground that Dürer was the first author to give attention to this subject.

§4.16 HENRY VIII ACCORDS THE FIRST ENGLISH PRINTING PRIVILEGE TO AN AUTHOR, THOMAS LINACRE

1514

In circa 1514 (the exact date is unknown), king Henry VIII granted what seems to be the first English printing privilege accorded to an author, Thomas Linacre, for his work *Progymnasmata Grammatices Vulgaria*, a collection of texts for rhetorical exercises. The book was printed by John Castell. In the colophon, it reads:

Imprinted in London on the South side of Poulys by John Rastell with the privilege of our most sovereign lord king Henry the VIII granted to the compiler thereof that no man in this his realm sell none but such as the same compiler make printed for the space of II years.

§4.17 ERASMUS DEFENDS THE IDEA OF PRINTING PRIVILEGES

January 22, 1522

Erasmus of Rotterdam proposes the idea of printing privileges in favor of his printer, Johannes Forben, of Basel, in a letter of January 28, 1522. A few years later Luther would also defend the rights of printers to exclusivity. However, both theologians were more concerned with the need to promote the dissemination of holy works of high quality and correction than to support the commercial rivalry of entrepreneurs. Nevertheless, Luther secured for his 1534 German translation of the Bible a privilege granted by the Elector of Saxony.

As soon as a work leaves Froben's printing press, if the commercial success seems certain, he [the counterfeiter] seizes a copy; the work is counterfeited and sold at a lower price. However Froben advances his funds and goes bankrupt. This misfortune would be prevented if the Emperor wished to prohibit the reprinting of what Froben had already printed, and prohibited it for two years. This term is short, but the printing press of Froben is worthy of this favor; nothing bad or seditious comes out of it.

§4.18 THE FRENCH PARLIAMENT GRANTS A PRIVILEGE TO A BOOKSELLER

November 29, 1539

Extracted from the records of the Parliament.

On the request submitted to the court, by Vincent Sertenas, merchant Bookseller, residing in this city of Paris. By which he requested that it would be allowed to have printed and displayed for sale a small treatise *L'aman mal traité de sa mie* [The lover poorly treated by his girlfriend], previously translated from the Spanish language to the French language. Which deals with the honest and chaste love of Arnalte and Lucenda: for recovering a great quantity of deniers he would have spent. For this reason, he requested inhibitions and prohibitions to all other Booksellers and Printers, to print and display the said Books for sale. In order that the applicant may recover those deniers he deemed convenient to spend, seen by the court the request, and the treatise whose printing is in question. And all considered, the court has permitted and permits that the applicant orders the printing and offer for sale of the mentioned treatise at a reasonable price, for the next two years. And it prohibits all other Booksellers and Printers to print and offer for sale the said treatise, under the penalty of confiscation of the books they would have printed, and of arbitrary fine. Done at the Parliament, on the twenty-ninth day of November, year of one thousand five hundred thirty nine.

§4.19 JACOB CROMBERGER OBTAINS ANOTHER PRIVILEGE—THIS TIME FROM CHARLES V, OF SPAIN, FOR PRINTING IN MEXICO

June 6, 1542

The same German printer, Cromberger, who made a fortune printing books under privileges in Spain and Portugal, obtained another privilege to carry out his business in New Spain (Mexico). The text that follows confirms that privilege and assigns it to Cromberger's widow and successors.

Real privilege chart to the wife and children of Juan Cromberger, confirming to them the one that was previously granted to him, so that only he could transfer books to New Spain and exercise the art of printing there.— Talavera, June 6, 1542.

The King. — Because on the part of you, the wife and children of Joan Conbergel [*sic*], printer, neighbor who went from the city of Seville, deceased, I have been informed that the said Joan Conbergel, at the request of our Viceroy of New Spain and the Bishop of Mexico, has sent to that land officers and printing and all necessary equipment, and printed books of Christian doctrine in all ways of science: and that, seen by the Bishops of that land the great benefit that followed from printing books, and that they be sent from these kingdoms, agreed and arranged with him that he had to make available in the city of Mexico books of all faculties and doctrines, and that it be given to him the profit of one hundred percent; that he may have a printing shop and be given for each printed folio a small quarter of silver, that each booklet has the value of half real, and for that, Us being served, we have provided that no other could sell books or booklets, or anything else printed, and that no other could print in New [Spain] except him or who your authorisation had, as it may seem in accordance with what had been agreed with him, of which before Us, on your behalf, has been presented, which said agreement had been seen by our President and ombudsmen of our Royal Audience of the said New Spain and had been approved by them; and that now you, in fulfillment of the mentioned agreement, given that Joan Convergel [*sic*] is dead, wish to do and fulfill what he was obligated to, and you have begged Us that, because the thing was so profitable in the service of God Our Lord, and ours, and the good of that land, we were served to prohibit that within twenty years no one could bring to New Spain books or booklets to sell, which you would give at the price that by the said Bishops had been fixed, and that furthermore We have provided that no one could have a printing shop in New Spain but you, or according to my mercy: which, seen by those of our Council of Indias, together with the agreement of the said Bishops and with the confirmation made on them by our President and Ombudsmen, it was agreed that I should give this chart, and I have agreed; therefore, you, the heirs, taking to the city of Mexico books of all faculties and doctrines according to the agreement, we defend and command that for the next ten years, running and being counted from January 1 of next year, of five hundred and forty-two years onwards, that no one nor any persons can take to New Spain to sell in it any printed book or booklet, of any science whatsoever, but you or whom you authorize, and if they take and sell, that they lose it and they be [conveyed] to our chamber and treasury, provided that neither you nor whom you authorize may take from those books more than one hundred percent of profit.

And moreover for the said time we give you license and faculty so that you or whom you authorize and not any other person, may have in New Spain a print shop and charge for each printed folio a small quarter of silver, so that each book is worth one half real and not more, according to the agreement the Bishops have granted you; hereby we determine that during the period of ten years no person may have a print shop in New Spain, unless it is you or whom you have determined.— Done in the town of Talavera, on the sixth day of the month of June of one thousand and five hundred and forty-two years.—F R. Ga. Car.^{lis} Hispalen.—By His Majesty's order. The Governor on his behalf — Joan de Samano.

§4.20 VENICE PASSES THE FIRST (?) COPYRIGHT STATUTE

February 7, 1544

Is the text that follows the first copyright statute? Even if it comes with an old taste, this Venetian Statute, enacted by the Great Council of Venice, of 1544, unequivocally makes the printing of any new book dependent on the previous permission, in writing, by the author or his/her successor. Even though the birth of modern copyright can be assigned to the Statute of Queen Anne, of 1710, copyright, in its essence, is not much different from this.

In 1603, the Senate of Venice adopted a detailed regulation covering the matter of the quality of the books as regards the need for their revision and correction, as well their printing characters (*see* Text 4.28).

MDXLIIII. 7th Day of February. In the Council.

The boldness and the greed for gains of some printers in our city have increased so much, that they dare to print whatever they like, and to name the composers of those things they print, without any knowledge by the latter, and even against their wish: Having this matter been brought to the attention of the heads of this Council, so that we immediately find a solution, which must be given now, and therefore;

It is ordered that no printer in our city dare to print, or sell any printed work in whatever language, unless the authorisation of its author, or his closest heirs, is expressed in an authentic document at the Reformatory of Our Study of Padua, to which the knowledge of that matter has been attributed, and that is stamped, and sell it, under the penalty of paying one ducato per each book and each author injured in the case it is printed against the present order, and of being imprisoned for one month, and that all books printed in that manner be confiscated and immediately burned, and the whistleblower who has brought the truth to light receive half of the mentioned fine, and the other half go to the Hospital of Mercy, and the present law be published over the stairs of San Marco and Rialto.

§4.21 IN THE MIDDLE OF THE SIXTEENTH CENTURY, FRANCE HAD ALREADY DEVELOPED A STANDARD FORMULATION OF PRINTING PRIVILEGES

August 11, 1551

The text that follows concerns a privilege granted by Henry II, of France, in 1551, to two booksellers of Lyon, for the publication of La Morosophie. The language of this privilege corresponds to what can be designated as a standard formulation of printers' rights, which the French administration developed through the sixteenth century.

Also noteworthy, given that the privilege was granted to two merchants, it ends with the record of the grant of a license by the grantees to the printer.

Henry by the grace of God King of France, to our beloved and loyal counselors, the people holding our courts of Parliament, provost of Paris, Sénéchaux of Lyon, Tolouse, Poitou and Provence: and to all our other justices and officers, or to their lieutenants, greetings and predilection. We have received the humble supplication of our dear and beloved Jean Mounier and Jean Perrin, booksellers in our city and university of Toulouse: containing that for some time now they would have rediscovered certain works, both in Latin in French. That is to say, a book entitled The Morosophy of William the Perriere Tolosan, containing a hundred Moral Emblems, illustrated with figures: and Latin verses, translated into as many French quatrains, dedicated to our very dear, and beloved cousin, the Duke of Vendome. Plus another book by the said author, entitled *The Considerations of the Four Worlds, Divine, Angelic, Celestial, and Sensible: in four Centuries, of French quatrains*. Which contain the Cream of Divine and Human Philosophy, dedicated to our dear and beloved Messrs. Pierre, Jacques, and Michel du Faur, brothers. Item another copy on Civil Law, of a named Antoine Govea, Doctor of Law: entitled *Antoni Goveani Jurisconsulti, de Iurisdictione libri duo, adversus Eguinarium Baronem Jurisconsultum, ad Petrum Castellanum Episcopum, Matesconen fem, et magnum Galliae elecmosynarium*. Which books they would like to print and advertise. But they doubt that, after the books will be printed, other booksellers or printers of the Kingdom will use them to make copies to print, sell, and distribute. And because they would be frustrated as regards their work, expenses, and efforts, if by us they had not been offered a suitable remedy. For that reason, these things considered, wishing that the good letters be spread throughout our Kingdom: liberally, at the supplication of Mounier and Perrin, desiring that the merit of their labor be not seized from them, nor the recovering of their expenses be prevented to them. For these causes and other good considerations, based on our certain science, special grace, full power and Royal authority: we have permitted and granted, permit and grant by these present [letters], to supplicants Jean Mounier and Jean Perrin, we wish and are pleased to allow them to print, or have printed, and offer for sale the books above specified, in large and small volumes, together or separately, as they see fit, for the time and term of the next consecutive ten years, counting from the day and date that the books will be finished to print, so many times, and in such number as they see fit: with express inhibitions, and defenses, to all booksellers and printers, merchants and any other of our said Kingdom, to print, to make print, or to put on sale or distribution in our said Kingdom, lands and lordships: except those that will have been printed by them or by their employees, or by their will and consent, under the penalty of confiscation of the books that will be printed and sold other than in the manner contained above, and an arbitrary fine. Thus we command, to each of you to whom it will concern, enjoin and commit that from our present grace, permission and grant, you do, allow and let the supplicants, to enjoy and use fully, and peacefully, during that period, as above it is said, ceasing and making to cease all disturbances and impediments on the contrary: for such is our pleasure: notwithstanding any ordinances, restrictions, orders, or prohibitions and letters contrary wise.

Given at Fontainebleau, on the eleventh day of August, the year of grace one thousand five hundred and fifty one, and of our kingdom the fifth. . . .

With the consent and agreement of the applicants above, the present Morosophie was completed, in Lyon, by Macé Bonhomme, this February 12, 1553.

§4.22 EDWARD VI GRANTS A PRINTING PRIVILEGE TO JOHN DAY

March 25, 1553

Edward the sixth by the grace of God King of England, France and Ireland, Defender of the Faith, and of the church of England and also of Ireland in earth the supreme head.

To all manner of Printers, Booksellers, and other our Officers, Ministers and Subjects, greetings.

We do you to understand, that of our grace especial, we have granted and given privilege and licence, and by these presents do grant and give privilege and licence, to our wellbeloved subject John Daye, of our City of London Printer, unto his factors and assigns, to Print, or cause to be printed, as well this Catechism in English, which we have caused to be set forth for the better instruction of youth, to be taught in English Schools, as also an A. B. C. with the Brief Catechism, already printed, any other privilege to the contrary in anywise notwithstanding.

And furthermore our pleasure is that the same John Day, his factors and assigns, shall and may have the only printing from time to time of the same Catechisms, in recompense of his industry pains and charges to be sustained in that behalf. Straightly forbidding by these presents all and singular our subjects, as well printers as book sellers, as all other persons within our Realms and dominions whatsoever they be, to print, or cause to be printed, within any our said dominions, these Catechisms aforesaid, or any of them, but only the said John Day, and his assigns, neither to buy any other sorts of impressions than such as shall be printed by the said John Day and his assigns, upon pain of our high displeasure, and that every offender therein shall forfeit to our use xls. for every such catechism, so printed, or bought, contrary to the true meaning of this our present licence and privilege, over and besides all such catechisms to be forfeited to whomsoever shall sustain the charges and sue the said forfeiture in our behalf.

Willing therefore and commanding all our officers and ministers as they tender our favour and will avoid our displeasure and indignation for the contrary, that they and every one of them (if need shall require) do aid and assist the foresaid John Day, his factors and assigns, in due exercising and execution of this our present licence and privilege with the effect according to the true meaning of the same. In witness whereof we caused these our letters to be made patents. Witness ourself at Westminster, the xxv day of March, the vii year of our Reign.

§4.23 ENGLAND CENTRALIZES THE BUSINESS OF PRINTING OF BOOKS IN THE COMPANY OF STATIONERS

May 4, 1557

As in France and Venice, the first English printers would be bestowed with privileges. But it did not take very long before the business of printing and selling books was concentrated under the guild of printers, incorporated under the name of Company of Stationers of London. According to the respective Charter, no book could be printed in England "or the dominions of the same, unless the same person at the time of his foresaid printing is or shall be one of the community of the foresaid mystery or art of Stationery of the foresaid City." Initially, as the Company's Charter itself states, the idea was to control the conformity of published books to the ideas of the Catholic Church.

The creation of the Company of Stationers, however, did not put an immediate end to individual printing privileges. The two regimes would coexist for a period, and naturally that would give rise to tensions. Tensions of a professional nature would also arise within the Company, which would favor the gains of a few wealthy printers, in detriment of others, who would end up ruined and unemployed. Various orders and statutes would be later enacted by the Parliament so as to attempt to overcome those tensions and confirm the Company's exclusive authority. These tensions would later give rise to the emerging of copyright law in England, which puts the focus of protection on authors and original works.

Charter of the Company of Stationers of London, May 4, 1557

The king and queen to all to whom etc. greeting.

Know ye that we, considering and manifestly perceiving that certain seditious and heretical books, rhymes and treatises are daily published and printed by divers scandalous, malicious, schismatical and heretical persons, not only moving our subjects and lieges to sedition and disobedience against us, our crown and dignity, but also to renew and move very great and detestable heresies against the faith and sound catholic doctrine of Holy Mother Church, and wishing to provide a suitable remedy in this behalf, of our special grace and from our certain knowledge and mere motion we will give and grant for ourselves, the heirs and successors of us the foresaid Queen, to our beloved and faithful lieges . . ., free men of the mystery or art of Stationery of our City of London, and the suburbs of the same, that they from hence forth may be in fact, deed and name one body by themselves for ever, and one perpetual community incorporated of one Master and two Keepers or Wardens in the community of the same Mystery or Art of Stationery of the foresaid City, and that they may have perpetual succession. . . .

And further we ordain, create, erect, make, and appoint by these presents the foresaid Master Wardens and community in deed and in name one body by themselves for ever, and one community for ever incorporated of one Master and two Keepers or Wardens and the community of the same mystery or art of Stationery of the foresaid city of London, and we incorporate the Master, Keepers or Wardens and community, and we will grant, create, erect, ordain, make, declare and appoint them by these presents to be a corporate body by the name of "The Master and Keepers or Wardens and Community of the mystery or art of Stationery of the City of London," for ever to endure really and in full; and that the same Masters, Keepers or Wardens and community may have for the future perpetual succession; and that the Master and Keepers or Wardens and community and their successors shall be for ever entitled, named, and called by the name of "The Masters and Keepers or Wardens and Community of the Mystery or Art of Stationery of the City of London" and by that name shall have power to plead and be impleaded and answer and be answered in all and several matters, suits and complaints, actions, demands and causes before any judges and justices, and in any courts and places; and they shall have a common seal to serve and make use of for their matters and business, and for the sealing of all and several their deeds and writings in any wise touching or concerning their affairs and business; . . .

Besides we will, grant, ordain, and appoint for ourselves and the successors of us the foresaid Queen that no person within this our realm of England or the dominions of the same shall practice or exercise by himself or by his ministers, his servants or by any other person the art or mystery of printing any book or anything for sale or traffic within this our realm of England or the dominions of the same, unless the same person at the time of his foresaid printing is or shall be one of the community of the foresaid mystery or art of Stationery of the foresaid City, or has therefore license of us, or the heirs or successors of us the foresaid Queen by the letters patent of us or the heirs or successors of us the foresaid Queen.

Further we will, grant, ordain, and appoint for ourselves, the heirs and successors of us the foresaid Queen to the foresaid Master, Keepers or Wardens and community of the mystery or art of Stationery of the City of London aforesaid and their successors for ever, that it shall be lawful for the Master and Keepers or Wardens aforesaid and their successors for the time being to make search whenever it shall please them in any place, shop, house, chamber, or building of any printer, binder or bookseller whatever within our kingdom of England or the dominions of the same of or for any books or things printed, or to be printed, and to seize, take, hold, burn, or turn to the proper use of the foresaid community, all and several those books and things which are or shall be printed contrary to the form of any statute, act, or proclamation, made or to be made; and that if any person shall practice or exercise the foresaid art or mystery contrary to the foresaid form, or shall disturb, refuse, or hinder the foresaid Master or Keepers or Wardens for the time being or any one of them for the time being, in making the foresaid search or in seizing, taking, or burning the foresaid books or things, or any of them printed or to be printed contrary to the form of any statute, act, or proclamation, that then the foresaid Master and Keepers or Wardens for the time being shall imprison or commit to jail any such person so practicing or exercising the foresaid art or mystery contrary to the foresaid form, or as is stated above, disturbing, refusing or hindering, there to remain without bail for the space of three months; and that the same person so practicing or exercising the foresaid art or mystery contrary to the foresaid form, or so, as is above stated, disturbing, refusing or hindering, shall forfeit for each such practicing or exercising aforesaid against the form aforesaid and for each such disturbance, refusal or hindrance a hundred shillings of lawful money of England, one half thereof to us, the heirs and successors of us the foresaid Queen, and the other half thereof to the foresaid Master, Keepers or Wardens and community. . . .

In witness of which thing we have caused to be made these our letters patent. Witnesses—the King and Queen at Westminster, the fourth day of May. By writ of privy seal, etc.

§4.24 FELIPE II, OF SPAIN, GRANTS A PRIVILEGE TO A PRINTER BASED IN BRUSSELS

1565

This privilege was granted by king Felipe II of Spain in the quality of sovereign of the Low Countries. Interestingly, the privilege covered not only the printing of the book concerned, but also its translation to other languages.

Excerpt from the Privilege

The King has allowed, and allows Guglielmo Silvio, Royal printer, that only he may print, sell and distribute through all these Low Countries the present *Descrittione delli paesi Bassi, cõmposta in Anversa by M. Lodovico Guicciardini*: And H. M. prohibits all Booksellers, Printers, and anyone else to print, or have printed in such countries of His, to sell, or to distribute the aforementioned *Descrittione* within the next ten years. Also prohibiting translating it, or having it translated into other languages for printing, without license, or the consent of the aforementioned Silvio under severe penalties, as it is widely contained in privileges; Given at Brussels, on the xxviij. of September. MDLXV. Bourgeois & I. de Facuwez.

§4.25 LUIS DE CAMÕES, THE PORTUGUESE POET, OBTAINS A PRINTING PRIVILEGE FOR HIS EPIC POEM, THE LUSIADS

September 24, 1571

In 1571, Sebastian, king of Portugal granted a privilege to Luís de Camões, for the exclusive printing of his epic poem, Os Lusíadas, for ten years.

I, the King, make known to those who see this Decree that I decide and it pleases me to give license to Luís de Camões so that he can have printed in this city of Lisbon, a work in eighth rhyme called Os Lusíadas, which contains ten perfect Cantos, in which by poetic order, in verse, the main deeds of the Portuguese in the parts of India are declared, after the navigation towards them has been discovered by the order from King Dom Manoel . . . who in holy glory may be, and with the privilege that in a period of ten years that shall commence from the day on which the printing of said work has finished onwards, it cannot be printed or sold in my kingdoms and lordships, nor brought from outside, nor taken to those parts of India to be sold, without permission of the said Luís de Camões or the person who has his power for that, under the penalty for who does otherwise to pay fifty cruzados and lose the printed volumes, or sell, half for the said Luis de Camões, and the other half for those who accuse them.

And before the mentioned work is sold, its price shall be determined by the board of my appellate judges of the palace, which shall be declared and imprinted on the first sheet of said work, so as to be known to all, and before being printed it shall be seen and examined by the general board of the holy office of the Inquisition, so that it be printed with their license, and if the said Luís de Camões adds a few more Cantos, they will also be printed with the license of the Holy Office, as stated above. And this Decree of mine shall also be printed at the beginning of the mentioned work, which I decide to be valuable and enforceable, as if it were a perfect letter on my behalf, signed by me and done by my Chancellery, regardless of the Rule of the second book, par. xx., which says that things whose effect is to last for more than one year shall be approved through letters, and if approved by decrees they shall be not valid. Gaspar de Seixas did it in Lisbon, on September 24, 1571. Jorge da Costa has done and written it.

§4.26 A WELL-KNOWN PRINTER'S TRADEMARK (THE FLORENTINE LILY FLOWER) IS COUNTERFEITED IN FRANCE

August 3, 1579

Business opportunities and market demand in the printing industry gave rise to fierce competition, and fierce and poorly controlled competition gave rise to many conflicts. The text that follows is an excerpt from the judgment of the Parliament of Paris, of 1579, settling a dispute between a Florentine printer, Philippe Tinghy, and Jeanne Joncti, the heiress of another Florentine printer, Jacques Joncti, both based in Lyon, involving the right to the exclusive use of the lily flower trademark.

On Monday, third day of August, one thousand five hundred seventy-nine, the President, between Philippes Tinghy, merchant bookseller living in Lyon, appealing from a sentence against him delivered by the Seneschal and people holding the presidential authority at Lyon, on the twenty-first day of March, one thousand five hundred and seventy-eight, and applicant of the homologation of a request submitted by him to the Court on the third day of June, one thousand five hundred and seventy-nine, on the one hand, and Miss Jeanne Joncty, residing at said Lyon, daughter and heiress by half of the late Jacques Joncty, also a Bourgeois living in said Lyon, appealed, and defendant against the homologation of the said request, on the other hand, the qualities of the parties not harming or prejudicing the parties. . . .

Brillon, on behalf of the King's Attorney General, says that it is necessary that the Court rules over the Parties, because the Privileges obtained on both sides have been verified; And this competition brings a division between them, which is one of their differences, and on the other [hand] concerning the mark, it is certain that it has been owned and peculiar to the late Jacques Joncti, Florentin national, and resident in France, who, through his inheritance, transmitted this mark to his daughter and heiress, who wants to continue his father's business: and with this purpose, in the month of September 1577, she obtained letters from the King, as it was necessary, by which she has been allowed to use the mark, exclusively against all others, which were verified in following January, 1578. From which time the Appellant, who is of the same nation, seeing the great course of the books and prints of the said Joncty, of whom he is said to have been a servant, obtained a Privilege to print certain books; and he affixed to those the mark of the Fleur-de-lis [lily flower], which was here verified, but five or six months after that of the respondent, and without hearing her: and the respondent says that this mark is hereditary in their house, and granted to her deceased father who has used it for a long time, and under it great books have been printed, that the Appellant cannot and must not illegally appropriate this mark, which is owned by and peculiar to the house of the respondent: that the marks of the Printers are of great importance to the success and the trade of the books, because the reputation of a good Printer is recognised by the mark, which, once he departs, must remain exclusively with the Appellant.

Now it is certain that on a similar dispute between two Counselors over their marks, the Court by Judgment ordered that it should remain with the person who had first taken it: and by other judgments the marks have always been kept by those who have used them the first, and who are known by their marks, on which their works have had some circulation: so that the Appellant cannot take this mark, nor use it, whatever the difference he says, by affixing the printer's name: which would only lead to confusion.

And it is reasonable that each one apart has its distinct and separate marks. In view of the privileges to print the books mentioned there, exclusively to each other, they are true monopolies and of great importance against the public liberty, especially to print again the books already printed hereafter, which must remain in the freedom of each and every one. . . .

That if they have bought some copies, or that by their art they have bound some new book, it is reasonable that they enjoy their privileges, but not old books for the impression of which it is necessary to open the door to each one; because otherwise it would be to impose high prices. By means of which the Court, if it pleases, as regards the mark and the shop sign, will keep it with the respondent. And as to the privileges, that everyone be allowed to print the books hereafter printed.

The Court, given that the appellant's solicitor and attorney did not know how to say valid causes, nor wanted to conclude, has dismissed and dismisses the appellation, ordered that the appealed will take her plain and full effect, and condemns the Appellant to the expenses of the cause of appeal, which shall be taxed without further journey, and in two écus and one twelfth of écu of a fine for the benefit of the King. [The Court] has evoked and evokes the main trial and dispute between the Parties: and stating the law, concerning the mark and the shop sign, it orders that it will remain with the Joncty, as having first occupied it.

And as regards the privileges, after having heard the King's Attorney General, [the Court] orders that there shall be no respect, except for the books which have not yet been printed hereafter; and as regards the others already printed, that they may be printed by all the Printers who will be able and will want to print them in full freedom. And homologating the request of the Attorney General, inhibits and forbids all Printers to have any books printed outside the Kingdom, on pain of forfeiture, and a fine of four thousand écus: and the Attorney General will have authority to inform about those who are said to have printed books outside this Kingdom; for the information made and reported, to decree against the guilty, as it will be to be done by reason.

§4.27 THE PUBLISHER OF MICHEL DE MONTAIGNE, THE FRENCH PHILOSOPHER, OBTAINS A PRINTING PRIVILEGE FOR HIS ESSAYS

May 9, 1579

Michel de Montaigne, one of the most influencing philosophers of the sixteenth century, had his essays first published in 1580, in Bordeaux. The privilege of exclusive printing (for the term of eight years) the first and second editions (1580 and 1582) of the essays was granted in 1579 to a printer of Bordeaux (S. Millanges), not to the author.

Excerpt from the Privilege

By privilege of the King, given in Paris on the 9th of May, 1579, it is permitted to S. Millanges, Ordinary Printer of the King, to print all new books: provided that they are approved by Monseigneur the Archbishop of Bordeaux, or his Vicar, and one or two doctors in theology, with very expresses prohibitions to all others of any quality, of printing, selling, or distributing them for eight years after the first print, without the consent of the said Millanges, as it is contained more broadly in the letters of the said. Signed De Puiberal.

§4.28 VENICE REVISES ITS "COPYRIGHT ACT" OF 1544

May 21, 1603

In 1603 the Senate of Venice adopted a detailed regulation covering the matter of the quality of the books as regards the need for their revision and correction, as well their printing characters. The regulation also determined the terms of exclusive protection for books printed in the city.

MDCIII. on xxi May. At Pregadi.

XX. Among the other arts that most greatly enhance the splendor of this City, that of Printing has always had preeminence, because with great accuracy, and labor carried out for a long time by its masters, has multiplied with great Public reputation, and very notable benefit to so many employees, engaged in the said Work. Today, as a result of the development that has occurred in this matter, and the devices having been taken to foreign States, with the continuous deviations of Masters and Workers, [the art of Printing] has been severely annihilated, and for the little care and greed of the Printers, who no longer have any interest in that the works be well printed, in good Form, and on good Paper, and [for that matter] due to the lack of sufficient Reviewers, ending in Works full of errors, it has lost that reputation, which used to give to Books of Venice great commercial success; therefore we should no longer delay in taking the appropriate Provision, and enact those norms that may best remove the above mentioned inconveniences; That the previous rules, which remain firm, and valid those Deliberations and Orders, which have up to now been enacted in relation to the Printing, not incompatible with the present, be in the future entirely observed as far as the subsequent Chapters are concerned. . . .

Who is registered in the aforesaid Art and prints any new Book in this city, not printed in any other place, will have the permission to print it, provided he informs those of the aforesaid Board that he will have been the first [to print], and wishes to have no privilege other than excluding others from printing it or selling it in the whole of Our Domain, for the next twenty years. As regards those [books] that will be printed in Italy, both near and beyond Monti, provided they are printed in accordance with the above mentioned License, they will have privilege for ten Years. And if any of those Registered [printers] wishes to print any Book of great esteem, as has happened several times, which is not for twenty Years after its printing, he shall have privilege for that of ten Years. And for those not printed ten Years before, [they shall have privilege] of five Years, with this express condition, that if these will not start printing these Works at the end of one month, after being given notice, that shall continue at least printing a half folio every day, and if they do not do so, except for the right impediment to be known by those of the aforementioned Board, of which they should report to the mentioned Reformers, are deemed deprived from the Privilege . . .

§4.29 MIGUEL DE CERVANTES, THE SPANISH NOVELIST, OBTAINS A PRINTING PRIVILEGE FOR HIS NOVEL, EL INGENIOSO HIDALGO DE LA MANCHA

September 26, 1604

The King. Because, on your part, Miguel de Cervantes, it has been reported to us that you have composed a book entitled *El Ingenioso Hidalgo de la Mancha*, which has cost you a lot of work, and is very useful, and helpful, you have asked us, and begged, that we give you the license and faculty for printing it, and privilege for the time we are served, or pursuant to our mercy. Which having been seen by those of our Council, because upon the mentioned book the diligences have been made according to the statute by us approved that deals with the printing of books, it has been agreed that we should order that this chart be given to you, for that reason, and he have agreed.

For which reason, for doing you good and mercy, we give you license and faculty, so that you, or the person that may have your authorisation, and not any other, may print the said book, entitled *El Ingenioso Hidalgo de la Mancha*, which is mentioned above, in all our Kingdoms of Castilla, for the time and period of ten years, that run and be counted from the said day of the date of our chart. Under penalty, that the person, or persons, who, without having your authorisation, print it, or sell it: or have it printed, or sold, for that reason lose the print that he has made, with the molds, and its equipment: and moreover he will incur in the penalty of fifty thousand maravedís, every time he does the contrary.

Of which penalty the third party be for the person who will accuse him: and the other third party, for our Chamber: and the other third party, for the judge who will sentence him. So much so that every time you make the said book to be printed, during the mentioned period of ten years, you bring it to our Council, together with the original one that has been seen, that each mold be initialed, and signed at its end, by Juan Gallo de Andrada, our Chamber scribe, of those who reside there, to know if the said print is in conformity with the original: or bring it if in public form, [as evidence that] a Reviewer appointed by our mandate has seen it, and corrected the said print, in accordance with the original, and that it has been printed according to it, and the errata by him designated is printed for each book of those that are thus printed, so that the price be set for each volume you decide to have.

And we order the Printer that, when he prints the said book, does not print the beginning, nor its first folio, nor delivers more than one single book, with the original, to the Author, or to the person at whose expense he prints it, and to no other, for that purpose of the said correction, and price setting, until the first book is corrected, and its price set by those of our Council: and [this] being done, and not otherwise, [he] may print the beginning, and the first folio, and successively put this chart of ours, and the approval, price, and errata, under the penalty of incurring in the penalties contained in the laws, and statutes of our Kingdoms. We order those of our Council, and any other of their law enforcers, that they keep, and comply with this chart, and with what is contained therein. Made at Valladolid, on the twenty-sixth day of September, of one thousand six hundred and four years. I the King.

§4.30 A COLLECTION OF FRENCH RULES ON PRINTING PRIVILEGES

1620

Unlike England, France opted for regulating the business of printing and selling books through specific regulations, rather than by setting a guild. Bouchel, a celebrated jurist, elaborated a consolidation of the rules that regulated the French industry of printing, in which he gathered a few norms, patent letters, and case law, adopted in the course of the sixteenth and seventeenth centuries at that were in force in 1620, date of the publication. Here are the excerpts concerning printing privileges.

Art. LXXVI.

It is forbidden for all Booksellers, Printers, and Binders to counterfeit the books upon which there will be a privilege received from the King: including to buy any of them so counterfeited from foreign merchants, or to have them brought in any manner whatsoever, under the penalties established by the privileges which would have been obtained.

Art. LXXVII.

It is equally forbidden for all Printers, Booksellers, and Binders to obtain any extension of the privileges for the printing of books, if there is no increase [in the contents] of the books whose privileges have expired.

Art. LXXVIII.

Once a Book has been made public, or printed outside the Kingdom, no one can obtain a special privilege to print it in this Kingdom.

§4.31 PRINTING PRIVILEGE GRANTED BY LOUIS XIII, OF FRANCE

November 12, 1637

As mentioned above, in the sixteenth and seventeenth centuries France developed a standard formulation of the rights expressed in printing privileges (*see* Text 4.22). The text that follows confirms this: a printing privilege granted by Louis XIII, of France, in 1637, to Mathurin Jousse, author of LE SECRET DE L'ARCHITECTURE, with language very similar to that text.

In 1639 the author assigned his privilege to the printer, George Griveau.

Extract from the Privilege of the King.

Louis by the grace of God, King of France and Navarre. To our loved ones and subjects. Counselors of people holding our Courts of Parliament, Bailiffs, Seneschals, Provosts, or their lieutenants, and to each of them in right oneself as it will belong, greetings.

Our beloved Mathurin Jousse, Engineer, and Architect in our city of Flèche, has shown us that he has worked intensively and extensively to elaborate and put in writing a Treatise on Perspective, and one on Geometric Traits, in two books and two volumes. The first entitled *La Perspective positive de Viator, Latine et Française, revue et augmentée, et réduite du petit au grand*. The second entitled *Le Secret d'Architecture, découvrant fidèlement les Traits Geométriques, coupés et*

> *dérobements nécessaires à toutes sortes d'entreprises dans les Bâtiments*. Enriched with various figures, with interpretations of them, with a large number of illustrations, both in detail and otherwise, which he added to the discourse for the intelligence of his intention: which Treaties the applicant would gladly have printed, and bring to light in the said form and manner. And fearing that after having worked for a long time and made the expenses that it suits him to do for the printing of them (without having our Letters of Privilege) some others undertake to have them printed and put on sale (which would make him completely frustrated of his toil). He humbly begged us to grant those to him. Therefore, wishing to make the applicant enjoy the costs of his work, dedication, and to recover the expenses that he wishes to incur in engraving those figures and prints, we have permitted and granted, permit and grant to the applicant, as he requests, to have printed, sold, and distributed by such persons as he thinks fit, the books, designs, and figures, jointly or separated in such characters and volumes, and as many times as he thinks fit, and to display them for sale, sell and distribute them in all places and venues of our Kingdom; and this for the time of nine years whole and completed, from the day that the books will be finished to print; during that period no engravers, book sellers, printers, imagers, and others can engrave, print, or have printed the said Treaties or Figures, nor sell and distribute them, of which We make express prohibitions and interdictions, under a penalty of fifteen hundred pounds of fine, payable half to Us, and half to the Party concerned, [in addition to] expenses, damages, and interests of the said applicant, and seizures of the copies. And so that they do not allege ignorance, We want that by having the present [letters] placed at the end of the copies, they are held for certified, with the responsibility nevertheless to send two copies of the said books to our Library of Cordeliers de Paris, and another to the hands of our beloved Chevalier, Keeper of the Seals of France, Sieur Seguier D'Aultry. For such is our pleasure . . . Given at Paris, the thirtieth day of March, the year of grace of one thousand six hundred and thirty-five. . . .

The said Jousse has assigned his Privilege to George Griveau, Ordinary Printer of the King, and of the Royal College of Flèche, to enjoy it, in accordance with the clauses contained and mentioned in the Privilege, according to the agreement made and concluded in front of Pierre la Fousse, Notary at the place of Flèche, dated the twelfth day of November, one thousand six hundred and thirty seven.

Completed to Print for the first time, the tenth day of June, one thousand six hundred and forty-two.

§4.32 LIKE FRANCE, ENGLISH ENACTS RULES ON THE PROTECTION OF PRINTERS' TRADEMARKS

1662

> As in France (*see* Text 2.31), but much later, the English Parliament would also enact rules on the protection of printers' distinctive marks. The text that follows is Section 6 of the so-called Licensing Act, which was signed by Charles II, in 1662.
>
> An Act for preventing the frequent Abuses in printing seditious treasonable and unlicensed Books and Pamphlets and for regulating of Printing and Printing Presses.

VI. Printers of Books, &c. to set their Names thereto, and declare the Name of the Author if required.

Penalty; No Person to print or forge the Name of the Person having sole Right to print any Book; Penalty.

And be it further enacted and declared That every person and persons that shall hereafter print or cause to be printed any Booke Ballad Chart Pourtracture or any other thing or things whatsoever shall thereunto or thereon print and set his or theire owne Name or Names and alsoe shall declare the Name of the Author thereof if he be thereunto required by the Licenser under whose Approbation the licensing of the said Booke Ballad Chart or Pourtraiture shall be authorized and by and for whom any such Booke or other thing is or shall be printed upon paine of Forfeiture of all such Books Ballads Charts Pourtraitures and other thing or things printed contrary to the Tenor hereof And the Presses Letters and other Instruments for printing wherewith such Book Ballad Pourtraiture or other thing or things shall be so imprinted or sett or prepared for the printing thereof to be defaced and made unserviceable And that no person or persons shall hereafter print or cause to bee imprinted nor shall forge put or counterfeit in or upon any Booke or Pamphlet the Name Title Marke or Vinnet of any other person or persons which hath or shall have lawfull Priviledge Authority or Allowance of sole printing the same without the free consent of the person and persons so priviledged first had and obtained upon pain that every person and persons so offending shall forfeit and lose all such Books and Pamphlets upon which such counterfeit Name or Marke shall be imprinted and shall further be proceeded against as an Offender against this present Act.

§4.33 ENGLAND ENACTS THE FIRST (?) COPYRIGHT ACT: THE STATUTE OF ANNE

April 10, 1710

The Statute of Anne, of 1710, laid down the foundations of modern copyright, even if it was still inspired by the rules that applied to industrial privileges (namely, the duration of protection). Like the Statute of Monopolies in the context of patents, the Statute of Anne also required the intervention of courts so as to be constructed in a manner that permitted the transition of copyright from a medieval institution to a modern, global one. After its entry into force, courts endorsed the view that the statute had not preempted common law copyright, of a perpetual nature. The best known opinion in this direction was the King Bench's decision in Millar v. Taylor, of 1769. This trend was overruled by the House of Lords' opinion of Donaldson v. Becket, of 1774, which held that the 1710 statute had eliminated perpetual protection for copyright. Therefore, to a certain extent, the Statute of Anne, which aimed at strengthening the rights of authors by ensuring their enforceability for a limited term, ended up limiting those rights by denying their perpetuity.

The Statute of Anne, April 10, 1710

An act for the encouragement of learning, by vesting the copies of printed books in the authors or purchasers of such copies, during the times therein mentioned.

I. Whereas printers, booksellers, and other persons have of late frequently taken the liberty of printing, reprinting, and publishing, or causing to be printed, reprinted, and published, books and other writings, without the consent of the authors or proprietors of such books and writings, to their very great detriment, and too often to the ruin of them and their families: for preventing therefore such practices for the future, and for the encouragement of learned men to compose and write useful books; may it please your Majesty, that it may be enacted, and be it enacted by the Queen's most excellent majesty, by and with the advice and consent of the lords spiritual and temporal, and commons, in this present parliament assembled, and by the authority of the same;

II. That from and after the tenth day of April, one thousand seven hundred and ten, the author of any book or books already printed, who hath not transferred to any other the copy or copies of such book or books, share or shares thereof, or the bookseller or booksellers, printer or printers, or other person or persons, who hath or have purchased or acquired the copy or copies of any book or books, in order to print or reprint the same, shall have the sole right and liberty of printing such book and books for the term of one and twenty years, to commence from the said tenth day of April, and no longer; and that the author of any book or books already composed, and not printed and published, or that shall hereafter be composed, and his assignee or assigns, shall have the sole liberty of printing and reprinting such book and books for the term of fourteen years, to commence from the day of the first publishing the same, and no longer; and that if any other bookseller, printer or other person whatsoever, from and after the tenth day of April, one thousand seven hundred and ten, within the times granted and limited by this act, as aforesaid, shall print, reprint, or import, or cause to be printed, reprinted, or imported, any such book or books, without the consent of the proprietor or proprietors thereof first had and obtained in writing, signed in the presence of two or more credible witnesses; or knowing the same to be so printed or reprinted, without the consent of the proprietors, shall sell, publish, or expose to sale, or cause to be sold, published, or exposed to sale, any such book or books, without such consent first had and obtained, as aforesaid: then such offender or offenders shall forfeit such book or books, and all and every sheet or sheets, being part of such book or books, to the proprietor or proprietors of the copy thereof, who shall forthwith damask, and make waste paper of them; and further, that every such offender or offenders shall forfeit one penny for every sheet which shall be found in his, her, or their custody, either printed or printing, published, or exposed to sale, contrary to the true intent and meaning of this act; the one moiety thereof to the Queen's most excellent majesty, her heirs and successors, and the other moiety thereof to any person or persons that shall sue for the same, to be recovered in any of her Majesty's courts of record at Westminster, by action of debt, bill, plaint, or information, in which no wager of law, essoin, privilege, or protection, or more than one imparlance shall be allowed.

And whereas many persons may through ignorance offend against this act, unless some provision be made, whereby the property in every such book, as is intended by this act to be secured to the proprietor or proprietors thereof, may be ascertained, as likewise the consent of such proprietor or proprietors for the printing or reprinting of such book or books may from time to time be known; be it therefore further enacted by the authority aforesaid, That nothing in this act contained shall be construed to extend to subject any bookseller, printer, or other person whatsoever, to the forfeitures or penalties therein mentioned, for or by reason of the printing or reprinting of any book or books without such consent, as aforesaid, unless the title to the copy of such book or books hereafter published shall, before such publication, be entered in the register book of the company of stationers, in such manner as hath been usual, which register book shall at all times be kept at the hall of the said company, and unless such consent of the proprietor or proprietors be in like manner entered as aforesaid, for every of which several entries, six pence shall be paid, and no more; which said register book may, at all seasonable and convenient time, be resorted to, and inspected by any bookseller, printer, or other person, for the purposes before-mentioned, without any fee or reward; and the clerk of the said company of stationers shall, when and as often as thereunto required, give a certificate under his hand of such entry or entries, and for every such certificate may take a fee not exceeding six pence.

III. Provided nevertheless, That if the clerk of the said company of stationers for the time being, shall refuse or neglect to register, or make such entry or entries, or to give such certificate, being thereunto required by the author or proprietor of such copy or copies, in the presence of two or more credible witnesses, That then such person and persons so refusing, notice being first duly given of such refusal, by an advertisement in the Gazette, shall have the like benefit, as if such entry or entries, certificate or certificates had been duly made and given; and that the clerks so refusing, shall, for any such offence, forfeit to the proprietor of such copy or copies the sum of twenty pounds, to be recovered in any of her Majesty's courts of record at Westminster, by action of debt, bill, plaint, or information, in which no wager of law, essoin, privilege or protection, or more than one imparlance shall be allowed. . . .

XI. Provided always, That after the expiration of the said term of fourteen years, the sole right of printing or disposing of copies shall return to the authors thereof, if they are then living, for another term of fourteen years.

§4.34 PRINTING PRIVILEGES FOR RELIGIOUS BOOKS INVALIDATED BECAUSE OF THEIR HIGH PRICES

1711

In his dictionary of case law, the celebrated French jurist Brillon mentions an interesting judgment that invalidated a printing privilege on a religious book because of the need for keeping its price low, so as to better disseminate the religious teachings it contained.

It is not difficult to see here a parallel with the debates on trade secrets (in the sixteenth and seventeenth centuries) and patents (today) for medicines, likewise attacked because of their alleged impact on high prices.

On the Privilege of Books; on those who print the Works whose Privilege has been granted to others. *See* the *Plaidoyez de Corbin, chap. 118*, where he observes that it has been devised by several Judgments, that the Privilege of the Hours was invalid because it is the daily bread of Christians, and that it is not advisable to submit it to the bidding of the market [*mettre enchère*].

§4.35 FRANCE IN THE DIRECTION OF COPYRIGHT: THE DAUGHTERS OF LA FONTAINE ARE RECOGNIZED AS SUCCESSORS IN TITLE TO THE PRIVILEGE FOR THE PRINTING OF HIS FABLES

September 14, 1761

In 1761, in France, privileges were still the tool that ensured exclusivity to printers. However, the following judgment by the King's Private Council has acknowledged a right of inheritance in the authors' works (the well-known Fables of La Fontaine) to his direct descendants—which suggests that the idea of copyright, as personal property, rather than a privilege, was already developing.

Judgment of the Private State Council of the King, which declares void the opposition made by the Booksellers of Paris to the privilege granted by his Majesty to the young ladies La Fontaine; and orders the Trustee and Deputies to register without delay the privileges and permissions granted by His Majesty.

September 14, 1761.

Extract from the Records of the Private State Council.

On the petition presented to the King, in his Council, by the young ladies Fontaine, asserting that on June 29 last, His Majesty had the kindness of granting them letters of Chancellery that allow them to have printed for fifteen years the Fables and Works of the late Mr. de la Fountaine, their ancestor; they have sent these letters to the Trustee of the Booksellers and Printers of Paris, so that he had them registered in the register of their community; but the Syndic has informed them that several Booksellers had opposed the registration. To remove this obstacle to the execution of the grace granted to the applicants, they are in the indispensable necessity to have recourse to His Majesty: It is true that no Bookseller or Printer has a remaining privilege for the printing of the works of Mr. de la Fontaine; the applicants were thus able to invoke the kindness of the King, to obtain the permission granted to them.

The suppliants descend in direct line of Mr. de la Fontaine: thus the works belong to them naturally by right of heredity, since there is no title, or privilege that deprives them of it; therefore the opposition of the Booksellers is untenable, so it is fair to dismiss it. To justify the facts stated in the present request, the applicants will add the letters of Chancellery, which grant them the permission in question, and a signed copy of the Trustee of Booksellers, on the opposition to the registration filed on July 13. The applicants begged that it might please His Majesty, without regard to the opposition filed by Messrs. Aumont, Babuty son, Barbou, Guillin, Brocas, Fournier, David, Davidts, Despilly, Humblot, Durand, Gibert, Knapen, Clerc father, Nyon, Prault eldest son, Savoye, Duchesne, Barrois, the widows David and Damonneville, Booksellers stating they are associated, to dismiss their opposition; to order that the Chancellery letters of June 29th last, be registered on the register of the Community of Booksellers of Paris, be registered; and to order that Mr. Aumont and associates pay the costs.

Considering the request signed by Roussel, Advocate of the applicants, and the documents mentioned above; heard the report of Mr. Taboureau des Reaux, Knight, Counselor of the King in his Councils, Master of the Ordinary Requests of his hotel, Commissioner for this designated, who has communicated it to Messrs. Commissioners appointed for the examination of the affairs of Chancellery and Library; The King in His Council, upon the opinion of Mr. Chancellor, has declared and declares null the act of opposition submitted on July 14th to the Syndic and Deputies of Printing and Library of Paris, at the request of the named Aumont, Babuty son, Barbou, Guillin, Brocas, Fournier, David, Davidts, Despilly, Humblot, Durand, Gibert, Knapen, Clerc father, Nyon, Prault eldest son, Savoye, Duchesne, Barrois, the widows David and Damonneville, all booksellers in Paris; prohibits the said Trustee and Deputies to have regard to such acts, enjoins them to inscribe without delay in their registers the privileges and permissions granted by His Majesty; except in the case the parties interested in appealing to Him [apply] for the report of the said privileges and permissions to be ordered, if there is the case, according to the opinion of Mr. Chancellor: And the present judgment shall be inscribed on the registers of the community of Printers-Booksellers of Paris, printed, published and displayed wherever necessary. Done at the King's Private State Council, held at Paris on the fourteenth of September, one thousand six hundred and sixty-one. Collated. Signed Cogorde.

§4.36 THE UNITED STATES GIVES COPYRIGHT THE STATUS OF CONSTITUTIONAL PROTECTION

1787

We the People of the United States, in Order to form a more perfect Union, establish Justice, insure domestic Tranquility, provide for the common defense, promote the general Welfare, and secure the Blessings of Liberty to ourselves and our Posterity, do ordain and establish this Constitution for the United States of America.

Article I

Section 8

The Congress shall have power

Clause 8

To promote the progress of science . . ., by securing for limited times to authors . . . the exclusive right to their respective writings . . . .

§4.37 THE UNITED STATES PASSES A STATUTE ON COPYRIGHT

May 31, 1790

Immediately after legislating on patents, the United States Congress passed a law on copyright. The statute would later be amended several times, starting in 1802. In 1831, a second amendment would extend protection to musical compositions.

Copyright Act, 1790

Section 1.

Be it enacted by the Senate and House of Representatives of the United States of America in Congress assembled, That from and after the passing of this act, the author and authors of any map, chart, book or books already printed within these United States, being a citizen or citizens thereof, or resident within the same, his or their executors, administrators or assigns, who halt or have not transferred to any other person the copyright of such map, chart, book or books, share or shares thereof; and any other person or persons, being a citizen or citizens of these United States, or residents therein, his or their executors, administrators or assigns, who halt or have purchased or legally acquired the copyright of any such map, chart, book or books, in order to print, reprint, publish or vend the same, shall have the sole right and liberty of printing, reprinting, publishing and vending such map, chart, book or books, for the term of fourteen years from the recording the title thereof in the clerk's office, as is herein after directed: And that the author and authors of any map, chart, book or books already made and composed, and not printed or published, or that shall hereafter be made and composed, being a citizen or citizens of these United States, or resident therein, and his or their executors, administrators or assigns, shall have the sole right and liberty of printing, reprinting, publishing and vending such map, chart, book or books, for the like term of fourteen years from the time of recording the title thereof in the clerk's office as aforesaid. And if, at the expiration of the said term, the author or authors, or any of them, be living, and a citizen or citizens of these United States, or resident therein, the same exclusive right shall be continued to him or them, his or their executors, administrators or assigns, for the further term of fourteen years; Provided, He or they shall cause the title thereof to be a second time recorded and published in the same manner as is herein after directed, and that within six months before the expiration of the first term of fourteen years aforesaid.

Section 2.

And be it further enacted, That if any other person or persons, from and after the recording the title of any map, chart, book or books, and publishing the same as aforesaid, and within the times limited and granted by this act, shall print, reprint, publish, or import, or cause to be printed, reprinted, published, or imported from any foreign Kingdom or State, any copy or copies of such map, chart, book or books, without the consent of the author or proprietor thereof, first had and obtained in writing, signed in the presence of two or more credible witnesses; or knowing the same to be so printed, reprinted, or imported, shall publish, sell, or expose to sale, or cause to be published, sold or exposed to sale, any copy of such map, chart, book or books, without such consent first had and obtained in writing as aforesaid, then such offender or offenders shall forfeit all and every sheet and sheets, being part of the same, or either of them, to the author or proprietor of such map, chart, book or books, who shall forthwith destroy the same: And every such offender and offenders shall also forfeit and pay the sum of fifty cents for every sheet which shall be found in his or their possession, either printed or printing, published, imported or exposed to sale, contrary to the true intent and meaning of this act, the one moiety thereof to the author or proprietor of such map, chart, book or books, who shall sue for the same, and the other moiety thereof to and for the use of the United States, to be recovered by action of debt in any court of record in the United States, wherein the same is cognizable. Provided always, That such action be commenced within one year after the cause of action shall arise, and not afterwards.

Section 3.

And be it further enacted, That no person shall be entitled to the benefit of this act, in cases where any map, chart, book or books, hath or have been already printed and published, unless he shall first deposit, and in all other cases, unless he shall before publication deposit a printed copy of the title of such map. chart, book or books, in the clerk's office of the district court where the author or proprietor shall reside: And the clerk of such court is hereby directed and required to record the same forthwith, in a book to be kept by him for that purpose, . . . For which the said clerk shall be entitled to receive sixty cents from the said author or proprietor, and sixty cents for every copy under seal actually given to such author or proprietor as aforesaid. And such author or proprietor shall, within two months from the date thereof cause a copy of the said record to be published in one or more of the newspapers printed in the United States, for the space of four weeks.

Section 4.

And be it further enacted, That the author or proprietor of any such map, chart, book or books, shall, within six months after the publishing thereof, deliver, or cause to be delivered to the Secretary of State a copy of the same, to be preserved

Section 5.

And be it further enacted, That nothing in this act shall be construed to extend to prohibit the importation or vending, Reprinting or publishing within the United States, of any map, chart, book or books, written, printed, or published by any person not a citizen of the United States, in foreign parts or places without the jurisdiction of the United States.

Section 6.

And be it further enacted, That any person or persons who shall print or publish and manuscript, without the consent and approbation of the author or proprietor thereof, first had and obtained as aforesaid, (if such author or proprietor be a citizen of or resident in these United States) shall be liable to suffer and pay to the said author or proprietor all damages occasioned by such injury, to be recovered by a special action on the case founded upon this act, in any court having cognizance thereof.

Section 7.

And be it further enacted, That if any person or persons shall be sued or prosecuted for any matter, act or thing done under or by virtue of this act, he or they may plead the general issue, and give the special matter in evidence.

§4.38 FRANCE PASSES A STATUTE ON COPYRIGHT

July 19-24, 1793

The French Revolutionary National Assembly contributed to the modernization of copyright: for the first time, copyright is acknowledged as property and the term of protection goes beyond the author's life.

Decree concerning the rights of property of writers of all kinds, composers of music, painters and designers, of 19-24 July 1793

The National Convention,

After hearing its Committee for Public Education, Decrees the following:

Art. 1. Writers of all kinds, composers of music, painters and designers, who will engrave paintings or drawings, will enjoy, during their entire life, the exclusive right to sell, to make sell, to distribute their works in the territory of the Republic, and to assign the property in whole or in part.

Art. 2. Their heirs or assignees shall enjoy the same right for a period of ten years after the death of the authors.

Art. 3. Peace officers shall be required to confiscate, on the request of and for the benefit of authors, composers, painters or designers and others, his heirs and assignees, all copies of editions printed or engraved without the formal written permission of the authors.

Art. 4. Any counterfeiter shall pay the true owner the sum equivalent to the price of three thousand copies of the original edition.

Art. 5. Any distributor of a counterfeit edition, if not recognized as a counterfeiter, shall pay the true owner an amount equivalent to the price of five hundred copies of the original edition.

Art. 6. Any citizen who brings to light any book, be it of literature or engraving, of any kind whatsoever, will be obliged to deposit two copies at the National Library or at the Cabinet of Prints of the Republic, of which he will receive a signed receipt. by the librarian; otherwise he cannot be admitted to justice for the prosecution of counterfeiters.

Art. 7. The heirs of the author of a work of literature or engraving, or any other production of the spirit or genius which belong to the fine arts, will have the exclusive property for ten years.

§4.39 THE IDEA OF PRINTING PRIVILEGES PROVED TO BE TIME RESISTANT

December 29, 1830

The appearance of printing privileges in the second half of the fifteenth century was explained by a combination of two factors: the need to incentivize and protect the printing industry that had just emerged; and the absence of a better legal regime. As said above, governments at that time resorted to a mechanism they were familiar with—that of industrial privileges. This reasoning was again of practical utility in the nineteenth century in Brazil: with its recently acquired independence, and given that it had not a copyright statute in force, the only legal regime available to promote the printing industry was that of industrial privileges.

This text concerns a printing privilege, granted in 1830, by Pedro I, Emperor of Brazil, under the 1830 act on industrial privileges

Imperial Letter—December 29, 1830

Granting José Paulo Figueirôa Nabuco the ownership and use for 20 years of several works on public administration, of which he is the author.

Dom Pedro, by Grace of God and Unanimous Acclamation of the Peoples, Constitutional Emperor and Perpetual Defender of Brazil. I make it known to those who this Letter of Mine see that, considering what José Paulo Figueirôa Nabuco, of My Council, represented to me, after having satisfied what is determined by the Letter of Law of August 28, 1830: I decide, after hearing the Prosecutor of the Crown, Sovereignty and National Treasury, to Grant to the mentioned José Paulo Figeirôa Nabuco, for a term of 20 years, the ownership and exclusive use of the chronological and systematic collection of the legislation of the Treasury and its appendix, of which he is the inventor, and also of another collection corresponding to the other branches of the public administration, and the index of the same collections, which he intends to publish, remaining in the enjoyment of the guarantees, and subject to the clauses and conditions expressed in the same Law. And for certainty of all that is said I ordered to give him this Letter signed by Me, and sealed with the seal of My Arms. Given at the Palace of Rio de Janeiro on the twenty-ninth day of December in the year of the birth of Our Lord Jesus Christ, one thousand eight hundred and thirty, ninth of the Independence and of the Empire.

Emperor with Signature and Seal.

§4.40 THE JUDICIAL CONSTRUCTION OF COPYRIGHT: A UNITED STATES COURT INTRODUCES THE NOTION OF FAIR USE

October 1841

In 1841 Judge Story, of the District Court of Massachusetts, set a fundamental building stone for the understanding of copyright: the concept of fair use.

Interestingly, it seems that neither the defendant nor the judge looked at the fact that the plaintiff claimed copyright in works of George Washington, not of his own. Indeed the opinion is clear that the organization of the offending work was very different from the first one. Therefore, another judge might have seen here a question of non-infringement, rather than of legitimate (hence, fair) use.

Folsom v. Marsh

Circuit Court, D. Massachusetts

October, 1841, Term 9, F. Cas. 342

Story, Circuit Justice. This is one of those intricate and embarrassing questions, arising in the administration of civil justice, in which it is not, from the peculiar nature and character of the controversy, easy to arrive at any satisfactory conclusion, or to lay down any general principles applicable to all cases. Patents and copyrights approach, nearer than any other class of cases belonging to forensic discussions, to what may be called the metaphysics of the law, where the distinctions are, or at least may be, very subtle and refined, and, sometimes, almost evanescent. In many cases, indeed, what constitutes an infringement of a patented invention, is sufficiently clear and obvious, and stands upon broad and general agreements and differences; but, in other cases, the lines approach very near to each other, and, sometimes, become almost evanescent, or melt into each other. So, in cases of copyright, it is often exceedingly obvious, that the whole substance of one work has been copied from another, with slight omissions and formal differences only, which can be treated in no other way than as studied evasions; whereas, in other cases, the identity of the two works in substance, and the question of piracy, often depend upon a nice balance of the comparative use made in one of the materials of the other; the nature, extent, and value of the materials thus used; the objects of each work; and the degree to which each writer may be fairly presumed to have resorted to the same common sources of information, or to have exercised the same common diligence in the selection and arrangement of the materials. Thus, for example no one can doubt that a reviewer may fairly cite largely from the original work, if his design be really and truly to use the passages for the purposes of fair and reasonable criticism. On the other hand, it is as clear, that if he thus cites the most important parts of the work, with a view, not to criticise, but to supersede the use of the original work, and substitute the review for it, such a use will be deemed in law a piracy. A wide interval might, of course, exist between these two extremes, calling for great caution and involving great difficulty, where the court is approaching the dividing middle line which separates the one from the other. So, it has been decided that a fair and bona fide abridgment of an original work, is not a piracy of the copyright of the author. . . . But, then, what constitutes a fair and bona fide abridgment, in the sense of the law, is one of the most difficult points, under particular circumstances, which can well arise for judicial discussion. It is clear, that a mere selection, or different arrangement of parts of the original work, so as to bring the work into a smaller compass, will not be held to be such an abridgment. There must be real, substantial condensation of the materials, and intellectual labor and judgment bestowed thereon; and not merely the facile use of the scissors; or extracts of the essential parts, constituting the chief value of the original work. . . .

In the present case, the work alleged to be pirated, is the Writings of President Washington, in twelve volumes, royal octavo, containing nearly seven thousand pages, of which the first volume contains a life of Washington, by the learned editor, Mr. Sparks, in respect to which no piracy is asserted or proved. The other eleven volumes consist of the letters of Washington, private and official, and his messages and other public acts, with explanatory notes and occasional illustrations by the editor. That the original work is of very great, and, I may almost say, of inestimable value, as the repository of the thoughts and opinions of that great man, no one pretends to doubt. The work of the defendants is in two volumes, duodecimo, containing eight hundred and sixty-six pages. It consists of a Life of Washington, written by the learned defendant, (the Rev. Charles W. Upham), which is formed upon a plan different from that of Mr. Sparks, and in which Washington is made mainly to tell the story of his own life, by inserting therein his letters and his messages, and other written documents, with such connecting lines in the narrative, as may illustrate and explain the times and circumstances, and occasions of writing them. Now, as I have already said, there is no complaint, that Mr. Upham has taken his narrative part, substantially, from the Life by Mr. Sparks. The gravamen is, that he has used the letters of Washington, and inserted, verbatim, copies thereof from the collection of Mr. Sparks. The master finds, by his report, that the whole number of pages in Mr. Upham's work, corresponding and identical with the passages in Mr. Sparks' work, are three hundred and fifty-three pages out of eight hundred and sixty-six, a fraction more than one third of the two volumes of the defendants. Of these three hundred and fifty-three pages, the report finds that three hundred and nineteen pages consist of letters of Washington, which have been taken from Mr. Sparks' work, and have never been published before; namely, sixty-four pages are official letters and documents, and two hundred and fifty-five pages are private letters of Washington. The question, therefore, upon this admitted state of the facts, resolves itself into the point, whether such a use, in the defendants' work, of the letters of Washington, constitutes a piracy of the work of Mr. Sparks. . . .

The question, then, is, whether this is a justifiable use of the original materials, such as the law recognizes as no infringement of the copyright of the plaintiffs. It is said, that the defendant has selected only such materials, as suited his own limited purpose as a biographer. That is, doubtless, true; and he has produced an exceedingly valuable book. But that is no answer to the difficulty. It is certainly not necessary, to constitute an invasion of copyright, that the whole of a work should be copied, or even a large portion of it, in form or in substance. If so much is taken, that the value of the original is sensibly diminished, or the labors of the original author are substantially to an injurious extent appropriated by another, that is sufficient, in point of law, to constitute a piracy pro tanto. The entirety of the copyright is the property of the author; and it is no defense, that another person has appropriated a part, and not the whole, of any property. Neither does it necessarily depend upon the quantity taken, whether it is an infringement of the copyright or not. It is often affected by other considerations, the value of the materials taken, and the importance of it to the sale of the original work. . . .

In short, we must often, in deciding questions of this sort, look to the nature and objects of the selections made, the quantity and value of the materials used, and the degree in which the use may prejudice the sale, or diminish the profits, or supersede the objects, of the original work. Many mixed ingredients enter into the discussion of such questions. In some cases, a considerable portion of the materials of the original work may be fused, if I may use such an expression, into another work, so as to be undistinguishable in the mass of the latter, which has other professed and obvious objects, and cannot fairly be treated as a piracy; or they may be inserted as a sort of distinct and mosaic work, into the general texture of the second work, and constitute the peculiar excellence thereof, and then it may be a clear piracy. . . .

In the present case, I have no doubt whatever, that there is an invasion of the plaintiffs' copyright; I do not say designedly, or from bad intentions; on the contrary, I entertain no doubt, that it was deemed a perfectly lawful and justifiable use of the plaintiffs' work. But if the defendants may take three hundred and nineteen letters, included in the plaintiffs' copyright, and exclusively belonging to them, there is no reason why another bookseller may not take other five hundred letters, and a third, one thousand letters, and so on, and thereby the plaintiffs' copyright be totally destroyed. Besides; everyone must see, that the work of the defendants is mainly founded upon these letters, constituting more than one third of their work, and imparting to it its greatest, nay, its essential value. Without those letters, in its present form the work must fall to the ground. It is not a case, where abbreviated or select passages are taken from particular letters; but the entire letters are taken, and those of most interest and value to the public, as illustrating the life, the acts, and the character of Washington. It seems to me, therefore, that it is a clear invasion of the right of property of the plaintiffs, if the copying of parts of a work, not constituting a major part, can ever be a violation thereof; as upon principle and authority, I have no doubt it may be. If it had been the case of a fair and bona fide abridgment of the work of the plaintiffs, it might have admitted of a very different consideration. . . .

§4.41 THE UNITED KINGDOM AMENDS ITS COPYRIGHT ACT

July 1, 1842

In 1842 the United Kingdom amended its Copyright Act and brought copyright to contemporary times (except for the detailed provisions on registration of works), with the rights lasting beyond the life of the author and the adoption of compulsory licenses. However, as old habits do not die easily, the various copyright terms are still presented in multiples of 7 years. The following text consists of excerpts from the 1842 Act.

The Copyright Act 1842

5 & 6 Vict. c. 45

An Act to amend the Law of Copyright.

Whereas is it expedient to amend the law relating to copyright, and to afford greater encouragement to the production of literary works of lasting benefit to the world: Be it enacted by the Queen's most Excellent Majesty, by and with the advice and consent of the Lords spiritual and temporal, and Commons, in this present parliament assembled, and by the authority of the same, that from the passing of this Act an Act passed in the eighth year of the reign of Her Majesty Queen Anne, intituled An Act for the Encouragement of Learning, by vesting the Copies of printed Books in the Authors or Purchasers of such Copies during the Times therein mentioned; and also an Act passed in the forty-first year of the reign of His Majesty King George the Third, intituled An Act for the further Encouragement of Learning in the United Kingdom of Great Britain and Ireland, by securing the Copies and Copyright of printed Books to the Authors of such Books, or their Assigns, for the Time therein mentioned; and also an Act passed in the fifty-fourth year of the reign of His Majesty King George the Third, intituled An Act to amend the several Acts for the Encouragement of Learning, by securing the Copies and Copyright of printed Books to the Authors of such Books, or their Assigns, be and the same are hereby repealed, except so far as the continuance of either of them may be necessary for carrying on or giving effect to any proceedings at law or in equity pending at the time of passing this Act, or for enforcing any cause of action or suit, or any right or contract, then subsisting. . . .

3. And be it enacted, that the copyright in every book which shall after the passing of this Act be published in the lifetime of its author shall endure for the natural life of such author, and for the further term of seven years, commencing at the time of his death, and shall be the property of such author and his assigns: provided always, that if the said term of seven years shall expire before the end of forty-two years from the first publication of such book, the copyright shall in that case endure for such period of forty-two years; and that the copyright in every book which shall be published after the death of its author shall endure for the term of forty-two years from the first publication thereof, and shall be the property of the proprietor of the author's manuscript from which such book shall be first published, and his assigns. . . .
5. And whereas it is expedient to provide against the suppression of books of importance to the public; be it enacted, that it shall be lawful for the Judicial Committee of Her Majesty's Privy Council, on complaint made to them that the proprietor of the copyright in any book after the death of its author has refused to republish or to allow the republication of the same, and that by reason of such refusal such book may be withheld from the public, to grant a licence to such complainant to publish such book, in such manner and subject to such conditions as they may think fit, and that it shall be lawful for such complainant to publish such book according to such licence. . . .
15. And be it enacted, that if any person shall, in any part of the British Dominions, after the passing of this Act, print or cause to be printed, either for sale or exportation, any book in which there shall be subsisting copyright, without the consent in writing of the proprietor thereof, or shall import for sale or hire any such book so having been unlawfully printed from parts beyond the sea, or, knowing such book to have been so unlawfully printed or imported, shall sell, publish, or expose to sale or hire, or shall have in his possession, for sale or hire, any such book so unlawfully printed or imported,

without such consent as aforesaid, such offender shall be liable to a special action on the case at the suit of the proprietor of such copyright, to be brought in any court of record in that part of the British Dominions in which the offense shall be liable to an action in the Court of Session in Scotland, which shall and may be brought and prosecuted in the same manner in which any other action of damages to the like amount may be brought and prosecuted there.

16. In actions for piracy the defendant to give notice of the objections to the plaintiff's title on which he means to rely And be it enacted, that after the passing of this Act, in any action brought within the British Dominions against any person for printing any such book for sale, hire, or exportation, or for importing, selling, publishing, or exposing to sale or hire, or causing to be imported, sold, published, or exposed to sale or hire, any such book, the defendant, on pleading thereto, shall give to the plaintiff a notice in writing of any objections on which he means to rely on the trial of such action; and if the nature of his defense be, that the plaintiff in such action was not the author or first publisher of the book in which he shall by such action claim copyright, or is not the proprietor of the copyright therein, or that some other person than the plaintiff was the author or first publisher of such book, or is the proprietor of the copyright therein, then the defendant shall specify in such notice the name of the person who he alleges to have been the author or first publisher of such book, or the proprietor of the copyright therein, together with the title of such book, and the time when and the place where such book was first published, otherwise the defendant in such action shall not at the trial or hearing of such action be allowed to give any evidence that the plaintiff in such action was not the author or first publisher of the book in which he claims such copyright as aforesaid, or that he was not the proprietor of the copyright therein; and at such trial or hearing no other objection shall be allowed to be made on behalf of such defendant than the objections stated in such notice, or that any other person was the author or first publisher of such book, or the proprietor of the copyright therein, than the person specified in such notice, or give in evidence in support of his defense any other book than one substantially corresponding in title, time, and place of publication with the title, time, and place specified in such notice.

17. And be it enacted, that after the passing of this Act it shall not be lawful for any person, not being the proprietor of the copyright, or some person authorized by him, to import into any part of the United Kingdom, or into any other part of the British Dominions, for sale or hire, any printed book first composed or written or printed and published in any part of the said United Kingdom, wherein there shall be copyright, and re-printed in any country or place whatsoever out of the British Dominions; and if any person, not being such proprietor or person authorized as aforesaid, shall import or bring, or cause to be imported or brought, for sale or hire, any such printed book, into any part of the British Dominions, contrary to the true intent and meaning of this Act, or shall knowingly sell, publish, or expose to sale or let to hire, or have in his possession for sale or hire, any such book, then every such book shall be forfeited, and shall be seized by any officer of customs or excise, and the same shall be destroyed by such officer; and every person so offending, being duly convicted thereof before two justices of the peace for the county or place in which such book shall be found, shall also for every such offense forfeit the sum of ten pounds, and double the value of every copy of such book which he shall so import or cause to be imported into any part of the British Dominions, or shall knowingly sell, publish, or expose to sale or let to hire, or shall cause to be sold, published, or exposed to sale or let to hire, or shall have in his

possession for sale or hire, contrary to the true intent and meaning of this Act, five pounds to the use of such officer of customs or excise, and the remainder of the penalty to the use of the proprietor of the copyright in such book.

18. And be it enacted, that when any publisher or other person shall, before or at the time of the passing of this Act, have projected, conducted, and carried on, or shall hereafter project, conduct, and carry on, or be the proprietor of any encyclopedia, review, magazine, periodical work, or work published in a series of books or parts, or any book whatsoever, and shall have employed or shall employ any persons to compose the same, or any volumes, parts, essays, articles, or portions thereof, for publication in or as part of the same, and such work, volumes, parts, essays, articles, or portions shall have been or shall hereafter be composed under such employment, on the terms that the copyright therein shall belong to such proprietor, projector, publisher, or conductor, and paid for by such proprietor, projector, publisher, or conductor, the copyright in every such encyclopedia, review, magazine, periodical work and work published in a series of books or parts, and in every volume, part, essay, article, and portion so composed and paid for, shall be the property of such proprietor, projector, publisher, or other conductor, who shall enjoy the same rights as if he were the actual author thereof, and shall have such term of copyright therein as is given to the authors of books by this Act; except only that in the case of essays, articles, or portions forming part of and first published in reviews, magazines, or other periodical works of a like nature, after the term of twenty-eight years from the first publication thereof respectively the right of publishing the same in a separate form shall revert to the author for the remainder of the term given by this Act: provided always, that during the term of twenty-eight years the said proprietor, projector, publisher, or conductor shall not publish any such essay, article, or portion separately or singly without the consent previously obtained of the author thereof, or his assigns: provided also, that nothing herein contained shall alter or affect the right of any person who shall have been or who shall be so employed as aforesaid to publish any such his composition in a separate form, who by any contract, express or implied, may have reserved or may hereafter reserve to himself such right; but every author reserving, retaining, or having such right shall be entitled to the copyright in such composition when published in a separate form, according to this Act, without prejudice to the right of such proprietor, projector, publisher, or conductor as aforesaid. . . .

20. And whereas an Act was passed in the third year of the reign of his late Majesty, to amend the law relating to dramatic literary property, and it is expedient to extend the term of the sole liberty of representing dramatic pieces given by that Act to the full time by this Act provided for the continuance of copyright: and whereas it is expedient to extend to musical compositions the benefits of that Act, and also of this Act; be it therefore enacted, that the provisions of the said Act of his late Majesty, and of this Act, shall apply to musical compositions, and that the sole liberty of representing or performing, or causing or permitting to be represented or performed, any dramatic piece or musical composition, shall endure and be the property of the author thereof, and his assigns, for the term in this Act provided for the duration of copyright in books; and the provisions herein before enacted in respect of the property of such copyright, and of registering the same, shall apply to the liberty of representing or performing any dramatic piece or musical composition, as if the same were herein expressly re-enacted and applied thereto, save and except that the first public representation or performance of any dramatic piece or musical composition shall be deemed equivalent, in the construction

of this Act, to the first publication of any book: provided always, that in case of any dramatic piece or musical composition in manuscript, it shall be sufficient for the person having the sole liberty of representing or performing, or causing to be represented or performed the same, to register only the title thereof, the name and place of abode of the author or composer thereof, the name and place of abode of the proprietor thereof, and the time and place of its first representation or performance.

21. And be it enacted, that the person who shall at any time have the sole liberty of representing such dramatic piece or musical composition shall have and enjoy the remedies given and provided in the said Act of the third and fourth years of the reign of his late Majesty King William the Fourth, passed to amend the laws relating to dramatic literary property, during the whole of his interest therein, as fully as if the same were re-enacted in this Act. . . .

23. And be it enacted, that all copies of any book wherein there shall be copyright, and of which entry shall have been made in the said Registry Book, and which shall have been unlawfully printed or imported without the consent of the registered proprietor of such copyright, in writing under his hand first obtained, shall be deemed to be the property of the proprietor of such copyright, and who shall be registered as such, and such registered proprietor shall, after demand thereof in writing, be entitled to sue for and recover the same, or damages for the detention thereof, in an action of detinue, from any party who shall detain the same, or to sue for and recover damages for the conversion thereof in an action of trover. . . .

25. And be it enacted, that all Copyright shall be deemed personal property, and shall be transmissible by bequest, or, in case of intestacy, shall be subject to the same law of distribution as other personal property, and in Scotland shall be deemed to be personal and moveable estate. . . .

§4.42 THE MOVEMENT TOWARDS INTERNATIONAL PROTECTION OF COPYRIGHT STARTS: FRANCE SIGNS AN AGREEMENT WITH SARDINIA

November 5, 1850

The significant increase in trade that took place at the peak of the Industrial Revolution awoke in governments the concerns over the absence of international protection of intellectual property, including copyright. Those concerns affected mainly those countries with overseas cultural and economic influence, in particular France, whose national idiom was, at that time, the language used for international deals. France was, therefore, the major power that first promoted the negotiation and signature of agreements covering those intellectual property areas of specific interest for its exporting industries: trademarks, designs, and copyright. The text that follows is the second amendment to what appears to be the first bilateral agreement on the protection of copyright, which was signed by France and Sardinia in 1843, and first amended in 1846.

Significantly, in its preamble, this second amendment makes it clear that there is a link between free trade and intellectual property: the reduction of tariffs for imports of articles embodying or displaying intellectual property.

Supplementary Convention concluded at Turin, November 5, 1850, between France and Sardinia, for the reciprocal guarantee of the ownership of works of art and spirit. Exchange of Ratifications on February 6th, 1851.

The President of the French Republic and His Majesty the King of Sardinia, having recognized that circumstances beyond the control of the High Contracting Parties have hitherto prevented the Special Conventions signed at Turin on August 28, 1843 and April 22, 1846, for the reciprocal guarantee, in Sardinia, of the ownership of works of art and of spirit, from producing the favorable results that had inspired their conclusion, and wishing to overcome, by mutual agreement, the practical difficulties that experience has revealed; on the other hand, His Majesty the King of Sardinia having consented to facilitate the entry into his States of books, engravings, litographies and musical works published in France, by lowering the tariffs currently collected, according to the law, for the importation of the said articles; the President of the French Republic and His Majesty the King of Sardinia have thought convenient to conclude, for this purpose, a special Convention, . . .

Art. 1. The two High Contracting Parties wishing to ensure the strict execution of the provisions of Article 6 of the Convention of August 6, 1843, which determine the prohibition, at the entry into each of the two States, of all works or objects of counterfeiting defined by Articles 1, 2 and 3 of the said Convention, oblige themselves to ensure that any attempt to fraudulently introduce such works or counterfeited objects through the borders of the two countries be repelled in an absolute manner. . . .

Art. 3. The recognition and verification of the nationality of works of art or of spirit shall be effected in the respective customs offices specially opened for this purpose, and with the assistance of the officials in charge in both countries of the examination of books arriving from abroad. . . .

§4.43 BILATERAL AGREEMENT BETWEEN FRANCE AND GREAT BRITAIN ON THE PROTECTION OF LITERARY AND ARTISTIC WORKS

November 3, 1851

Pursuant to the movement that led to the signature of a significant number of bilateral agreements on copyright, France and Great Britain signed a convention, in 1851. Like the agreement between France and Sardinia (*see* Text 4.42), this convention also stated its association with trade and tariffs.

Convention concluded at Paris, on November 3rd, 1851, between France and Great Britain, for the reciprocal guarantee of the property of the works of literature and art. Exchange of Ratifications, January 8, 1852.

The President of the French Republic and Her Majesty the Queen of the United Kingdom of Great Britain and Ireland, equally animated by the desire to extend to both countries the enjoyment of copyright for works of literature and fine arts that may be published for the first time in one of them, and H.B.M. having consented to extend to books, engravings and musical works published in France, the reduction that the law allows her to grant, under certain conditions, concerning the rate of the tariffs currently levied upon importation into the United Kingdom of these same articles published in a foreign country;

The President of the French Republic and H. British. M. thought it appropriate to conclude, for this purpose, a special Convention, . . .

Art. 1. From the date on which, in accordance with the provisions of Article 14 below, the present Convention shall become executing, authors of works of literature or of art to which the laws of one of the two countries at present guarantee and will guarantee in the future the right of ownership or of author, shall have the right to exercise such rights in the territories of the other country, for the same period of time and within the same limits as would be exercised in the territory of this other country itself, the right attributed to authors of works of the same nature that would be published there, so that the reproduction or counterfeiting, in one of the two States, of any work of literature or of art published in the other, will be treated in the same way as the reproduction or counterfeiting of works of the same nature originally published in that other State, and that the authors of one of the two countries will have the same action and enjoy the same guarantees against the counterfeiting or the unauthorized reproduction in the courts of the other State, as those the law grants or could grant in the future to the authors of the latter country.

It is understood that these words "works of literature or of art," used at the beginning of this article, include the publications of books, dramatic works, musical compositions, drawings, paintings, sculptures, engravings, litographies and any other production of literature and fine arts.

The representatives or successors in title of the authors, translators, composers, painters, sculptors or engravers, shall in all respects enjoy the same rights as the present Convention accords to authors, translators, composers, painters, sculptors or engravers themselves.

Art. 2. The protection granted to original works is extended to translations. It is understood, however, that the purpose of this article is simply to protect the translator as regards his own translation, and not to confer the exclusive right of translation of any work, except in the case and limits provided by the next article.

. . .

Art. 4. The stipulations of the preceding articles shall also apply to the performance of dramatic works and the performance of musical compositions, in so far as the laws of each country are or shall be applicable, in this respect, to dramatic and musical works represented or performed publicly in these countries for the first time. However, in order to be entitled to legal protection, as far as the translation of a dramatic work is concerned, the author must publish his translation three months after the registration and the deposit of the original work.

It is understood that the protection stipulated by this article is not intended to prohibit imitations made in good faith, or the appropriation of dramatic works in the respective scenes of France and England, but only to prevent counterfeited translations. The matter of imitation or counterfeiting will be determined in all cases by the courts of the respective countries, according to the legislation in force in each of the two States.

Art. 5. Notwithstanding the provisions of Articles 1 and 2 of this Convention, articles taken from newspapers or periodical collections published in one of the two countries may be reproduced or translated in the newspapers or periodical collections of the other country, provided that the source from which they will have been drawn is indicated. However, this permission shall not be understood as extending to the reproduction, in one of the two countries, of newspaper articles or of periodical collections published in the other, the authors of which would have stated, in a visible manner, in the same newspaper or collection where they have made them appear, that they forbid their reproduction.

Art. 6. The importation and sale in either of the two countries of any counterfeit of works enjoying the privilege of protection against counterfeiting, under Articles 1, 2, 3 and 5 of this Convention, shall be prohibited, whether these counterfeits originate in the country where the work has been published, or in any other foreign territory.

Art. 7. In the event of violation of the provisions of the preceding articles, the counterfeited works or objects shall be seized and destroyed, and the persons who are guilty of these offenses shall be liable in each country to the penalty and prosecution that are or would be prescribed by the laws of that country against the same offense committed in respect of any work or production of national origin.

Art. 8. Authors and translators, as well as their legally designated representatives or successors in title, shall in both countries be entitled to the protection stipulated in the preceding articles, and the right of author may only be claimed in one of the two countries after the work has been registered in the following manner, namely: . . .

Art. 11. In order to facilitate the execution of the present Convention, the two High Contracting Parties undertake to communicate to one another the laws and regulations that may be subsequently established in the respective States, in respect of the rights of authors, for the works and protected by the provisions of this Convention.

Art. 12. The provisions of the present Convention shall in no way affect the right that each High Contracting Party expressly reserves to itself to monitor and defend, by legislative or internal measures, the sale, the circulation, the representation and the exhibition of any work or of any production in respect of which either country considers it appropriate to exercise this right. . . .

Art. 13. Nothing in this Convention shall be deemed to affect the right of either High Contracting Party to prohibit the importation into its own States of books which, according to its domestic laws or stipulations subscribed with other powers, are or would be declared to be counterfeits or copyright infringements.

Art. 14. Her Excellency H. B. M. undertakes to recommend to Parliament the amendment of a law authorizing her to bring into force those provisions of the present Convention that need to be approved by a legislative act. When this law has been adopted, the Convention will be implemented from a date to be fixed by the two High Contracting Parties.

Done at Paris on the 3rd of November of the year of grace 1851.

§4.44 FRANCE EXTENDS COPYRIGHT PROTECTION TO FOREIGN WORKS

1852

As it had promised to Great Britain, in the 1851 Convention (*see* Text 4.43), France has given statutory recognition to that Convention. But France went further, and, in 1852, enacted a decree extending the provisions of the Criminal Code of 1810 on piracy to the counterfeiting of foreign works.

Article 1. Counterfeiting on French territory of works published abroad and mentioned in Article 425 of the Penal Code, constitutes a [criminal] offense.

Article 2. The same applies to the distribution, the exportation and the shipping of counterfeit works. The export and the dispatch of these works are an offense of the same kind as the introduction into French territory of works which, having been printed in France, have been counterfeited abroad.

Article 3. The offenses mentioned in the preceding articles shall be punishable in accordance with Articles 427 and 429 of the Penal Code.

Article 463 of the same code may be applied.

Article 4. Nevertheless, the prosecution will be admitted only under the fulfillment of the conditions required with respect to works published in France, in particular by Article 6 of the law of July 19, 1793.

§4.45 THE GENESIS OF THE BERNE CONVENTION ON THE PROTECTION OF LITERARY AND ARTISTIC PROPERTY

September 8, 1886

In the second half of the nineteenth century a number of countries had already adopted protection of copyright (e.g., France, the United Kingdom and the United States; Italy, in 1865; Germany, in 1870 and 1876; Spain, in 1881; and Belgium, in 1886). But an obstacle remained: international exchange of goods had grown, and with it, international exchange of culture and science. However, such an exchange was not accompanied by the recognition of rights in works printed abroad, except for those countries that had signed bilateral agreements on the protection of copyright. But they were very few and the territorial coverage of those agreements was, therefore, too small.

This situation led to the signature of an international convention on the protection of literary and artistic property, as signed in 1886, and ratified in 1887, in Berne, Switzerland. The Convention was later reformed several times, with its first major overhaul taking place in Berlin, in 1908. In Berlin as well as in the successive revisions (Rome, 1928; Brussels, 1948; Stockholm, 1967; and Paris, 1971), the Conventional copyright's scope was expanded beyond the right to publish, translate and make adaptations or arrangements, so as to include the right to perform in public, to recite, to communicate, to broadcast and to make reproductions. Administered by the World Intellectual Property Organization (WIPO), successor to the International Bureau that was established in 1886, the Union then created had 177 Members in 2019.

The following texts explain the genesis of the Berne Convention and describe the main points that were in the minds of delegations, as follows: (i) Édouard Clunet describes the origins of the Convention: (ii) Louis Renault reports on the intervention of the head of the Swiss delegation at Berne, in 1986; and (iii) the first articles of the Convention, in their original version.

(i) Soon, the initiative of those concerned makes up for the insufficiency of Parliaments. The authors meet and give to their aspirations the formula of votes that the legislator is called to translate into articles of law. Here the era of the Congresses opens. It begins with the Congress on Literary and Artistic Ownership held in Brussels from September 27 to 30, 1858, where we note the following vote: "It is desirable that all countries adopt legislation on a uniform basis for the ownership of works of literature and art."

In 1861, the Antwerp Art Congress states the following: "In order to bring about an agreement among governments in order to generalize the protection of artistic property, the Congress refers to the continuation of the efforts that governments are making for this purpose by way of negotiation." On the proposal of Mr. Wervoot (Belgium) the Congress adopts the following resolutions:

1. The Congress considers that the principle of the international recognition of artistic works in favor of their authors must take place in the legislation of all civilized peoples;

2. This principle must be admitted from country to country, even in the absence of reciprocity;
3. The assimilation of foreign artists to national artists must be absolute and complete.

During the celebrations of the third centenary of Rubens, a new international artistic congress was held in Antwerp, in August 1877, and included in his program this question: "Research of the bases of an international legislation intended to protect the property rights on the works of art and to repress the frauds and the counterfeits." In the last session of August 21, 1877, upon the initiative of our honorable friend M. Rolin-Jacquemyns, President of the Institute of International Law, and since Minister of the Interior in Belgium, the Congress welcomed a proposal in the sense of coming to an agreement with the Institute "for the purpose of obtaining a law which would have an international character."

On the occasion of the International Universal Exhibition organized by France in 1878, two Congresses were held that year in Paris: the literary one, thanks to the initiative of the Society of French Authors; the other artistic, under the auspices of the French Government. The Literary Congress voted for the assimilation of treatment between works of foreign origin and those of national origin. International issues were the object of a broader exam in the Artistic Congress. On the proposal of M. Clunet, the Congress took this resolution (Article 20): "It is to be hoped that a general Union will be formed between the various states of Europe and overseas, which will adopt uniform legislation on artistic property. The Congress expresses the wish that the convention that will establish this Union is inspired by the resolutions it has adopted and gives them a definitive solution."

It is this wish that is fulfilled today by the Convention of the International Union for the Protection of Literary and Artistic Works, which has just adopted the diplomatic instrument signed at Berne, by ten States, on September 9, 1886. . . .

It was in 1883 that the [Literary and International Artistic] Association gave the measure of its influence, and its action closely associated with the Union Convention, object of our examination.

At the Congress of Rome in 1882, the Association, assisted by Mr. Paul Schmidt, speaking on behalf of the German Writers Society, decided that an extraordinary conference would be held in 1883 in Berne with a view to preparing the formation of a general Union for the protection of intellectual property, and the elaboration of a draft, able to serve as a basis for the discussions of a diplomatic conference.

The Swiss Government, which is always ready when it comes to supporting a liberal and elevated idea, welcomed this project and granted its official patronage to the Conference. On September 10, 1883, the Conference opened in the State Hall of the Federal Council at Berne; under the chairmanship of the Federal Councilor Mr. Numa Droz, whose name is authoritative in Europe in all matters relating to intellectual or industrial property. . . .

Two weeks later, on September 26, 1886, the Association held its annual congress in Amsterdam, and Mr. Pouillet published in a report the summary of the work of the Conference in a report. We borrow from this remarkable work the following excerpts: . . .

The Berne Conference, after interesting debates, admitted two principles: first, it demands that any work published, represented or executed in any of the States of the Union be immediately protected after the completion of the prescribed formalities by the law of the country where the work has originated, and without any other formality in all the other States of the Union. The work published in one of the States of the Union is deemed to appear at the same time in all the others.

> A second principle that the conference has deemed useful, even indispensable, to proclaim is that of the exclusive right, which must be acknowledged to the author, on every translation of his work as well as on the original work itself.
>
> Beside these two principles that the conference has proclaimed loudly, several declarations of detail have found their place, especially as regards the adaptation, this particular and perfidious form of the imitation of theater plays; the conference expressed the wish that it should be considered a real counterfeit.
>
> The conference thus declared that the right of authors is exercised even on manuscript or unpublished works. . . .
>
> But on the other hand, it would certainly be a great gain to reach at this moment a general agreement by which the superior principle and, so to speak, of natural law would be proclaimed: that the author of a literary or artistic work, whatever his nationality and the place of reproduction, must be protected everywhere on par with the nationals of each nation.
>
> This fundamental principle, which does not conflict with any existing convention, once admitted, and the General Union constituted on this basis, it is beyond doubt that under the influence of the exchange of views that would be established among the States of the Union, the most shocking differences existing in international law would be erased successively in order to make room for a more uniform regime, and consequently safer for the authors and their rightful successors in title. . . .
>
> Encouraged by the welcome given to its advances, the Federal Government decided to convene a diplomatic conference for September 8, 1884, in Bern.
>
> The conference decided to base its work on the program of the Federal Government, but to precede the detailed examination of the articles with a general discussion on the principles that would be introduced during the Convention.
>
> To this end, the German delegation presented a questionnaire containing fourteen essential points and requested that beforehand it should be discussed whether, instead of concluding a convention based on the principle of national treatment, it would not be preferable to seek as soon as possible a codification regulating in a uniform manner for the whole of the proposed Union, and in the framework of a convention, the totality of the provisions concerning the protection of the copyrights. . . .
>
> The draft elaborated in 1884 was submitted to the examination of a second diplomatic conference held at Berne in 1885. . . .

The representative of the Government of Switzerland thus characterized the situation in his opening speech:

> The establishment of a General Union for the Protection of Copyrights, on the basis of the assimilation of foreigners to nationals, and the abolition of the multiple formalities currently required, does not seem to meet any opponents. If differences of opinion arise, they relate to other more or less important points of the project, and in particular to those that have the effect of modifying certain provisions of the domestic laws.

Of course, gentlemen, the object of our convention is to secure property rights reciprocally for the nationals of the various countries of the Union; therefore, for filling the gaps that national legislations may contain, it is necessary to unify to a certain extent the principles of literary and artistic property that have a truly international character. Everyone is convinced of this, but there are differences as to the extent to which unification must take place. Those who at home apply very advanced principles, which are also great suppliers of intellectual products for other countries, would like to see this unification be achieved at the first attempt, on the points that are dearest to them, the most complete ideal.

Others, guided by the necessity of a situation that must be taken into account, are willing to take a step forward, but cannot take a great one for the first time. These are serious difficulties, but which, in my opinion and, I believe it, in yours, are not insurmountable. The authors and the artists naturally demand the most protection possible; for their part, jurists and lawmakers discuss, from a theoretical and practical point of view, the good foundation of rights, in part new ones, about which their recognition is requested.

What dominates, however, the conflict of opinions and interests in these regions, as well as in the official spheres, is the feeling that a universal Union for the Protection of Copyrights is a necessity of our time.

Following a general discussion that occupied three plenary sessions, the conference had to recognize that if it wanted to see the greatest number of countries enter the Union it had to codify substantive law only to the extent that this codification could be accepted by those countries whose membership would be a guarantee of success for the common work. Called to choose between a restricted Union, comprising only the most advanced countries in the field of the protection of literary and artistic works, and a Union embracing almost all the important countries from the point of view of literature and the arts, the Conference has considered that the latter alternative had more advantages than the other, and consequently has given preference to it. . . .

Following the commitment made, the articles voted in 1885 have been considered as acquired, and therefore proposals likely to bring new provisions have been rejected. Exception has been made for a simple editorial correction proposed by Switzerland. . . .

On September 9, 1886, in the State Council Chamber in Berne, the convention was signed by the representatives of ten states: Germany, Belgium, Spain, France, Great Britain, Haiti, Italy, Liberia, Switzerland, Tunisia.

(ii) Federal Councilor Numa Droz opened the meeting with the following speech:

> Gentlemen,
> Three years ago, under the auspices of the International Literary Association, a gathering of writers, artists and jurists from various countries was held in this room to study the basis of a Universal Convention for the protection of copyright. A draft has been elaborated by common agreement and handed over to the Swiss Federal Council, which agreed to accept the mission of transmitting it to the Governments of other States and at the same time has taken the initiative of a Diplomatic Conference in order to found an International Union, similar to those already existing in other areas, in particular for the protection of industrial property.
>
> This initiative has been generally welcomed. The following year, on September 8, 1884, I had the honor to welcome, on behalf of the Federal Council, the representatives of Germany, Austria-Hungary, Belgium, Costa Rica, France, Great Britain, Haiti, Paraguay, the Netherlands, El Salvador, Sweden and Norway, as well as Switzerland. Other States, which had

shown their sympathy for the proposed work, had not been able to send their Delegates to Berne in consequence of various circumstances.

The Federal Government had replaced the rough project of the International Literary Association with a more comprehensive program, which was further developed by the Conference. A draft Convention came out of these laborious deliberations; it was, as well as a final report signed by all the Delegates present, transmitted by the Federal Council to the Governments of all the civilized countries, with the request that they examined it and gave definitive instructions to their Delegates for a new Conference.

On September 7th, 1885, we had the pleasure of welcoming the representatives of the following countries: Germany, Belgium, Spain, the United States of America, France, Great Britain, Haiti, Honduras, Italy, the Netherlands, Sweden and Norway, Switzerland and Tunisia.

The work had made rapid progress in the minds. In fact, as the moment of conclusion drew nearer, the more difficulties of a general understanding arose. The most advanced countries in the field of the protection of literary and artistic works naturally desired an international codification that corresponded as much as possible to their ideal. Others said they could not follow them so far in a first step.

Each country, moreover, was stuck to certain peculiarities of its domestic legislation and was reluctant to sacrifice too much of its autonomy. The work of the Conference must have been even more thorough and more intense than the first time. Reciprocal concessions had to be made; and when, after many meetings, the final agreement was reached, we felt that we had drawn up a Convention that deserved to be approved by all, as a work of genuine progress, wisely taking into account the possibilities of the moment, according to authors real protection, and capable, without essential modifications, of the improvements that experience will indicate and that the future will be able to claim. It was unanimously acknowledged that the agreed text should be definitive and therefore it would not bear further amendments.

Today, you are called, Gentlemen, to transform, by your signatures, this draft Convention into a diplomatic act. Allow me to pay a well-deserved tribute to all those present and absent who have collaborated effectively in this important Treaty designed to stimulate the endeavours of human genius, through the legitimate protection of their work.

Yes, gentlemen, it was necessary, in order to arrive at this happy result, the legal science, the practical light, the spirit of conciliation, the conscientious work of the Delegates to the two Diplomatic Conferences that preceded this one. To be fair, I should name each of them and note the part he has taken in the overall discussions or in detail . . . .

The International Union for the Protection of Literary and Artistic Works, as it stands in its beginning, is a remarkable part of humanity. It will rule over copyright in a territory of about five hundred million people. It embraces in Europe the principal countries of literary and artistic production, and soon, we have the firm hope, it can also register the accession of the United States of America, which occupies in the world a rank so distinguished, and in this respect the statement of sympathy contained in a recent message from President Cleveland and the presence among us of Minister Winchester assure us that it will soon be so, . . .

Finally, some States have stated that the Convention did not interest them, as they do not have national literature and that they wanted to be able

> to enjoy freely the intellectual products of others. I believe that these States are in a wrong path and that they are mistaken about their true interests. By recognizing copyright, they would encourage national production, they would cease to simply be tributaries of other peoples, and to be subject exclusively to intellectual influence coming from outside; soon there would be between them and us exchanges of ideas from which everyone would benefit, because the arts and letters need to be constantly renewed; the modern man gets more used to seek the food of his mind as well as of his body under all the skies and in all climates, and who knows what treasures the literary and artistic genius of the new peoples could bring to light if that was sufficiently stimulated and supported.
>
> Be that as it may, Gentlemen, we can trust the future of our work. It is the solemn consecration of a principle of right and justice; it has the effect of tightening the bonds that must unite humanity; it will certainly contribute to encourage, to multiply the most noble productions of the human genius; it is therefore, for all these reasons, a work of civilization that honors our time.
>
> Switzerland is proud, Gentlemen, to have presided over the development of this work and to have been judged worthy by you to pursue in a more immediate manner its realisation by becoming the seat of the international body that must serve as a center for the Union. I testify to you our deep gratitude and I am happy to salute, in the name of our people, the new creation, daughter of the ideal and future mother of many progresses that will come out of this Conference. . . .

(iii) The first two articles of the 1886 Convention read:

> Article I
>
> The Contracting States are constituted into an Union for the protection of the rights of authors over their literary and artistic works.
>
> Article II
>
> Authors of any of the countries of the Union, or their lawful representatives, shall enjoy in the other countries for their works, whether published in one of those countries or unpublished, the rights which the respective laws do now or may hereafter grant to natives.
>
> The enjoyment of these rights is subject to the accomplishment of the conditions and formalities prescribed by law in the country of origin of the work, and cannot exceed in the other countries the term of protection granted in the said country of origin.
>
> The country of origin of the work is that in which the work is first published, or if such publication takes place simultaneously in several countries of the Union, that one of them in which the shortest term of protection is granted by law.
>
> For unpublished works the country to which the author belongs is considered the country of origin of the work. . . .

§4.46 THE UNITED STATES AMENDS ITS COPYRIGHT ACT AND EXTENDS PROTECTION TO FOREIGN WORKS

March 3, 1891

The 1891 amendment of the copyright statute improved and modernized the United States system, extending it to foreign authors, but kept three features that linked it to the regime of industrial privileges that preceded the birth of copyright: the need for registering the protected works; the terms of protection (in multiples of 14 years); and the requirement that certain works (books, photographs, chromos, and lithographs) be printed in national territory (known as the manufacturing or the local exploitation requirement). This last imposition was later extended to Canadian territory. It was part of the US copyright system until the 1980s, when a panel in the General Agreement on Tariffs and Trade (GATT) ordered the United States to drop it on the ground that it was incompatible with the national treatment principle of the 1947 GATT Agreement.

An Act to amend title sixty, chapter three, of the Revised Statutes of the United States, relating to copyrights

Be it enacted by the Senate and the House of Representatives of the United States of America in Congress assembled, that section forty-nine hundred and fifty-two of the Revised Statutes be, and the same is hereby, amended so as to read as follows:

Sec. 4952. The author, inventor, designer, or proprietor of any book, map, chart, dramatic or musical composition, engraving, cut, print, or photograph or negative thereof, or of a painting, drawing, chromo, statuary, and of models or designs intended to be perfected as works of the fine arts, and the executors, administrators, or assigns of any such person, shall, upon complying with the provisions of this chapter, have the sole liberty of printing, reprinting, publishing, completing, copying, executing, finishing, and vending the same; and, in the case of a dramatic composition, of publicly performing or representing it, or causing it to be performed or represented by others. And authors or their assigns shall have exclusive right to dramatize or translate any of their works, for which copyright shall have been obtained under the laws of the United States.

Sec. 2. That section forty-nine hundred and fifty-four of the Revised Statutes be, and the same is hereby, amended so as to read as follows:

Sec. 4954. The author, inventor, or designer, if he be still living, or his widow or children, if he be dead, shall have the same exclusive right continued for the further term of fourteen years, upon recording the title of the work or description of the article so secured a second time, and complying with all other regulations in regard to original copyrights, within six months before the expiration of the first term. And such person shall, within two months from the date of said renewal, cause a copy of the record thereof to be published in one or more newspapers, printed in the United States, for the space of four weeks.

Sec. 3. That section forty-nine hundred and fifty-six of the Revised Statutes be, and the same is hereby, amended so as to read as follows:

Sec. 4956. No person shall be entitled to a copyright unless be shall, on or before the day of publication, in this or any foreign country, deliver at the office of the Librarian of Congress, or deposit in the mail within the United States, addressed to the Librarian of Congress, at Washington, District of Columbia, a printed copy of the title of the book, map, chart, dramatic or musical composition, engraving, cut, print, photograph, or chromo, or a description of the painting, drawing, statue, statuary, or a model or design, for a work of the fine arts, for which he desires a copyright; nor unless he shall also, not later than the day of the publication thereof, in this or any foreign, country, deliver at the office of the Librarian of Congress, at Washington, District of Columbia, or deposit in the mail, within the United States, addressed to the Librarian of Congress, at Washington, District of Columbia, two copies of such copyright book, map, chart, dramatic or musical composition, engraving, chromo, cut, print, or photograph, or in case of a painting, drawing, statue, statuary, model, or design for a work of the fine arts, a photograph of the same:

Provided, That in the case of a book, photograph, chromo, or lithograph, the two copies of the same required to be delivered or deposited as above, shall be printed from type set within the limits of the United States, or from plates made therefrom, or from negatives, or drawings on stone made within the limits of the United States, or from transfers made therefrom. . . .

Sec. 13. That this act shall only apply to a citizen or subject of a foreign state or nation when such foreign state or nation permits to citizens of the United States of America the benefit of copyright on substantially the same basis as its own citizens; or when such foreign state or nation is a party to an international agreement which provides for reciprocity in the granting of copyright, by the terms of which agreement the United States of America may, at its pleasure, become a party to such agreement. The existence of either of the conditions aforesaid shall be determined by the President of the United States by proclamation made from time to time as the purposes of this act may require.

Approved, March 3, 1891.

§4.47 A DISCUSSION THAT HAS NOT GONE AWAY: SHOULD NEWS BE COPYRIGHTED?

1925 and 1934

We have seen above that the bilateral Convention between France and Great Britain (1851) reserved copyright protection to articles published in newspapers (provided their authors claimed such property), thus implying that mere news would be out of protection. Since then, initiatives aiming at clarifying and/or improving copyright protection have left news out of its scope. But this does not mean that there have not been other attempts to protect news. Actually, the first attempts were based on the notion of unfair competition, to the extent that the lack of protection would permit rival newspapers to eliminate the competitive advantage of those who obtained the news first, without any corresponding efforts.

Voices in favor (and against) such protection were heard at two of the Conferences aiming at revising the Paris Convention for the Protection of Industrial Property. The texts that follow reflect the debates on this topic held (i) at The Hague, 1925, and (ii) in London, 1934.

(i) Presentations on the Reasons and Proposals submitted by the Dutch copyright administration and the International Bureau.

IX. Repression of Unfair Competition (Art 10*bis*)

> We first thought of inserting in the few examples of acts of unfair competition listed in paragraph 2 the usurpation of the daily news that represent mere press information. Indeed, these news are not governed by the laws concerning literary property, because they lack what constitutes the foundation of the copyright: the creative activity and the personal originality of the thought or the expression; on the other hand, these factual communications are nonetheless of great economic value and are the subject of commercial transactions (subscriptions, etc.) as well as rivalries between commercial enterprises (agencies).
>
> The Convention of Literary Union could not take them under its aegis. However, by stipulating in Article 9, paragraph 3, of the revised Berne Convention that "the protection of the present Convention does not apply to news of the day," the Review Conference meeting in Berlin in 1908 declared (Minutes, at 252) that, outside the field of copyright, [there are] commercial issues that are covered by industrial propriety, particularly the field of unfair competition, of which the plunder of the news of the day bears all the signs.

Encouraged by this declaration, the first International Congress of Information Agencies, meeting in Berne in June 1924, expressed the wish to see included in the regime of Article 10*bis* of the Paris-Washington Convention the "reproduction and the use, with a goal of profit, of news of the day containing political, commercial, economic and financial information."

But, however desirable such a solution may be of better delimiting the sphere of action of the two industrial and literary Conventions, we have had to convince ourselves that such a reform would at present meet a strong resistance and therefore seems premature; so we have given up on making a proposal about this.

Serbia-Croatia-Slovenia — In the explanatory memorandum . . . reference is made to the plan originally devised by the drafters of the Conference Program of including in the examples of acts of unfair competition the usurpation of the news of the day that represent simple press information, which newspapers or telegraphic agencies publish. However, this plan, whose realization is declared to be desirable in principle, has been abandoned as premature in anticipation of strong resistance on this point.

However, the Administration of Serbia-Croatia-Slovenia has received from the Ministry of Foreign Affairs, Press Section, along with the text of the resolution of the First International Congress of Information Agencies, held in Berne from 6 to 11 October 1924, a special note requesting its support, by its national Delegation, at the Hague Conference, the votes expressed in that resolution, and it has decided to follow up this request by proposing to the Conference the addition to Article 10*bis* of a new paragraph as follows:

> All news obtained by a newspaper or a news agency, regardless of their form, content or the method by means of which they would have been transmitted shall be protected against any act qualified as of unfair competition, as long as their commercial value will subsist.
>
> If this drafting was considered to be too broad, it could be replaced alternatively by the following text: "All news obtained by a newspaper or news agency, bearing the title of the newspaper or agency, will be protected against any

> act qualifying as an act of unfair competition, as long as their commercial value remains."
>
> . . . [The President] recalls that it was necessary to insert in the minutes a declaration made at the General Committee by the Delegation of the Kingdom of the Serbs-Croats-Slovenes, to which he subsequently gave the floor.

Mr. Choumane (Kingdom of the Serbs-Croats-Slovenes) reads the following statement:

> Well before the beginning of the Conference, the State Administration of Serbs, Croats and Slovenes sent an amendment to the International Bureau, tending to repress unfair competition in the trade of news of the day and information obtained by any international agencies.

This wish has been printed in leaflet VII of the International Bureau and reproduced in the Program of the Conference. But during the work of the Sub-Commission, it was only at the second reading that we drew the attention of the Conference to our amendment. Because the proposal of the Honorable Delegate of France, Mr. Maillard, that the question be referred to a Study Committee, has not been accepted by any of the Delegations, we have withdrawn our amendment. But, having the desire to do something for the protection of this right of telegraphic agencies, we have the honor to propose now a simple vote, which will have effect only in the future.

It is well known, today better than ever, that the various news of the day represent a fairly considerable commercial value. Many international telegraph agencies have been set up for trading with this information.

It is therefore fair to guarantee them fair trade and to repress all acts that tend to unfairly compete with them. Our Delegation has the honor to point out again to the honorable Delegates that its proposal must be understood in the sense that the protection of the news of the day and the information relates to the news and information that have not yet been published by the agency.

We are happy to be able to declare that the Delegation of Spain has declared that it accepts in principle the vote that we propose.

Mr. Mendez de Vigo (Spain) said that the Delegation of Spain, which had previously approved the declaration that the Delegation of the Kingdom of the Serbs, Croats and Slovenes had just made, supported it fully. . . .

(ii)

Counterproposals, Convention, Article 10*bis*.

Czechoslovakia: Add to paragraph (3) a 3rd (new) [proviso] thus conceived:

> 3rd The unauthorized reproduction of press reports of any kind, during the twenty-four hours following their first publication, provided their nature of currentness gives them commercial value.
>
> Variant:
>
> 3rd The disclosure, unauthorized and with a commercial purpose, of press information, regardless of its content and mode of transmission, during a twenty-four hour period.

Reasons: The need to protect the press against unfair competition has long been felt. The press Bureaus that make reports and the newspapers that acquire the news in a fair manner are interested in that third parties (newspapers, news agencies that are inadequately equipped, etc.) do not seize them without authorization and do not use them for their benefit. The abuses committed in this area were denounced on the occasion of the first International Congress of Information Agencies, held in Berne from June 6 to 11, 1924 (Congress in which were represented the largest press Bureaux of twenty-five countries in Europe and the United States), where a resolution was voted aimed at obtaining the insertion in Article 10*bis* of a new paragraph protecting those concerned from such unlawful acts.

The Yugoslav Administration made a proposal to this effect at the Hague Conference, which did not obtain consensus. The Conference of Press Experts convened in Geneva in 1927 by the League of Nations also affirmed the need to protect press information; the London Congress, 1932, of the International Association for the Protection of Industrial Property, voted in respect of Article 10*bis* the following resolution:

> "The Congress considers that in certain cases the disclosure of press information for commercial purposes, without authorization, may constitute unfair competition;" and the Vienna Congress of 1933 of the International Chamber of Commerce expressed their support for the insertion in the Convention of the Union of "a provision tending to treat as unfair competition any publication of press news obtained otherwise than by the regular and permissible routes mentioned in the resolutions of the Conference of press experts held in Geneva in 1927, as long as this information keeps a nature of currentness giving it commercial value."

3. Press information. The German Administration had proposed the following new 4th [subparagraph]:

> 4th The disclosure, unauthorized and with a commercial purpose, of press information, regardless of their content or mode of transmission, made before the end of the day following the day of first publication, as well as any disclosure for commercial purposes made without indication of the source.

The Czechoslovak Administration had made a similar proposal, which the Delegation of that country withdrew in favor of the German proposal, with the object of facilitating unanimity.

The Italian Delegation recalled that the protection of press information, which has not been hitherto recognized in the Paris Convention or the Berne Convention, is the subject by major press organizations, which are industrial in nature, of claims that should deserve the attention of the lawmaker. He spoke in favor of the principle of the obligation to cite the source of the information, when the disclosure has been made for a commercial purpose, but against the fixing of a time limit for reproduction, because a too absolute rule could harm the public interest and imply the recognition of the ownership of information, which is unacceptable both for legal reasons and for the reason that the same news may arrive at the same time to more than one person. The Italian Delegation maintained that it was necessary not to protect the news itself, but its priority, that is, the effort of the one who came first, sometimes thanks to a considerable financial sacrifice, to bring the information to the public.

The French Delegation expressed itself in the same direction. It recognized that efforts aiming at protecting press information under the aegis of the Union for the Protection of Industrial Property, which could not fall within the scope of the Berne Convention, because the notion of the ownership of a new is inadmissible, deserved to be seconded, but it expressed the fear that it would be difficult to find a satisfactory formula.

However, in view of the interest of the question, it asked that the Conference should once again issue a vote. The Delegation of the United States questioned the advisability of introducing into the Convention a provision dealing with press information, which does not fall under the provision that Article 2 gives about the words "industrial property." It stated that a provision of this nature could hardly be incorporated into national laws, which could not foresee all acts of unfair competition, involving not only manufacturers and traders, but also authors, doctors, and even lawyers.

The Spanish and Portuguese delegations considered that the subject was rather within the competence of the Berne Convention. The Belgian, Hungarian and Polish Delegations (the national law of the latter country already deals with the activities covered by the German proposal), supported the principle of the German proposal. The Austrian, British and Danish delegations recognized the importance of the question, but considered that it was not yet ripe enough to be decided within the framework of the Convention. The representative of the International Chamber of Commerce noted that the desire to protect press information is obvious, but that the discussions provoked by the I.C.C. had not lead to a satisfactory result.

A vote by roll call on the German proposal gave the following results: yes: 13; no: 5 (Austria, Denmark, Finland, Japan, United States); abstentions: 13.

4. T.S.F. [wireless telegraphy]—The Czechoslovak Delegation proposed. . . . to ban also

"Any commercial use of a radioelectric transmission without the previous authorization of the broadcaster."

This proposal was rejected by hands raised, by 12 votes to 2.

§4.48 THE ROME CONVENTION INCREASES THE PROTECTION OF THE RIGHTS OF PERFORMERS AND PHONOGRAM PRODUCERS, BUT NOT OF BROADCASTERS

October 26, 1961

In 1961 the international community, gathered at WIPO, was successful in harmonizing minimum standards for the protection of performers, producers of phonograms, and broadcasting organizations. The standards were at a minimum level, and corresponded to those generally available in some WIPO Member States. In the case individual countries had higher standards, the 1961 treaty applied national treatment, thus extending those higher standards to the nationals of the other countries. The 1961 treaty mirrored a situation that corresponded to the technology used at that time for transmitting audio and video signals. Since then, in response to technological evolution, the international standards of protection of performers and producers of phonograms have been raised: in 1994, under the TRIPS Agreement; in 1996, under the WIPO Treaty on Performers and Producers of Phonograms (known as the WPPT); and in 2012, under the Beijing Treaty. But broadcasters have not benefited from new rules, and the exponential growth of communication media that have become available since 1996 has left that industry without adequate protection on the international level. Thus far broadcasters have not been able to raise the standards of protection in WIPO, and negotiations in that respect continue at its Standing Committee on Copyright and Related Rights (the SCT). But, at a bilateral level, some countries have been able to introduce new rules on broadcasting into free trade agreements.

The language of the second article of the Rome Convention speaks for itself as regards the dissatisfaction of broadcasting organizations concerning the lack of international protection, given that such protection is almost confined to national treatment. It is true that Article 2 refers to the possibility of Parties adopting higher standards, which the Convention provides for in various provisions, but those are still insufficient, given, as said above, the exponential growth of communication methods that have been developed since 1961.

Rome Convention

International Convention for the Protection of Performers, Producers of Phonograms and Broadcasting Organizations

Done at Rome on October 26, 1961

The Contracting States, moved by the desire to protect the rights of performers, producers of phonograms, and broadcasting organisations,

Have agreed as follows: . . .

Article 2

[Protection given by the Convention. Definition of National Treatment]

1. For the purposes of this Convention, national treatment shall mean the treatment accorded by the domestic law of the Contracting State in which protection is claimed:
   (a) to performers who are its nationals, as regards performances taking place, broadcast, or first fixed, on its territory;
   (b) to producers of phonograms who are its nationals, as regards phonograms first fixed or first published on its territory;
   (c) to broadcasting organisations which have their headquarters on its territory, as regards broadcasts transmitted from transmitters situated on its territory.
2. National treatment shall be subject to the protection specifically guaranteed, and the limitations specifically provided for, in this Convention. . . .

§4.49 THE UNITED STATES SUPREME COURT SETS A (LOW) STANDARD FOR ORIGINALITY

March 27, 1991

The notion that works must stand on originality in order to be copyrightable is not new. However, in 1991 the United States Supreme Court set a threshold, which, even if not an objective standard, gives nevertheless a good guidance as a way to separate what is copyrightable from what it should not be. That threshold, referred to as the "sweat of the brow" standard, means that copyrightability should not be a product of mere efforts, be they financial or other, in generating the work. There must be more than that, even if there is no need it be very significant.

Feist Publications, Inc. v. Rural Telephone Service Co., Inc.

499 U.S. 340 (1991)
O'Connor, J., delivered the opinion of the Court.
I

Rural Telephone Service Company, Inc., is a certified public utility that provides telephone service to several communities in northwest Kansas. It is subject to a state regulation that requires all telephone companies operating in Kansas to issue annually an updated telephone directory. Accordingly, as a condition of its monopoly franchise, Rural publishes a typical telephone directory, consisting of white pages and yellow pages. The white pages list in alphabetical order the names of Rural's subscribers, together with their towns and telephone numbers. The yellow pages list Rural's business subscribers alphabetically by category and feature classified advertisements of various sizes. Rural distributes its directory free of charge to its subscribers, but earns revenue by selling yellow pages advertisements.

Feist Publications, Inc., is a publishing company that specializes in area-wide telephone directories. Unlike a typical directory, which covers only a particular calling area, Feist's area-wide directories cover a much larger geographical range, reducing the need to call directory assistance or consult multiple directories. The Feist directory that is the subject of this litigation covers 11 different telephone service areas in 15 counties and contains 46,878 white pages listings—compared to Rural's approximately 7,700 listings. Like Rural's directory, Feist's is distributed free of charge and includes both white pages and yellow pages. Feist and Rural compete vigorously for yellow pages advertising.

As the sole provider of telephone service in its service area, Rural obtains subscriber information quite easily. Persons desiring telephone service must apply to Rural and provide their names and addresses; Rural then assigns them a telephone number. Feist is not a telephone company, let alone one with monopoly status, and therefore lacks independent access to any subscriber information. To obtain white pages listings for its area-wide directory, Feist approached each of the 11 telephone companies operating in northwest Kansas and offered to pay for the right to use its white pages listings. . . .

Unable to license Rural's white pages listings, Feist used them without Rural's consent. Feist began by removing several thousand listings that fell outside the geographic range of its area-wide directory, then hired personnel to investigate the 4,935 that remained. These employees verified the data reported by Rural and sought to obtain additional information. As a result, a typical Feist listing includes the individual's street address; most of Rural's listings do not. Notwithstanding these additions, however, 1,309 of the 46,878 listings in Feist's 1983 directory were identical to listings in Rural's 1982-1983 white pages. . . . . Four of these were fictitious listings that Rural had inserted into its directory to detect copying.

Rural sued for copyright infringement in the District Court for the District of Kansas taking the position that Feist, in compiling its own directory, could not use the information contained in Rural's white pages. . . .

This case concerns the interaction of two well-established propositions. The first is that facts are not copyrightable; the other, that compilations of facts generally are. Each of these propositions possesses an impeccable pedigree. That there can be no valid copyright in facts is universally understood. The most fundamental axiom of copyright law is that "no author may copyright his ideas or the facts he narrates." *Harper & Row, Publishers, Inc.* v. *Nation Enterprises*, 471

U.S. 539, 556 (1985). Rural wisely concedes this point, noting in its brief that "facts and discoveries, of course, are not themselves subject to copyright protection." . . . At the same time, however, it is beyond dispute that compilations of facts are within the subject matter of copyright. Compilations were expressly mentioned in the Copyright Act of 1909, and again in the Copyright Act of 1976.

There is an undeniable tension between these two propositions. Many compilations consist of nothing but raw data—*i. e.*, wholly factual information not accompanied by any original written expression. On what basis may one claim a copyright in such a work? Common sense tells us that 100 uncopyrightable facts do not magically change their status when gathered together in one place. Yet copyright law seems to contemplate that compilations that consist exclusively of facts are potentially within its scope.

The key to resolving the tension lies in understanding why facts are not copyrightable. The *sine qua non* of copyright is originality. To qualify for copyright protection, a work must be original to the author. *See Harper & Row, supra*, at 547–549. Original, as the term is used in copyright, means only that the work was independently created by the author (as opposed to copied from other works), and that it possesses at least some minimal degree of creativity. . . . To be sure, the requisite level of creativity is extremely low; even a slight amount will suffice. The vast majority of works make the grade quite easily, as they possess some creative spark, "no matter how crude, humble or obvious" it might be. . . . Originality does not signify novelty; a work may be original even though it closely resembles other works so long as the similarity is fortuitous, not the result of copying. To illustrate, assume that two poets, each ignorant of the other, compose identical poems. Neither work is novel, yet both are original and, hence, copyrightable. *See Sheldon* v. *Metro-Goldwyn Pictures Corp.*, 81 F. 2d 49, 54 (CA2 1936).

Originality is a constitutional requirement. The source of Congress' power to enact copyright laws is Article I, § 8, cl. 8, of the Constitution, which authorizes Congress to "secure for limited Times to Authors . . . the exclusive Right to their respective Writings." In two decisions from the late nineteenth century—*The Trade-Mark Cases*, 100 U.S. 82 (1879); and *Burrow-Giles Lithographic Co.* v. *Sarony*, 111 U.S. 53 (1884)—this Court defined the crucial terms "authors" and "writings." In so doing, the Court made it unmistakably clear that these terms presuppose a degree of originality. . . .

It is this bedrock principle of copyright that mandates the law's seemingly disparate treatment of facts and factual compilations. "No one may claim originality as to facts." . . . This is because facts do not owe their origin to an act of authorship. The distinction is one between creation and discovery: The first person to find and report a particular fact has not created the fact; he or she has merely discovered its existence. To borrow from *Burrow-Giles*, one who discovers a fact is not its "maker" or "originator." . . . "The discoverer merely finds and records." . . . Census takers, for example, do not "create" the population figures that emerge from their efforts; in a sense, they copy these figures from the world around them. . . . Census data therefore do not trigger copyright because these data are not "original" in the constitutional sense. . . . The same is true of all facts—scientific, historical, biographical, and news of the day. "They may not be copyrighted and are part of the public domain available to every person." *Miller, supra*, at 1369.

Factual compilations, on the other hand, may possess the requisite originality. The compilation author typically chooses which facts to include, in what order to place them, and how to arrange the collected data so that they may be used effectively by readers. These choices as to selection and arrangement, so long as they are made independently by the compiler and entail a minimal degree of creativity, are sufficiently original that Congress may protect such compilations through the copyright laws. . . . Thus, even a directory that contains absolutely no protectable written expression, only facts, meets the constitutional minimum for copyright protection if it features an original selection or arrangement. . . .

This inevitably means that the copyright in a factual compilation is thin. Notwithstanding a valid copyright, a subsequent compiler remains free to use the facts contained in another's publication to aid in preparing a competing work, so long as the competing work does not feature the same selection and arrangement. As one commentator explains it: "No matter how much original authorship the work displays, the facts and ideas it exposes are free for the taking. . . . The very same facts and ideas may be divorced from the context imposed by the author, and restated or reshuffled by second comers, even if the author was the first to discover the facts or to propose the ideas." . . .

It may seem unfair that much of the fruit of the compiler's labor may be used by others without compensation. As Justice Brennan has correctly observed, however, this is not "some unforeseen byproduct of a statutory scheme." *Harper & Row*, 471 U.S., at 589 (dissenting opinion). It is, rather, "the essence of copyright," *ibid.* and a constitutional requirement. The primary objective of copyright is not to reward the labor of authors, but "to promote the Progress of Science and useful Arts." Art. I, § 8, cl. 8. Accord, *Twentieth Century Music Corp.* v. *Aiken*, 422 U.S. 151, 156 (1975). To this end, copyright assures authors the right to their original expression, but encourages others to build freely upon the ideas and information conveyed by a work. *Harper & Row, supra*, at 556-557. This principle, known as the idea/expression or fact/expression dichotomy, applies to all works of authorship. As applied to a factual compilation, assuming the absence of original written expression, only the compiler's selection and arrangement may be protected; the raw facts may be copied at will. This result is neither unfair nor unfortunate. It is the means by which copyright advances the progress of science and art. . . .

The "sweat of the brow" doctrine had numerous flaws, the most glaring being that it extended copyright protection in a compilation beyond selection and arrangement—the compiler's original contributions—to the facts themselves. Under the doctrine, the only defense to infringement was independent creation. A subsequent compiler was "not entitled to take one word of information previously published," but rather had to "independently work out the matter for himself, so as to arrive at the same result from the same common sources of information." . . . "Sweat of the brow" courts thereby eschewed the most fundamental axiom of copyright law—that no one may copyright facts or ideas. *See Miller* v. *Universal City Studios, Inc.*, 650 F. 2d, at 1372 (criticizing "sweat of the brow" courts because "ensuring that later writers obtain the facts independently . . . is precisely the scope of protection given . . . copyrighted matter, and the law is clear that facts are not entitled to such protection").

Decisions of this Court applying the 1909 Act make clear that the statute did not permit the "sweat of the brow" approach. The best example is *International News Service* v. *Associated Press*, 248 U.S. 215 (1918). In that decision, the Court stated unambiguously that the 1909 Act conferred copyright protection only on those elements of a work that were original to the author. International News Service had conceded taking news reported by Associated Press and publishing it in its own newspapers. Recognizing that § 5 of the Act specifically mentioned " 'periodicals, including newspapers,' " § 5(b), the Court acknowledged that news articles were copyrightable. *Id.* at 234. It flatly rejected, however, the notion that the copyright in an article extended to the factual information it contained: "The news element—the information respecting current events contained in the literary production—is not the creation of the writer, but is a report of matters that ordinarily are *publici juris*; it is the history of the day.". . .

The question that remains is whether Rural selected, coordinated, or arranged these uncopyrightable facts in an original way. As mentioned, originality is not a stringent standard; it does not require that facts be presented in an innovative or surprising way. It is equally true, however, that the selection and arrangement of facts cannot be so mechanical or routine as to require no creativity whatsoever. The standard of originality is low, but it does exist. . . . As this Court has explained, the Constitution mandates some minimal degree of creativity, *see The Trade-Mark Cases*, 100 U.S., at 94; and an author who claims infringement must prove "the existence of . . . intellectual production, of thought, and conception." *Burrow-Giles, supra*, at 59-60.

The selection, coordination, and arrangement of Rural's white pages do not satisfy the minimum constitutional standards for copyright protection. As mentioned at the outset, Rural's white pages are entirely typical. Persons desiring telephone service in Rural's service area fill out an application and Rural issues them a telephone number. In preparing its white pages, Rural simply takes the data provided by its subscribers and lists it alphabetically by surname. The end product is a garden-variety white pages directory, devoid of even the slightest trace of creativity.

Rural's selection of listings could not be more obvious: It publishes the most basic information—name, town, and telephone number—about each person who applies to it for telephone service. This is "selection" of a sort, but it lacks the modicum of creativity necessary to transform mere selection into copyrightable expression. Rural expended sufficient effort to make the white pages directory useful, but insufficient creativity to make it original.

§4.50 A UNITED STATES FEDERAL COURT DETERMINES THAT THE INHERENT RIGHT TO SAY "NO" IS THE ESSENCE OF INTELLECTUAL PROPERTY AND ITS PROCOMPETITIVE ROLE

1994

The text that follows is a groundbreaking opinion issued by the District Court of Massachusetts and confirmed by the Court of Appeals for the 1st Circuit. The action of copyright infringement was filed by Data General Corp., provider of maintenance services for the computers it manufactured. Data General created a copyrighted software program (ADEX) that provided for an efficient diagnosis of problems in its MV computers. It used that software to maintain its own computers and licensed it exclusively to in-house technicians of companies that owned Data General equipment, which could perform their own maintenance.

The defendant, Grumman Systems, provided services of maintenance of computers (including those of the plaintiff). But Data General would not license ADEX to its own service customers or to the customers of maintenance providers, such as Grumman. There was not another source for ADEX.

There were two other diagnostics software available on the market but they were not fully functional substitutes. Unable to have legal access to ADEX, the defendant copied and used them in its business.

Sued on copyright infringement by Data General, Grumman alleged that ADEX provided a natural competitive advantage to the plaintiff, which, being the manufacturer, knew better than anyone else the characteristics of its computers.

Therefore, ADEX became an essential facility, and therefore Data General's refusal to give access to that software to potential competitors was a violation of antitrust law.

The text that follows is a short excerpt from the opinion written by District Court Judge Skinner, where he asserts the procompetitive effect of copyright.

Data General Corp. v. Grumman Systems

761 F. Supp. 185 (D. Mass., 1991), *aff'd*, 36 F.3d 1147 (1st Cir. 1994)

The case law has consistently affirmed that a manufacturer is under no obligation to pre-disclose or disclose its knowledge about its products so that competition may arise in the related peripheral hardware, software, and repair services markets. *See Berkey Photo v. Eastman Kodak, supra.* The underlying thrust of Grumman's essential facilities claim is that if it cannot force DG to share its knowledge, the essential facilities doctrine requires DG to share the fruits of its knowledge. As the First Circuit stated in a different factual context, "this view of the essential facilities doctrine, however, considerably overstates its scope." . . . . DG does not have monopoly power in the sale of computer systems and thus is not using a bottleneck to create another monopoly. The "bottleneck" of its superior knowledge in the design of DG computers is insufficient to invoke the essential facilities doctrine; a better mousetrap is not necessarily an essential facility. The Sherman Act has not been interpreted to require manufacturers to abandon their advantage in creating accessories to their systems. If manufacturers of complex and innovative systems were required to share with competitors the development of accessories, because they had a possibly absolute advantage through producing the system, the incentives of copyright and patent laws would be severely undermined. Not only would the manufacturer, who is in the best position to create these accessories, have less incentive to do so, but also the impetus for competitors to reverse engineer and produce competing solutions would be reduced.

§4.51 UNFAIR COMPETITION IS EXTENDED SO AS TO COMPLEMENT COPYRIGHT LAW

2010 and 2011

In 1994 WTO Members raised the international standards of protection of copyright by means of a number of norms included in the TRIPS Agreement. Two years later, in 1996, through the so-called "Internet Treaties"(the WIPO Copyright Treaty—WCT, and the WIPO Performances and Phonograms Treaty—WPPT), WIPO Member States raised the standards of copyright for works, performances and phonograms in the digital environment. But a few States of the United States, in 2010 and 2011, went much farther in strengthening that protection not only by extending the scope of the repression of unfair competition to software but also by applying those new standards regardless of the place where infringement has occurred (thus, applying extraterritoriality).

Louisiana Revised Statutes

TITLE 51 — TRADE AND COMMERCE

RS 51:1427 — UNFAIR OR DECEPTIVE TRADE PRACTICES OR ACTS; STOLEN OR MISAPPROPRIATED COMPUTER SOFTWARE; VIOLATIONS

§1427. Unfair or deceptive trade practices or acts; stolen or misappropriated computer software; violations

A. It shall be unlawful for a person to develop or manufacture a product, or to develop or supply a service using stolen or misappropriated property, including but not limited to computer software that does not have the necessary copyright licenses, where that product or service is sold or offered for sale in competition with those doing business in this state.

B. Any violation of this Section shall be an unfair method of competition and unfair practice or act and shall subject the violator to any and all actions and penalties provided for in this Chapter. For the purpose of this Section, a violation shall occur each time such a product or service is sold or offered for sale.

Revised Code of Washington

RCW 19.330.020

Unfair acts.

Any person who manufactures an article or product while using stolen or misappropriated information technology in its business operations after notice and opportunity to cure as provided in RCW 19.330.050 and, with respect to remedies sought under RCW 19.330.060(6) or 19.330.070, causes a material competitive injury as a result of such use of stolen or misappropriated information technology, is deemed to engage in an unfair act where such an article or product is sold or offered for sale in this state, either separately or as a component of another article or product, and in competition with an article or product sold or offered for sale in this state that was manufactured without violating this section. A person who engages in such an unfair act, and any articles or products manufactured by the person in violation of this section, is subject to the liabilities and remedial provisions of this chapter in an action by the attorney general or any person described in RCW 19.330.060(5), except as provided in RCW 19.330.030 through 19.330.090.

[2011 c 98 § 2.]

RCW 19.330.010

Definitions.

The definitions in this section apply throughout this chapter unless the context clearly requires otherwise. . . .

(7)(a) "Stolen or misappropriated information technology" means hardware or software that the person referred to in RCW 19.330.020 acquired, appropriated, or used without the authorization of the owner of the information technology or the owner's authorized licensee in violation of applicable law, but does not include situations in which the hardware or software alleged to have been stolen or misappropriated was not available for retail purchase on a stand-alone basis at or before the time it was acquired, appropriated, or used by such a person. . . .

§4.52 MARRAKESH TREATY TO FACILITATE ACCESS TO PUBLISHED WORKS FOR PERSONS WHO ARE BLIND, VISUALLY IMPAIRED, OR OTHERWISE PRINT DISABLED

June 27, 2013

The coming into force of the TRIPS Agreement, in 1994, and the subsequent agreements (mostly of a bilateral and regional nature) that increased the harmonized protection of intellectual property, has given rise to complaints that the concessions towards higher standards of protection had gone too far. Those complaints were heard mainly in connection with pharmaceutical patents and the attendant issues of access to health. However, worries have also been expressed in connection with copyright and its allegedly negative impact on access to culture and education. The problem of access to works by those visually impaired gained momentum in the middle of the first decade of this century, when some delegations brought the debate to WIPO. The allegation was that there was a concentration of visually impaired people in poor countries, and therefore there was the need for facilitating the translation of copyrighted works through technical means. Many developed countries had already internally enacted provisions in that sense, with exceptions to copyrights that facilitate that access.

The result was the Marrakesh Treaty. The text that follows reproduces the Preamble of the treaty, which gives a very precise idea of the principles and objectives that inform it.

The Marrakesh Treaty entered into force in 2016.

Marrakesh Treaty to Facilitate Access to Published Works for Persons Who Are Blind, Visually Impaired, or Otherwise Print Disabled

Preamble

The Contracting Parties,

Recalling the principles of non-discrimination, equal opportunity, accessibility and full and effective participation and inclusion in society, proclaimed in the Universal Declaration of Human Rights and the United Nations Convention on the Rights of Persons with Disabilities,

Mindful of the challenges that are prejudicial to the complete development of persons with visual impairments or with other print disabilities, which limit their freedom of expression, including the freedom to seek, receive and impart information and ideas of all kinds on an equal basis with others, including through all forms of communication of their choice, their enjoyment of the right to education, and the opportunity to conduct research,

Emphasizing the importance of copyright protection as an incentive and reward for literary and artistic creations and of enhancing opportunities for everyone, including persons with visual impairments or with other print disabilities, to participate in the cultural life of the community, to enjoy the arts and to share scientific progress and its benefits,

Aware of the barriers of persons with visual impairments or with other print disabilities to access published works in achieving equal opportunities in society, and the need to both expand the number of works in accessible formats and to improve the circulation of such works,

Taking into account that the majority of persons with visual impairments or with other print disabilities live in developing and least-developed countries,

Recognizing that, despite the differences in national copyright laws, the positive impact of new information and communication technologies on the lives of persons with visual impairments or with other print disabilities may be reinforced by an enhanced legal framework at the international level,

Recognizing that many Member States have established limitations and exceptions in their national copyright laws for persons with visual impairments or with other print disabilities, yet there is a continuing shortage of available works in accessible format copies for such persons, and that considerable resources are required for their effort of making works accessible to these persons, and that the lack of possibilities of cross-border exchange of accessible format copies has necessitated duplication of these efforts,

Recognizing both the importance of rightholders' role in making their works accessible to persons with visual impairments or with other print disabilities and the importance of appropriate limitations and exceptions to make works accessible to these persons, particularly when the market is unable to provide such access,

Recognizing the need to maintain a balance between the effective protection of the rights of authors and the larger public interest, particularly education, research and access to information, and that such a balance must facilitate effective and timely access to works for the benefit of persons with visual impairments or with other print disabilities,

Reaffirming the obligations of Contracting Parties under the existing international treaties on the protection of copyright and the importance and flexibility of the three-step test for limitations and exceptions established in Article 9(2) of the Berne Convention for the Protection of Literary and Artistic Works and other international instruments,

Recalling the importance of the Development Agenda recommendations, adopted in 2007 by the General Assembly of the World Intellectual Property Organization (WIPO), which aim to ensure that development considerations form an integral part of the Organization's work,

Recognizing the importance of the international copyright system and desiring to harmonize limitations and exceptions with a view to facilitating access to and use of works by persons with visual impairments or with other print disabilities,

Have agreed as follows: . . .

§4.53 THE EUROPEAN UNION EXTENDS COPYRIGHT PROTECTION TO PRESS PUBLICATIONS ONLINE

April 17, 2019

The debate over the possibility of protecting press news against their reproduction did not vanish after the rejection of its coverage by copyright and by the repression of unfair competition. The rising of the Internet and the appearance of a myriad of websites and blogs containing snippets of information obtained by copying and pasting news extracted from news agencies and online magazines and periodicals have led to a clear understanding of the economic losses that those practices cause. Albeit under vast criticism, the European Union has put an end to such practices. The text that follows consists of an excerpt from the preamble and one provision of the Copyright Directive of 2019 that provides for the protection of the news of the day under a copyright approach—but mainly under an unfair competition rationale.

Directive (EU) 2019/790 of the European Parliament and of the Council of 17 April 2019 on copyright and related rights in the Digital Single Market

(54) A free and pluralist press is essential to ensure quality journalism and citizens' access to information. It provides a fundamental contribution to public debate and the proper functioning of a democratic society. The wide availability of press publications online has given rise to the emergence of new online services, such as news aggregators or media monitoring services, for which the reuse of press publications constitutes an important part of their business models and a source of revenue. Publishers of press publications are facing problems in 17.5.2019 L 130/103 Official Journal of the European Union EN licensing the online use of their publications to the providers of those kinds of services, making it more difficult for them to recoup their investments. In the absence of recognition of publishers of press publications as rightholders, the licensing and enforcement of rights in press publications regarding online uses by information society service providers in the digital environment are often complex and inefficient.

Article 15. Protection of press publications concerning online uses

1. Member States shall provide publishers of press publications established in a Member State with the rights provided for in Article 2 and 3(2) of Directive 2001/29/EC for the online use of their press publications by information society service providers.

   The rights provided for in the first subparagraph shall not apply to private or non-commercial uses of press publications by individual users.

   The protection granted under the first subparagraph shall not apply to acts of hyperlinking. The rights provided for in the first subparagraph shall not apply in respect of the use of individual words or very short extracts of a press publication.
2. The rights provided for in paragraph 1 shall leave intact and shall in no way affect any rights provided for in Union law to authors and other rightholders, in respect of the works and other subject matter incorporated in a press publication. The rights provided for in paragraph 1 shall not be invoked against those authors and other rightholders and, in particular, shall not deprive them of their right to exploit their works and other subject matter independently from the press publication in which they are incorporated.

   When a work or other subject matter is incorporated in a press publication on the basis of a non-exclusive licence, the rights provided for in paragraph 1 shall not be invoked to prohibit the use by other authorised users. The rights provided for in paragraph 1 shall not be invoked to prohibit the use of works or other subject matter for which protection has expired.
3. Articles 5 to 8 of Directive 2001/29/EC, Directive 2012/28/EU and Directive (EU) 2017/1564 of the European Parliament of the Council (19) shall apply

mutatis mutandis in respect of the rights provided for in paragraph 1 of this Article.

4. The rights provided for in paragraph 1 shall expire two years after the press publication is published. That term shall be calculated from 1 January of the year following the date on which that press publication is published. Paragraph 1 shall not apply to press publications first published before 6 June 2019.
5. Member States shall provide that authors of works incorporated in a press publication receive an appropriate share of the revenues that press publishers receive for the use of their press publications by information society service providers.

CHAPTER 5

Industrial Designs

§5.01 FRANCE DETERMINES, FOR THE FIRST TIME, THE EXCLUSIVITY OF INDUSTRIAL DESIGNS

August 1664

One of the first legal acts determining the protection of industrial designs was a decree signed by Louis XIV, in the context of a permission for the establishment of a carpet factory in Beauvais. It is also probable that the idea for the temporary exclusivity in designs has been inspired by Colbert—the same politician who had the idea of creating a patent office at the Palace of the Louvre (*see* Text 1.27).

Decree for the establishment of a tapestry factory in Beauvais (excerpt)

Vincennes, August 1664.

As one of the most important works of peace that God has pleased to give us, is that of restoring all kinds of commerce in this kingdom, and of putting it in a condition to dispense with the recourse to foreigners for things necessary for the use and convenience of our subjects: so we have hitherto forgotten nothing that would be able to procure this advantage, by all the means that we have judged to be proper for the success of this grand design: among which means is that of the re-establishment of the manufactory of tapestries, in the manner of those of Flanders, whose manufacture had been introduced before in our good city of Paris and others of this kingdom, by the care of the late King Henri-le-Grand, our very honored ancestor, appearing with reason of a very great consequence; and our dear and well-loved Sieur Colbert, our counselor in all our councils, superintendent and general organizer of our buildings, arts and manufactures of France, having made known to us that the restoration of this factory and manufacture of said tapestries could not be better entrusted to no one more capable of leading him to a happy end than Louis Hinard, a merchant upholsterer and bourgeois of Paris, recognized as one of the most skillful in the industry, not only in the said manufacture, but also in the commerce of that kind of merchandise, if it pleased us to grant him permission to establish the manufactory in our city of Beauvais, or any other of our province of Picardy, whichever he sees fit, which he will judge the most convenient to enjoy by him, his heirs and successors in title, during the time and in accordance with the provisions dictated by the conditions and articles he has us for this purpose presented.

For these reasons . . . we have allowed Hinard to establish the said manufactory and manufacture of all kinds of tapestries of *verdures* and characters of high and low level. We wish that the said Hinard, his heirs and successors in title enjoy the said permission and establishment for 30 years: and this to the exclusion of and privately from all others, under the penalty of a fine of 10,000 pounds, confiscation of their goods, and all costs, damages and interest, all applicable to the benefit of said Hinard. . . . And because it is necessary for such establishment that the mentioned Hinard and his associates can easily maintain in the premises of said establishment all the workers and other people who will be employed by them, we allow them to take and establish in such places such number as they see fit of painters, dyers, beer brewers, bakers, masters or companions; who will enjoy the same privileges and exemptions as the so-called upholsterers. We wish that the wool and dyeing substances that will be purchased by the said Hinard and associates and their agents, within the kingdom, . . . be and may be by them brought and transported to the place of the said establishment without being subject to the payment of any fees. To which effect we allow those mentioned to put and carry a blanket of our colors and coat of arms on their carts, boats and other things used for the transportation, both said wools and dyeing substances as well as the tapestries that will be manufactured by them: which will be marked by them by working and weaving the said tapestries with the mark given to them by the said superintendent, and without any one being able to use the said mark for other tapestries, nor copy the designs on which they will be made, under the penalty of a fine of 10,000 pounds, and of confiscation.

§5.02 IN ANOTHER INITIATIVE LINKED TO THE TAPESTRY INDUSTRY (AUBUSSON), FRANCE REAFFIRMS THE EXCLUSIVITY OF INDUSTRIAL DESIGNS

May 28, 1732

It seems that the idea of granting exclusivity to the industrial designs created in Beauvais has produced good results. Several decades later, through a patent letter, the same protection would be granted to the designs created for the tapestries of Aubusson. A few years later a similar patent letter would be issued in connection with the manufacture of tapestries of Feuilletin, which competed with Aubusson. In 1736 the French State Council issued a judgment ordering the two manufactures to stop copying each other's marks.

Patent Letters, Concerning the Manufacture of Tapestries of Aubusson.

Given at Compiegne, May 28, 1732. Registered in Parliament.

XXVI

We prohibit all Painters, Merchants, Master manufacturers and workers of Tapestries, to copy or to make copy the designs that are made or purchased at the expense of Merchants or Master manufacturers, under the penalty of the fine of five hundred pounds against each offender. . . .

XXVIII

We wish that in accordance with the Letters patent of the month of July 1665, a Painter be sent to the City of Aubusson and maintained [there] at our expense, for making the designs of tapestries which will be manufactured there; to train pupils, and to inspect the workers of the said Manufacture, for the beauty and regularity of the shades of the said tapestries.

§5.03 THE PROTECTION OF INDUSTRIAL DESIGNS IS EXTENDED TO THE SILK INDUSTRY, BASED IN LYON

1744

In 1744 Louis XV, of France, approved the regulations of the silk industry, in Lyon, confirming a number of regulations previously imposed by the magistrates of that city, prohibiting the unauthorized copy of designs. Lyon had benefited from the immigration of skilled Italian artisans, who, lured by promises of privileges, brought their skills and tools, and founded the silk industry in that city. Soon the silk industry would become the chief economic activity of Lyon.

Statutes and Regulations for the Community of Master Merchants, and Master Workers in fabrics made of gold, silver and silk, and other mixed of silk, wool, fur, yarn and cotton, of the city and suburbs of Lyon; and for the manufacture of the said fabrics.

Title IX

XII

Similar prohibitions are imposed to the said master workers to sell, give or lend, for whatever cause and under any pretext whatsoever, the designs entrusted to them for manufacturing, under the penalty of a fine of one hundred pounds and the forfeiture of the master's status, and even of corporal punishment; for the payment of which fine the said master workers shall be subject to imprisonment [*contraint par corps*], by virtue of the Consulate's judgment that will have condemned them to it.

XIII

Similar prohibitions are made to all designers and other persons whomever, to remove and copy, to cause the removal and copy directly or indirectly, and in any way whatsoever, any design on fabrics, both old and new, or on design plans of the said fabrics; under the penalty of a fine of one thousand pounds against the designer who would have removed or copied the said designs, and of the same fine against the person who had caused them to be removed or copied, and in addition to the seizure of the fabrics which were made upon the removed or copied designs; the said seizure applicable half in favor of the said community, and half in favor of the master whose designs would have been removed or copied.

§5.04 A LAWSUIT INVOLVING THE INFRINGEMENT OF INDUSTRIAL DESIGNS IN LYON

April 29, 1749

Protection of industrial designs was taken seriously by the French authorities, as the text that follows shows. The significant growth in commercial rivalry in luxury goods, such as silk cloth, had persuaded merchants and manufacturers—and authorities, as well—of the importance of designs as tools of differentiation.

Judgment of the King's State Council which confirms, with fine and costs, a judgment of the Judges of the Consulate of Lyon, which condemns the Sieur Ribier, Merchant Manufacturer of Silk Cloths in Lyon, with the penalties brought by Articles XIII and XIV of the Regulations of 1744, concerning the Manufacture of Silk Cloths of Lyon, for having removed one design from Sieur Duperet & Company, also Merchant Manufacturers in Lyon, and having had made Silk Cloths with the same design.

Of April 29 1749.

Extracted from the Records of the State Council

Between Aymé Ribier, Merchant Manufacturer in Cloths of Gold, Silver and Silk of the City of Lyon, Appellant of a Judgment of the Consulate of the City of Lyon of June 13, 1747, according to the Requests by him presented to the State Council on January 9, 1748 and January 22, 1749, on one side; and Jean-Baptiste Duperet & Company, also Merchants Manufacturers in Gold, Silver and Silk Cloths of the said city of Lyon, Respondents and Defendants, on the other side. . . .

The definitive and *inter partes* judgment of the Consulate of Lyon, of June 13t^{h}, 1747, rendered after having heard the advice of the Masters and Guards, who said that as a result of the clarifications and observations found in the Minutes above mentioned, they believed that the said Duperet & Company are the first Inventors and first Manufacturers of the Design and Druggets in question; by which Judgment, deciding on the merits of the dispute of the Parties, reserved by the said inter partes judgment of the previous 31st of May, that the said Duperet & Company are declared inventors of the Design in question, and the first makers of the Druggetts upon the said Design; and consequently, given the infringement committed by the said Ribier by having it copied and having worked upon it, against the provisions of Articles XIII and XIV of the Regulations for the Manufacture of Silk Cloths of Lyon, the said Ribier is condemned to the penalties and fines against him pronounced by the Judgment of the 24th of the said month of May, which would be executed for that purpose, and, moreover, ordered to pay the costs. . . .

The King in His Council, ruling on the whole, without regard to the appeal filed by the said Aymé Ribier of the said Judgment of the Consulate of Lyon of June 13, 1747, or to all his requests, in which His Majesty has declared it non receivable and ill-founded, and which He has dismissed, has ordered and orders that the said Judgment shall be executed in accordance with its form and content: Condemns the said Ribier to the fine of 75 pounds and to the costs . . . Done at the King's State Council, held at Versailles on the twenty-ninth of April, one thousand seven hundred and forty-nine. . . .

§5.05 GREAT BRITAIN AWAKENS FOR THE IMPORTANCE OF PROTECTING INDUSTRIAL DESIGNS

June 1, 1787

Copyright in artistic designs, such as engravings and etchings, was already recognized in England, through a number of statutes passed by the Parliament. But their use as esthetic formats for consumer goods had still to wait several years. Great Britain was confident in the power of its manufactures for winning the trade wars against other European powers and the United States. The first British Act granting protection for designs was passed in 1787. It was a very limited Act, however. It would apply to certain fabrics only, and it would not extend to articles of manufacture (only after 1839 those designs would receive protection). Moreover, the term of protection was very narrow, which would make this Act ineffective. Interestingly, it provided for the exhaustion of rights.

An Act for the encouragement of the arts of designing and printing linens, cottons, calicoes, and muslins, by vesting the properties thereof in the designers, printers, and proprietors, for a limited time.

Whereas it may be expedient, for the encouragement of the arts of designing original patterns for printing linens, calicoes, cottons, and muslins, to vest the property thereof in the designers, printers, or proprietors, for a limited time; for which purpose may it please your Majesty that it may be enacted; and be it enacted by the King's most excellent majesty, by and with the advice and consent of the Lords spiritual and temporal, and commons, in this present parliament assembled, and by the authority of the same. That, from and after the first day of June one thousand seven hundred and eighty-seven, every person who shall invent, design, and print, or cause to be invented, designed, and printed, and become the proprietor of any new and original pattern or patterns for printing linens, cottons, calicoes, or muslins, shall have the right and liberty of printing and reprinting the same for the term of two months, to commence from the day of the first publishing thereof, which shall be truly printed with the name of the printer or proprietors at each end of every such piece of linen, cotton, calico, or other person whatsoever, from and after the fifth day of June one thousand seven hundred eighty-seven, within the time limited by this act, shall print, work, or copy, such original patter or patterns, or cause to be printed, worked, or copied, such original pattern or patterns, or shall print or reprint, or cause to be printed or reprinted, any such pattern or patterns, and shall publish, sell, or expose to sale, or in any other manner dispose of, or cause to be published, sold, or exposed to sale, or in any other manner disposed of, any linen, cotton, calico, or muslin, so printed without the consent of the proprietor or proprietors thereof, first had and obtained in writing, signed by him or them respectively in the presence of two or more witnesses, knowing the same to be so printed or reprinted without the consent of the proprietor or proprietors of such pattern, then every such proprietor or proprietors shall and may: if the offence be committed in England, by and in a special action upon the case, to be brought against the person or persons so offending, recover such damages as a jury on the trial of such action, . . .; and if the offence be committed in Scotland, every such proprietor or proprietors shall and may, . . . provided nevertheless, that it shall and may be lawful for any person or persons who shall hereafter purchase any plate or plates, block or blocks, for printing, from the original proprietors thereof, to print, reprint, and expose for sale, or cause to be printed, reprinted, and exposed for sale, from the said plates or blocks, without being liable for any action on that account. . . .

§5.06 FRANCE ESTABLISHES A FORMAL SYSTEM OF REGISTRATION OF INDUSTRIAL DESIGNS IN LYON

March 18, 1806

As awareness of the importance of protecting industrial designs as an element of competitive advantage grew, French authorities paid increased attention to legal security around those designs and their associated rights. One aspect of that attention was the setting of a formal registry of designs in Lyon.

Law of March 18, 1806 establishing a council of prud'hommes in Lyon (excerpts)

Title II

. . .

Section III

On the conservation of the property of the designs

Art. 14.—The council of prud'hommes is charged with the conservative measures of the property of the designs.

Art. 15.—Any manufacturer, who wants to be able to claim, subsequently, before the commercial court, the property of a design of his invention, will be required to deposit in the archives of the council of prud'hommes a specimen under envelope, bearing its stamps and signature, on which will also be affixed the stamp of the council of prud'hommes. . . .

Art. 17.—In case of dispute between two or more manufacturers on the property of a design, the council of prud'hommes shall open the envelopes deposited by the parties; it will provide a certificate indicating the name of the manufacturer who will have the priority of the date.

Art. 18.—In depositing his sample, the manufacturer shall declare whether he intends to reserve the exclusive ownership for one, three or five years, or to perpetuity; this statement shall be noted. On the expiry of the period of time indicated by the said declaration, if the reservation is temporary, any packet of samples deposited under seal in the archives of this council must be sent to the registry of arts of the city of Lyon, and the samples contained therein be added to the collection of the registry. . . .

§5.07 COMPETITION FOR FOREIGN MARKETS WITH OTHER COMMERCIAL POWERS SPURS GREAT BRITAIN TO INCREASE PROTECTION FOR INDUSTRIAL DESIGNS

1839, 1842, 1843

A movement led by the calicoe manufacturers (soon embraced by other sectors of the British industry) got the attention of Parliament. Their major concerns were that insufficient protection facilitated piracy and counterfeiting; and that such situation favored the French industry, which, albeit less productive, had developed art and taste in consumer goods, and had the preference of consumers.

As a result of that pressure, the Parliament in 1839 passed a statute extending the protection of designs to all industrial articles, increasing the term, and requiring registration. A few years later amendments would be introduced to improve the system further. However, England kept for several decades a dual system of protection, based on the distinction between designs for ornamental purposes and designs for the shape and configuration of useful articles. Only in 1883 would the Parliament reunite the two notions under one single concept—that of designs "applicable to any article of manufacture, or to any substance artificial or natural, or partly artificial and partly natural" (*see* Text 5.11).

The texts that follow are excerpts from a treatise on copyright in designs authored by James Emerson Tennent (1804-1869), chair of the Committee of the House of Commons on the Copyright of Designs, and who, sensitive to the plea of the industry, sponsored and successfully promoted the legislative changes.

To the Honourable The Commons of the United Kingdom of Great Britain and Ireland, in Parliament Assembled,

The humble Petition of the undersigned Printers of Calicoes and other woven Fabrics, Merchants, Manufacturers, Engravers, and others, carrying on business in and near Manchester, in the County of Lancaster.

Sheweth,

That your Petitioners have learnt with the greatest satisfaction the introduction of a bill into your honourable house for extending the protection given to original designs, or patterns, printed upon woven fabrics, from the term of three months to twelve, thereby giving to the original inventor, or proprietor of such designs, a right of property for a reasonable time in the produce of his skill, or capital, of which he has hitherto been unjustly deprived.

That your Petitioners are all deeply interested in, and many of them wholly dependent on the welfare and prosperity of the print trade, which is one of the great staple manufactures of the country, and they most respectfully and earnestly submit to the consideration of your honourable house, that whilst the various fabrics themselves enjoy that natural protection which the law affords to property, yet, by a strange anomaly, the original designs or patterns which give to these fabrics a great portion of their value, and which are equally the produce of labour, skill, and capital, are left almost wholly unprotected, the inventors or proprietors of such designs having no proprietary interest in them beyond a few weeks, when they become the common property of the trade. . . .

Four years ago, a Select Committee of your honourable house investigated the subject of arts and manufactures, and in an interesting Report, accompanied by most important evidence disclosing this humiliating fact, that however much the manufacturers of this country surpass their continental rivals in the goodness and cheapness of their productions, they are immeasurably below them in the taste and elegance of their designs. The fact is incontestable, and your Petitioners ascribe it mainly to the want of adequate protection, for no one will devote much time, attention, and money, to an object of which, if unsuccessful, he must bear the loss, and of which, if it succeeds, he must share the profit with the public.

Without protection, Schools of Design, your Petitioners venture to predict, will accomplish nothing; protection, without schools, may do much, but both united would give a stimulus to this deficient branch of our national industry, which would soon place the productions of this country on a level with those of the most distinguished nations. . . .

Wherefore your Petitioners humbly pray that the Bill now before your Honourable House may be passed into a Law,

And your Petitioners will ever pray. . . .

That the present limited term of three months is utterly inoperative as any protection to the trade, I have already exhibited proofs, not merely in the complaints of the sufferer whose property has been wrested from him, but in the confessions of those who have made the pirated copies, and the declaration of the merchants who have purchased them as a systematic trade. Mr. Brookes, who has accumulated wealth as a calico printer, avows, that down to a very late period his business consisted of an indiscriminate appropriation of the designs of others, notwithstanding the law of copyright, which he boldly set at defiance.

And Mr. Lucas, with all the unreserve of a man speaking of an ordinary line of business, admits that his extensive trade in printed calicoes is carried on with pirates alone; that so ordinary a matter is it to disregard the law, that it never enters into his head when he wants a lot of goods copied, to ask the question whether the designs be pirated property or not; and that he never meets the slightest difficulty in obtaining any quantity he requires, provided he finds the price to suit him, and that as to the present term of three months, "he never felt it to be any protection to the printer at all."

The present term of three months is stated, by those printers and designers who have petitioned the House of Commons for its extension, to be utterly inadequate for their protection, either in the home market or the foreign, or in that in which goods are suited conjointly for both, and that it fails to afford them that remunerative property in their inventions which the law designed and professes to confer. . . .

The improvement of the art of design by increased protection will, at the same time, augment the consumption both at home and abroad; abroad, because the Americans and others now buy French goods, under the feeling that they are superior in style to ours, whilst taste, if improved, added to our existing facilities for cheaper production, would ensure us the preference; and at home, because dresses would be more frequently changed and bought by the upper classes, on the same principle which leads to the purchase of a painting, to gratify taste and fancy, "as a dress, after all, is not a mere covering, else we should have no printed dresses at all;" and those whose trade now is to copy patterns, being compelled, as they will be, to produce originals, "the trade generally will be increased, from the circumstance of there being a greater number of producers than at present;" and Mr. Ross declares that "parties always buy a large quantity where there is a large assortment and variety." . . .

But, independently of pecuniary advantage to be gained by the suppression of copying, strong objections have been made to its continuance, on the moral ground of its dishonesty and injustice, as well as on the temptation which it holds out to servants and others, to purloin the designs entrusted to them by their masters, for sale to other houses, a practice of which serious complaints were made by various witnesses examined before the committee, cases having occurred in which, from this circumstance, copies of printed goods have been published by a rival house, almost simultaneously with the appearance of the original.

Those printers who think humility of price is the sole and only introduction to public favour, are opposed to the alteration of a law that in general gives an unjust advantage to the pilferer over the honest producer. Those who see taste and superior elegance opening the door to French manufactures in every quarter of the globe, perceive their own inferiority, and whilst they are conscious of their powers and capabilities, pray only for protection and encouragement to develop them.

The petitioners for copyright are those who, though they produce in the aggregate the smallest number of pieces because their works are the most elaborately beautiful, are nevertheless those who, in proportion to their production, give the greatest amount of employment. On the other hand, the opponents of extension are those who produce the coarsest and most ordinary articles those mountains of cloth, whose superficies is counted by "miles" instead of yards, but which are produced by little labour, affording but scanty employment, and the whole value of the article, cloth, printing, and profit inclusive, falls short of the mere wages of labour of printing alone, of most styles of the former class.

§5.08 WILLIAM E. GLADSTONE SPEAKS IN DEFENSE OF INDUSTRIAL DESIGNERS

October 26, 1863

William Ewart Gladstone, (1809-1898), the prestigious British politician and Prime Minister, added his voice in defense of the commercial value of artistic excellency. He did so in a speech he gave at the Foundation of the Wedgwood Institute. Josiah Wedgwood (1730-1795), founder of the famous manufacture of china, porcelain, and other objects of daily use, was the first British entrepreneur to integrate designing into the production and commercialization of consumer goods. Gladstone has acknowledged that element of the success of the British industrialist and called the attention for France's leadership in using industrial designs as a factor for securing international markets. Interestingly, Wedgwood did not pay particular attention to intellectual property. During his life he obtained (and enforced) one patent only (in 1769, on a method of producing Etruscan vases) because he disliked the costs of enforcing patents. He preferred the advantages of being the first on the market (known as the "head start"), which would keep him constantly innovating, but with the attendant price of being the constant (and defenseless) subject of imitation.

. . . We may consider the products of industry with reference to their utility, or to their cheapness, or with regard to their influence upon the condition of those who produce them, or, lastly, with reference to their beauty, to the degree in which they associate the presentation of forms and colors, agreeable to the cultivated eye, with the attainment of the highest aptitude for those purposes of common life for which they are properly designed. . . . We come, then, to the last of the heads which I have named: the association of beauty with utility, each of them taken according to its largest sense, in the business of industrial production. And it is in this department, I conceive, that we are to look for the peculiar pre-eminence, I will not scruple to say the peculiar greatness, of Wedgwood. . . .

Now in the application of beauty to works of utility, the reward is generally remote. A new element of labor is imported into the process of production; and that element, like others, must be paid for. . . .

The beautiful object will be dearer than one perfectly bare and bald; not because utility is curtailed or promised for the sake of beauty, but because there may be more manual labor, and there must be more thought, in the original design—*Pater ipse colendi/Haud facilem essem viam voluit.*

Therefore the manufacturer, whose daily thought it must and ought to be to cheapen his productions, endeavoring to dispense with all that can be spared, is under such temptation to decline letting beauty stand as an item to lengthen the account of the costs of production. So the pressure of economical law tells severely upon the finer elements of trade. And yet it may be argued that, in this as in other cases, in the case for example of the durability and solidity of articles, that which appears cheapest at first may not be cheapest in the long run. And this for two reasons. In the first place, because in the long run mankind are willing to pay a price for Beauty. I will seek for a proof of this proposition in an illustrious neighbouring nation. France is the second commercial country of the world; and her command of foreign markets seems clearly referable, in a great degree, to the real elegance of her productions, and to establish in the most intelligible form the principle that taste has an exchangeable value; that it fetches a price in the markets of the world.

But there seems to be another way by which the law of nature arrives at its revenge upon the shortsighted lust for cheapness. We begin, say, by finding beauty expensive. We accordingly decline to pay a class of artists for producing it. Their employment ceases; and the class itself disappears. Presently we find by experience that works reduced to utter baldness do not long satisfy. We have to meet a demand for embellishment of some kind. But we have now starved out the race who knew the laws and modes of its production. Something, however, must be done. So we substitute strength for flavor, quantity for quality; and we end by producing incongruous excrescences, or even hideous malformations, at a greater cost than would have sufficed for the nourishment among us, without a break, of chaste and virgin art. . . .

Depend upon it that all false, all sham work, however it may last for a little, the effect of it is ultimately to destroy reputation, to take away confidence, and to act most injuriously upon those who have adopted the trick. But, apart from that, I have the strongest conviction that all along the English industry has been defective in the matter of beauty. The quality under which we generally hear that described—the form under which we generally hear that important element described—is under the name of taste. Well, taste is nothing in the world except the faculty which devises according to the laws of beauty, which executes according to the laws of beauty. In France the standard of taste, taken as a whole, in French production is very much higher than in the productions of England and depend upon it, it is the taste of the French which fetches the price in the market as well as the other qualities of what they produce, and which has immensely contributed to give to France its very high place in the commerce of the world—because I dare say you know that France is at this moment, and for some time has been, the second country in the world as regards the export of her domestic productions. Well, it is this want which the schools of art in England aim at supplying. It is a great national want, a national want that has been felt at all times, and a national want that is now especially felt, because of the depression of British commerce and because of the increased difficulties in finding a way into the markets of many foreign countries. Now, it seems a very singular thing that this want should exist, because it is admitted that England is a country which, in the products of beauty in its highest forms, shows no deficiency at all. . . .

§5.09 THE EXAMPLES OF FRANCE AND GREAT BRITAIN ARE FOLLOWED: GERMANY PASSES A LAW ON THE REGISTRATION AND PROTECTION OF INDUSTRIAL DESIGNS

January 11, 1876

Like England, other exporting countries did not take long to realize the competitive advantages stemming from the esthetical appearance of articles, and the importance of industrial design protection in that regard. Germany, in 1876, passed its first law on industrial designs. Soon, other European countries would do the same.

Interestingly, this German statute has a provision dealing with designs created under an employment contract. This reveals that, in the last quarter of the nineteenth century, the topic of inventions and creations by employees had already become a common feature of intellectual property (*see* Text 1.44).

Law of January 11, 1876, concerning copyright in industrial designs and models

Article 1—The right to reproduce, in whole or in part, an industrial design or model belongs exclusively to the author of that design or model.

Only productions new and original are considered designs or models in the sense of this law.

Art. 2.—For designs carried out by designers, painters, sculptors, etc., employed in a German industrial establishment, at the order or on behalf of the owner of the said establishment, this owner shall be considered, unless otherwise agreed, as the author of the design or the model.

Art. 3.—The right of the author is transmitted to his heirs. This right may be alienated, in whole or in part, by contract or by disposition of last will.

Art. 4.—It is not considered counterfeit to freely use any parts of a design or a model to produce a new design or model.

Art. 5.—Any reproduction of a design or model, which occurs without the consent of the rightholder (article 1-3), and which is intended to be distributed, is prohibited.

It is still admitted that there is infringement:

(1) If the reproduction was obtained by a process different from that used to produce the original work, or if it is intended for a branch of industry other than that to which the original belongs;
(2) If the reproduction has proportions or colors other than those of the original, or if it differs from the original only by changes that can be discerned only by means of a particular attention;
(3) If the reproduction did not take place directly, according to the original work, but indirectly, according to a reproduction of this same work.

Art. 6.—It is not considered counterfeit:

(1) The hand-copy of a design or of a model, provided that the copy is not intended for commercial distribution and sale;
(2) The reproduction in the plastic industry of drawings intended for the textile industry, and vice versa;
(3) The reproduction in the body of a writing of designs or industrial models.

Art. 7.—The author of a design or of a model is protected against counterfeiting only if he has declared his design or model to be registered in the register for that purpose, and has deposited in the hands of the authority responsible for keeping the register a sample or a figurative representation of the design or of the model. . . .

Art. 8.—The protection against counterfeiting that this law grants to the author of the design or the model, can last, at the option of the author, from one year to three years, as from the day of the declaration (Art. 7).

The author is entitled, by paying the fixed fee . . ., to obtain an extension of the term of protection, as long as this period is not more than fifteen years. The extension of the term of protection is recorded in the register of designs.

The author may exercise the right conferred to him by paragraph 2 of this article, either at the time of his declaration or at the expiration of the third year and the tenth year of the term of protection.

Art. 9.—The registration of drawings is carried by the authorities that are in charge of keeping the registers of commerce (*Handelsregister*).

The author must make the declaration and the deposit of the design in the court of his principal establishment, or, if he does not possess any commercial reason registered (on the commercial register), in the competent court of his domicile.

Authors who do not have an establishment or domicile in Germany must make the declaration and deposit at the Commercial Court of Leipzig. . . .

Art. 16.—This law applies to all designs of national authors, provided that the objects made from such designs have been made in Germany, regardless of whether they are distributed in Germany or abroad.

Foreign authors who have their industrial establishment in the territory of the German Empire enjoy the protection of the present law for objects which have been manufactured in Germany.

In any case, the protection that foreign authors can invoke is regulated by existing international treaties. . . .

§5.10 GREAT BRITAIN AND AUSTRIA-HUNGARY SIGN A BILATERAL AGREEMENT COVERING THE RECIPROCAL PROTECTION OF INDUSTRIAL DESIGNS

December 5, 1876

As it happened with copyright and trademarks, international protection of designs started at the bilateral level, before reaching multilateral harmonization. Both France and Great Britain would press for the protection of industrial designs by their trading partners, on the basis of national treatment. *See also* Texts 2.56 and 2.62.

Treaty of Commerce between Great Britain and Austria-Hungary.

Signed at Buda-Pesth, December 5, 1876.

Article VI.

Trade-Marks, &c. — National Treatment.

The subjects of one of the two High Contracting Parties shall enjoy in the territories of the other the same protection as native subjects with regard to rights of ownership over trade and manufacture marks, and other distinctive marks of goods or their packages, as well as over patterns and designs for manufactures.

The subjects of Her Britannic Majesty will not, however, be able to claim in Austria-Hungary the exclusive right to a mark or other indication on a pattern or design unless they have deposited two specimens of it in the Chambers of Commerce at Vienna and Buda-Pesth.

§5.11 GREAT BRITAIN UNIFIES THE PROTECTION OF DESIGNS FOR ORNAMENTAL PURPOSES AND OF DESIGNS FOR THE SHAPE AND CONFIGURATION OF USEFUL ARTICLES

August 25, 1883

An Act to amend and consolidate the Law relating to Patents for Inventions, Registration of Designs and of Trade Marks.

Be it enacted by the Queen's most Excellent Majesty, by and with the advice and consent of the Lords Spiritual and Temporal, and Commons, in this present Parliament assembled, and by authority of the same, as follows: . . .

Part III.

Designs.

Registration of Designs.

47.(1.) The comptroller may, on application by or on behalf of any person claiming to be the proprietor of any new or original designed not previously published in the United Kingdom, register the design under this part of the Act.

48.(1.) On application for registration of a design the applicant shall furnish to the comptroller the prescribed number of copies of drawings, photographs or tracings of the design sufficient, in the opinion of the comptroller, for enabling him to identify the design; or the applicant may, instead of such copies, furnish exact representations or specimens of the design. . . .

50. (1.) When a design is registered, the registered proprietor of the design shall, subject to the provisions of this Act, have copyright in the design during five years from the date of registration. . . .

58. During the existence of copyright in any design—

(a) It shall not be lawful for any person without the licence or written consent of the registered proprietor to apply such design, or any fraudulent or obvious imitation thereof, in the class or classes of goods in which such design is registered, for purposes of sale, to any article of manufacture, or to any substance, artificial or natural, or partly artificial and partly natural; and

(b) It shall not be lawful for any person to publish or expose for sale any article of manufacture or any substance to which such design, or any fraudulent or obvious imitation thereof, shall have been so applied, knowing that the same has been so applied without the consent of the registered proprietor.

60. In and for the purposes of this Act—

"Design" means any design applicable to any article of manufacture, or to any substance artificial or natural, or partly artificial and partly natural, whether the design is applicable for the pattern, or for the shape or configuration, or for the ornament thereof, or for any two or more of such purposes, and by whatever means it is applicable, whether by printing, painting, embroidering, weaving, sewing, modelling, casting, embossing, engraving, staining, or any other means whatever, manual, mechanical, or chemical, separate or combined, not ebbing a design for a sculpture, or other thing within the protection of the Sculpture Copyright Act of the year 1814 (54 George III. c. 56).

"Copyright" means the exclusive right to apply a design to any article of manufacture, or to any such substance as aforesaid, in the class or classes in which the design is registered.

§5.12 FOR THE FIRST TIME, THE HARMONIZED PROTECTION OF INDUSTRIAL DESIGNS IS DEBATED ON A MULTILATERAL LEVEL

October 6 to 31, 1958

At the 1958 revision of the Paris Convention for the Protection of Industrial Property, the International Bureau renewed a proposal that France had, unsuccessfully, submitted at the revision of London, in 1934: to affirm an obligation to accord protection to industrial designs under an industrial property regime. The motivation behind the proposal was a clarification of the dual protection of designs, under copyright and industrial property. Designs have been mentioned in the Paris Convention since its first version, of 1883, but with the only substantive consequence of their being accorded national treatment. Members of the Union remained, nevertheless, free to opt for not establishing a particular regime for designs under an industrial property approach, namely by prohibiting their use as designs and patterns of manufactured goods. This was the subsidiary rule that resulted (and still results) from Article 2(5) of the Berne Convention—albeit with the natural limitations of the application of copyright to eminently utilitarian objects whose shapes obey ornamental purposes. After 1958, Members were obliged to establish such an industrial property regime for industrial designs.

However, the other proposals of the Bureau, which concerned a definition of designs and a minimum term of protection, were rejected by the Contracting Parties. Today, Article 5*quinquies* of the Paris Convention does not go beyond saying that "Industrial designs shall be protected in all the countries of the Union." On a multilateral level, minimum standards of protection would be introduced almost forty years later, in the GATT Uruguay Round (*see* Text 5.13).

Preparatory Work and Debates

Industrial designs, definition, protection

(Article 5*quater* new, eventually new Article 7*ter*)

Item XI of the Program

A) Proposition with explanation of reasons

I. We are dealing here only with industrial designs and models (*Patterns and Designs, Geschmacksmuster*).

Their characteristic is to produce an *aesthetic effect* and serve as a *type for an industrial production*. From the moment the *technical effect* becomes preponderant, it is no longer an industrial design or model, but an invention, if the level of invention (*degree of invention, Erfindungshohe*) is sufficient; where applicable, a utility model (*utility models, Gebrauchsmuster*) in countries with this category of "small inventions" . . . .

The industrial design can therefore be defined in the following way: Any layout of lines (= design = two dimensions) or any plastic form (= model = three dimensions), combined or not with colors, provided they serve as a type for the industrial production of an object.

> II. The International Chamber of Commerce (Meetings in Paris in 1950 and Vienna in 1953) proposed a new Article *5quater*. The purpose of this article was primarily to give a definition of industrial designs and models, that is to say, to specify the subject matter of the protection to be granted in this matter by the Union States.

Indeed, the Paris Convention of 1883 (Article 1, proviso 2) lays down a general rule according to which the protection of industrial property concerns, in particular, industrial designs.

In Articles 4, 11 and 12, it also refers to industrial designs and models in relation to other forms of industrial property, without, however, giving any definition, for which it relies on the legislation of the Union States.

However, the various domestic laws are still far from converging. It is therefore difficult to refer to the national law of each country to know the mode and extent of protection. Most countries have both copyright laws and industrial design protection laws. Some countries, on the other hand, do not have yet a law on industrial designs and models and protect works of art applied to the industry according to the rules of copyright. Finally, other countries, such as France, considering the impossibility of making a clear distinction between artistic work and industrial work, grant both protections cumulatively. Accumulation has the effect of providing more extensive protection, because copyright laws, unlike those governing industrial property, provide for a longer term and require no filing formality.

Without wishing to go deeper in the questions raised by Article 2, proviso 5, of the Berne Convention, in the text revised at Brussels on June 26, 1948, we note that there is now a tendency to no longer regard industrial designs and models as an independent branch of industrial property and to assimilate them either to inventions or utility models, or to artistic works or trademarks. One would like to apply the principle of the unity of art and obtain a broader protection.

However, Article 2, proviso 5, of the Berne Convention, has given each country of the Union for the Protection of Literary and Artistic Property the power to exclude the works of art applied to industry from all or part of the coverage of their copyright law, if they are protected as industrial designs or models.

In this respect, the systems of protection, as we have observed above, vary greatly from one country to another. It may happen, for example, that a work protected only in a certain country as a design or model may be so in another Union country under the Copyright Act, provided that it is a truly artistic work.

The line between an industrial design and an artistic product is sometimes difficult to determine, because the artistic value does not prevent the author from having an interest in his work enjoying industrial protection. However, this is not a reason to deny particular protection to a combination of dots or lines, or to a layout of lines with a plastic form, regardless of the intrinsic artistic value, when they are incidental to an industrial object.

For a true application of the principle of assimilation, all Unionist countries should protect as industrial designs the works of art applied to industry. One cannot admit, without risking great confusion, the existence of two different laws whose respective fields of application are not clearly distinguished.

The desired goal could be achieved through a definition of industrial designs and models in the text of the Convention. Is this a timely proposal? . . .

We propose to adopt a new Article 5*quater* providing for the obligation to protect industrial designs and models (proviso 1); this article would then give a definition of the industrial design or model (proviso 2) and lay down the essential conditions for its protection (provisos 3 and 4). . . .

Proposed Text

Art. *5quater* new.

1. Industrial designs and models shall be protected.
2. Any line arrangement (design) or any plastic form (model), combined or not with colors, to be used as a type for the industrial production of an object, constitutes a design or model.
3. The novelty of designs shall be assessed in the light of the actual situation in the country where protection is claimed.
4. The term of protection shall be at least five years. Each national law may provide for its renewal or provide protection for a longer term. . . .

§5.13 MINIMUM STANDARDS OF INDUSTRIAL DESIGN PROTECTION GAIN MULTILATERAL RECOGNITION IN THE TRIPS AGREEMENT

April 15, 1994

The section of the TRIPS Agreement that covers industrial designs is not particularly remarkable, except that it pays special attention to designs for textiles. The reason was that the introduction of this section in the Agreement is owed to the initiative of a few GATT Contracting Parties with particular interests in the fashion industry.

Beyond that, the industry in general does not see differences in the level of protection of industrial designs with great concern. A great deal of industrial designs are applied in articles that have a very short life cycle, and therefore a formal system for their registration and protection is less important than other systems of direct or indirect appropriation, such as secrecy, head start, and reputation. This is the reason that explains that in the myriad of bilateral free trade agreements that have been signed between the major trading partners one cannot find provisions increasing the standards of protection of industrial designs.

The only concern that has emerged in the last years as regards industrial designs and that has deserved the attention of courts and parliaments is the alleged anti-competitive consequence of registering designs for parts of complex products (car, printers, cameras, etc.) (*see* Text 5.14).

Agreement on Trade-Related Aspects of Intellectual Property Rights (TRIPS Agreement)

Part II Standards concerning the Availability, Scope and Use of Intellectual Property Rights

Section 4: Industrial Designs

Article 25

Requirements for Protection

1. Members shall provide for the protection of independently created industrial designs that are new or original. Members may provide that designs are not new or original if they do not significantly differ from known designs or combinations of known design features. Members may provide that such protection shall not extend to designs dictated essentially by technical or functional considerations.
2. Each Member shall ensure that requirements for securing protection for textile designs, in particular in regard to any cost, examination or publication, do not unreasonably impair the opportunity to seek and obtain such protection. Members shall be free to meet this obligation through industrial design law or through copyright law.

Article 26

Protection

1. The owner of a protected industrial design shall have the right to prevent third parties not having the owner's consent from making, selling or importing articles bearing or embodying a design which is a copy, or substantially a copy, of the protected design, when such acts are undertaken for commercial purposes.
2. Members may provide limited exceptions to the protection of industrial designs, provided that such exceptions do not unreasonably conflict with the normal exploitation of protected industrial designs and do not unreasonably prejudice the legitimate interests of the owner of the protected design, taking account of the legitimate interests of third parties.
3. The duration of protection available shall amount to at least 10 years.

§5.14 THE EUROPEAN UNION DIRECTIVE ON DESIGNS

December 12, 2001

In 2001, the European Union adopted a Directive on the region-wide registration and protection of industrial designs. The text that follows transcribes a few recitals of the Directive's preamble that clarify two important points: designs of parts of complex products that are necessary for reparation purposes are not registrable; and two systems of protection have been established: one, informal, for short-lived designs, and another, formal, for designs that last longer on the market. The topic of designs for complex products has been a controversial one within the Union, some of its Members retaining in their national laws full protection for those designs.

Council Regulation (EC) No 6/2002

of 12 December 2001

on Community designs

Whereas: . . .

(10) Technological innovation should not be hampered by granting design protection to features dictated solely by a technical function. It is understood that

this does not entail that a design must have an aesthetic quality. Likewise, the interoperability of products of different makes should not be hindered by extending protection to the design of mechanical fittings. Consequently, those features of a design which are excluded from protection for those reasons should not be taken into consideration for the purpose of assessing whether other features of the design fulfil the requirements for protection.

(11) The mechanical fittings of modular products may nevertheless constitute an important element of the innovative characteristics of modular products and present a major marketing asset, and therefore should be eligible for protection.

(12) Protection should not be extended to those component parts which are not visible during normal use of a product, nor to those features of such part which are not visible when the part is mounted, or which would not, in themselves, fulfil the requirements as to novelty and individual character. Therefore, those features of design which are excluded from protection for these reasons should not be taken into consideration for the purpose of assessing whether other features of the design fulfil the requirements for protection.

(13) Full-scale approximation of the laws of the Member States on the use of protected designs for the purpose of permitting the repair of a complex product so as to restore its original appearance, where the design is applied to or incorporated in a product which constitutes a component part of a complex product upon whose appearance the protected design is dependent, could not be achieved through Directive 98/71/EC. Within the framework of the conciliation procedure on the said Directive, the Commission undertook to review the consequences of the provisions of that Directive three years after the deadline for transposition of the Directive in particular for the industrial sectors which are most affected. Under these circumstances, it is appropriate not to confer any protection as a Community design for a design which is applied to or incorporated in a product which constitutes a component part of a complex product upon whose appearance the design is dependent and which is used for the purpose of the repair of a complex product so as to restore its original appearance, until the Council has decided its policy on this issue on the basis of a Commission proposal.

(14) The assessment as to whether a design has individual character should be based on whether the overall impression produced on an informed user viewing the design clearly differs from that produced on him by the existing design corpus, taking into consideration the nature of the product to which the design is applied or in which it is incorporated, and in particular the industrial sector to which it belongs and the degree of freedom of the designer in developing the design.

(15) A Community design should, as far as possible, serve the needs of all sectors of industry in the Community.

(16) Some of those sectors produce large numbers of designs for products frequently having a short market life where protection without the burden of registration formalities is an advantage and the duration of protection is of lesser significance. On the other hand, there are sectors of industry which value the advantages of registration for the greater legal certainty it provides and which require the possibility of a longer term of protection corresponding to the foreseeable market life of their products.

(17) This calls for two forms of protection, one being a short-term unregistered design and the other being a longer term registered design.

(18) A registered Community design requires the creation and maintenance of a register in which will be registered all those applications which comply with formal conditions and which have been accorded a date of filing. This registration system should in principle not be based upon substantive examination as to compliance with requirements for protection prior to registration, thereby keeping to a minimum the registration and other procedural burdens on applicants.

(19) A Community design should not be upheld unless the design is new and unless it also possesses an individual character in comparison with other designs.

§5.15 A UNITED STATES COURT CLARIFIES THE DICHOTOMY FUNCTION V. ORNAMENT

April 19, 2016

Fundamentally, the law of industrial designs has crystalized around one single topic, which is the definition of the subject matter of protection, and, in particular, the search for the solution for the conundrum imposed by the dichotomy function v. ornament. The text that follows is an opinion of the Court of Appeals for the Federal Circuit (CAFC), which puts the controversy in an adequate perspective: protected designs are the ornamental shapes of products, whether these are functional or not. For a design to be deemed functional, the function has to be in the product, not in the design (in the sense that a change in the shape does not alter the product's utility or operation).

Sport Dimension, Inc. v. The Coleman Company Inc.

United States Court of Appeals for the Federal Circuit

Stoll, Circuit Judge

Coleman is an outdoor sporting equipment company that sells an array of products, including personal flotation devices. Coleman owns United States Design Patent No. D623,714 ("D'714 patent"). It claims "[t]he ornamental design for a personal flotation device," . . .

Sport Dimension is a sports equipment and apparel company that sells water-sports-related equipment, including its Body Glove® line of personal flotation devices. Sport Dimension's Body Glove® Model 325 is the accused device . . .

Sport Dimension's accused personal flotation devices, like Coleman's design, have two armbands connected to a torso piece. But, unlike Coleman's design, the torso section in the Body Glove® device extends upwards to form a vest that goes over a person's shoulders.

Sport Dimension filed a declaratory judgment action in the Central District of California requesting judgment that it did not infringe the D'714 patent and that the patent is invalid. The district court issued two rulings that we now review. . . .

Second, the district court adopted Sport Dimension's proposed claim construction, as follows:

> The ornamental design for a personal flotation device, as shown and described in Figures 1-8, except the left and right armband, and the side torso tapering, which are functional and not ornamental.
>
> Notably, this construction eliminates several features of Coleman's claimed design, specifically the armbands and the side torso tapering. The court "found that the armbands, the armband attachments, the shape of the armbands, the tapering of the armbands, and the tapering off the side torso were all elements that serve a functional rather than ornamental purpose in the D'714 patent." J.A. 3. In light of the court's claim construction order, Coleman moved for entry of judgment of noninfringement in favor of Sport Dimension so that it could appeal the claim construction. The court entered judgment, and Coleman timely appealed. . . .
>
> We have often blessed claim constructions, for example, where the court helped the fact finder "distinguish between those features of the claimed design that are ornamental and those that are purely functional." *Id.* (citing *OddzOn Prods., Inc. v. Just Toys, Inc.*, 122 F.3d 1396, 1405 (Fed. Cir. 1997)). Of course, a design patent cannot claim a purely functional design—a design patent is invalid if its overall appearance is "dictated by" its function. *Id.* at 668. But as long as the design is not primarily functional, "the design claim is not invalid, even if certain elements have functional purposes." . . . That is because a design patent's claim protects an article of manufacture, which "necessarily serves a utilitarian purpose." . . . So a design may contain both functional and ornamental elements, even though the scope of a design patent claim "must be limited to the ornamental aspects of the design." . . . "Where a design contains both functional and nonfunctional elements, the scope of the claim must be construed in order to identify the non-functional aspects of the design as shown in the patent." . . .

In *OddzOn*, *Richardson*, and *Ethicon*, we construed design patent claims so as to assist a finder of fact in distinguishing between functional and ornamental features. But in no case did we entirely eliminate a structural element from the claimed ornamental design, even though that element also served a functional purpose. . . .

The district court's construction in this case conflicts with that principle of design patent claim construction because it eliminates whole aspects of the claimed design. In its construction, the district court improperly excluded the left and right armband and the torso side tapering:

> The ornamental design for a personal flotation device, as shown and described in Figures 1-8, *except the left and right armband, and the side torso tapering*, which are functional and not ornamental.
>
> J.A. 3 (emphasis added). The court explained that the armbands and tapered torso "serve a functional rather than ornamental purpose," and thus excluded them from the claim scope. *Id.* . . .
>
> We thus look to the overall design of Coleman's personal flotation device disclosed in the D'714 patent to determine the proper claim construction. The design includes the appearance of three interconnected rectangles, as seen in Figure 2. It is minimalist, with little ornamentation. And the design includes the shape of the armbands and side torso tapering, to the extent that they contribute to the overall ornamentation of the design. As we discussed above, however, the armbands and side torso tapering serve a functional purpose, so the fact finder should not focus on the particular designs of these elements when determining infringement, but rather focus on what these elements contribute to the design's overall ornamentation. Because of the design's many functional elements and its minimal ornamentation, the overall claim scope of the claim is accordingly

narrow. *See Ethicon Endo-Surgery,* 796 F.3d at 1334 (endorsing a "limited" claim scope for a design with functional elements).

We therefore reject the district court's claim construction, vacate the stipulated judgment of noninfringement, and remand for consideration of infringement and, if necessary, validity consistent with the proper claim construction. . . .

Index

S

T

U

V

W

Y

Credits

1.01. L. Borchardt, Die Geschichte der Zeitmessung und der Uhren, vol. I, part 2 (W. Gryter & Co., 1920). Source: < archive.org >. Michel Dessoudeix, Lettres Égyptiennes—La Naissance du Nouvel Empire de Kamosis à Thoutmosis II (Actes Sud, 2010). Alexandra von Lieven, *The Movement of Time. News from the "Clockmaker" Amenemhet*, in Renata Landgrávofá and Jana Mynárová (eds.), Studies in Honour of Anthony J. Spalinger on the Occasion of his 70th Feast of Thoth (Charles Univ. in Prague, 2016). Source: < www.academia.edu/28449812/von_Lieven_Clockmaker_Amenemhet.pdf >.

1.02. Athenaeus of Naucratis (end of the 2nd, beginning of the 3rd century AD), The Deipnosophists, or Banquet of the Learned, Book XII, Chapters 17 and 20 (excerpts), [Transl. C.D. Yonge]. Source: < archive.org >.

1.03. Diodorus of Sicily (1st century AD), History, Book XIV, 42.1-43.1 [C.H. Oldfather, Diodorus of Sicily, vol. VI, at 129-131 (William Heinemann Ltd. 1954)]. Source: < archive.org >.

1.04. Plutarch, Life of Marcellus, chaps. XIV-XIX, *in* William Stearns Davis, Readings in Ancient History—Rome and the West, at 72, 74-75 (Allyn and Bacon, 1913). Source: < archive.org >.

1.05. Diodorus of Sicily, Diodorus of Sicily in Twelve Volumes, with an English Translation by C. H. Oldfather, vol. I, at 51 (Book I.15.1-7) (Harvard Univ. Press 1933). Source: < archive.org >.

1.06. Morris Hicky Morgan (transl.), Vitruvius—The Ten Books of Architecture, Book IX, Introduction, and Book X, Chapter XVI (excerpts), at 251 and 315-316 (Dover Publ., 1914).

1.07. Pliny the Elder (1st century AD), Natural History, Book XI [E. Littré, Histoire Naturelle de Pline, vol. I, at 369 and 387 (Firmin-Didot & Cie., 1877)]. Source: < gallica.BnF.fr >.

1.08. The Code of Justinian (sixth century AD), translated by Samuel P. Scott (Cincinnati, 1932). Source: < droitromain.univ-grenoble-alpes.fr/Anglica/ codjust_Scott.htm > .

1.09. Calendar of Patent Rolls, Henry III, at 138. Source: < sdrc.lib.uiowa .edu/patentrolls >

1.10. Calendar of Patent Rolls, Edward III, vol. 2, at 161. < babel.hathitrust.org >

1.11. The Cloth Act, 1337. *Statutes of the Realm*, 11th Edward III c 5. Source: < archive.org > .

1.12. Francesco Scipione, *Notizie sopra Jacopo e Giovanni Dondi dall'Orologio*, in Saggi Cientifici e Letterari dell'Academia di Padova, vol. II, at 469, 473-474 (1789). Source: < archive.org > .

1.13. Frank D. Prager and Gustina Scaglia, Brunelleschi—Studies of his Technology and Inventions, at 111-112 (Dover Public, 1970).

1.14. Calendar of Patent Rolls, Henry VI, Part II, at 255. Source: < sdrc.lib.uiowa.edu/patentrolls/h6v5/body/Henry6vol5page0255.pdf > .

1.15. Giulio Mandich, *Venetian Patents (1450-1550)*, 30 J.P.Off. Soc'y 166, 176-177 (1948).

1.16. Nicolás García Tapia, *Pedro Azlor, Médico de Isabel la Católica, y su Patente de Invención*. Source: < asclepio.revistas.csic.es > .

1.17. Henrique da Gama Barros, História da Administração Pública em Portugal nos Séculos XII a XV, vol. 9, at 13 (Tipografia Castro Irmão, 1922). Source: < purl.pt/6787 > .

1.18. Augustin Thierry, Recueil des Monuments Inédits de l'Histoire du Tiers État, 1ère Série, Région du Nord, vol. 2, at 608 (Firmin Didot Frères, 1853). Source: < gallica.BnF.fr > .

1.19. Augustin Thierry, Recueil des Monuments Inédits de l'Histoire du Tiers État, 1ère Série, Région du Nord, vol. 2, at 620 (Firmin Didot Frères, 1853). Source: < gallica.BnF.fr > .

1.20. M.L. Cimber and F. Anjou, Archives Curieuses de l'Histoire de France depuis Louis XI jusqu'à Louis XVIII, vol. 10, at 419-423 (Beauvais, 1836). Source: < www.numelyo.bm-lyon.fr > .

1.21. Arrêt du Conseil d'Etat et lettres patentes du Roi, du 6 mars 1610 contenant le privilège octroyé à Claude du Caire. Source: < gallica.BnF.fr > .

1.22. Arrêt du Conseil d'Etat et lettres patentes du Roi, du 6 mars 1610 contenant le privilège octroyé à Claude du Caire. Source: < gallica.BnF.fr > .

1.23. Isambert, Taillandier and Decrusy, Recueil Général des Anciennes Lois Françaises, depuis l'an 420 jusqu'à la Révolution de 1789, vol. 16, mai 1610—mai 1643, at 18-21 (Belin-Leprieur, 1829). Source: < gallica.Bn-F.fr > .

1.24. Isambert, Taillandier and Decrusy, Recueil Général des Anciennes Lois Françaises, depuis l'an 420 jusqu'à la Révolution de 1789, vol. 16, mai 1610—mai 1643, at 32-33 (Belin-Leprieur, 1829). Source: < gallica.Bn-F.fr > .

1.25. The Statutes: Revised Edition, vol. I, Henry III to James II, AD 1235-6—1685, 693-694 (George Edward Eyre and William Spottiswoode, 1875). Source: <archive.org>.

1.26. Pierre Clément, Lettres, Instructions et Mémoires de Colbert, vol. 2, at 694-695 (Imprimerie Impériale, 1863). Source: <gallica.BnF.fr>.

1.27. Ernest Maindron, L'Académie des Sciences, at 18, 14-15 (Félix Alcan, 1888). Source: <gallica.BnF.fr>.

1.28. Antonio Delgado da Silva, Colecção da Legislação Portuguesa desde a Última Compilação das Ordenações—Legislação de 1750 a 1762, at 795 (Tipografia Mairense, 1830). Source: <www2.senado.leg.br/bdsf/ >.

1.29. Isambert *et alii*, Recueil Général des Anciennes Lois Françaises depuis l'An 420 jusqu'à 1789, vol. 22, at 387-388 (Belin-Leprieur, 1836). Source: <gallica.BnF.fr>.

1.30. William Carpmael, Law Reports of Patent Cases, vol. 1, at 35 (A. Macintosh, 1843). Public domain. Source: <archive.org>.

1.31. William Woty, The Patent, A Poem (printed for the author by G. Kearsley, 1776). Source: <books.google.com>.

1.32. Benjamin Vaughan Abbott, Decisions on the Law of Patents for Inventions Rendered by English Courts, Since the Beginning of the Seventeenth Century, vol. 1, at 43 et seq. (Charles R. Brodix, 1887). Source: <archive.org>.

1.33. Clinton Rossiter (org.), The Federalist Papers, at 271-272 (New American Library, 1961). <archive.org>

1.34. Source: <www.ipmall.info>.

1.35. M. de Boufflers, Rapport Fait à l'Assemblée Nationale au Nom du Comité d'Agriculture et de Commerce, dans la Séance du jeudi au soir 30 décembre 1790, sur la propriété des auteurs de nouvelles découvertes ou inventions en tout genre d'industrie, at 3-5 (Imprimerie Nationale, 1791). Source: <gallica.BnF.fr>.

1.36. Blanc-St. Bonnet, Code des Brevets d'Invention, de Perfectionnement et d'Importation, at 33 and 71 (Audin, 1823). Source: <gallica.BnF.fr>

1.37. Les Archives de la Révolution Française. Source: <gallica.BnF.fr>.

1.38. Blanc-St.-Bonnet, Code des Brevets d'Invention, de Perfectionnement et d'Importation, at 100 (Audin, 1823). Public domain. Source: <gallica.BnF.fr>.

1.39. William Carpmael, Law Reports of Patent Cases, vol. I, at 156 (A. Macintosh, 1843). Public domain. Source: <archive.org>.

1.40. Collecção das Leis do Brazil, at 45-47 (Imprensa Nacional, 1891). Source: <www2.camara.leg.br/>.

1.41. William Carpmael, Law Reports of Patent Cases, vol. 1, at 353-354 (A. Macintosh, 1843). Source: <archive.org>.

1.42. Nuno Pires de Carvalho, 200 Anos do Sistema Brasileiro de Patentes, at 89-90 (Lumen Juris, 2009).

1.43. Richard Peters (org.), The Public Statutes at Large of the United States of America, From the Organization of the Government in 1789, to March 3,

1845, Arranged in Chronological Order, at 117 (Little, Brown & Co., 1856). < archive.org > .

1.44. Source: < supreme.justia.com > .

1.45. Michel Pelletier, Brevets d'Invention, Marques de Fabrique, Modèles et Dessins, Nom Commercial, Concurrence Déloyale, at 345 et seqs. (Baudry et Cie, 1893). Source: < gallica.BnF.fr > .

1.46. Source: < supreme.justia.com > .

1.47. Source: < supreme.justia.com > .

1.48. Source: < supreme.justia.com > .

1.49. Ministère des Affaires Etrangères, Conférence Internationale pour la Protection de la Propriété Industrielle, at 15-16 (Imprimerie Nationale, 1883). Source: < gallica.BnF.fr > .

1.50. Earl W. Hayter, *The Western Farmers and the Drivewell Patent Controversy*, 16 Agricultural History 1, at 16-17 (January 1942). Earl W. Hayter, The Patent System and Agrarian Discontent, 1875-1888, 34 The Mississippi Valley Historical Review 1, at 62-64 (June, 1947). Scientific American, January 8, 1887, vol. LVI, No. 2, first page. Source: < archive.org > .

1.51. Source: < advance.lexis.com. >

1.52. Source: < gutenberg.net.au/ebooks06/0601981h.html > (Project Gutenberg Australia).

1.53. Source: < www.worldlii.org/int/other/UNGA/1961/ >

1.54. Arpad Bogsch, *Summary History of the Patent Cooperation Treaty* (1966-1995), in WIPO, The First Twenty-Five Years of the Patent Cooperation Treaty, 1970-1995 (PCT), at 10-11 (WIPO, 1995). Source: < www. wipo.int > .

1.55. Source: < www.wto.org > .

1.56. WO/GA/26/4, of August 18, 2000, Annex II. Source: < www.wipo.int > .

1.57. Source: < www.wto.org > .

1.58. Source: < www.wipo.int > .

1.59. Source: < supreme.justia.com > .

1.60. Source: < www.uspto.gov > .

1.61. Source: < www.uspto.gov > .

2.01. James B. Pritchard (ed.), The Ancient Near East—An Anthology of Texts & Pictures, at 191-2 (Princeton Univ. Press, 2011)—translator J.J. Finkelstein.

2.02. Translation by L.W. King. Source: < avalon.law.yale.edu > .

2.03. Gustave Glotz, Le Travail dans la Grèce Ancienne—Histoire Economique de la Grèce, at 171-173 (Felix Alcan, 1920). Source: < gallica.BnF.fr > .

2.04. The first slogan is engraved on a Greek kylix (a shallow bowl), sixth century BC, found in Medellin, Badajoz, Spain, and on display at the Archeological Museum of Madrid, Spain. Second slogan: Robert Étienne, Pompéi, at 428 (Hachette, 1998). The third slogan appeared in a photo of published by the Historia Magazine 33, at 10, National Geographic Society (Spain).

2.05. C. H. Oldfather (transl.), Diodorus of Sicily in Twelve Volumes, with an English Translation by, vol. I, at 51 (Book I.15.1-7) (Harvard Univ. Press 1933). Source: < archive.org > .

2.06. Alexander Kerr (transl.), The Republic of Plato—Book IV, at 14 (Charles H. Kerr & Co., 1904). Source: < archive.org > .

2.07. Walter C.A. Ker, Martial Epigrams, vol. II, at 403 (William Heinemann, 1920). John Bostock and H.T. Riley (transl.), The Natural History of Pliny, vol. III, at 85, and vol. VI, at 287 (Henry G. Bohn, 1855). Source: < archive.org > .

2.08. John Bostock and H.T. Riley (transl.), The Natural History of Pliny, Book XXXIII, XLIX, vol. VI, at 287 (Henry G. Bohn, 1855). Source: < archive.org > .

2.09. Bartolo da Sassoferrato, Tract on Insignia and Coats of Arms, extracted from Osvaldo Cavallar, Susanne Degenring, and Julius Kirshner, A Grammar of Signs (Univ. of California at Berkeley, 1994), © for the translation The Regents of the University of California. Reproduced with permission.

2.10. Gustave Fagniez, Documents relatifs à l'Histoire de l'Industrie et du Commerce en France, vol. 1, at 211-212 (Alphonse Picard & Fils, 1898). Source: < gallica.BnF.fr > .

2.11. Calendar of Patent Rolls, Edward I, 1272-1281, at 181. Source: < babel.hathitrust.org > .

2.12. The Statutes of the Realm published by Command of His Majesty King George the III, vol. 1, at 140-141 (Dawsons of Pall Mall, 1810, reprinted 1963). Source: < babel.hathitrust.org > .

2.13. Decrusy, Isambert, and Jourdan (orgs.), Recueil Général des Anciennes Lois Françaises Depuis l'An 420 jusqu'à la Révolution de 1789, vol. IV—1327-1357, at 452 (Berlin-Le-Prieur and Verdière, w/d). Source: < gallica.BnF.fr > .

2.14. Gustave Fagniez, Documents relatifs à l'Histoire de l'Industrie et du Commerce en France, vol. 2, at 287-289 (Alphonse Picard et Fils, 1900). Source: < gallica.BnF.fr > .

2.15. Gustave Fagniez, Etudes sur l'Industrie et la Classe Industrielle à Paris au XIIIème et XIVème Siècles, at 387-388 (Slatkine Reprints, 1975). Public domain. Source: < gallica.BnF.fr > .

2.16. Augustin Thierry, Recueil des Monuments Inédits de l'Histoire du Tiers Etat, Région du Nord, vol. I, at 678 (Firmin Didot Frères, 1850). Source: < gallica.BnF.fr > .

2.17. Augustin Thierry, Recueil des Monuments Inédits de l'Histoire du Tiers Etat, Région du Nord, vol. I (Firmin Didot Frères, 1850). Public domain. Source: < gallica.BnF.fr > .

2.18. Augustin Thierry, Recueil des Monuments Inédits de l'Histoire du Tiers État, vol. 2, at 34-35 (Firmin Didot Frères, 1853). Source: < gallica.BnF.fr > .

2.19. Emilio Motta, *Per la Storia del'Arte dei Fustagni nel Secolo XIV*, in Archivio Storico Lombardo, 2nd series, vol. 7, year 17, at 140 et seq. (Fratelli Dumolard, 1890). Source: < archive.org > .

2.20. Fagniez, Gustave, Documents relatifs à l'histoire de l'industrie du commerce en France, vol. II, 14th and 15th centuries, at 181 (Alphonse Picard et Fils, 1900). Source: < gallica.BnF. fr > .

2.21. M. de Vilevault, Ordonnances des Rois de France de la Troisième Race, vol. 11, at 11-14 (Imprimerie Royale, 1769). Source: < gallica.BnF.fr > .

2.22. Gustave Fagniez, Documents Relatifs à l'Histoire de l'Industrie et du Commerce en France, vol. 2, at 215 (Alphonse Picard et Fils, 1900). Source: < gallica.BnF.fr > .

2.23. Calendar of Patent Rolls, Henry VI, 1422-1429, at 140. Source: < sdrc.lib.uiowa.edu/patentrolls > .

2.24. Ruy de Pina (1440-1522), Chronica d'El-Rei D. Affonso III, pp. 17-18 (Escriptorio, 1907). Source: < archive.org > .

2.25. Ouin-Lacroix, Histoire des Anciennes Corporations d'Arts et Métiers et des Confréries Réligieuses de la Capitale de la Normandie, at 580, 707, 584, 575, and 664 (in the same order) (Lecointe Frères, 1850). Source: < gallica.BnF.fr > .

2.26. A. Germain, Histoire du Commerce de Montpellier, vol. 2, at 387-390 (Jean Martel Aîné, 1861). Source: < gallica.BnF.fr. >

2.27. The Statutes of the Realm published by Command of His Majesty King George the III, vol. 2, at 456-457 (Dawsons of Pall Mall, 1816, reprinted 1963). Source: < babel.hathitrust.org > .

2.28. A. Germain, Histoire du Commerce de Montpellier antérieurement à l'Ouverture du Port de Cette, vol. 2, at 430-433 (Jean Martel Ainé, 1861). Source: < gallica.BnF.fr > .

2.29. Pierre Mouton *et alii*, Recueil des Statuts, Ordonnances, Règlements et Privilèges, accordés en faveur des Marchands Orfèvres Jouailliers de la Ville & Fauxbourgs de Paris, dont ils ont joui depuis l'an 1435, jusqu'en la présente année 1688 (Lambert Rouland, 1688). Source: < gallica.BnF.fr > .

2.30. Claude Raillard, Extraits des Principaux Articles des Statuts des Maitres Horlogers de la Ville et Fauxbourgs de Paris des Années 1544, 1583, 1646, 1707, & 1719, Enregistrés en Parlement, at 44-45 (1752). Source: < gallica.BnF.fr > .

2.31. Code de la Librairie et Imprimerie de Paris, ou Conférence du Règlement Arrêté au Conseil d'Etat du Roi, Le 28 Février 1723, avec les Anciennes Ordonnances, Édits, Déclarations, ARRÊTS, Réglements et Jugements Rendus au Sujet de la Librairie et de l'Imprimerie, depuis l'an 1332, jusqu'à présent, at 89 (Saugrain, 1744). Pierre Guenois, La Grande Conférence des Ordonnances et Edits Royaux, vol. I, at 1030, 1033, 1036, 1047 (Estienne Richer, 1636). L. Bouchel, Recueil des Statuts er Règlements des Marchands Libraires, Imprimeurs, et Relieurs de la Ville de Paris, at 65-66 (François Julliot, 1620). Source: < gallica.BnF.fr > .

2.32. François Husson, Artisans Français—Les Serruriers—Etude Historique (Marchal & Billard, 1902). Source: <gallica.BnF.fr>.

2.33. A.E. Bland *et alii*, English Economic History—Select Documents, at 300-301 (G. Bell & Sons, Ltd, 1921). Public domain. Source: <archive.org>.

2.34. Edict du Roy pour une reformation, police, et règlement sur les façons et teintures des draps (Frederic Morel, 1572). Source: <gallica.BnF.fr.>.

2.35. Noel Fail, Mémoires des Plus Notables et Solemnels Arrêts du Parlement de Bretagne (new edition, 1753). Source: <gallica.BnF.fr>.

2.36. Keith M. Stolte, How Early did Anglo-American Trademark Law Begin? An Answer to Schechter's Conundrum, 8 Fordham Int. Prop., Media & Entert. L. J. 2, at 533 and 535 (1997). The original source of these two reports is J.H. Baker & S.F.C. Milsom, Sources of English Legal History—Private Law to 1750, at 615-618 (Oxford Univ. Press, 1986). Source: <archive.org>.

2.37. Joseph Garnier, Analecta Divionensia—Documents Inédits pour Servir à l'Histoire de France et Particulièrement a Celle de Bourgogne, Correspondance de la Mairie de Dijon, vol. 2, at 113-115 (J.-E. Rabutot, 1870). Source: <gallica.BnF.fr>.

2.38. Alderman Charles Haskins, J.P., The Ancient Trade Guilds and Companies of Salisbury, at 371-374 (Bennett Brothers, 1912). Source: <archive.org>

2.39. Articles du Traité Fait en Angleterre, entre les Rois de France & d'Espagne, & les Archiducs de Flandres, pour le rétablissement du Commerce. 1604. Source: <gallica.BnF.fr>.

2.40. Antoine Mornac, In Senatu Parisiensi Patroni Observaciones, vol. 4, at 384 (Montalant, 1721). Source: <gallica.BnF.fr>.

2.41. Reports of Sir George Croke, of the Courts of King's Bench and Common Pleas, of Such Selected Cases as were adjudged during the Reign of James the First (4th ed., Grimston, 1791). Source: <archive.org>.

2.42. Extracted from Bain, Ebenezer, Merchant and Craft Guilds—A History of the Aberdeen Incorporated Trades, at 224 (J.&J.P. Edmond & Spark, 1887). Public domain. Source: <archive.org>

2.43. Augustin Thierry, Recueil des Monuments Inédits de l'Histoire du Tiers État, vol. 3, at 118, 126 (Firmin Didot Frères, 1856). Source: <gallica.BnF.fr>.

2.44. Alex J. Warden, Burgh Laws of Dundee, at 26 (Longmans, Green, & Co., 1872). Source: <archive.org>.

2.45. Claude Blondeau and Gabriel Gueret, Journal du Palais ou Recueil des Principales Decisions de Tous Les Parlemens et Cours Souveraines de France, vol. 1, at 901-904 (Denys Thierry & Jean Guignard, 1701). Source: <gallica.BnF.fr>.

2.46. Regimento da Fábrica dos Panos de Portugal, ordenado no anno de 1690 (Oficina de Miguel Deslandes, 1690). Source: <purl.pt/14991>.

2.47. Coûtumes du Pays et Région d'Anjou Conférées avec les Coûtumes Voisines et Corrigées sur l'Ancien Original Manuscrit, avec le Commentaire de Me Gabriel du Pineau, *Questions et consultations, Chapter XXXVIII*, at 142-145 (Charles Osmont, 1698). Source: <gallica.BnF.fr>.

2.48. Pierre Jacques Brillon, Dictionnaire des Arrêts ou Jurisprudence Universelle des Parlements de France et Autres Tribunaux, vol. 2, at 71 (Guillaume Cavelier, 1711). Source: <archive.org.>.

2.49. Danby Pickering, The Statutes at Large, From the Ninth to the 15th Year of King George II, vol. 17, at 296 et seq. (Joseph Bentham, 1765). Source: <archive.org>.

2.50. Rowland Cox, Trade-Mark Cases, at 2-3 (The Riverside Press, 1881). Source: <archive.org>.

2.51. Toussaint Joseph-Charlot, Recueil des Satuts, Lettres Patentes, Édits, Déclarations du Roy, Arrêts du Conseil, du Parlement, Sentences de Police, et d'Autres Juges, at 81-83 (Veuve Lamesle, 1750). Source: <gallica.Bn-F.fr>.

2.52. Colecção das Leis, Decretos, e Alvarás, Que Comprehende o Feliz Reinado DelRei Fidelíssimo D. José o I Nosso Senhor, vol. I, at 333 (A.R. Galhardo, 1797). Source: <digitalis-dsp.uc.pt>.

2.53. Isambert *et alii*, Recueil Général des Anciennes Lois Françaises depuis l'An 420 jusqu'à 1789, vol. 22, at 321-322 (Belin-Leprieur, 1836). Source: <gallica.BnF.fr>.

2.54. Jourdan *et alii*, Recueil Général des Anciennes Lois Françaises depuis l'an 420 jusquà la Révolution de 1789, du 3 mars 1781 au 1er janvier 1785, at 245-246 (Belin-Leprieur, 1827). Source: <gallica.BnF.fr>.

2.55. J. Patricio Sáiz González, Legislación Histórica sobre Propriedad Industrial—España (1759-1929), at 77-78 (OEPM, 1996). Source: <books-.google.com>.

2.56. L. Dufet and H. Agnus, Recueil Général des Traités de Commerce Conclus entre la France et les États Suivants: Angleterre, Belgique, Brésil, Chine, Japon, Nicaragua, Salvador, Îles Sandwich, Suisse et Turquie, at 1 et seq. and 159 et seq. (Duffet et Cie., 1861). Source: <gallica.BnF.fr>.

2.57. Émile Barrault, Marques de Fabrique et Noms Commerciaux—Guide Pratique du Fabricant, du Négociant et du Commerçant, at 30-39 (1859). Public domain. Source: <gallica.BnF.fr>.

2.58. The Weekly Reporter 1862-1863 (Eleventh Year), Containing Cases Decided in the Superior Courts of Equity and Law, vol. XI, at 745-746 (Ware and Grove, 1863). Public domain. Source: <books.google.com>.

2.59. Lewis Boyd Sebastian, The Law of Trademarks and Their Registration, and Matters Connected Therewith, Including a Chapter on Goodwill, Together with Appendices, at 288 (Stevens and Sons, 1878). Source: <books.google-.com>.

2.60. Rowland Cox, Trade-Mark Cases, at 157-158 (The Riverside Press, 1881). Source: <archive.org>.

2.61. Michel Pelletier, Droit Industriel—Brevets d'Invention, Marques de Fabrique, Modèles et Dessins, Nom Commercial, Concurrence Déloyale, at 363 (Baudry et Cie., 1893). Source: <gallica.BnF.fr>.

2.62. Gaston de Bernhardt, Handbook of Treaties, &c., Relating to Commerce and Navigation between Great Britain and Foreign Powers, Wholly or Partially in Force on July 1, 1907, pág. 24 (Harrison and Sons, Londres, 1908). Source: < gallica.BnF.fr > .

2.63. Eugène Pouillet, Traité des Marques de Fabrique et de la Concurrence Déloyale en Tous Genres, at 1193 (Marcal & Godde, Successeurs, 1912). Source: < gallica.BnF.fr > .

2.64. Source: < www.loc.gov/law/help/us-treaties/bevans/m-ust000002-0043.pdf > .

2.65. Nuno Pires de Carvalho, IP and Antitrust—The Competition Policies of Intellectual Property in Eighty Cases, at 43 et seq. (Wolters Kluwer, 2015).

2.66. 48 Revista de Direito Mercantil 69 (1982).

2.67. *Compilation of Written Submissions and Oral Statements—Prepared by the Secretariat*, MTN.GNG/NG11/W/12/Rev.1, of 5 February 1988, at 13-14. Source: < www.wto.org > .

2.68. Source: < curia.europa.eu/jcms/jcms/j_6/en/ > .

2.69. Source: < www.wto.org > .

3.01. Code of Hammurabi, transl. L.W. King. Source: < avalon.law.yale.edu/ancient/hamframe.asp > .

3.02. Diodorus of Sicily, Histoire Universelle, vol. I, at 167 (translated [into French] by Abbot Terrasson, De Bure, 1737). Source: < gallica.BnF.fr > .

3.03. The Code of Justinian, translated by Samuel P. Scott (Cincinnati, 1932). Source: < droitromain.univ-grenoble-alpes.fr/ > .

3.04. Calendar of Patent Rolls, Edward III, vol. 3, 1334-1338. Source: < babel.hathitrust.org > .

3.05. Calendar of Patent Rolls, Edward III, vol. 3, 1334-1338, at 494. Source: < sdrc.lib.uiowa.edu/patentrolls/ > .

3.06. A.E. Bland *et alii*, English Economic History—Select Documents, at 147-148 (G. Bell & Sons, Ltd, 1921). Source: < archive.org > .

3.07. Paul Frankel, *The Secret of Mediaeval Masons*, 20 The Art Bull. 46 (1945). Source: < www.jstor.org > .

3.08. Louis Caillet, *Contrat d'apprentissage passé avec Pierre Gobert, drapier de Romans, le 8 juin 1535, par Simon de Despit*, in Nouvelle Revue Historique de Droit Français et Étranger, vol. 35, at 565-568 (1911). Source: < gallica.BnF.fr > .

3.09. Alfred Franklin, Dictionnaire Historique des Arts, Métiers et Professions exercés dans Paris depuis le Treizième Siècle, at 439 (H. Welter, 1906). < gallica.BnF.fr >

3.10. Isambert *et alii*, Recueil Général des Anciennes Lois Françaises depuis l'An 420 jusqu'à 1789, vol. 13, at 184-185 (Belin-Leprieur, 1836). Source: < gallica.BnF.fr > .

3.11. Recueil des Édits, Déclarations, Lettres-Patents et Arrêts du Conseil, Enregistrés au Parlement de Metz, vol. 5, at 142-143 (Veuve Antoine & Fils, 1788). < gallica.BnF.fr >

3.12. Ebenezer Bain, MERCHANT AND CRAFT GUILDS—A HISTORY OF THE ABERDEEN INCORPORATED TRADES, at 255 (J. & J. P. Edmond & Spark, 1887). Source: < archive.org > .

3.13. J.H. Aveling, THE CHAMBERLENS AND THE MIDWIFERY FORCEPS—MEMORIALS OF THE FAMILY AND AN ESSAY ON THE INVENTION OF THE INSTRUMENT, at 132-136 (excerpts) (J. & A. Churchill, 1882). Source: < archive.org > .

3.14. Nicolas de Blégny, LE REMÈDE ANGLOIS POUR LA GUÉRISON DES FIÈVRES, PUBLIÉ PAR L'ORDRE DU ROI, AVEC LES OBSERVATIONS DE MONSÏEUR LE PREMIER MÉDECIN DE SA MAJESTÉ, SUR LA COMPOSITION, LES VERTUS, ET L'USAGE DE CE REMÈDE, at 5-12 (Estienne Michallet, 1683). < gallica.BnF.fr >

3.15. H. Omont, *Un Charlatan Italien sous Louis XIV*, in BULLETIN DE LA SOCIÉTÉ DE L'HISTOIRE DE PARIS ET DE L'ILE-DE-FRANCE, 1893, at 137-138 (H. Champion, 1893). Source: < gallica.BnF.fr > .

3.16. Jacquemart, Albert, and Blant, Edmond, HISTOIRE ARTISTIQUE, INDUSTRIELLE ET COMMERCIALE DE LA PORCELAINE, Part I, 463-465 (J. Techemer, 1861). Public domain. Source: < gallica.BnF.fr > .

3.17. Arrêt du Conseil du Roi (Imprimerie Delaguette, 1748). Source: < gallica-.BnF.fr > .

3.18. J.-S.-G. Nypels, LE DROIT PÉNAL FRANÇAIS PROGRESSIF ET COMPARÉ—CODE PÉNAL DE 1810, at 287 (Bruylant-Christophe et Cie., 1863). Source: < gallica.BnF.fr > .

3.19. Rowland Cox, TRADE-MARK CASES, at 10 (The Riverside Press, 1881). Source: < archive.org > .

3.20. J.H. Merivale, REPORTS OF CASES ARGUED AND DETERMINED IN THE HIGH COURT OF CHANCERY, FROM THE COMMENCEMENT OF MICHAELMAS TERM, 1815, TO THE END OF THE SITTINGS AFTER MICHAELMAS TERM, 1817, vol 3, at 157 et seq. (A. Strahan, 1819). Source: < books.google.com > . 1817 English Reports Decisions. Source: < www.commonlii.org/uk/cases/EngR/1817/ > . Edward Jacob, and John Walker, REPORTS OF CASES ARGUED AND DETERMINED IN THE HIGH COURT OF CHANCERY, during the Time of Lord Chancellor Eldon, vol. 1, at 394-395 (A. Strahan, 1821). Source: < archive.org > . Nicholas Simon and John Stuart, REPORTS OF CASES DECIDED IN THE HIGH COURT OF CHANCERY BY THE RIGHT HON. SIR JOHN LEACH, VICE-CHANCELLOR OF ENGLAND, vol. 1, at 74-76 (J. & W. T. Clarke, 1824). Source: google books. Edmund H. Bennett and Chouncey Smith (eds.), ENGLISH REPORTS IN LAW AND EQUITY: CONTAINING REPORTS OF CASES IN THE HOUSE OF LORDS, PRIVY COUNCIL, vol. 6 (1851), at 14-36 (Charles C. Little and James Brown, 1852). Source: < babel.hathitrust.org > .

3.21. W.H. Dunbar, George Dingwall Fordyce, and John de Maria, REPORTS OF CASES DECIDED IN THE SUPREME COURTS OF SCOTLAND AND IN THE HOUSE OF LORD ON APPEAL FROM SCOTLAND, BEING A CONTINUATION OF THE SCOTTISH JURIST, vol. 8 at 321-322 (M. Anderson, 1836). Source: < archive.org > .

3.22. Union Internationale pour la Protection de la Propriété Industrielle, Actes de la Conférence réunie à la Haye du 8 octobre au 6 novembre 1925, at 479 (Bureau International de l'Union, 1926). Source: < gallica.BnF.fr > .

3.23. Source: < advance.lexis.com > .
3.24. Source: < supreme.justia.com > .
3.25. Source: < www.wto.org > .
3.26. Source: Government Publishing Office, < www.govinfo.gov > .
3.27. IP/C/M/83/Add.1, of January 30, 2017, paragraphs 49-56. Source: < docs.wto.org > .
4.01. Vitruvius, The Ten Books on Architecture, transl. by Morris, Hicky, Book VII (excerpt). (Dover Publications, 1960, originally published by the Harvard Univ. Press in 1914).
4.02. Walter C.A. Ker, Martial Epigrams, vol. I, at 63-65 (William Heinemann, 1919). Henry G. Bohn, The Epigrams of Martial Translated into English Prose, Each Accompanied by One or More Verse Translations, from the Works of English Poets, and Various Other Sources, at 62 (Henry G. Bohn, 1860). Source: < archive.org > .
4.03. John Earl of Orrery, The Letters of Pliny the Younger with Observations on Each Letter, vol. II, at 251 (2nd ed., James Bettenham, 1751). Source: < archive.org > .
4.04. Walter C.A. Ker, Martial Epigrams, vol. II, at 239 (William Heinemann, 1920). Source: < archive.org > .
4.05. J. Raleigh Nielson, *The Boy Poet Sulpicious—A Tragedy of Roman Education*, 11 The School Review 384, 385 (May, 1903). Source: < www.jstor.org/stable/i244555 > .
4.06. Arthur Murphy, The Works of Caius Tacitus, vol. III, at 322-323 (John Stockdale, 1805). Source: < archive.org > .
4.07. Montalembert, The Monks of the West—From St. Benedict to St. Bernard, vol. 3, at 117-122 (William Blacwood and Sons, 1867). Source: < archive.org > .
4.08. R. Fulin, *Documenti per Servire alla Storia della Tipografia Veneziana*, in Archivio Veneto vol. XXIII, at 99 (1882). Source: < archive.org > .
4.09. Isambert, Decrusy and Armet, Recueil Général des Anciennes Lois Françaises, depuis l'an 420, jusqu'à la Révolution de 1789, vol. 5, 1438-1483, at 710-712 (Belin-Leprieur and Verdière, 1828). Public domain. Source: < gallica. BnF.fr > .
4.10. R. Fulin, *Primi Privilegi di Stampa in Venezia*, in Archivio Veneto, vol 1, at 163-164 (Marco Visentini, 1871). Source: < archive.org > .
4.11. Venâncio Deslandes, Documentos para a Historia da Typographia Portugueza nos Séculos XVI e XVII, at 4 (Imprensa Nacional, 1888). Source: < archive.org > .
4.12. Giorgio Vasari, Lives of the Most Eminent Painters, Sculptors, and Architects, vol. 3, at 492-493 (transl. Jonathan Foster, Bell & Daldy, 1865). Source: < archive.org > .
4.13. Tito de Noronha, Ordenações do Reino, at 60-62 (Imprensa Portuguesa, 1873). Source: < archive.org > .
4.14. Meraud Grant Ferguson, *'In Recompense of his Labours and Inuencyon': Early Sixteenth-Century Book Trade Privileges and the Birth of Literary*

Property in England, 13 Transactions of the Cambridge Bibliographical Society 17 (2004). Source: < www.jstor.org > .

4.15. George Haven Putnam, Books and Their Makers during the Middle Ages, vol. 2, at 409-411 (G.P. Putnam's Sons, 1897). Source: < archive.org > .

4.16. Arthus W. Reed, *The Regulation of the Book Trade before the Proclamation of 1538*, 15 Transactions of the Bibliographical Society 157, 174 (1920). Source: < archive.org > .

4.17. Edmond Werdet, Histoire du Livre en France Depuis les Temps les Plus Reculés Jusqu'en 1789, Deuxième Partie—TRansformation du Livre, 1470-1789, at 22 (E. Dentu, 1861). Source: < gallica.BnF.fr > .

4.18. Lamant mal traicte de sa mye, Acuerdo olvido (without designation of the printer; s.d.). Source: < www.bne.es/en/Catalogos/BibliotecaDigitalHispanica/Inicio/ > .

4.19. Jose Toribio Medina, La Imprenta en México (1539-1821), vol. 8, at 384-385 (Printed at the author's home, 1911). Source: < www.bne.es/en/Catalogos/BibliotecaDigitalHispanica/Inicio/ > .

4.20. Horatio F. Brown, The Venetian Printing Press—An Historical Study based upon Documents for the Most Part Hitherto Unpublished, at 211 (John C. Nimmo, 1891). Source: < archive.org > .

4.21. Mathurin Jousse, Le Secret de l'Architecture (George Griveau, 1542). Public domain. Source: < gallica.BnF.fr > .

4.22. Rev. Joseph Ketley (edit.), The Two Lithurgies, A.D. 1549, and A.D. 1552, with Other Documents Set Forth by Authority in the Reign of King Edward the Sixth, at 487-488 (Cambridge, 1849). Source: < archive.org > .

4.23. Edward Arber (ed.), A Transcript of the Registers of the Company of Stationers of London, 1554-1640 A.D., vol. I, at XXVII (Privately Printed, 1875). Source: < archive.org > .

4.24. Descrittione di M. Lodovico Guicciardini Patritio Fiorentino, Di Tutti Paesi Bassi, Altrimenti Detti Germania Inferiore (Guglielmo Silvio, 1567). Source: < archive.org > .

4.25. Luís de Camões, Os Lusíadas, at 3 (António Gonzales, 1572). Source: < purl.pt/1 > .

4.26. Laurens Bouchel, La Bibliothèque ou Trésor du Droit Français, ou sont traitées les matières Civiles, Criminelles & Beneficiales, tant reglées par les Ordonnances & Coutumes de France, que decidées par Arrêts des Cours Souveraines, 2nd vol., at 712-713 (Jacques Dallin, 1667). Source: < books-.google.com > .

4.27. Essais de Messire Michel Seigneur de Montaigne, Livre Premier et Second (Millanges, 1580). Source: < gallica.BnF.fr > .

4.28. Horatio F. Brown, The Venetian Printing Press—An Historical Study based upon Documents for the Most Part Hitherto Unpublished, at 218-220 (John C. Nimmo, 1891). Source: < archive.org > .

4.29. Miguel de Cervantes Saavedra, El Ingenioso Hidalgo Don Quixote de la Mancha, at 3 (Juan de la Cuesta, 1605). Source: < www.bne.es/en/Catalogos/BibliotecaDigitalHispanica/Inicio/ > .

4.30. L. Bouchel, Recueil des Statuts er Règlements des Marchands Libraires, Imprimeurs, et Relieurs de la Ville de Paris, at 65 (François Julliot, 1620). Source: < gallica.BnF.fr > .

4.31. Mathurin Jousse, Le Secret de l'Architecture (George Griveau, 1542). Source: < gallica.BnF.fr > .

4.32. Statutes of the Realm: Volume 5, 1628-80, at 428-435. Originally published by Great Britain Record Commission, s.l, 1819. Source: < www.british-history.ac.uk/statutes-realm/vol5/pp428-435#h3-0006 > .

4.33. Source: < avalon.law.yale.edu/18th_century/anne_1710.asp > .

4.34. Pierre Jacques Brillon, Dictionnaire des Arrêts ou Jurisprudence Universelle des Parlements de France et Autres Tribunaux, vol. 2, at 409 (Guillaume Cavelier, 1711). Source: < archive.org. > .

4.35. Source: < gallica.BnF.fr > .

4.36. Source: < constitutionus.com/ > .

4.37. Source: < www.copyright.gov/about/1790-copyright-act.html > .

4.38. Eugène Chausson, La Propriété Littéraire—Sa Législation en France et à l'Étranger—Son Véritable Caractère, at 41 (Sevin, 1895). Source: < gallica.BnF.fr > .

4.39. Coleção das Decisões do Governo do Império do Brasil 1830, at 59. Source: < www2.camara.leg.br > .

4.40. Source: < advance.lexis.com > .

4.41. Catherine Seville, Literary Copyright Reform in Early Victorian England: The Framing of the 1842 Copyright Act, at 258 et seq. (Cambridge Univ. Press, 1999). Source: < archive.org > .

4.42. M. de Clerq, Recueil des Traités de la France, vol. 6, 1850-1855, at 37 (A. Durand and Pedone-Lauriel, 1880). Source: < gallica.BnF.fr > .

4.43. M. de Clerq, Recueil des Traités de la France, vol. 6, at. 125 et seq. (A. Durand et Pedone-Lauriel, 1880). Source: < gallica.BnF.fr > .

4.44. Charles Fliniaux, Législation et Jurisprudence concernant la Propriété Littéraire et Artistique, at 89 (Ernest Thorin, 1878). Source: < gallica.BnF.fr > .

4.45. Edouard Clunet, Etude sur la Convention d'Union Internationale pour la Protection des Oeuvres Littéraires et Artistiques, at 5 et seq. (Marchal et Billard, 1887). Louis Renault (org.), Archives Diplomatiques—Recueil Mensal International de Diplomatie et Histoire, vol. 20, at 157-161 (F.-J. Féchoz, 1886). Source: < gallica.BnF.fr > . George Haven Putnam, The Question of Copyright, at 287 et seqs. (2nd ed., G.P. Putnam's Sons, 1896). Source: < archive.org > .

4.46. The Statutes at Large of the United States of America, from December 1889, to March 1891, vol. 26, at 1106 et seq. (Government Printing Office, 1891). Source: < archive.org > .

4.47. Actes de la Conférence Réunie à la Haye du 8 Octobre au 6 Novembre 1925, at 253-254, 350-351 and 580-581 (Bureau International de l'Union, 1926). Actes de la Conférence Réunie à Londres du 1er Mai au 2 Juin 1934, at

289-291 and 420-421 (Bureau de l'Union Internationales pour la Protection de la Propriété Industrielle, 1934). Source: <gallica.BnF.fr>.

4.48. Source: <www.wipo.int>.

4.49. Source: <supreme.justia.com>.

4.50. Source: <law.justia.com>.

4.51. Source: <law.justia.com/codes/louisiana/2011/rs/title51/rs51-1427/>. Source: <app.leg.wa.gov/RCW/>.

4.52. Source: <www.wipo.int>.

4.53. Source: <eur-lex.europa.eu>.

5.01. Pierre Clément, Lettres, Instructions et Mémoires de Colbert, vol. 2, at 786-787 (Imprimerie Impériale, 1863). Source: <gallica.BnF.fr>.

5.02. Lettres Patentes Concernant la Manufacture de Tapisseries d'Aubusson, 1732. Source: <gallica.BnF.fr>.

5.03. Statuts et Règlement pour la Communauté des Maîtres Marchands, & Maîtres Ouvriers à façon en étoffes d'or, d'argent & de soie, & autres mêlées de soie, laine, poil, fil & coton, de la ville & fauxbourgs de Lyon; & pour la fabrique des dites étoffes. Du 19 Juin 1744. (excerpts). Source: <gallica.BnF.fr>.

5.04. Arrêt du Conseil d'Etat qui confirme, avec amende & dépens, une Sentence des Juges de la Conservation de Lyon, du 29 Avril 1749. Source: <gallica.BnF.fr>.

5.05. Danby Pickering, The Statutes at Large, From Magna Carta to the End of the Eleventh Parliament of Great Britain, vol. 36, at 260-262 (John Archdeacon, 1787). Source: <archive.org>.

5.06. Michel Pelletier, Droit Industriel—Brevets d'Invention, Marques de Fabrique, Modèles et Dessins, Nom Commercial, Concurrence Déloyale, at 380-381 (Baudry et Cie., 1893). Source: <gallica.BnF.fr>.

5.07. J. Emerson Tennent, A Treatise on the Copyright for Designs for Printed Fabrics, with Considerations on the Necessity of its Extension, at at xi-xv, 67-68, 93, 94, 265-266 (Smith, Elder and Co., 1841). Source: <archive.org>.

5.08. David J. Brewer, Edward A. Allen, and William Schuyler (eds.), The World's Best Orations from the Earliest Period to the Present Time, vol. 6, at 2283 (Ferdinand P. Kaiser, 1899). E.E. Brown (org.), The Might of Right—From the Writings of William Ewart Gladstone, XXVIII, XXX (excerpts) (D. Lothrop & Co., 1880). Source: <archive.org>.

5.09. Charles Constant, Code Général des Droits d'Auteur sur les Oeuvres Littéraires et Artistiques, at 61 et seq. (G. Pedone-Lauriel, 1888). Source: <gallica.BnF.fr>.

5.10. Gaston de Bernhardt, Handbook of Treaties &c., Relating to Commerce and Navigation between Great Britain and Foreign Powers, at 27 (Harrison and Sons, 1908). Source: <archive.org>.

5.11. James J. Eston, The Law of Patents, Designs, and Trade-Marks As Contained in the Act 46 & 47 Vic. Cap. 57 (Waterlow Bros. & Layton, 1883). Source: <archive.org>.

5.12. Union Internationale pour la Protection de la Propriété Industrielle, Actes de la Conférence Réunie à Lisbonne du 6 au 31 Octobre 1958, at 865-866 (Bureau de l'Union Internationale pour la Protection de la Propriété Industrielle, 1963). Source: < gallica.BnF.fr > .

5.13. Source: < www.wto.org > .

5.14. Source: < ec.europa.eu > .

5.15. Source: < www.cafc.uscourts.gov/node/20430 > .

www.ingramcontent.com/pod-product-compliance
Ingram Content Group UK Ltd.
Pitfield, Milton Keynes, MK11 3LW, UK
UKHW020238290926
15470UKWH00002B/609

9 789403 517544